LONDON REVIEW OF BOOKS

ANTHOLOGY ONE

London Review
OF BOOKS

ANTHOLOGY ONE

WITH AN INTRODUCTION BY

KARL MILLER

JUNCTION BOOKS
LONDON

When the idea of an anthology of items from the *London Review of Books* was first considered it became quickly apparent that the number of pieces which deserved to be reprinted very greatly exceeded the limits of a single volume. We have been severely selective, and the result is not meant to be the best of the first two years of the *London Review of Books,* but one of perhaps half a dozen volumes that could compete for that distinction. In addition to the strengths of any individual piece we had to think of its contribution to the balance and sequence of the whole book. The ultimate responsibility for the selection that has resulted is mine, though I have paid attention to the views of the paper's editors, and to those of the contributors themselves.

Michael Mason
Editorial Director
Junction Books

© 1981 London Review of Books

First published in Great Britain by
Junction Books Ltd
15 St John's Hill
London SW11

ISBN 0 86245 045 4 (hard)
      0 86245 046 2 (paper)

Typeset by Photo-Graphics, Yarcombe, Nr. Honiton, Devon.
Printed and Bound in Great Britain by
Whitstable Litho Ltd., Whitstable Kent

Contents

Preface

The *London Review of Books* started when, though hardly where, Times Newspapers left off, in consequence of their pay dispute of 1979. Some of those who were worried by the silence that fell when the presses stopped were already exercised by deteriorations they had perceived in the coverage given in this country to new books. Steps were talked of, and taken — among them, the devising of a paper which I was asked to edit. We were, and still are, a part-time editorial staff of only three people, together with a part-time designer. We set ourselves to get the paper out three weeks after the decision to proceed was reached, and, chasing for authors and subjects and type-faces through the August haze, we very nearly failed to make it. The *New York Review of Books* financed us, and we were folded at first into the copies of that paper which were distributed in Europe. The understanding was that the Americans would probably retire from the venture in due course, and this they did: the British Arts Council has since taken their place as a source of finance. Meanwhile the *Times* and the *Times Literary Supplement* had resumed publication.

From the point of resumption to the end of William Rees-Mogg's term as editor of the *Times*, the advent of the *London Review* was never mentioned, as far as I know, in his pages, where, to the last rumour or tremor, every pay or status dispute in the newspaper industry was always patiently chronicled. The editor may not have heard of us, since we had ceased to figure in the publicity and press agency reports which furnish so much of the news in newspapers: or he may have felt that we were not the sort of news that is worth printing. Small papers are accustomed to such silences on the part of large papers — and of broadcasting channels — which are often quite keen to benefit from their initiatives. All the same, it is clearly wrong that the creation of a paper, however small, should be disregarded in favour of small pieces of pay dispute. Wrong, but typical of the times in which we live, when the failures which occur up and down the country are preferred by the media to the efforts that are made. Mary-Kay Wilmers, Susannah Clapp and Peter Campbell, who have been with the paper from the first and have survived a number of rough rides, rightly think that we should be grateful for the readers we have gained: they have no hard feelings, and would not approve of this note of complaint. Let it stand as a mark of pain, as bruises from our rough rides: from the experience, for example, of seeking regional outlets for the paper, of struggling to have it displayed on London news-stands hung with foreign publications, and of then being assured by the trade that we were doing harm to newsagents by encouraging readers to interest themselves in postal subscriptions. This was like being knocked down and then being thundered at for trying to get up.

If it was to be expected that we should be almost invisible to newspapers, and to the BBC, the Vice-Chairman of whose Board of Governors the inattentive Rees-Mogg has now predictably become, it was also to be expected that we should at once be told that we were boring, and not as good as the *New York Review of Books*. We had barely begun when I learned, as one does, that the Mistress of a Cambridge college had spoken to that effect. No editor is unfamiliar with the sentiment that the only good paper is the dead one of the same name that preceded the paper he edits: the sentiment can readily be adapted to meet the case of new ventures, and to communicate the lust for failure natural during a recession. In the early days, we were for ever being rumoured to be going out of business, or to be having rows.

Michael Mason of Junction Books has chosen what he takes to be the least boring of the articles and reviews we have carried to date, the date being the summer of 1981 — so that those who have not read the paper will be in a position to judge for themselves whether the reproaches were justified. They may possibly wonder why we make the effort, why we go to these pains. The main reason is the pleasure we get when we have something to print that strikes us as true and fresh, and as needing to be said, and when we print a new writer. A case in point was the article by Barbara Everett (18 June-1 July 1981) in which she elucidated Henry James's dependence on the art and preoccupations of Romanticism. Such thoughts have been inhibited by an orthodoxy in respect of James's work which has invoked the English novel of morals and manners, the defeat of morals and manners at the hands of Modernism, and James's own estimate of what he had accomplished: and they are thoughts that needed to be expressed. A further joy was the issue of 6-19 August 1981, which came close to the kind of thing we have been aiming at. Here Sean O'Faolain wrote, idiosyncratically and truthfully, about life, death, and the cult of the hunger strike as this has shown itself, early and late, in his native country of Ireland, and in India; while Mary-Kay Wilmers examined the cult of death pursued by Henry James's sister Alice; Peter Laslett wrote about motherhood and about an alleged new fatherhood, Sheldon Rothblatt about ideas of decline in British society; A.W.F. Edwards discussed hereditary genius, and an attempt to personalise and politicise the inauguration of statistical theory in Victorian England.

These discussions and others — on medicine and sexuality — were made to coincide; they were tuned to one another on the page. It is our policy to do this — more than is usual in literary journalism. It is also our policy to do our best to identify the books that matter most — conscious that we can't hope to succeed in every instance — and to devote ourselves at length to the questions raised by these books. We mix the discussion of books with related concerns and with poetry and prose fiction. Both policies have helped to shape the present anthology.

This has been a thin-skinned preface, and one reason for that has been touched on. There is another. Having worked as an editor for long spells, and been away from it for five years, I notice that I am getting old, and less unmoved by those connoisseurs of mass-circulation journalism for whom it is critical that we retain each one of our mostly terrible daily papers, for whom Jimmy Goldsmith's news-magazine *Now!* was beautiful, both because it was big money and because it was always being said to be about to fail, and eventually did, and who look down on the minority press. The small papers of this country have done a good job, and have had little to be ashamed of. What *has* been shameful, in recent times, is the politicising and destruction of the literary content of the *New Statesman*. This item in the deteriorations which have been feared is just as bad and sad, in its own small-circulation way, as the collapse into ineptitude of the editorial direction of the BBC — which has responded to a violent time by continuing to fill its programmes with fantasies of criminal violence.

It has been a pleasure to work again with those with whom my friends and I used to work in the past, including the remote past, out of which have come some marvellous old writers. I am grateful to them all for giving us a paper. To return to journalism after an absence is to be aware of a different scene from the one I remember from earlier days — to be aware of a cruel and stupid, and yet more interesting world, in which there is more to write about but in which older editors may suppose that there are fewer people to write about it, a world altogether unforeseen, in which there are rumours of a wish to die, in which young men kill themselves for political reasons, and also, we are told, because there is no work. The confidence that your house would never be attacked by rioters, or by policemen, is gone. No interval since the war can compare with the past year or two, during which the country has been tuned to the beating hearts of individuals in crisis — to the on-and-off of the *Times* resumption, to the drama of the American hostages in Iran, to the IRA's programme of hunger strikes, to the temper of John McEnroe on the Wimbledon Centre Court. Time after time, we have been maintained, manipulated, as in some hospital, at fever pitch. The Fifties can look in comparison a time of pastoral calm, when the rioters principally apparent to the high culture were Philip Larkin and Kingsley Amis.

Sociology and Marxism mattered in those days, in the sense that they produced many books. But Marxism still matters to publishers, and there is some of the old sociological determinism in the current absorption, on the Left, in literary theory. The literature which counts for the Left in question is a literature which has to be 'undone' by analysis of the tendencies inherent in the language available to its authors, while another Left wants to cancel Britain's association with the democracies of Europe, and to curtail the authority of the Labour Party's elected representatives in the House of Commons: such undoings are discussed in the anthology that follows. As our opening issue indicates, the *London Review* saw promise in Social Democracy before the movement was launched. Now that the movement has had a deserved initial success, we may become, as becomes a small paper, even more invisible to it than we are now. But it may need all the help it can get. In this quarter as in others, the press is on the hunt for failures and quarrels, and the collaboration with the Liberals is providing it with a thriving subject-matter of this kind. 'If they quarrel, they fail,' the *Observer* has said of these allies: but newspapers would rather that they did quarrel. If they do, they will be behaving no differently from other political groups. Politicians, even those calm and studious persons whom one may remember from twenty-five years ago, have always been inclined, and obliged, to fall out. But what politicians now do, for the most part, and most unproductively, is fight. They no longer write. They no longer think.

The public spirit proclaimed, and indeed present, in 19th-century political life is no longer easy to find, even in those places where it has yet to be undone by analysis. This may not be enough to deliver the message that Britain has experienced a catastrophe, with a theory to explain it. But it has contributed to the worst fault of the material we have published so far — which is the failure to sustain a political discussion, and to engage with the idea of a national decline and fall.

Karl Miller

Merry Wife of Windsor

Patricia Beer

The most terrifying comment made on the Abdication may well be that of Lord Beaverbrook, writing twenty years after the events in which he played such a prominent part: if the British people, he said, had been less absorbed in the affair of Edward VIII and Mrs Simpson the energy thus saved might have been used to avert world war. Possibly the same remark might be made today, for popular, even best-selling, books and plays are still being written about the protagonists.

One of the first books about Mrs Simpson, as she still was, must have been Edwina H. Wilson's *Her name was Wallis Warfield*, for it was published, in New York, in December 1936, before the issue was decided. ('Suppose — just suppose — an American girl should become Queen of England!') The volume is worth looking at, for it sets the style of much that has been written since, and the tone is of an unpretentious idiocy which is engaging rather than otherwise. Everything British is explained as if to educationally-subnormal Martians.

There is a great deal, of course, about following the dictates of one's heart and people drawing other people to them like magnets, but that is only the background. What was irresistible to the readers (the book went into three printings in a fortnight) was the account of Mrs Simpson's furs, nail varnish, jewellery and accomplishments — 'she can complete a jigsaw puzzle in half the time the average person takes.' The readers need not despair, however. 'Those who envy Wallis Simpson her success' are given hints to guide them, for example: 'A wise hostess never entertains at the same time her bridge-playing friends and those who shun the game.'

All this is accurate and well-researched, no doubt, but in one respect Edwina H. Wilson is wrong. In spite of her assertions that whatever happens Mrs Simpson 'IS queen — QUEEN OF ROMANCE', her subordinate clauses give her away. A propos of *their* first meeting she writes: 'It was — at least it may have been — a night to make history.' Clearly if Mrs Simpson does not bring it off, the waters will close over her. In fact, they never have.

Writers concerned with the politics of the Abdication obviously

1

do not indulge, at any length or at all, in revelations about Mrs Simpson's favourite colour. Lord Beaverbrook, in *The Abdication of Edward VIII* (published in 1966 though written earlier, and arguably the best book on the subject), gives an account of his first meeting with Mrs Simpson which is not dismissive — in fact it is quite eloquent and certainly intriguing — but is appropriately succinct:

She appeared to me to be a simple woman. She was plainly dressed and I was not attracted to her style of hairdressing. Her smile was kindly and pleasing, and her conversation was interspersed with protestations of ignorance of politics and with declarations of simplicity of character and outlook, with a claim to inexperience in worldly affairs. Throughout the evening she only once engaged in political conversation, and then she showed a liberal outlook, well maintained in discussion, and based on a conception which was sound.

Whether the emphasis is on politics or on gossip, the body of literature about the Windsors is large, repetitious and with a few exceptions boring. (If one has occasion to study it, a good way of keeping oneself going is to concentrate on how very variously a concept can be expressed provided the language is competently loaded: Stanley Baldwin said of Edward VIII, 'He has the secret of youth in the prime of age,' whereas Ernest Simpson just called him Peter Pan.) In contributing *The Duchess of Windsor,*[1] Diana Mosley has set herself a harder task than most. Her aims are good or at least interesting; their realisation was impossible.

There is bound to be an element of moral judgment in any account of the Windsors, but the Duchess has had the worst of it. The Duke, after the first accusations of dereliction of duty wore off, has been blamed principally for silliness, which is commonly supposed not to be a moral quality. Geoffrey Bocca's *She might have been Queen* (1955), for instance, bears out the title by recording the long series of fatal mistakes made by the King/Duke at the time of the Abdication; it reads like a nightmare school report to the effect that Windsor could have done better. The Duchess, on the other hand, has been saddled with all of the Seven Deadly Sins, except perhaps Sloth.

If people feel that the Duchess should be defended then it is obviously correct for them to make the attempt, and Lady Mosley

---

[1]Diana Mosley, *The Duchess of Windsor* (Sidgwick & Jackson, 1980).

would seem a natural for the task, possessing qualifications for both the political and the personal approach. She is connected with a long tradition of knight-errantry on the Windsors' behalf: Sir Oswald led his Blackshirts through the East End in support of the King. And her own political views dispose her to a lenient interpretation of such incidents as the Windsors' respectful visit to Nazi Germany. She has known the Duchess for many years in France and can supply all the details about table decorations, weight-watching and centre partings that readers are still assumed to need. But an apologia at book length tends to defeat its own ends, unless there is some new material or a powerful argument. A listing of good qualities is not enough, especially when some of the claims strain credulity: I cannot believe that Mrs Simpson divorced Mr Simpson for his own good. The best method, surely, is the one used by A.J.P. Taylor in his editorial foreword to Beaverbrook's book: he feels that Mrs Simpson was unfairly blamed; he says so and says why, briefly.

Lady Mosley's other aim is 'to try and discover something about the woman who inspired such a deep and lasting love and the man who lavished it on her'. She clearly thinks that deep, lasting love, and especially this particular example of it, is a freak that calls for investigation, but it may be that, like the ability to dress well and serve good food (talents of the Duchess's about which she is particularly repetitious), it is more common than she supposes. But if a deep, lasting love really has to be regarded not as natural but as some kind of infatuation or obsession then it is not much good examining the object of it. It certainly seems to have been a happy marriage; Lady Mosley, with a rare approach to shrewdness, points out that photographs in which the Duke looks sad were mostly taken at family funerals.

In any case, as some people defy photography, the Duchess seems to defy any description which is simultaneously favourable, interesting and convincing. In the early Fifties, both Windsors published memoirs, and neither the Duke's account of his wife, in *The King's Story*, nor hers of herself, in *The heart has its reasons*, makes her seem even tangible: but as both books were written by ghosts that may account for it.

The Duchess of Windsor is a curiously unworldly book. Lady Mosley really did have special knowledge of her subject: there is footnote after footnote saying 'in conversation with the author' and 'in a letter to the author'. But her confidential informants seldom tell her anything very penetrating, and they are clearly a communicative set, for over the years they must have told it to the women's magazines, the popular press and most of the rival biographers. Some of her other informants are 'ordinary people' as in 'Nothing that happened afterwards ever altered the love that ordinary people bore King Edward VIII.' I suppose these ordinary people are the ones that British election manifestos address as being the objects of the candidate's deepest concern; and I do not imagine that Lady Mosley knows many of them. I know several, and they tell me she is wrong, on this point and others.

She is on the wrong tack from the start — from the epigraph, in fact, which reads: 'The more alive one is, the more one is attacked.' She has apparently come to the conclusion that any form of criticism necessarily indicates that the criticised person has superior vitality and extraordinary talents. It is a comfortable belief, and would be a life-saver if the case was one's own, but when applied generally it can lead to misinterpretation. Lady Mosley really seems to believe that the infrequency of the Duchess's visits to England was masterminded by 'those in the know' who feared her, perhaps throne-toppling, popularity. 'What if the Duchess, with her breezy, friendly manner, went down all too well?'

Lady Mosley is so vehement in her denunciation of spitefulness, as directed towards the Duchess, that it is no surprise at all to find her being spiteful herself: about George V, about George VI, and particularly about Queen Mary: 'It is easy to understand why it was Queen Mary who most resented the Abdication. She was imbued with a sense of the importance of being royal, and she never recovered from having been a Serene Highness among Royal Highnesses.' As an Englishwoman living in France, Lady Mosley is ready with a special set of sneers about the way the Royal Family dress: 'The Duchess in her Paris clothes looked like the denizen of another planet among the flowery toques and pastel overcoats.'

I was quite startled to find how much these jibes annoyed me. I was at school at the time of the Abdication and we were unmoved by the event except as an occasion to exchange jokes at the back of the gymnasium. (Q. Why has the King bought a tin-opener? A. Because what he wants is in Cannes.) Nor have I been particularly concerned since. But Lady Mosley's book makes me feel, after more than forty years and in the presence of infinitely more impor-tant controversies, that I ought to be taking sides.

What Sort of Traitors?
The British Spy Opera

Neal Ascherson

The other day, I found myself in a taxi queue with Anthony Blunt.
He looked frayed but fervently cheerful, much as if he had just
been dug out of the ruins of his own bombed house. Never mind
the furniture, the books and the glass: the ceiling had come down,
but the dear old family dining-table had taken the strain. Nobody is
going to try him, nobody is going to bump him off. The worst that
can happen now is abuse by newspapers, and that will only hasten
the process of reconciliation with his friends. Newspapers are 'they'
and we, after all, are 'we'. As Andrew Boyle relates,[1] it turned out
that a great many old acquaintances of Burgess and Maclean were
much more horrified — felt, indeed, much more betrayed — by the
fact that the late Goronwy Rees gave a version of their flight to the
People than by the flight itself. When Stephen Spender showed the
Daily Express a friend's letter about Burgess, he was held to have
disgraced himself.

This book is a great feat. Andrew Boyle went through archives
and memoirs in two continents, but above all persuaded people to
talk — people in the know, who had given out little or no information before. So much has been written about the Two and then the
Three and now the Baker's Dozen, as far as one can see, that it
hardly seemed possible that Boyle could do more than rehash old
evidence or bomb the rubble. How wrong! It wasn't so much that
he flushed out Professor Blunt: smart fellows about Cambridge
and St James's seem to have known all about Blunt for years. It
was — first — that Boyle opened out the whole American dimension of the affair, through the FBI/CIA files and the secret
chronicles of James Jesus Angleton — that rather Jamesian secret
agent, an American from an English public school, who began by
admiring the style of SIS and ended by discovering how many of
them were traitors or bunglers. And secondly, it was that so many
British spooks, retired or still in the trade, decided that Andrew
Boyle was the man to whom they would finally spill their lapfuls of
wizened beans.

---

[1] Andrew Boyle, *The Climate of Treason* (Hutchinson, 1980).

There must be a connection here. The British Intelligence services don't divulge the sort of stuff they gave Boyle out of the kindness of their hearts. Most 'authoritative' books about them have rather the status of Palace memoirs by governesses and grooms: as a brass watch for long service, a few veterans of relatively menial status are allowed to publish mendacious and exaggerated books (some of the books about Ultra, for instance) which grossly overstate either the importance of some operation or the credit due to SIS, or both. But *The Climate of Treason* is not one of these hagiograms. They really talked: David Footman, Nicholas Elliott, Sir Robert Mackenzie, George Carey-Foster, Sir Frederick Warner, agents and diplomats on the security side, and a large anonymous group of Intelligence men from both branches of the service, retired and active.

The reason can be guessed at. Boyle's American breakthrough depended upon the Freedom of Information Act, which brought him baskets of US intelligence material on matters still secret in Britain, but also upon anonymous CIA sources who were anxious to enlighten him on — especially — the Philby and Maclean affairs. What he discovered suggested that the business was even more humiliating for SIS than had been supposed by the public, and that the injury it dealt to Anglo-American Intelligence co-operation was correspondingly graver than had been understood. At the British end, one can assume, news of what Boyle had got his hands on led to a decision for a *Flucht nach vorn* — a controlled but corrective release of more British material about the Cambridge spies.

Boyle's discovery, essentially, was that the Americans had identified Maclean and Philby as Soviet spies by 1948. They did not pass on their information to the British, partly because they no longer trusted them, and partly because the CIA agent in charge of the case, Angleton, was the sort of counter-intelligence cat so fascinated by mice that he would almost prefer to let them escape with the cheese than to pounce. Angleton was tipped off after the war by Jewish Intelligence to the effect that a British physicist working on nuclear weapons development in the States was a Soviet spy. This was the man Boyle calls 'Basil', or 'the fifth man'. He was easily turned round by the Americans, after he had confessed that he was helping Maclean to collect and assess for the Russians information about nuclear weapons co-operation (Donald Maclean was at this time in the British Embassy in Washington). When Kim Philby arrived in Washington in 1949, as the SIS liaison man with American Intelligence, the double-agent 'Basil' was able to confirm the suspicions of James Jesus Angleton that Philby was working for the other side. None of this went to the British. In a paroxysm of information avarice, Angleton decided that the Brits could find out the hard way. They already knew, through the chance error of a Soviet cipher clerk, that there had been a diplomatic leak in their Washington Embassy, and years of cryptographic detective work would eventually lead them to Maclean. So why should Angleton share his best sources with the British, in whose barrel, no doubt, other rotten apples nested? Although 'Basil' was a British citizen, it does not appear that SIS were told anything about his espionage, let alone his 'turning', until after Burgess and Maclean had fled in 1951.

Boyle's careful account of these later years, when the Cambridge spies were coming to the end of their free run, shows how astonishingly ineffective security was in their case — even allowing for the presence of Philby at the top of the M16 counter-espionage department. Mosaic-work, the logical assembling of a pattern of guilt, played only a minor part in their detection. It was mostly luck, and almost all the luck came from a series of defecting Soviet agents, starting with Krivitsky in 1937 (who had already warned that the USSR had spies in the British diplomatic service) and ending with Golitsin in 1961, the man who finally gave SIS the proof that Kim Philby had been a Soviet agent for the whole of his working life. Meanwhile evidence that the British loyalty of the Cambridge spies was wobbly lay scattered across the land. Nobody cared to pick it up. They could have stood in Piccadilly Circus and screamed that they were Communists, to no effect. In fact, they more or less did so: the old Gargoyle, where Maclean howled drunkenly at Goronwy Rees that 'you were one of US, but you ratted!', wasn't far away. Nor were all the flats and pubs where Guy Burgess and Donald Maclean had told people exactly what they were, and at the top of their voices. But the reaction was always much the same, always the nanny's pursed lip: 'Overtired again! Don't look at Master Guy or Master Donald, it only encourages them...' The British reaction, that is. James Jesus Angleton was different. When Kim Philby, after being decorated at Buckingham Palace, said that what Britain needed was a good stiff dose of socialism, James Jesus wondered if he might not be a Communist.

In all the new details he adds to the story, Andrew Boyle doesn't clear up a point which must be of central importance in the history of the Cambridge spies. We have been offered a series of books about the Ultra triumph, about the breaking of the Enigma codes and the work at Bletchley Park, about the constellation of Cambridge genius which was assembled there. What we don't know, and it's a very relevant question, is how much the Russians were told. The Americans were informed, indeed participated. But did the Russians get Ultra after the Nazi invasion of June 1941 transformed them into allies?

Boyle is ambiguous. At one point he observes that 'Stalin and his underlings' were '...being told nearly everything they required to know at first hand,' rendering information from their agents within British Intelligence unnecessary. But later on he quotes Muggeridge's account of a 1944 row, in which Victor Rothschild and Kim Philby protested that Ultra intercept material was being withheld from the Russians. Boyle goes on to say that it was 'standard practice' to withhold Ultra from the Soviet Union, but that it was reaching Moscow anyway through 'Lucy', the Soviet espionage centre in Switzerland. This is additionally puzzling, because 'Lucy' has been described as a personal German source, not a code-break. But in any case, the significance for Boyle's main story is obvious. If in the years 1941-3, when the Russians were carrying almost the whole burden of the war against Germany, they were dying in substantial numbers because they were denied the war's most important source of secret information, the actions of the Cambridge spies at that time must appear in a better light. What justification could the British advance for withholding this information — the military radio traffic of the enemy — from their own ally? Only one: that Britain's best interest was to stand aside and watch Nazi Germany and Soviet Russia slaughter each other to the last man. Nearly forty years later, we have drifted so far to the right that many young people of liberal mind can accept that as a good policy. Why choose between Hitler and Stalin? One dictatorship was as bad as the other. But the 'climate' then was very different. The appeasers who hoped that Hitler and Stalin could be set at each others' throats, and thought that a Nazi victory in that particular contest might even be preferable, had lost a political battle. Churchill ruled instead, ready to make a favourable reference to Hell in the House of Commons if the Devil were prepared to join the anti-Nazi coalition. To accept that Ultra could be shared with the Americans but not with the Russians would have seemed, then, like an admission that, after all, Cliveden still ruled from the back seat. This is a point of historical fact which ought to be settled.[2]

Boyle is a bit of a prig. Nobody gets away with anything. Political hindsight dominates. Communists, Tories, imperialists, idealists all get the back of his hand: there are no heroes. He certainly makes the case that treachery doesn't pay in personal terms (although we know little about Blunt's inner torments, if any). Burgess, Maclean and Philby all took to drink in the most satisfactorily Victorian way. Maclean driven to the verge of madness by Presbyterian guilt. As for Marx, he was 'inhuman' and wrote 'turgid tomes'; even Donald Maclean's book *British Foreign Policy after Suez*, written after his flight, has to be dismissed as 'somewhat ponderous'. (Unfair: it's penetrating and very readable.) But Boyle's study of the three main personalities is more impressive. Guy Burgess turns out to have been a much more forceful figure than the 'Etonian mudlark and sick toast of a sick society' version. Maclean, for all his convulsions of conscience and drunken violence, clung more persistently than the others to the hope that he was not just a spy and a traitor but the representative of a serious alternative for Britain. Kim Philby, in contrast, is diminished: he had skill and sang-froid, but little of political originality or inner conflict to hold attention.

British Intelligence, in Boyle's chronicle, remains as weird a community as ever, in spite of all the author's new information and captures of confidence. Amateurism, class prejudice and what Boyle calls 'the sad pleasures of sodomy' composed its peculiar flavour. The circumstances of my own unhappy brush with the service only confirm it. My background was 'right', and I was duly recommended as a likely lad by a Cambridge don (Boyle rids us of the myth that Cambridge tutors recruited assiduously for Russia, but does not add that they recruit assiduously for the home side). There followed a lunch at the Reform Club, where this 23-year-old ass received the proposal that he should go to the new Communist state of Betelgeuse in order to write a biography of its ferocious leader. An argument about where Betelgeuse was had to be settled by a visit to the *Times* Atlas, dated 1910, in the Club library. My real assignment, they said, was to approach leading Betelgeusians

---

[2] I have been told since writing this that Ultra-based information was passed to the Russians — though not all of it, and without disclosing its source in radio intercepts — through the British Embassy in Moscow on a regular basis. 'Lucy', according to my informants, had nothing to do with Ultra.

and 'get them round to our point of view'. Uneasy, I objected that I knew nothing of the place or its language. 'Old D. will put you in the picture,' they chortled, returning to their port. A few days later, I was summoned to meet D. in his home. After a silent but delicious dinner, D. asked me to sit next to him on the sofa. I supposed that I was at last to be put in the picture, but D. merely grasped me tightly and wordlessly by the penis. I extracted myself and ran away, and after some days of great confusion, wrote to say that perhaps I was not mature enough for this service.

An outfit like that — and these events took place years after the 'flight of the diplomats' — deserves everything it gets. I suppose there was a wild brilliance about the Betelgeuse project, which would almost certainly have cost me my head. But what most impresses me, in retrospect, is their sublime confidence that after that lunch and dinner I would still be their loyal man and true. This was a service which, even then, still assumed that people of our sort didn't let us down. It is not surprising that SIS were so incredulous, in the face of plain evidence of internal treachery, at the suggestion that somebody one had been at Cambridge with or whose father one had known could be a 'mole'.

And these assumptions about class loyalty, it seems to me after reading Boyle, also relate to the final question: why did the Cambridge spies spy? It would be silly to argue that Communism had little to do with it, but the Communist Party of Great Britain was clearly not the point, nor the source of inspiration. Even if their Soviet recruiters and controllers had wished it, none of these three (or indeed four) had the stamina to become active CP members, to sell the *Daily Worker* anywhere but on King's Parade, to throw themselves into the problems of who should be elected to the Executive Committee or the Political Committee. They didn't have the *partinost*, or 'party spirit', of friends like James Klugman or John Cornford. To put it crudely, the CP in Britain was beneath them. They were unwilling in the end to leave the Establishment, and became prominent figures in the BBC, the Foreign Office, Intelligence and so forth — just as they were destined to. Except that they also spied.

They all leave one with the odd impression, even Philby in his early years, that they became Soviet agents *faute de mieux*. What they needed was something else: a British movement of total opposition to the régime which was both respectable and formidable. They needed a *divided* Establishment, an alternative régime-in-waiting which they could join. Continental republics know this dualism. In France or Italy, Maclean would probably have been a prominent Communist with a bourgeois life-style, and quite possibly a good desk in the Foreign Ministry whose contents he would not have felt moved to microphotograph each night. In Britain, still an *ancien régime* in this respect, Labour did not offer such an alternative, while the price of CPGB activity would obviously be impotence and ostracism. The spies didn't see why they should be impotent and ostracised.

The Thirties were a decade of rapid social change and improvement in popular living standards, as well as a time of poverty and misery for many. But Britain remained governed, financed, exploited and largely represented by the upper class. There was no alternative ruling group, waiting in the wings with its own governors, financiers, civil servants, generals and even spooks. Labour was a party which, as far as the student leftist could see, would deferentially leave the old élite in place. The Cambridge spies wanted something else for Britain, something which now sounds absurd: a socialist revolution which would both smash the patrician hegemony to which the spies were such guilty heirs, and restore British greatness and independence. Objectively, we can now see them as Stalin's pawns. They don't seem to have taken that view, even with a thrill of masochism. The future spies sought a centre of full-blooded, total opposition to the status quo in Britain. They could find such a centre only abroad, in Moscow.

They really were traitors. Swedish colonels, West German bureaucrats who betray secrets to the East, are not in their league. They usually do it for money, or because they are under pressure or because they have some personal grievance. Nor are their fellow citizens as fascinated by their treachery as the British public are by the tale of the upper-crust spies. Philby, Burgess, Maclean and Blunt were doing something more fundamental: they betrayed what their counry was doing but by the same act destroyed the way their country did things. After them, the delicate muscle-tissue of the executive, uncritical trust moving in sheaths of class loyalty and schoolmate confidence, never worked so well again. This isn't to say that state servants do not still use it. They do, but with misgivings and with much greater difficulty. The damage done by the spies here was irreparable in the long run, but if one considers that the old-boy system was overdue for replacement, one could argue that the Cambridge spies betrayed their friends, in this instance, but not necessarily their country.

At the edge of the story, other elements of motive — even stranger — can be sensed. A certain crude psychologism fits, the spies savaging their Patria as substitute for an absent or unconvincing father. But there is another approach. Birth, the accident of birth in the privileged upper tenth of a caste society, imprisoned these men in a cell with the gnawing rat of guilt. Nothing they could do in life would efface the original sin of that unfair birth — except rebirth. Not just the Communist faith but the actual existence of the Soviet Union — isolated, hated, mysterious — glowed to them across Europe as a second chance for themselves as well as for humanity. Cross that snowy frontier, die for the old world, awake purified in a new one clutching 'a white stone with a new name writ thereon...'

In the end, there is Protestantism, English and Scottish, in these men. Boyle leaves us with the picture of an aging Burgess in Moscow, slowly picking out on the piano hymn tunes from his schooldays:

My soul, there is a country
Far beyond the stars,
Where stands a winged sentry
All skilful in the wars...

If thou canst get but thither
There grows the flower of peace
The Rose that cannot wither,
Thy fortress and thy ease.

Changes

Seamus Heaney

As you came with me in silence
to the pump in the long grass

I heard much that you could not hear:
the bite of the spade that sank it,

the slithering and grumble
as the mason mixed his mortar,

and women coming with white buckets
like flashes on their ruffled wings.

The cast-iron rims of the lid
clinked as I uncovered it,

something stirred in its mouth.
I had a bird's eye view of a bird,

finch-green, speckled and white,
nesting in dry leaves, flattened, still,

suffering the light.
So I roofed the citadel

as gently as I could, and told you
and you gently unroofed it

but where was the bird now?
There was the single egg, pebbly white,

and from the rusted bend of the snout
tail-feathers splayed and sat tight.

So tender, I said, 'Remember this.
It will be good for you to retrace this path

when you have grown away and stand at last
at the very centre of the empty city.'

A Free Translation

Craig Raine

(for Norma Kitson)

Seeing the pagoda
of dirty dinner plates
I observe my hands

under the kitchen tap
as if they belonged
to Marco Polo:

glib with soap
they speak of details
from a pillow book,

the fifty-seven ways
in which the Yin
receives the Yang.

Rinsed and purified
they flick off drops
like a court magician

whose stretching fingers
seek to hypnotise
the helpless house...

This single bullrush
is the silent firework
I have invented

to amuse the children.
Slow sideboard sparkler,
we watch its wadding

softly fray.
Your skein of wool
sleeps on the sofa,

a geisha girl
with skewered hair,
too tired to think

of loosening ends,
or fret forever
for her Samurai,

whose shrunken ghost
attacks the window pane —
still waspish

in his crisp corselet
of black and gold
hammered out by *Domaru.*

In coolie hats,
the peasant dustbins
hoard their scraps,

careless of the warrior class...
It is late, late:
we have squeezed

a fluent ideogram
of cleansing cream
across the baby's bottom.

It is time to eat
the rack of pork
which curves and sizzles

like a permanent wave
by Hokusai
time to bend

to a bowl of rice,
time to watch
your eyes become

Chinese with laughter
when I say that
orientals eat with stilts.

Taylorism

Norman Stone

'Like Goering with culture, I reach for my revolver when offered philosophies of history,' wrote A.J.P. Taylor some years ago, when the 'What is History' theme was going the rounds. He likes to parade himself as a simple, practical man — 'an old-fashioned, penny-counting historian'. He thinks that history's only function is 'fun', dismisses the rest as 'sales-talk' and believes that we study history 'for pleasure, not instruction'.

The fact is that he has himself given the world a great deal of both. As Chris Wrigley's large and thorough bibliography of his works[1] shows, he has been more prolific, on a wider range of subjects, than any of his contemporaries except perhaps for E.H. Carr. He has written two standard works of reference in Oxford series: *English History 1914-1945* and *The Struggle for Mastery in Europe 1848-1918* — now a generation old, but still the best place to go if you want to know what, say, the Schleswig-Holstein question was about. Taylor's *Bismarck,* his *Habsburg Monarchy* and his famous *Origins of the Second World War* are all classics, which are regularly reprinted and which have something fresh to say each time you look at them. He was and is a wonderful lecturer. He has combined all of this with a journalistic sideline that would have occupied other men full-time. And yet he is generous with his time when it comes to virtually unpaid, humdrum academic work — giving occasional lectures, or contributing reviews to the scholarly journals. He will shortly be 75, and it is a good time to consider his career as a whole.

Taylor's public stance has always been a radical one, and he has quoted more than once the French revolutionary's motto: *je suis contre.* He has made his reputation in debunking Establishments — the Habsburg Monarchy, statesmen, generals, diplomats or politicians. In his *English History* he was even surprisingly good on bankers. He approves, in good radical style, of the People: he writes warmly, for instance, of the working classes' generosity of spirit at the time of the General Strike, when they stood by the miners though this would bring no obvious advantage. But, oddly,

---

[1]Chris Wrigley, *A.J.P. Taylor: A Complete Annotated Bibliography* (Harvester, 1980).

he is not very interested in social history, probably feels that it can be made up once you get the political side right, and writes off sociology as nonsense. He is concerned with individuals and their decisions, and so has written mainly about Establishments, even if he disapproves of them. There is some tension between what interests him and his own attitudes to it — a tension that makes him the outstanding historian of the Macmillan era. It is maybe not surprising that, with such attitudes, he should have been associated with the Beaverbrook empire and become a great popularising historian.

But though Taylor has always been a popular historian, he is still a professional one, of extraordinary technical gifts. His most obvious strength is his style, which tells, even in his briefest comments. He likes short sentences, with short words, and he is sparing with adjectives or adverbs. He likes homely words (he is, for instance, the only historian who regularly uses the word 'fancy'). His paragraphs are dramatic: you always want to know what happens next.

Above all, he has a wit and irony that English history has not known since Gibbon. Here he is, introducing a very complex subject, the political crisis of 1931, which, occurring in the context of the Slump and the collapse of the pound, split the existing Labour government and brought about a 'National' coalition of Labour Right and Conservatives: 'The new age got off to a good start. A crisis of muddle which no one properly understood led to a general election of unrivalled confusion. A National government, which had been formed to save the pound, failed to save it; presented themselves as the saviours of the country on the basis of this failure; and had their claim accepted by a great majority of the electors.' He has no rival in the acid footnote that often sums up, in the shortest possible space, an issue of which the rest of us might be tempted to make a meal. *English History* contains a classic, in the context of British strategy during the 'phoney war' of 1930-40. One essential element in that extraordinary strategy was the belief that Hitler's economic system was collapsing, and that blockade would finish it off. Only one man, the Cambridge economist Claude Guillebaud, really understood that what Hitler had done was to stumble on the economics of public spending. He published a book saying as much, and was almost imprisoned under the 18B regulation as a pro-Nazi. In a footnote which cast a glow over Guillebaud's last years, Taylor acknowledged his achievement and added: 'His reputation never recovered from this recognition of the truth.'

Style can be a dangerous thing, as Taylor himself pointed out about the later Shaw ('verbal felicity, nothing to say'). There are times when the sheer verbal excitement of a Taylor paragraph can detract from its meaning: you remember the phrases, not what they are saying. The tension builds up as these short sentences follow each other; quite often, you cannot put the book down. But sometimes you find yourself turning to a far less agile writer — a May or a Macartney on the Habsburgs, an Otto Pflanze on Bismarck — to understand the context, and to appreciate what Taylor achieved in simplifying it all. Taylor's two books on the world wars are astonishing feats of clarity and compression. He himself regards his *Second World War* as, technically, his best piece of work, in that he succeeded in combining the German and the Japanese wars in a coherent, concise account. Both books can safely be put into the hands of an intelligent 14-year-old who wants to know what happened. Both also have something to say to a specialist, because Taylor is an inspired 'guesser' of things.

I have found this myself on several occasions, for my own interests — coincidentally — have followed Taylor's. Some years ago, when I was writing an article on Hungarian politics at the turn of the century, I hit upon an insoluble problem: why had the Government lost the election of 1904? Hungarian governments did not lose elections: they jotted down the names of successful candidates, and then let the police organise for them to be elected. The problem in Hungarian politics was to keep the government bloc together, and to stop the small opposition from obstructing parliamentary business. Taylor found the answer: the Government had deliberately lost that election, in order to foist responsibility on the opposition and thereby stop the Habsburg Army from intervening. After laboriously going through the sources, I found that Taylor was quite right.

A similar inspired guess in his *First World War* put me onto an important truth about Russian railways: they came under crippling strain in wartime circumstances, not because the network or rolling-stock was too poor — on the contrary, they could stand comparison even with Germany — but because the Army authorities used an excessive amount of railway transport to carry fodder for horses, particularly cavalry horses that were next to useless in the field. When I checked up on this, I found that Taylor had put me on the right lines. The German Army used only a fifth of its railway transport for fodder: the Russian army used half. You do not need much more explanation of the supply crisis, whether civilian or military, that preceded the revolution in 1917. Taylor's ability to intuit things after which the technicians have to lumber — in his *Second World War* there is a similar intuition about Soviet tank strength in the early summer of 1942 — marks a true leader in historical writing. It is maybe no surprise that Taylor's only hero in modern England is Lloyd George — also a man 'above the parties' who could tell the technicians what to do. Perhaps it was this that made Taylor so interested in Adolf Hitler.

On the strength of his *Origins of the Second World War*, Taylor was accused of being a Nazi sympathiser — an accusation that is not worth refuting. He said that 'Hitler' was not a sufficient explanation for the outbreak of war in September 1939: the British were also responsible. For some years after Hitler had come to power, they tried to bring him into some kind of political and economic partnership that would uphold the European order and maybe make Hitler less dreadful at home. They lured him up the garden path and then slammed the door in his face when he tried to take Danzig, which everyone regarded as legitimately German. When the British declared war on him, Hitler was obviously dismayed; he insulted Ribbentrop for misleading him. At the same time, since he and not the British had an alliance with Russia, he could stand the pace, and even suspected that the British had only declared war on him to save face. This interpretation transfers much of the problem from Berlin to London. When the book came out, this was regarded as scandalous. But the interpretation is now commonplace, and we have moved on.

It was Taylor's picture of Hitler that was really disturbing. Earlier writers had seen Hitler as an evil genius, revealing his plans in *Mein Kampf*, planning to destroy German democracy, militarise Germany, annihilate the neighbouring countries to south and east, and embark on a conquest of the world. Taylor saw something different — still evil, but not in the Hollywood sense that was apparently required. A year or two before, he had written a *Bismarck* that also clashed with customary opinion: Bismarck turned out to be a man who despised ideas, a master gambler who profited from the weakness of two Establishments — the German Liberals and the Habsburgs — at one go. Taylor had been reading the various documents on Hitler as they came out, and saw that

Hitler was much more of a short-term opportunist than anyone had supposed. His rearmament, about which he boasted, was sufficient only for a short war with a weak state; it was Austrians or Czechoslovaks or Englishmen who kicked off the crisis that led to German occupation of Austria or the Sudetenland or the destruction of the Czech state; it was Hitler's expectation that the same would happen over Poland that led him to miscalculate in September 1939; the various documents used at Nuremberg to hang leading Nazis for conspiracy to cause war were fraudulent — especially in the case of the Hossbach Memorandum of November 1937; finally, *Mein Kampf*, which so many writers had taken seriously as Hitler's blue-print, was simply the kind of bad-tempered vapouring you could hear in any Munich beerhouse or Viennese café. To be fair, that was Hitler's own judgment of it: it had been written in prison, when he had nothing better to do, and he wished he had not written it at all.

Taylor would never, of course, deny that Hitler intended to restore Germany as the Great Power in Europe; nor would he deny that Hitler probably meant to expand at Russia's expense. How did it then happen that he found himself involved in a war with the Western Powers? It was a good enough question, and Taylor's answer was a coherent one, based on better documentation than his opponents had.

True, he overstated his position. It was an unnecessary provocation to say that war broke out in September 1939 because Hitler launched a diplomatic manoeuvre a day later than he should have done. In his desire to show how much combustible material lay around in eastern Europe for Hitler to use, Taylor sometimes oversimplified. It was true, as Taylor says, that the Austrian crisis of 1938 was kicked off when Schuschnigg, the Austrian Chancellor, asked to see Hitler; similarly it was the Czechoslovak leader, Benes, who kicked off the crisis that led to Munich in September 1938 and Hitler's annexation of the Sudetenland. But these statesmen were responding to situations that Hitler had created. In March 1939, the Czechoslovak state broke up altogether when the Slovaks declared their independence. Taylor seems to think that this happened more or less as a consequence of a nationality quarrel between Czechs and Slovaks, and in a sense he is right. But he forgot that there had been severe German pressure on the Slovaks for some months. He quotes a remark that Hitler made to a Slovak Fascist early in 1939, to the effect that he, Hitler, wished he had known about the Slovak movement before. This remark can only have been a face-saver: Hitler had been studying how to use Slovak nationalism to break up Czechoslovakia for the previous two months, and his agents had been at work. None of this really dents Taylor's case, but it gave hostages to fortune which his critics could use — a great deal less scrupulously than Taylor had used his own evidence.

One great strength — perhaps the greatest — in *Origins* was a standard Taylorian anti-Establishment theme. The key to that book lies in its first hundred or so pages, demonstrating the weakness of the international Establishment between the wars, and especially the gap between its rhetoric and its ambitions. 'Self-determination of peoples' had been a con-trick so far as the defeated peoples of 1918 had been concerned; so was the League of Nations. 'Reparations', the Gold Standard, German Democracy, the Little Entente were all of them bogus — like the Maginot Line which was set up, at great expense, to defend it all. Taylor had a wonderful time in these first pages of *Origins*, demonstrating the hollowness and even the contradictions of the post-war settlements. It was almost as if they invited a Hitler. It probably is as true to say that Hitler was a creation of his own success as that his success was his creation.

There were gaps, inevitably, in *Origins*. Taylor's Hitler was rather too passive, a man on the make who was led into situations. It is almost certainly right not to bother too much with *Mein Kampf* in a direct sense: but it said a great deal about the moral framework in which its author operated (and for that matter its readers). Taylor tended to be weak on 'atmosphere', to stick perhaps too closely to the kind of documentation he had used to such effect in his earlier works of diplomatic history. He was certainly right in saying that Hitler did not go to war to solve some great economic and social crisis — T.W. Mason's efforts to demonstrate this have been a boring failure — but he might have considered the long-term causes of the Second World War. Still, his facts have stood up astonishingly well. Almost the only area where there has been a modification worth mentioning concerns Hitler's armaments. It now turns out that German armament in the 1930s was quite low, not because Hitler wanted it to be, but because the Nazi state was not good at producing the goods. Hitler would say that he wanted the skies darkened by aircraft. His planners would knock a third off his figure; then the producers would manufacture a third less than that; and Goering would step in and scrap the whole programme, substituting other aircraft.

Origins offers no pattern — only muddle and misunderstanding, and an arms-race exploding into war. Taylor was (and is) a keen unilateral disarmer, and 1939 was maybe a parable for him. So, demonstrably, was 1914. In his short book on the outbreak of the First World War — *War by Timetable* — he more or less made out that the crisis of July 1914 began with German 'brinkmanship', but developed into war because the Great Powers, especially Germany, were caught by the intricate technicalities of their mobilisation programmes. Negotiations had to be cut short because generals became nervous that if they wasted time in talking, their enemies would steal a march on them when it came to mustering troops for the railway movements which everyone knew would decide the outcome of the war. This is of course quite fair at one level. But the atmosphere of mistrust and Russo-German rivalry in which such panics could occur matters at least as much: it made the difference, between, say, 1911 and 1914. To account for an atmosphere of this kind is not easy.

A.J.P. Taylor makes something of a virtue out of not confronting long-term questions. In a splendid metaphor, he said that looking for long-term causes of things was like ascribing motor accidents to the existence of the internal combustion-engine. We would forgive him the sentiment for the sake of the metaphor. He dislikes explanations 'which explain everything and nothing' (and said some very sensible things on Marxism in his introduction to the *Communist Manifesto*). He writes rudely about Acton's pontificating — it leads straight to *1066 and All That* — and he is not much less rude about Burckhardt. His own grasp is sometimes weaker when he has to tackle a larger theme than usual — say, 'Fascism'. There are signs that he is occasionally uneasy about this: he can say surprisingly favourable things about the history of technology, and he once said of the famous Dutch historian, Geyl, that he was one of very few historians who would stop the historian apologising to the philosopher.

It is a pity that he did not get an Oxford chair just at the moment when he might have developed his range to cover longer-term historical subjects. Still, even if he was treated by Oxford with the same kind of grotesque misappreciation that E.H. Carr had received, it was by his own choice that he abandoned the Oxford position he still had, and spent the next few years largely on journalism and writing textbooks.

One fruit of that period is Taylor's uncharacteristically lengthy life of Beaverbrook, who caught him as he fell or propelled himself from Oxford's good graces. It was an extremely laudatory life — Taylor's only exercise in that genre. But I do not know that this connection did A.J.P. Taylor very much good — any more than it did Michael Foot, Harold Nicolson, Robert Bruce-Lockhart, Tom Driberg or any of the other literati who seem to have lost a dimension in the service of that heterogeneous collection of unlikeable lost causes that Beaverbrook picked up. Taylor wrote that the *Express* was what England would have been without its class system. (He also said of Chaplin — another acquisitive little man who did splendid things in his youth before degenerating into a bad-tempered and slushy old money-bags — that he was 'as timeless as Shakespeare and as great'.) Taylor had in fact been trapped in a position he himself must have found deeply uncomfortable, as chaplain on a pirates' ship. He was happier when it was the other way about.

The extraordinary thing about this connection is that, although he was caught up in the Beaverbrook empire, Taylor did not care a fig for the social careerism, expense-account lunches and general splashing of money that might have made sense of it all. He was out of place in that world. Was it that Beaverbrook's exuberance and ebullience could cut through the emotional constraints of the Nonconformist North of England? Was it that he offered his own version of power? Was it just that he made a fuss of Taylor at a bad time?

This latest volume of Taylor's essays[2] begins with an autobiographical essay that explains everything short of that. His origin, Dissenting middle-class stock in the North of England, accounts for a great deal: 'On the one hand you reject established views — religious in earlier times, political and social in our own. On the other hand, you have no inner conflict in doing so. Indeed you would have a conflict only if you accepted them.' His only hero is the People, or perhaps the common-sense characters who spoke for them and aspired to become their managers — Bright, Brougham, Peel (he even contrives to say some good things about C.P. Snow). He inhabits an oddly Dickensian world, in which the British Empire is represented by a Major Bagstock, the Civil

---

[2] A.J.P. Taylor, *Politicians, Socialism and Historians* (Hamish Hamilton, 1980).

Service by the Tite Barnacles, the bourgeoisie by the Veneerings, religion by the Reverend Melchisedech Howler. In his *English History* the only people he respects are managers, especially if they are slightly neurotic, as Baldwin (like Bismarck) was. As for the rest, the Church of England, like the Habsburg Monarchy, might as well take itself off to Hollywood; so maybe should the British Monarchy, though not so fast; the universities produce little, and that little is not read; the Army does not come off very well, though the Navy does. It is altogether a Little Englander's view of the recent English past: if the People were freed of all the claptrap of Empire, Peerage, Church, Civil Service, Ancient Universities, then all would be well. He ends his *English History* on a note of hope, as the Labour Government comes in: 'Men no longer sang "England Arise". But England had arisen just the same.'

This same attitude underlay what he said about the Habsburg Monarchy a generation ago. Most Englishmen who write about the Habsburgs do so dazzled by the romance and gloss of a thousand-year-old empire whose head could claim the Mandate of Heaven, and use it to enjoin on his subjects a suitable consciousness of the futility of human endeavour — particularly political endeavour, and particularly where it meant limiting the power of the Mandate of Heaven. Taylor was different. He seems to have peered across the fog of Middle European history and espied there faces that reminded him of the government front bench. He lived in Vienna for two years, learnt the language (and many others) thoroughly, but seems to have gained no affection at all for the place. Metternich's aphorisms ('most men would do better while shaving'), German liberalism, Archduke Franz Ferdinand's promise, Magyar nationalism, most of the Croats (they regarded their horses as 'more national than their peasants') and virtually all of Viennese culture ('daring arguments, tame conclusions') are put to flight in a marvellous essay, the only heroes of which are the manager, Tito, and the saint (or maybe mismanager) Michael Karolyi, whom Taylor knew. This dislike of Establishments also led him to write badly of the Prussians; until a few years ago, he was a notorious German-hater. He was also extraordinarily rude about the Italians — Prussians at heart, but with an element of southern frivolity thrown in. It was maybe understandable that he should have regarded Soviet Russia, for a time, as the great hope. Here was a People, demonstrably Managed. At the end of the war, he thought that 'we can be more confident of the future of the Anglo-Russian alliance when we have learnt to think of Trieste as Trst.' By 1954, he was calling Russia 'the greatest catastrophe of my lifetime'. In other words, he has been honest all the way through, even it is has led him into trouble and self-contradiction.

In the end, the country where Taylor belongs most is probably the one he has written about least — France. He admits that he learnt much of his style from the great French historian, Albert Sorel; he could probably be brought to admit that he owed much to another French writer of distinction, Louis Eisenmann, whose *Compromis austro-hongrois* he once described as the finest historical work of this century. France of the Third Republic had a solid patriotism, not one captured by imperialist ranters or militarists. It was anti-clerical. It had an intellectual élite that was honest, hard-working, egalitarian, humane, and vertically, though not horizontally, puritanical. That élite set some sort of standard for the kind of ex-peasant politician on the make who kept the Republican show on the road. The exoneration of Dreyfus, Taylor says, brought more glory to France than Napoleon did.

At bottom, A.J.P. Taylor is a romantic individualist. It is this which makes him so uneasy with institutions. It is this, too, which seems to have caused his increasing breach with the Left. His *English History* carefully catalogued the blunders and the have-your-cake-and-eat-it attitudes of the Left in the Thirties. He has nothing at all in common with the methods or ideology of the new left-wing historians; and he probably regards the present-day constellation in the Labour Party as every bit as unscrupulous and dreary — and more dangerous, because more comprehensive — as any interest group of the past. He has become something of a pessimist, and says: 'Now I regard the state and still more the future of my country gloomily. Indeed I often wonder whether it is worth while writing history at all.' He would have deserved well of the Republic, if we had had one.

G.M. Trevelyan's Two Terrible Things

John Vincent

G.M. Trevelyan (1876-1962) burnt all his papers. His 'Autobiography of an Historian' (1949) is as the title suggests both narrow and concise. The sketch by a pupil, J.H. Plumb, published in 1951, is a survey of the books rather than the man. Mrs Moorman, herself the biographer of Wordsworth as well as a loyal daughter, rightly considers this is not enough, and has retrieved letters, chiefly early and chiefly to his brother, the Labour Minister, Sir Charles Trevelyan, which show the forces that inspired G.M. Trevelyan's history.[1] Her study makes her father accessible as a human being for the first time, relieves him from the imputation of being too much of a paragon to be interesting, and shows him, without hindsight and Whig interpretation, as a writer of distinct ideological and quasi-religious purpose, more aware of his limitations and his lack of self-confidence than of the recognition the world awarded. He now appears as a liberal bigot whom no socialist, Christian or conservative could consider nonpartisan.

Mrs Moorman's book concentrates on the period before his return to Cambridge as Regius Professor (a Baldwin appointment) in 1927. Only two of her ten chapters concern his life after 1927, whether from discretion or from lack of materials is not made quite clear. Lord Trevelyan, a diplomatist, throws more light on Trevelyan and his family in 'The Master', an essay semi-humorous in tone, set among a cluster of sketches of various Trevelyans from successive epochs.[2] The first part of Lord Trevelyan's book concerns Khrushchev, Nasser, Chou, and such celebrities, the second is family history; no one will complain of either section who enjoys worldly understatement. Mrs Moorman and Lord Trevelyan together give us a picture of great interest.

G.M. Trevelyan was a third-generation arriviste. His grandfather, Sir Charles Trevelyan, Trollope's Sir Gregory Hardlines, pushed his way from nothing to the top of the Civil Service, marrying Macaulay's sister on the way. His father pushed his

---

[1] Mary Moorman, *George Macaulay Trevelyan: A Memoir* (Hamish Hamilton, 1980).

[2] Humphrey Trevelyan, *Public and Private* (Hamish Hamilton, 1980).

way into high politics, marrying a cotton fortune on the way.
G.M. Trevelyan himself was pushed into the Mastership of Trinity
in 1940 (one of Brendan Bracken's best appointments). His
seigneurial attitude, his rural disposition and habits, his distance
from mundane academics, all reflected the reverence for tradition
and continuity which often afflicts younger sons of cadet branches.
There had indeed always been Trevelyans at Nettlecombe, but that
elder branch of the family luckily died out in 1879, bringing a
further injection of upward social mobility and broad acres to a
dynasty which had begun with a penniless clerk in India in 1830. By
1900 G.M. Trevelyan saw his family almost as haughty Border
Lords: 'It is a rule that no Trevelyan ever sucks up either to the
press, or the chiefs, or the "right people". The world has given us
money enough to enable us to do what we think right; we thank it
for that and ask no more of it.' The Trevelyans were synthetic
Border Whigs as Sir W. Scott was a synthetic Border Tory.

It is doubtful whether the great families of Northumbria quite
saw the Regius Professor and Cambridge master as the
representative of landed tradition — the mask he wore in
Cambridge. For one thing, his Tory acquaintance was apparently
limited beyond belief. For another, his brother the Labour
Education Minister combined the rights of man with the *droit de
seigneur*, and with the diddling of the National Trust on the
principle that property was a crime, but sponging and bad
landlordship were not. G.M. Trevelyan had a David and Saul
relationship of some intensity with his brother Charles, the
wenching socialist baronet, who suffered from depression and
aristocratic bad temper and wilfulness. If anything could have cured
him of progressivism, it would have been the sight of his brother;
but G.M. Trevelyan's innocence was too fundamental to be
disturbed by facts. 'Three years consummate misery' at Harrow
made him loathe 'aristocratic curs' and embrace Democracy. From
there, he went on to three significant and consistent positions.
Before 1914 he embodied the ferment engendered by the new
Liberalism. Between the wars he embodied the new liberal
conservatism and its sustaining myths. In the 1940s he represented
Churchillian continuity and Englishness in the intellectual sphere.
The clue to his development was religious.

G.M. Trevelyan was the strongly agnostic son of a mildly
'nothingarian' father. The grandparents were Evangelical Anglican
on one side, Unitarian on the other. All three Trevelyan brothers

were unbelievers, but with George it was much more than mere absence of belief, it was a creed in its own right. 'Two terrible things have happened this week,' he was heard to say, 'my son has bought a motorbike and my daughter has become a Christian.' As a young don, he was turned down on religious grounds by the first great love of his life, the daughter of a great Anglican family. In the aftermath of this rejection, he thought 'a definitely agnostic atmosphere is essential for my free development of work and of life.' His daughter, the wife of a historian bishop with whom Trevelyan got on rather well, not surprisingly softens the outlines, notes his regular attendance at Chapel when Master of Trinity (1940-51), and records his saying: 'If there had been more sensible clergymen in Cambridge in my time I could have become a churchman.'

But the Trevelyan who attended Chapel as an official duty — Trinity was worth a mass — had essentially the same outlook as the Harrow schoolboy who had refused to be confirmed. He preached a sermon in Trinity in 1945, but it was not a Christian sermon. To say he was merely anti-clerical is only partly true, though he retained the old Evangelical family feeling against high churchmen, for his definition of anti-clericalism was pretty capacious. Talking in old age of Lucretius, he burst out: 'And doesn't it strike you as extraordinary that Lucretius should have lived and written only a few years before the greatest outburst of clericalism that the world has ever seen?' Trevelyan's judgment of Christianity was probably formed essentially by his experience of it as a university party at Cambridge: his knowledge of it in other contexts was slight, though he did once stoop to arrange an honorary degree for Dorothy Sayers. But his main reason for opposing Christianity was that he believed in something else, and did so to the end.

He really believed in Carlyle, Shelley, Meredith, civic altruism, the countryside, Garibaldi, and the lives of heroes teaching by example. If he had not been more gentleman than intellectual, he might have become a Comtean; as it was, he remained a Carlylean. His last two publications were attempts to put Carlyle and Meredith before the public of the 1950s; he had been trying to do the same thing in his *The Meredith Pocket Book* of 1906. His Clark Lectures of 1953, his last sustained composition, showed how little two wars had affected his creed. He defended Scott as the great social historian who had made Carlyle and Macaulay possible, vindicated Shelley against Arnold, and preached a religion of poetry: 'It is joy, joy in our inmost hearts. It is a passion like love or it is nothing.' He fused England, poetry, joy, youth and landscape in a single sacramental experience. If this is rather like Arnold, dynastic connections are not far to seek: his wife was the great-niece of the poet, and her mother, Mrs Humphry Ward of *Robert Elsmere* fame, had even composed a special free-thinkers' marriage service for G.M. Trevelyan's wedding. The late Victorian child was truly father to the Master of Trinity. Trevelyan was as strongly opposed to modernity, urban modernity, as any Christian. If he could move people 'to seriously question the value of modern life, I shall be quite satisfied'. He was as explicitly sacramental as any Christian. He saw the modern passion for mountains, rocks and moors as 'one of the sacraments prepared for man or discovered by man'. In this he had all the seriousness and severity of his Evangelical ancestors. He was a pious pagan who took his paganism with a deep reverence, without any touch of hedonism. He felt kinship with Meredith, Shelley and Carlyle because they — Meredith particularly — seemed to him to be pious pagans who had faced the problems of life without religion with a religious outlook. He even believed in a pagan version of life after death. The statue of Garibaldi in every Italian town was 'the symbol of the hope of resurrection after centuries of death'. At times of difficulty, his thoughts turned to Garibaldi, as the orthodox might look to Christ.

He believed, rather more oddly, in Shelley as a teacher rather than a poet: 'For centuries to come, the eyes of men...will be turned to the funeral pyre of Shelley on the shore of the blue Mediterranean.' Not till Dowden in the 1880s had revealed the full extent of Shelley's caddishness did the educated young take him fully to their hearts. For the generation that preceded the Liberal victory of 1906, Shelley was a thinker, no less. This takes some explaining. Enough now to say that for Trevelyan poetry and the countryside contained the means by which the few were to save the many. His ideal was 'the wedding of the modern democratic spirit, the spirit of duty in its highest form, to modern literature'. The masses were to be given a religion, Shelley was to be its Cranmer, and *Sartor Resartus*, 'the greatest book in the world', its Thirty-Nine Articles.

While the intellectuals of Continental Europe were discovering socialism and irrationalism, Trevelyan and his English generation were trying to create a new spirituality to fill the vacuum left by the departure of Gladstone and his public Christianity. They had four options before them: religiose literary paganism, altruistic civic idealism, the countryside and music. Music as a vehicle for lay spirituality had to wait for the wireless. Altruism was part of the Trevelyan ethic. His letters to his brother were signed successively 'God Save Ireland', 'God Save The People', and 'Ich Dien', despite the Irish having threatened, in their progressive way, to kill him in infancy.

The countryside was more than enjoyment to Trevelyan. It was a public doctrine. His ruralism was offered as a remedy for the ills of an urban people, as an emblem of a common Englishness and as a therapy for the human condition. He believed that 'without natural beauty the English people will perish in the spiritual sense.' Walking was his equivalent to meditation or praying. His essay 'Must England's beauty perish?' (1929) and his lecture 'The Call and Claims of Natural Beauty' (1931) were his contribution to the making of the Baldwin consensus. At another level, they were part of the response by the intelligentsia to the motor-car, while it is truistic to remark that they involved an attempt at social control. His ruralism was based on the same odd premise as that of Dr Leavis — namely, that if urban mass culture is wrong, something else must, from polemical necessity, be right. Trevelyan's emphasis on the scenic, national, vivid, tonic quality of the past as an alternative to a drab present linked him between the wars with G.M. Young, Baldwin, Kipling, Arthur Bryant, Helen Waddell, John Buchan and Vaughan Williams, who together form a cultural unity which needs discussion. During the second war, the same qualities made his *Social History* (1944) as much an expression of the wartime thirst for other worlds as *Brideshead Revisited* or *The Unquiet Grave,* and brought him a publisher's cheque for £27,000 of which £25,000 went in tax.

Trevelyan's politics were formed, not in response to the resurgent Liberalism of 1906, but to the period of eclipse which followed the Home Rule split of 1886. His father, as a young radical of the 1860s, had been able to see the intelligent artisan as the prime mover towards a better world (though G.O. Trevelyan had to buy an estate for the duration of the 1865 election in order to encourage deferential radicalism). By the 1890s, the artisan read the *Daily Mail*, voted Tory, was in the hands of the brewers, and delighted in the Boer War. The artisan was no longer intelligent. Liberals were in a dilemma. What does a party of the people do when the people are against them, and they against the people?

Where his father had supported reform because the urban masses were good, Trevelyan turned to it because they were bad. Like other contributors to Masterman's once famous *Heart of the Empire,* he used Matthew Arnold's reactionary cultural criticism to reach progressive conclusions. He called for 'good intellectual food for habitual consumption, to meet this terrible free trade in garbage'. His remedies for the traditionless 'false consciousness' of the town worker were not collectivist. Instead, he looked to 'the enthusiastic *effort of individuals* in the spheres of economy, social work, religion, education, literature, journalism and art' as the means by which 'the glorious world of the future will be built up'.

His political creed implied a cultural programme, and his historical writing was a matter of putting into practice the politics of his youth. Always a naive liberal pessimist — in 1901 he saw 'the world going to ruin, for causes much more fundamental than the mere South African error' — he never really came out of his shell in party-political terms. His autobiography, however, perhaps suppresses some element of political motive in his leaving Trinity, and moving to London in 1903. The cover story, true as far as it goes, that he gave up being a don in order to write books, overlooks his founding of an independent Liberal periodical in 1902, his commitment to the Working Men's College in London, his being seen by Beatrice Webb as the rising hope of political Liberalism, and his refusal to be Director of the London School of Economics in 1908. If he turned to books rather than practical politics, it was because his political analysis laid down that books were politically more effective.

His aversion to Christianity entered into his party politics. He did not like Liberal 'bondage to Non-Conformity', though he fought hard for the party in 1906 and 1910, and was personally behind such demagogic stunts as the 'Big Loaf' poster. He warmed to Labour for the idiosyncratic reason that it was the first time a party had 'a secular religious background' which would 'counteract the enormously paralysing effect of religious humbug in England'. As early as 1912 he wished MacDonald premier, thinking 'he had more sense than the rest of the Labour men and all the government put together.' He never actually joined Labour, and socialism meant nothing to him. He was pleased with the 1924 Labour government, partly because it contained 'a good deal of old Liberal blood', partly because it showed the inexhaustible suppleness of our ancient constitution. In the early 1920s he was president of the

Berkhamsted Liberal Association, resigning in 1926 because Asquith was too harsh against the General Strike. By 1945 he felt, 'I should as soon see Labour win as not,' though he took little pleasure in what followed.

If he seems quite narrowly to have escaped the role of an Attlee, whom he much resembled in outlook, he also narrowly escaped being cast in the difficult part of the emotionally committed regional specialist, patronising emergent nationalisms and mixing governmental assignments with propagandist work. He might, in short, have become Seton-Watson, with whom he travelled in the Balkans. The collapse of Serbia saved him from becoming a Serbian expert; the rise of Mussolini brought his career as a writer on Italy to an end, and redirected his energies into English channels. He was not at his best in foreign politics.

He began, unlike his pro-Boer father, as a humane imperialist in the Boer War: that is, he wanted England to win and the Boers to thrive. He was an Edwardian Little Englander. 'The worst danger of all is the claim...that if France goes to war, we must,' he wrote on 28 July 1914. Germany he saw as the ultimate bulwark against Russian barbarism. 'Sir Edward Grey has betrayed us,' he wrote on 5 August 1914. On this issue, shattered though he was at the time, he came to change his mind. In *Lord Grey of the Reform Bill* (1920) he saw the war as having 'been fought on the principles of Fox and Grey', and in 1937, writing the life of the Foreign Secretary who had taught his wife her knowledge of birds, he accepted that 'we were wrong and Grey was right.'

His main war work was as Commandant (1915-18) of the Friends' Ambulance Unit in Italy, a self-financing but not wholly Quaker body which was not short of liberal romantics. There is little to be said about this beyond that Trevelyan ran a very good front-line ambulance service, though Henry James, a close family friend, perhaps rather overdid it when he wrote: 'I think incessantly of George and yearn over him...and in fact figure him as the backbone, quite, of that long and in some ways perhaps rather limp peninsula.' Trevelyan's courage and ability to command are beyond doubt; the details, to which Mrs Moorman gives too much space, matter little.

Trevelyan was in Italy, not as a pacifist subterfuge (he was 38 in 1914), but because, perhaps less creditably, he believed in Italy's war. He really believed that it was worth redeeming Trento and Trieste. He came to feel Shelley and Byron would have approved of

Italy's imperialist war, and he saw the Austria of 1914 (with its universal franchise which Britain still lacked) in terms of the black legend of literary liberalism. Trevelyan had swallowed hook, line and sinker the attitudes of one party to a quarrel, which is little to the credit of one who made the traditional Whig claim for political history that 'the knowledge of past transactions, coolly viewed from the distance of later years, will provide the best education in life and politics.' Trevelyan, having idolised Garibaldi for marching on Rome, was not in the best position to criticise Mussolini, 'that man of genius' as he called him, though he hoped, in a lecture, that the new man on a white horse would restore freedom along with order and discipline.

Mussolini might have led Trevelyan to have second thoughts about his beloved Risorgimento, and to become more conscious of the resemblances between the liberal and the fascist dictatorships, especially as seen through Catholic eyes. Both regimes used the same clichés of secular modernity, action, nation-building and self-sacrifice. In fact, the advent of Mussolini only led Trevelyan to stop thinking on Italian subjects, as perhaps was to be expected from the title of his anthology, *English Songs of Italian Freedom* (1911). His Garibaldian creed, which was at its height between 1905 and 1920, was based not so much on love of Italy as on dislike of Christianity. He wrote his three Garibaldi books, which so caught the mood of the pre-1914 Liberal revival, as a bigoted partisan, 'feeling inexpressibly the unreality of all historical events except only those performed in a red shirt'. He would have been as surprised by Christian Democratic Italy as by Lampedusa's *The Leopard*.

In his other works, as Mrs Moorman reveals, he saw himself as more than a technical historian unravelling the story of the past. His *Wycliffe* (1899) reflected, by its very choice of subject, the polemical anti-clericalism that marked his journalism at the time. His *John Bright* (1913), begun about 1909-10, reflects the constitutional struggles of 1909-11, and a belief that his subject was 'a wonder and a world's desire — more like Garibaldi than the Prince Consort'. He feared being a person 'who wrote three amusing volumes about Garibaldi and then tailed off', because 'any fool can tell the story of Garibaldi interestingly.' He was also aware that 'I have not yet tackled the art of telling politics,' and derived immense help from his father over the Reform crisis of 1866-67. ('By his help, and by that alone, I can make that really live.') Trevelyan was conscious, as we should be, that in his biographies he was working far in advance of the other historians of the day, who rarely ventured beyond the younger Pitt.

His textbook on the *Nineteenth Century* (1922), a landmark in its day, cannot in his eyes have been quite anodyne, for he noted 'the Church papers restore my self-respect by their disapproval.' His *History of England* (1926) was conceived in wartime Italy in a political as much as in an academic manner. 'In this age of democracy and patriotism, I feel strongly drawn to write the history of England as I feel it, for the people.' He saw 'a vision of the evolution of English society and character and habit', and thought he might help 'some unlearned people to have it too'. His life of *Grey of the Reform Bill* (1920) was conceived in terms of the Whig apostolic succession. 'I was born and bred to write about Grey and the Reform Bill, and I believe it is the best way now of doing Fox justice, to show that it was he who made the Reform Bill possible.' And, for good measure, 'Pitt was really such a mean cad, and the world doesn't know it and thinks it a "Whig tradition".' The life of Grey, he added, was 'awfully exciting and so deeply connected with everything that happened since and is happening'. Trevelyan's journeyman work as historiographer to the Whig Party was undertaken, not to fill in time, but from deep excitement. Even his short *The English Revolution, 1688-1689* (1938), task-work for the Home University Library, filled him with zeal: 'It is one of the most amazing stories in the world and never grows old to me.'

Trevelyan's occasional ventures into public life were highly successful. If he was a man of sometimes strange ideas, he was in practical matters a pillar of common sense and effective zeal. He was chairman of the Estates Committee of the National Trust and president of the Youth Hostels Association. He persuaded the Forestry Commission to leave central Lakeland alone. He wrote one of George V's Jubilee speeches. His wife saved nine acres of Coram's Fields in central London from development. By buying farms in Langdale and at Housesteads, he secured some of the most important parts of the Lake District and the Roman Wall. His Mastership of Trinity was a happy affair, certainly for him. He was *de facto* chairman of the Oxford and Cambridge Royal Commission of the 1920s, Asquith, the real chairman, falling asleep at meetings. His public recognition came unsought and to some extent preceded his achievements, but in the event was justified by the productivity and range of his output in his fifties and sixties.

The man who had nervously declined the far from onerous duties of a Cambridge reader in 1911, when he was 35, found himself in age able to cope with running Trinity in wartime while writing the great *Social History* (though the suggestion for the book came from his publisher). Mrs Moorman and Lord Trevelyan write about the man, not the books, and about the young man of ideas, not the elder statesman. This is not therefore the time to celebrate or to analyse his history, only what lay behind it.

His period (1900-40, say) was one in which university history slept. The great technical advances of the Victorians had been made. The impetus had spent itself by 1900. Lesser men, administrators of historical fact, continued the work of Maitland, Stubbs and Acton without knowing why. History, as a university subject, was at its most institutionally successful (with Classics in decline) between the wars, just when it was most intellectually empty. The effects of an intellectual vacuum of this kind are curious. One result was Guy Burgess; another the Master of Trinity. Both were amateur doctrinaires reacting against an absence of intellectual environment and doing it rather badly. But, if Shelley and Meredith and Carlyle were tactically not the best of all possible cards to play, the strategic impulse to make an empirical subject yield a doctrinal harvest was a sound one, and Trevelyan stands high above his generation for being guided by instinct, prejudice and family tradition in the matter.

The day before he died, Trevelyan had Macaulay's Third Chapter read to him. His last words were 'Peterloo'. The nurse asked: 'What about Peterloo, Master?' He replied, '1819,' and did not speak again.

Montereale

Christopher Hill

This is not quite another *Montaillou*.[1] Professor Ginzburg's book deals with an isolated heretical individual, not with a heretical community. But it shares some of the qualities of that marvellous book. It reveals an almost equally startling body of wholly unorthodox ideas existing within a nominally Roman Catholic society. The Middle Ages, it has been unkindly said, appear to be 'the age of faith' because nearly all the evidence which survives was written by monks and priests. We might extend this to the couple of centuries after the invention of printing: they appear to be centuries of faith because priests controlled the censorship. It is very difficult to find out what ordinary people thought. They may have accepted the orthodoxy of their betters, though there are many indications that this was not the case. But if they did hold unorthodox views there was no prospect of getting them printed, except when the orthodox refuted and denounced them. Only in the present generation have historians like Robert Mandrou and Peter Burke seriously attempted to ascertain what was going on beneath the surface. In *Montaillou* Le Roy Ladurie utilised one lucky cache of evidence. Professor Ginzburg has found another.

Domenico Scandella, known as Menocchio, lived from 1532 to 1599 or 1600. He was a miller, who spent nearly all his life in Montereale, a small hill town in the Friuli, part of the Venetian republic. The occupation of miller set Menocchio apart. 'The mill was a place of meeting, of social relations, in a world that was predominantly closed and static.' Like the ale-house, 'it was a place for the exchange of ideas,' and millers were 'an occupational group exceptionally receptive to new ideas and inclined to propagate them'. Millers were prominent in medieval heretical sects and among 16th-century Anabaptists. Ginzburg describes another miller living at the same time in the mountains of Modena who had similar heresies to Menocchio.

Venice was the most liberal and anti-clerical state in Italy: early 17th-century Englishmen regarded Venetians almost as honorary Protestants. The republic's bourgeois patrician government

---

[1] Carlo Ginzburg, *The Cheese and the Worms: the Cosmos of a 16th-Century Miller* (Routledge & Kegan Paul, 1980).

exploited the fierce hostility which existed between nobles and peasants in the Friuli, on the whole supporting the latter. The Friuli was unique in Europe in having a representative body for the peasantry alongside the *Parlamento* of their betters. Menocchio benefited from Venetian anti-clericalism when he was first on trial for heresy in 1584: the inquisitor was reminded that Venetian regulations required the presence of a secular official at all trials by the Inquisition. So by 16th-century standards Menocchio lived in a relatively free society; and his village was tucked away in the mountains.

Professor Ginzburg has drawn on the account of Menocchio's interrogation, which is often full enough to be printed as dialogue. Menocchio was a loner who thought a lot for himself. He knew some of his thoughts were dangerous, but he found the captive audience of his judges irresistible, and poured out his ideas to them with the wildest imprudence, only occasionally checked by a transparent cunning. The inquisitors seem to have been flabbergasted by what they heard, and to have tried hard to make coherent sense of it so as to be able to identify Menocchio's heresies.

Eleven books were mentioned in Menocchio's trial. Some he owned, others he borrowed. We should not underestimate the importance of printing in bringing new ideas to people like Menocchio. An Italian translation of the 14th-century *Travels of Sir John Mandeville* revealed to him the existence of the quite different civilisations and religions of Islam, India and China. He also probably read the Koran, of which an Italian translation appeared in Venice in 1547. This is another example of the republic's relative liberalism: the Koran did not appear in English until 1649.

Professor Ginzburg emphasises that Menocchio's reading was 'one-sided and arbitrary, almost as if he was searching for confirmation of ideas and convictions that were already firmly entrenched'. John Bunyan, likewise uneducated, faced similar problems after the publication of the Koran in England. Professor Ginzburg compares Montaigne, a contemporary operating at a very different intellectual level, who drew sceptical conclusions from reading descriptions of the natives of America. From Mandeville, Menocchio extracted the view that there were good men in all religions: but 'since I was born a Christian I want to remain a Christian, and if I had been born a Turk I would want to live like a Turk.' From the rather surprising source of Boccaccio's

Decameron Menocchio drew the conclusion that 'each person holds his faith to be right, but we do not know which is the right one.' (Menocchio had read the *Decameron* in an edition published before the Counter-Reformation censorship got busy on it; only the story which prompted this conclusion — a story the censors blotted out — remained in his memory.)

Tolerance, respect for the views of others, seems to have been one of the ideas for which Menocchio sought confirmation from his reading. From an even less plausible source, *Il Fioretto della Bibbia*, Menocchio 'got my opinion that, when the body dies, the soul dies too, since out of many different kinds of nations some believe in one way, some in another'. It is a non-sequitur: but it illustrates one of Menocchio's most steadfast convictions. The inquisitors could easily lead him into logical traps, but could not get him to renounce his deeply-held ideas.

So the problem which Professor Ginzburg attacks is to identify and account for these convictions, which Menocchio did not get from his reading but brought to it.

In Menocchio's talk we see emerging, as if out of a crevice in the earth, a deep-rooted cultural stratum so unusual as to appear almost incomprehensible. This case...involves not only a reaction filtered through the written page, but also an irreducible residue of oral culture. The Reformation and the diffusion of printing had been necessary to permit this *different* culture to come to light. Because of the first, a simple miller had dared to think of *speaking out,* of voicing his own opinions about the Church and the world. Thanks to the second, *words* were at his disposal to express the obscure, inarticulate vision of the world that fermented within him. In the sentences or snatches of sentences wrung out of books he found the instruments to formulate and defend his ideas.

'Can't you understand, the inquisitors don't want us to know what they know!' he exclaimed to a fellow villager.

But what was the 'oral culture' that the Reformation and printing had released? What were the ideas which Menocchio brought to his reading? Here what strikes me as most remarkable is the extent to which Menocchio's ideas can be paralleled by those held in Montaillou two and a half centuries earlier, and by ideas which lurked underground in England from at least the Lollards of the 15th century until they burst out into the open in the freedom of the 1640s, when priestly censorship broke down. They included rejection of the Trinity, of the divinity of Christ, of the sacrifice of the Cross; denial of the immortality of the soul, of the existence of a local heaven or hell, of the virgin birth, of the sanctity of marriage. Menocchio was hostile to Latin as the language of a privileged class, and thought that 'Holy Scripture has been invented to deceive man.' The Apocryphal gospels were no less authoritative. He rejected images, ceremonies, the sacraments, saints' days, the power, wealth and economic oppressiveness of the Church, and a mediating priesthood: laymen had a right to preach. More positively, Menocchio accepted a sort of materialist pantheism, such as was to be reproduced in mid-17th-century England by Ranters and Gerrard Winstanley. 'Everything that can be seen is God...We are gods.' Menocchio had a wide tolerance and was impatient of theological niceties. 'We should be concerned about helping each other while we are still in this world' rather than about prayers for the dead. 'It's more important to love our neighbour than to love God.' 'He who does no harm to his neighbour does not commit sin,' even if he blasphemes. It is a morality rather than a religion. Many of these views were held by Anabaptists in the Friuli in the mid-century; Menocchio may have been in contact with such groups, though this cannot be proved. He owned a vernacular Bible, a prohibited book.

His ideas are also reminiscent of those of the great anti-Trinitarian heretic Servetus, whom Calvin burned after Servetus had escaped the Inquisition. There is no evidence that Menocchio had read Servetus, whose heresies certainly circulated widely in Italy, not only among the learned. Servetus's emphasis on the humanity of Christ, his belief that the Holy Spirit meant right reason in man, and that God was in all things, including human beings, may underlie Menocchio's outburst:

What do you imagine God to be? God is nothing else than a little breath ... Air is God ... I believe that the [Holy Spirit] is in everybody ... What is this Holy Spirit? ... This Holy Spirit can't be found.

Yet even if such contacts could be established, they are not enough to account for Menocchio's heresies. The fact that so many of them can also be encountered in 14th-century Montaillou, in 15th and 17th-century England, and among large numbers of 16th-century heretics all over Europe, suggests that Professor Ginzburg is right in postulating the existence of 'an oral culture that was the patrimony not only of Menocchio but also of a vast segment of 16th-century society'. Its beliefs were loosely formulated and varied from place to place: but the evidence for its existence is very strong. Professor Ginzburg stresses that the peasant culture existed in its own right, and was not merely the cast-off ideas of a higher culture. Indeed, he suggests that we should see 'a circular relationship composed of reciprocal influences, which travelled from low to high as well as from high to low'. Apparent echoes of Wyclif, Anabaptists or Servetus in Menocchio may tell us more about the origins of their heresies than about Menocchio's contacts. Professor Ginzburg suggests that the inquisitors were being unnecessarily clever in hearing echoes of Wyclif in Menocchio's belief in the mortality of the soul. But Anabaptists probably inherited this belief from the Hussites, who took it from English Lollards. All three may have drawn on longer-lasting peasant beliefs.

Some of the most interesting pages in this fascinating book grapple with the problem of identifying the ideas of this oral peasant culture. By definition they could not be printed in a censored press. 'The thoughts, the beliefs and the aspirations of the peasants and artisans of the past reach us (if and when they do) almost always through distorting viewpoints and intermediaries.' Ginzburg speaks of 'the tenacious persistence of a peasant religion intolerant of dogma and ritual, tied to the cycles of nature, and fundamentally pre-Christian'. Only in the 1640s in England could Levellers, Diggers, Ranters, early Quakers and other sectaries get some popular ideas into print. Ginzburg identifies rationalism, scepticism, materialism, egalitarian utopianism and religious naturalism as permanent characteristics of this culture.

Books, as we have seen, were not 'sources' for Menocchio. 'Between himself and the printed page' was 'a filter that emphasised certain words while obscuring others'. And this filter 'continually leads us back to a culture that is very different from the one expressed on the printed page — one based on an oral tradition'. Menocchio insisted that his opinions 'came out of *his* head'. 'I did not believe that paradise existed because I did not know where it was.' The title of Ginzburg's book derives from Menocchio's idea that the world was not created by God but 'produced by nature', 'from the most perfect substance of the world'. From this original chaos the angels and God himself were produced by spontaneous generation, 'just as maggots are produced from a cheese'. Professor Ginzburg points out that the doctrine of spontaneous generation of life from inanimate matter was a 'tendentiously scientific' idea, the possibility of which was not refuted until more than a century later. He draws attention to Thomas Burnet's use in *The Sacred Theory of the Origin of the Earth* (1681) of the metaphor of cheese-making.

So we are brought back to the two-way transmission of ideas from popular to upper-class culture: the problem of 'the popular roots of a considerable part of high European culture, both medieval and post-medieval'. Professor Ginzburg refers to Rabelais, Breughel, Anabaptists and Servetus: he reminds us that Giordano Bruno was burnt at the same time as Menocchio. He suggests that after the Peasants' War in Germany and the reign of the Anabaptists in Münster (the 1520s and 30s) a determined effort was made to re-establish upper-class ideological hegemony, which took 'various forms in different parts of Europe, but the evangelisation of the countryside by the Jesuits, and the capillary religious organisation based on the family achieved by the Protestant churches. can be traced to a single current', ending in the 'repression and effacement of popular culture'.

Yet if we think of our great heretical poet Milton, it is remarkable how many of his unorthodox ideas reproduce in a more sophisticated form those of Menocchio: Milton's rejection of creation *ex nihilo*, his doctrine of creation out of a pre-existent chaos, his theological materialism, his anti-Trinitarianism (often attributed to the influence of Servetus), denying the equality of the Son to the Father, his belief that 'all men are Sons of God,' his passionate hatred of idolatry, his rejection of monogamy. Milton's rebel angels argued that they were not created by God but were 'self-begot'. Milton's heresies are traditionally attributed to Classical sources: Ginzburg's remarkable book reinforces the suggestion that we should think rather about Milton's relationship to popular culture.

The Cheese and the Worms is enthralling reading. The translation, which must have been difficult, reads excellently. The translators have, however, added a gratuitous note in which they tell us that Menocchio had a fair trial. The practice of recording what the victim 'might utter during the torture, even his sighs, his cries, his laments and tears', so useful for the historian, was 'designed to discourage irregularities'. Menocchio was tortured and burnt under 'what was, for the times, an essentially moderate code of law'. Professor Ginzburg more wisely limited himself to remarking on the presence of a lay observer at Menocchio's first trial, when torture was not used. There appears to be no evidence relating to this point in his second trial, but Rome found it necessary to insist that 'the jurisdiction of the Holy Office over a case of such importance can in no way be doubted', which suggests that the secular authority was trying to save Menocchio. He was burnt at 'the express desire of his Holiness', Pope Clement VIII.

There is one consoling moment in this grim conclusion. Menocchio was subjected to the torture of the strappado for half an hour, in order to make him reveal the names of his 'accomplices'. First he said, 'Let me down, and I'll think about it,' but he still could not recall any names: he almost certainly had no followers. Jerked up again, he promised to talk, and named the Count of Montereale, lord of his village, and to this story he stuck. That last piece of peasant shrewdness was enough: the inquisitors were not anxious to get involved with a count. So Menocchio was not tortured again, so far as we know, until he died in the fire.

Grand Old Man: Harold Macmillan's Services and Disservices

Robert Blake

Biographies of living people seldom come off. There is much to be said for gathering information about a person while he is still alive, as Mr Alastair Horne is now doing in the case of Mr Macmillan. But to publish in the subject's lifetime is difficult. There are things in some people's careers which it is impossible even to mention while they are living and many more which it is hard to treat in proper perspective. To steer the course between defamation and flattery, while at the same time avoiding grey caution, is not always easy. In spite of these and other problems Mr George Hutchinson has been remarkably successful in this short and admirably written biography.[1] It is a portrait which is recognisable and vivid, essentially sympathetic but not uncritical. A valuable by-product is the author's decision to reprint Iain Macleod's piece from the *Spectator* about the manoeuvres for the succession in 1963. Since it takes more than one-eighth of his total of 150 pages, this may seem disproportionate, but it ought to be available somewhere in book form. It is one of the most remarkable articles ever written by an ex-minister.

Macleod's account raises another major problem for the contemporary biographer. There can be no doubt that Mr Macmillan, on his sick bed at King Edward's Hospital for Officers and despite the aftermath of a major operation, was determined at almost all costs to prevent Mr R.A. Butler succeeding him. His illness would have given him every excuse to resign at once and proffer no advice to the Queen at all on such a matter. Constitutionally, he was not obliged to give it, and Bonar Law declined to do so in somewhat similar circumstances in 1923. Mr Macmillan must have had the strongest motives for acting as he did. Iain Macleod's account, which has so far never been seriously disputed, shows vividly the lengths to which he was prepared to go.

Obviously, this antipathy between these two major figures is something that needs an explanation. It is not like that between

---

[1] George Hutchinson, *The Last Edwardian at No 10: An Impression of Harold Macmillan* (Quartet, 1980).

Disraeli and Gladstone, or Pitt and Fox: they belonged to opposite parties. Nor does it resemble the hostility between Ernest Bevin and Aneurin Bevan, or between Neville Chamberlain and Winston Churchill, who represented conflicting attitudes within the same party. It is not obvious that Mr Macmillan and Mr Butler differed to any great extent on matters of policy. There were disagreements, but on style and details, not content. The reasons for Mr Macmillan's determination to stop Mr Butler succeeding him have to be conjectured, but a contemporary biography by the nature of the genre cannot give us the whole story and it will be many years before we have it, if we ever do.

However this may be, it is pleasant to record that at various societies and gatherings the two great men still meet each other with the enigmatic courtesy and cryptic urbanity that one would expect, though does not invariably find, in the world of country houses, London clubs and Oxford and Cambridge colleges. The idea, spread by some, that Lord Butler (as he now is) was more 'middle-class', and therefore more acceptable to the rank and file of the Conservative Party, than Mr Macmillan with his alleged 'grouse-moor image' is rubbish. The difference between Marlborough and Eton means nothing in this context. Both men have been for most of their lives rich, confident and self-assured. Neither belongs to the aristocracy, though Mr Macmillan married into it. And what does 'aristocracy' really mean in a world of endless absorption and assimilation? All this chip-on-the-shoulder fussication about social class, exploited brilliantly by Harold Wilson in the early 1960s, seems strangely *vieux jeu* today. No one cares.

Yet it was effective in its day. Harold Macmillan had an ear for the rhetoric of opposition. He and Sir Harold Wilson have always been on cordial terms. They are, seen in relation to one aspect of politics, birds of a feather. They have something of the same capacity for wit, style and oratory. Mr Macmillan is better, for he knows when to stop, and he can listen. Nevertheless, both stem from the same tradition of British politics. They descend from Disraeli, just as Attlee descended from Campbell-Bannerman, Gaitskell from Gladstone, Mr Heath from Peel. Disraeli was the greatest leader of the opposition in all history. Harold Macmillan never had to play that part, but who can doubt how good he would have been if the task had fallen his way.

Mr Macmillan's career, like that of everyone who gets to the top, was based on luck as well as on merit. In the 1930s, he was regarded as a bit of a bore. The writings that he contributed towards the reconstruction of the British economy are not calculated to set the Thames on fire — dull, ponderous, meritorious and yawn-producing. He resigned the Conservative Whip in 1936 when sanctions against the Italian conquest of Abyssinia were abandoned. Few people were startled when he accepted it again a year later, but this was because few noticed that he had ever resigned it. He became a part of the group against 'appeasement', but he was not an outstanding or very important figure. He received minor office in 1939 as Parliamentary Secretary to the Minister of Supply under Lord Beaverbrook, who soon invited him to stay *en garçon* (though that would not have been Lord Beaverbrook's expression) at Cherkeley, his château-styled abode in Surrey. He replied that he only went to stay at other people's houses with his wife (Lady Dorothy, daughter of the Duke of Devonshire). Silence ensued. He never spent a night at Cherkeley, though he never quarrelled with Lord Beaverbrook.

The fascinating problem about the careers of those who get to the top in politics is the turning-point, the moment when they seem to be suddenly on their way up. Of course with some people there is no such moment. They rise by a sort of gradual inevitability. With Mr Macmillan there were two turning-points. The first came when Churchill in 1942 appointed him Minister Resident at Allied Headquarters in North-West Africa. It is not too much to say that the job 'made' him. It was essentially a position which depended on the influence its occupant could exert, not the power, which was negligible. Macmillan had an American mother and he spoke excellent French. As Churchill's principal link with Eisenhower, he played a key part in the diplomacy of the Mediterranean theatre. He made a life-long friend of the American commander, but there was another important personage on the scene, and Mr Macmillan had to convey some disagreeable decisions to him. He could hardly have guessed how strangely, even balefully, his career was to be entwined with that of General de Gaulle twenty years later.

If his wartime service put him into the front rank of post-war Conservative politicians, it still remained unlikely that he would get to the very top. When Churchill bowed out — much later than anyone expected — it was obvious that Anthony Eden would succeed him and Eden was three years younger than Mr Macmillan. Moreover, few people would have put him even as high as being the runner-up to Eden. Mr Butler, who was younger than either of them, would have been tipped by most for the succession. When both Churchill and Eden were ill in the summer of 1953, he, not Mr Macmillan, was regarded as the most likely next prime minister. In the event, both recovered and the question did not arise.

The second turning-point in Mr Macmillan's career was Suez, and his role in those still mysterious events is one of the most controversial in his career. It is doubtful whether the full truth about Suez will ever be known. The Cabinet minutes conceal it, for they have been drafted for that very purpose, and the horde of researchers who will home in on the Public Record Office in 1987 are likely to be much disappointed. It may be that some member of the Cabinet will one day give us a candid account. Kilmuir has not done so, nor have Eden, Mr Macmillan, Lord Butler or Lord Home. The nearest to the knuckle has been Selwyn Lloyd, but even he leaves many unanswered questions, though at least he says what anyone would guess: that the object of the exercise was not to 'part the combatants' or extinguish a 'forest fire' but to bring down Nasser.

It is widely believed that Harold Macmillan was one of the foremost exponents of the strong line against the Egyptian dictator. He says in his memoirs that he takes full responsibility for the Cabinet's policy, and he was certainly a member of the Prime Minister's committee dealing with the day-to-day decisions which culminated in one of the worst fiascos of modern British history. Yet it is also alleged — and has never been contradicted — that Mr Macmillan was one of the first to cry halt, just when the Anglo-French force, having taken Suez, was heading unresisted towards Port Tewfik and within a few hours could have controlled the Canal. American financial pressure is supposed to have been the reason. But was this unpredictable? Did the Americans ever show anything but deep disapproval of the use of force against Egypt? And did not Mr Macmillan hold the post of Chancellor of the Exchequer — of all offices, the one that should have been best informed about finance? Mr Hutchinson does not touch on this delicate question, which the posthumous biographer of Mr Macmillan will have to face and answer. However, these stories of what occurred in Cabinet did not circulate at once — and time was crucial. Mr Butler, who had never concealed his scepticism about Suez, was the loser despite the fact that he was right — or perhaps because of it. Most Conservatives knew that the Government had made a hash of things but they did not want to be led by the man who had said so all along, although he had not made it a resignation issue. And Mr Butler was never the man to be discreet. This is one of the many qualities which makes his company so enjoyable: the world of London's social and dining clubs and the salons of fashionable hostesses could hardly fail to be aware of his views, and at this juncture they were fatal to his chances.

There can be no doubt that for the immediate crisis the Conservatives chose — or rather found chosen for them — the right man. It is difficult to think of anyone else who could have rallied their fortunes, then at their nadir, to such an extent that, less than three years after the Suez debacle, the Party won its third consecutive election by an increased majority. It is most unlikely that Mr Butler or any other potential runner would have brought off such a startling coup. Mr Macmillan's methods are a striking indictment of the folly of those fashionable socio-political scientists, aped of course by trendy journalists, who said then and still say that Parliament has become a meaningless charade and that the House of Commons has no relevance to the great issues of the day. Mr Macmillan knew that prestige and confidence radiate outwards. The public does not read Hansard, as it is supposed to have done — though I do not believe it — in the 19th century, but the man — or woman — who dominates the House does in some mysterious unanalysable way make an imprint on the country. It is not easy to say just how this is done, but the process occurs, and Mr Macmillan, one of the greatest Parliamentarians since the days of his own hero, Disraeli, soon acquired a mastery in the House which rippled centrifugally over the whole electorate. Not that he neglected the direct approach. He was and still is of all our political figures one of the finest performers on television — urbane, witty, eloquent, moving.

What did he actually do with the power which came to him almost by accident and which he confirmed with such brilliance in 1959? Here again we face the problems of the contemporary biographer and the recent historian. Although it is well over twenty years since he became Prime Minister and more than sixteen since he left office, judgments on his record are anything but agreed. Nor is this surprising if one looks back into the history of historiography. How much sense would most judgments about Lloyd George have made in 1938, or about Balfour in 1922, or about Disraeli in 1896? No doubt there were some which would now seem prescient, but many more that were wrong-headed, perverse, inadequate or downright silly.

Mr Macmillan can be seen from one point of view as an enlightened Whig determined to avoid the unemployment which had horrified him at Stockton in the 1920s, softening the acerbities of class conflict by emollient measures, bowing to liberal aspirations for colonial autonomy, encouraging the spread of higher education, resisting Treasury austerity. But he can also be seen as the prisoner of a past in which unemployment mattered far more than in 1960, as a man who betrayed white minorities all over Africa, replacing them by regimes which found gardens and turned them into deserts, as the creator of a dozen or more second-rate universities, and, above all, as the man who missed the chance to halt inflation. The resignation of the entire Treasury team, Peter Thorneycroft, Enoch Powell and Nigel Birch, in 1958, dismissed as a little local difficulty, has come to symbolise, especially in the monetarist mood of today, a fatal turning point towards the downward path into stagflation and excessive public expenditure — all the tendencies which Margaret Thatcher is trying to reverse, although it is nice to know that personally she gets on admirably with the Grand Old Man. But who can say how all this will appear to people ten or twenty years hence? For that matter, who can guess what will be thought, even in five years' time, of the EEC which Mr Macmillan, vetoed by De Gaulle, failed to enter but made into a prime objective of the Conservative Party?

What is reasonably certain is that Mr Macmillan, however one may judge his motives, inflicted a grave injury on the Conservative cause during his last hours in office. The next general election was crucial. If the Conservatives had gained a fourth successive victory, even with a reduced majority, surely Labour would have had to rethink its whole position and face the dilemma of either moving into a centrist role, like that of the Democrats in America, or degenerating into a doctrinaire rump doomed to perpetual opposition. Conservatism would have benefited from each of these alternatives. Sir Alec Douglas-Home, with all the disadvantages (at that time) of his 14th earldom and his alleged sponsorship by a 'magic circle', only barely lost in 1964. Who can seriously doubt that Mr Butler would have won? Here Mr Macmillan did a lasting disservice to his party. The Labour leaders once in office no longer needed to think. They merely needed to manoeuvre. The course of recent history might have been very different if the verdict had gone the other way. Whether Mr Butler would have made a good prime minister is another question.

Preconditions for an Irish Peace

Garret FitzGerald

When Ireland was divided politically by the Government of Ireland Act 1920, this event was taken much less seriously by most Irish people than might have been expected in view of the generation-long political turmoil that had preceded it. The decision was taken in an effort to reconcile the divergent aspirations of the Nationalist majority in the island as a whole and of the Unionist minority largely concentrated in the six north-eastern counties.

The Nationalist majority in Ireland, then engaged in a struggle for the independence of the whole island, was not greatly impressed by the establishment of a provincial parliament and government in the North, especially as the attempt to implement the remainder of the Act by establishing a similar parliament and government in the South was an abysmal failure. Opinion may also have been affected by the fact that the opening of this Northern Parliament was the occasion for a speech by King George V, owing much to his personal initiative and offering an olive branch to the Irish Nationalist tradition that quickly led to a Truce, and, five months later, 6 December 1921, to a Treaty between the United Kingdom Government and the separatist administration — those who had been operating an 'underground' government throughout most of Ireland for several years past.

The Treaty recognised the whole of Ireland as a unit to be accorded sovereignty as a self-governing Dominion of the British Commonwealth a year later, albeit with an option for the six north-eastern counties to quit this new all-Ireland state within one month of its establishment, by the vote of a majority of the Northern Provincial Parliament. The vote was passed on the very day following the establishment of this all-Ireland state.

The stormy debate that ensued in the Dail — the democratically-elected Parliament of the new state which had emerged from clandestinity after the Truce — centred on the monarchical form of the proposed state, and specifically on the Oath of Allegiance to the Crown. Only a couple of speakers from the North adverted to the political division, which appears to have been assumed by all concerned to be purely temporary in character, partly because of a fallacious belief that Northern Ireland was too small to be viable,

49

and partly because the concept of a divided Ireland was too unhistorical to be taken seriously. In the North also, there existed a widespread, but not publicly proclaimed, belief among Unionists that the division of the island would be temporary, and would give them a breathing-space during which to prepare to live with their neighbours within a single-political framework.

Some reflection of this widespread assumption of the temporary nature of the division, and of the continuing acceptance of a broader unity within the island, is to be found to this day in the fact that so many Irish institutions continue to be organised on an all-Ireland basis: not merely the Churches, Roman Catholic and Protestant, but also the trade-union movement, the banking system (despite the new phenomenon of currencies with two different parities), and sports like rugby and hockey. Certain organisations which existed before 1920 have, of course, split on a North-South basis for one reason or another, and almost all new organisations coming into existence since then have been organised separately in the two parts of the island: but the important symbols of a basic unity remain intact, and are not found anomalous by the vast majority of Northern Unionists. Why, given this background, has the division between North and South proved so long-lasting, and, in the past decade, such a potent source of violence?

First, the division created its own new vested interests, as should have been, but was not, foreseen. Second, the two new political units moved fairly rapidly away from each other in important respects. Partly at least, this reflected the difference in ethos between the Christian denominations to which the majorities in the two areas gave their allegiance.

In the North, quite apart from a desire to maintain and indeed intensify the Protestant character of society in the area, there was a deep fear of the Nationalist minority within their borders, and of the island-wide Nationalist majority, and this led its exclusively Unionist governments to discriminate against Catholics with regard to employment, and — in some cases with a view to enhancing their local parliamentary majority — with regard to the location of housing, and, arguably also, its availability. As a result, because differential unemployment induced differential emigration, the threateningly large minority of Catholic children — approaching 50 per cent of the total — never converted itself into an equivalent proportion of the adult population, the Catholic proportion of which has, until recently, remained only a little above 30 per cent.

In the South, with a population which, when the first Census was taken in 1926, contained only 6 per cent of Protestants, the new state insensibly, and insensitively, allowed itself to drift towards a Catholic, Gaelic ideal which corresponded to the aspirations of the great majority of its people. Great care was taken to protect the rights of the Protestant minority: by giving them half the seats in the relatively powerful Senate or Upper House in the early years, by protecting their lives and property against attack by extreme elements during the Civil War that followed the Treaty in the South, by leaving untouched the possession of all pre-Reformation church property by the Anglican Church of Ireland, and, for example, by providing additional grants for school transport for Protestants in view of their dispersion at a low density throughout the rural population.

Protestant opinion in the South was reassured by these measures, and was reluctant to protest at changes in the Constitution or laws which had no directly damaging effect on their interests, but which introduced Catholic teaching in various forms: contraception was banned in 1935, and a bar on divorce legislation was introduced in the new Constitution of 1937. Other laws made the Irish language an essential element for the School Leaving Certificate, and for entry into the public service: provisions designed to repay the debt due by the Nationalist political movement to the Irish-language revival of the late 19th and early 20th centuries, through which many of the Nationalist leaders had come to know each other and to develop their ideas of a separate Irish state. These were provisions which made the new state more alien still to Northern Protestants.

What had been separated by Britain was further divided by Irishmen largely unconscious of the significance of their acts. One other factor helped to make the political division more lasting than it might have been: the South remained neutral in the Second World War, fearful lest participation on the Allied side might have rekindled the ashes of the post-Treaty Civil War, which had ended only half a generation earlier. Some would argue that the ending of Ireland's membership of the Commonwealth by the declaration of a Republic in 1949 further divided South from North: but common participation in the Commonwealth in earlier decades had not done much to foster reunification.

Such is the background to the crisis of the past decade. Obstacles to a normalisation of political relations within Northern Ireland

and to a rapprochement between North and South — the latter attempted in the mid-1960s — had been twofold: the reluctance of the Northern minority to participate in the institutions of the Province, extending at periods to abstention from its Parliament; and a recurrent 'anti-partition' campaign emanating from the Republic, and designed either to persuade, or through international pressure, to force, Britain to reunify Ireland, whatever the wishes of the majority of its population.

These phenomena, combined with a sense of themselves as the *real* minority in the island of Ireland as a whole, has encouraged the perpetuation and even intensification of a siege mentality among Northern Unionists, whose 'Establishment' saw advantages in encouraging working-class Protestant fears of Catholics as a means of diverting attention from any potential movement to the left among the mass of the workers.

Against this background, two preconditions for progress towards political normality were, first, a decision by the Northern Nationalist minority to accept the existence of the Province and its administration as a fact, and a willingness, not merely to work with this system, but to insist on their rights within it; and, second, the abandonment by political parties in the Republic of both of their (in any event mutually contradictory) policies of trying, on the one hand, to construct a Gaelic, Catholic state that would be totally alien to Northern Protestants, and, on the other hand, to secure British coercion of the Northern Unionists into an all-Ireland state.

In the late 1960s and early 1970s, these preconditions began to be fulfilled. The Nationalist minority in Northern Ireland turned away from the sterile politics of intermittent abstentionism, and the enthusiasms of a new generation that had benefited from post-war free education were channelled into a civil rights movement inspired by what was happening in the United States. By demanding civil rights within the existing political context, this movement was in fact accepting this context, at least until a majority in Northern Ireland should decide in favour of a united Ireland, whenever that might be.

The opportunity thus provided for reconciliation in Northern Ireland, with an agreement to differ as to a future relationship with the Republic, was not grasped or understood by the Unionist leaders, who felt threatened by the demand for equal rights from the minority and who, in August 1969, directed their local forces of order to intervene against the civil rights movement with such violence that the British Army had to be sent in to restore order and to protect the minority from the police, and from Unionist mobs who followed them on a rampage of destruction.

Out of this situation emerged two new political forces. The first was a Nationalist political party in Northern Ireland which has ever since commanded the support of the vast majority of Northern Nationalists. The SDLP rejects the old Nationalist stance. It advocates participation in the institutions of Northern Ireland, and reunification with the Republic on a basis of the consent of a majority of the people of Northern Ireland. The second force to emerge was the Provisional IRA, which, at the end of 1969, broke away from the Marxist Official IRA, and, in the summer of 1970, began to secure some minimal support, or at least tolerance, in Nationalist 'ghetto' areas after the British Army's curfew and search in a major Nationalist area of Belfast. This was carried out in a manner that decisively alienated many among the minority from the force which had come to their rescue, at the request of several of their lay and religious leaders, less than a year before.

In the Republic, the events of 1969 had a traumatic impact. After some initial uncertainty in the face of the massive violence in Belfast and Derry in August of that year, the political parties in the Republic rapidly faced realities to which they had closed their eyes for decades. They opted — immediately and decisively in the case of Fine Gael and Labour (then in opposition), and more slowly and ambivalently in the case of Fianna Fail (then, as it is now once again, in government) — for a policy of reunification only by consent, rejecting the older policies of attempting to persuade or to force Britain to 'hand over' the North against its will.

So the two preconditions for a start to a solution of the Irish problem were fulfilled, both in the North and in the Republic. But the acitivities of the Provisional IRA represented a new and disturbing element, which made it very difficult to reap any benefits.

Moreover, two crucial events supervened which altered the whole scenario. First there was the internment by the Northern Unionist Government in August 1971 of some hundreds of Nationalists, the majority of whom turned out to be innocent of any involvement with the IRA, and about half of whom were brutalised — a small number by methods which included psychological techniques later found by the European Commission on Human Rights (but not, on appeal, by the Court) to be torture. Second, there was the killing in

Derry, at the end of January 1972, of 13 young men by soldiers of the Parachute Regiment. This event was filmed and televised throughout Ireland and the world, and, because of the close links that existed between local British Army leaders and the provincial Unionist administration, it had a decisive effect on British politicians' attitudes towards the retention of this administration. Within two months the British Conservative Government abolished the provincial Parliament and Government in Northern Ireland, and introduced direct rule from Westminster, pending agreement on some more equitable and successful method of self-government for the Province.

In this new situation, there were two further preconditions for success — additional, that is, to the continuation of the preconditions already referred to with respect to the Northern Nationalist minority and the political parties of the Republic. These were, first, that Northern Unionist politicians should be convinced of Britain's determination never to permit a restoration of self-government without at least a period of power-sharing, so that the Nationalist minority could gain a sense of participation in the running of the affairs of the community to which they had been unwillingly attached over half a century earlier; and, second, that the IRA should be convinced of Britain's determination to refuse any dealings with them in any circumstances, and of the British Government's determination to retain its political responsibility for Northern Ireland until an internal solution was found.

Neither of these two new preconditions has been realised. This has produced the deadlock which we now face. The Conservative Government of Mr Heath succeeded in securing agreement at Sunningdale, in December 1973, to a power-sharing executive in Northern Ireland, and to a consultative Council of Ireland to bring together Northern and Southern politicians. But this agreement (whose effective implementation had not been helped by an overemphasis by some politicians in the Republic on the significance of the Council of Ireland as a harbinger of future unification) was undermined by the resistance of some Unionist politicians who had excluded themselves from this consensus, and, above all, by the failure of the new British Labour Government, under Harold Wilson in May 1974, to face what in its early stages was a very shaky Workers' Strike against the new Executive.

The consequent collapse of the Executive, as its Unionist members became aware of Britain's failure to suppress the rebellion — for that is what it became — had a traumatic effect on the whole Northern Ireland situation. The weakness of will then demonstrated in support of an existing power-sharing administration was widely interpreted as evidence that the will would be lacking to bring into existence any other similar type of devolved government in the future.

The situation that followed was not necessarily irretrievable, as may be seen from the almost fortuitous way Unionist politicians subsequently impaled themselves on an anti-power-sharing hook, and by the efforts a number of them made at different stages to get off this hook. What has prevented any progress towards this aim in the years since then has in part been the half-hearted way the British Government of the day pursued the principle of 'no devolution without power-sharing'. Particularly unfortunate was the ambivalence of its attitude towards Northern Unionist representatives at Westminster during the period of the 'hung' Parliament — from the spring of 1976 especially, when discussions between representatives of the Labour Government and Westminster Unionists destroyed the credibility of this already somewhat tattered principle.

There was no way in which devolutionist Unionists in Northern Ireland, frustrated at their exclusion from any political role, could give vent to this frustration by 'unhooking' themselves from their anti-power-sharing position, so long as their colleagues at Westminster were reporting back success in efforts to wring from the Labour Government a promise of extra seats at Westminster for Northern Ireland after the subsequent General Election. These Westminster Unionist MPs could also report an apparent weakening of the line on 'no devolution without power-sharing' on the part of both the main parties, who were competing for the support, in some cases the abstention, of Northern Ireland Unionist or Loyalist MPs, in a Parliament where the Government was in a minority.

One of the two additional preconditions for a settlement was eroded, therefore, because of the exigencies of domestic British politics. This was the process which later drew from Speaker 'Tip' O'Neill the metaphor 'making Northern Ireland a football in British politics'. While hardly technically accurate, his language nevertheless correctly reflected the unhappy fact that domestic British interests had taken precedence over those of Northern Ireland at a crucial period for that Province.

The result, predictable to almost anyone close to the Northern Ireland scene, was the erosion of the Unionist Party itself, divided between apparently successful Westminster integrationists and clearly unsuccessful domestic devolutionists, and devoid of the kind of imaginative leadership called for by such a difficult situation. Dr Ian Paisley's extremist Democratic Unionist Party was the inevitable gainer: British failure to pursue unambiguously the clear-cut policy of 'no devolution without power-sharing' had played straight into his hands.

The second precondition for a resolution of the Northern Ireland problem after the abolition of the Stormont Parliament and Government was that the British Government would be equally unambiguous in rejecting discussion or negotiation with the IRA. The capacity of the IRA to sustain a guerrilla campaign year after year depends upon access to arms and explosives — all too easy, this, in a world where all the great powers lavish them competitively on regimes of every kind — and upon the maintenance by the forces of order — through forms of interrogation at Castlereagh Barracks, for instance — of a sufficient element of alienation among at least a proportion of the Nationalist minority. But the continued activity of the IRA depends most of all upon the hope that at some point a British government will seek to negotiate a cease-fire with them, on terms involving an agreement that Britain will withdraw from Northern Ireland, with or without the consent of a majority of its population.

This hope has been generated, and kept alive, by successive British politicians. The process started when, as Leader of the Opposition, Sir Harold Wilson visited Dublin, allegedly to meet the leaders of the democratically-elected government of that state and of the opposition parties, but, in fact, to make direct contact with leaders of this murderous conspiracy against the Irish state and against the peace of Northern Ireland and its people. Feelings in Ireland were bitter at what was seen as a betrayal of hospitality and an undermining of the Irish democratic system by a political guest. Courtesy towards Britain and the Leader of its Opposition may have inhibited the full expression of this resentment. It was, however, made very plain after the subsequent decision of the Conservative Secretary of State for Northern Ireland, Mr William Whitelaw, to invite the leaders of the IRA to meet him in London: a serious mistake by a British political leader who otherwise distinguished himself in this most exacting portfolio, and came nearer to solving the Irish problem at Sunningdale in December, 1973, than anyone before or since.

The process of building up the hopes and expectations of the IRA continued regardless of Irish protests under Mr Whitelaw's successor, Mr Merlyn Rees, who authorised discussions by his officials with what were described as members of the political party representative of the Provisional IRA, Sinn Fein. These discussions gave rise to a widespread and demoralising belief that agreements were reached which promised a measure of immunity, for a period, to certain IRA leaders in Northern Ireland.

The damage done by these repeated contacts with terrorist leaders or representatives can scarcely be underestimated. The boost to the morale of the IRA, with whom no government of the Republic has had truck, was inestimable, and it is hard to say how many years of refusal of further contact will be required to undo this damage, and to convince the IRA that their violence is futile, and that no future British government will discuss or negotiate with them.

It is the failure to meet the two preconditions — a resolute pursuit of the policy of 'no devolution without power-sharing', in order to bring the Unionists to terms with reality, and an equally resolute pursuit of the policy of no dealings with terrorists over the heads, or behind the backs, of the democratically-elected politicians of the two parts of Ireland — which has led to the present impasse.

Even the maintenance hitherto, in the face of these events, of the two other preconditions for a solution — support by the vast bulk of the minority population for a party which is prepared to work devolved government in the present context, pending agreement among the people of Northern Ireland as to a new political relationship with the rest of the island, and a firm commitment on the part of all the democratically-elected political parties of the Republic to the proposition of reunification only with the consent of a majority in Northern Ireland — is insufficient to provide of itself the basis for a solution when the other two preconditions have been so undermined.

What kind of way forward can one envisage? First, a clear-sighted recognition that there can be no 'military' solution in advance of a political solution. The conditions which favour the persistence of IRA activities — including those aspects of the handling of security in Northern Ireland which continue to alienate a section of the minority from 'law and order' — can be removed only by the coming into being in Northern Ireland of an administration which draws its authority from the consent of the great bulk of both sections of the community.

The Loyalist 'veto' on this — the insistence of the Official Unionist and Democratic Unionist Parties that they will accept no form of devolution that does not permit them to govern by a simple majority, and thus, for an indefinite future, to exclude the chosen political representatives of the Nationalist minority from any role in government, as they were excluded from 1920 until 1972 — has been encouraged by British weakness in 1974 at the time of the Workers' Strike, and since then by the role of the Unionist and other Loyalist MPs who held the balance of power in the 'hung' Parliament at Westminster.

A determined effort will be required to undo the effects of these acts and omissions. The IRA hope to divert attention away from this focus of political action and towards the security issue, and to embroil the United Kingdom and Irish Governments in fruitless arguments about the details of security co-operation, which is already closer than between any other two countries I can readily recall. Wise politicians on either side of the Irish Sea are unlikely to fall into this trap.

There is one fact to which the British Government could usefully direct its own attention. The vast majority of people in Northern Ireland are sick of the violence of the past ten years, and would accept any reasonable way out of their present situation. Whatever 'hooks' some of their politicians may be on, the people are 'unhooked', and are relatively open-minded. It cannot be without significance that despite the negative attitudes to power-sharing of the political parties whose candidates they choose as their representatives at election times, the great majority of Northern Protestants have responded favourably to questions about the acceptability of some form of power-sharing on every one of the five occasions when such questions were put to them in public opinion polls between 1973 and 1978. A sizable proportion of Catholics have also expressed themselves as being satisfied to remain in the United Kingdom, for the time being at any rate, and to leave the issue of North-South relations to be determined when peace has been restored.

A British government seeking a political solution may thus decide to be guided by two considerations: the avoidance of further repressive action likely to alienate those whose consent to a solution is needed, and the direction of political efforts towards enabling the modest and moderate aspirations of the great majority of people in Northern Ireland to find appropriate expression — through channels that cannot be blocked by politicians' vetoes.

In the meantime, the Republic has its part to play: not merely, as it is currently fashionable to emphasise, in security matters, where the interest it has in preserving its own democratic system against terrorism is a sure guarantee of performance, but also in reassuring the beleaguered Northern Protestant population that what the vast majority in the Republic at present seek is nothing but peace, reconciliation, and such political links between North and South as a majority in Northern Ireland may in time freely decide to be beneficial to their part of Ireland.

Not everyone in the Republic is reconciled to these objectives, and they are admittedly more limited than those that have been expressed over many decades, without much thought of the consequences, by generations of political leaders who have never fully faced the reality of a politically-divided Ireland. A recent speech by a young Government party deputy, the granddaughter of Eamonn de Valera, Prime Minister of the Irish state for periods of over twenty years, has given expression to the frustrations of a minority in the Republic who hark back to the simplicities of irredentist nationalism. While prompt and decisive counter-action by the Prime Minister Jack Lynch within his Fianna Fail Party pre-empted this threat to the maintenance by the Party of these objectives, which are in harmony with those of the two opposition parties, the persistence of an unthinking irredentism among a section of that Party, and of Irish political opinion, cannot be ignored, and could once again become a significant factor in Irish politics if a resolution were not found within a measurable period to the problem of devolved self-government in Northern Ireland. In Northern Ireland too, the persistent failure to resolve the problem of devolved self-government deprives of any role all politicians save the dozen who get elected to Westminster, and places a great strain on the SDLP's ability to hold the support of the great bulk of the Nationalist minority for its moderate policies.

Quite apart from the atrocious effects of a continued IRA campaign of violence, and the evidence that this is now for a second time provoking a backlash of counter-terrorism from Loyalist paramilitaries, there is the danger of a general degradation of the political situation in Ireland if the new British government does not act decisively to halt the drift of recent years, and to give to the people of the North, in the face of the intransigence of some of their politicians, a form of devolved self-government that will command the consent of a majority of the members of both sections of the community. The achievement of this difficult task has been notably aided by the visit of the Pope, by the passionate and unambiguous way in which he denounced the attempt to find a solution to the Northern Ireland problem by violent means, by the extraordinary endorsement his words secured among the several hundred thousand Catholics from Northern Ireland present at his address, and by the positive reactions of many Protestants to his speech. The longing for peace of the minority within Northern Ireland, as of the majority, is now manifest, and provides a more favourable atmosphere for a new political initiative than anyone could have expected at this time.

Living and Dying in Ireland

Sean O'Faolain

One of the more surprising things about the life-ways of primitive societies is their persistence: so much so that one of them can frighten us by suddenly resurfacing a thousand years after it seemed to be stone dead. Up to that disconcerting moment the most we are inclined to allow the remote past is that it may linger on as a sanctified revival or a quaint reconstruction. It does not trouble us if we find that some of our dearest religious rites are as old as Babylon — Baptism, for instance. We could easily accept that the Druidic costumes we see at the modern Welsh cultural assemblies called Eisteddfoddu refer back to ceremonies initiated long before Christ. It would amuse us to be told that every time we spit out a 'Pooh!' or a 'Pfoo!' in the heat of argument we are echoing the habit of those fourth-century heretics known as Messalians, who cultivated spitting as a religious practice in the belief that the air is filled with legions of miniature demons. So at any rate W.E.H. Lecky suggests in his *The Rise and Influence of Rationalism in Europe*, quoting the learned 19th-century French scholar Alfred Maury, author of such abstruse books as *Fées dans le Moyen Age* and *Histoire de la Magie*. There is, however, one serious caveat attaching to every archaism. However slight such perdurables may be, however sweetened by the passage of time, it is wise to presume the co-existence of others not at all tempered by age. The Hunger Strike is one such.

Linguistic scholars have proved that this practice flourished more than two thousand years ago all over the Indo-European world: that is to say, throughout Europe, the vast expanses of Asia and scattered places elsewhere — almost a third of the globe. A small modern reflection of this ancient diffusion was noted during May of this year by such press agencies as AP, AFP, UPI who reported that two hundred young people were starving themselves, some unto death, in hospitals, prisons, churches, labour camps, public places in France, Spain, Italy, Turkey, the USSR, West Germany, Corsica and Ireland, in protest against various forms of, as they saw it, oppression. They mostly concentrated on prison conditions, although six Basques were also demanding an amnesty for all Basque prisoners, 21 Tunisians in Paris were protesting against their expulsion, and others like the Irish were demanding to be treated as prisoners of war. Before the month was out one German was dead, and four Irishmen. A death-way then? Or a life-way? In the imagery of the Sermon on the Mount, the broad way that leadeth to destruction? Or the narrow way that leadeth unto life? Or since living and dying imply one another, a way of asserting values, personal, racial, national, even philosophical, common to both living and dying. Those reports from press agencies mentioned above were, one notes, entitled 'Hunger strikers' aims vary.'

Consider my own country. The main proof that this lethal practice flourished here in pre-Christian times derives from the ancient Irish Laws which recognised and strove to regulate the rite of 'fasting against a person of exalted state in order to enforce a claim against him'. This elegantly succinct definition I take from the long essay entitled 'Irish History and Irish Law' by Dr Daniel Binchy, doyen of the Celtic School in the Dublin Institute for Advanced Studies, who after fifty years of what he modestly describes as 'long-term drudgery' — that is, single-minded scholarly toil — presented to the world in 1980 a meticulous transcription of the extant legal sources of the oldest law tracts known to the West.[1] His six volumes are, alas, as yet untranslated and unannotated: not that those words 'as yet' should evoke any larger hopes. It is doubtful if there are as many as six Celtic scholars left to the world who can read Binchy's text with complete assurance. Anything I may say here about these laws, or any customs with which they deal, derives from Binchy's long essay and the other labourers in his field to whom he refers, as far back as that almost legendary figure Johann Kaspar Zeuss, who in virtual solitude composed or induced in 1853, unaided, out of his vast erudition, the first-ever grammar of a tongue one word of which he had never heard spoken and which was even then beginning to disappear. Among others of our time who, against every obstacle, kept a firm grip on the linguistic key to those primitive laws were Rudolph Thurneysen, Whitley Stokes, who drew attention to the fact that 'fasting against' still prevailed in some areas of India, Osborn Bergin, Myles Dillon, whose knowledge of Sanskrit drew attention to the French Sanskritist Louis Renou's very early dating

---

[1] D.A. Binchy, *Corpus Iuris Hibernici*, 6 vols. (Institute for Advanced Studies, Dublin, 1981).

of the Hindu practice of aggressive fasting — namely, between 600 and 300 BC — and that erudite linguist and fervent nationalist, titular head of the infant IRA at the time of the 1916 Rising, Eoin MacNeill, who engagingly began to write his *Prolegomena to the Study of 'The Ancient Laws of Ireland'* in Mountjoy Prison, Dublin, in 1921, and, 'time' being a colloquialism to professors as well as prisoners, as engagingly chose not to publish it until 46 years later.

Professor Binchy's article on 'Irish History and Irish Law' is entirely factual and particular about the practice of 'fasting against': but in introducing it he does make one particularly striking general observation which, I believe, casts a revealing light on the Irish way of living and dying, whether around 500 BC or at the start of this century, allowing, of course, for those changing fashions in dying and those varying attitudes to living which historians like Philippe Ariès have been exploring so imaginatively and suggestively in recent years.[2] Speaking of the old Irish jurists, Binchy says: 'Naturally they were unaware that what they were describing was the vestigal remnant of an extremely ancient usage rooted in primitive magic...' Which means that while they thought they were merely describing established rules governing certain dangerous contests between protest and power, we cannot fail to hear, even if we are armed only with a smattering of anthropology, an underground or background whisper of a very different order. For example, the old jurists at one point give a useful list of three alternatives open to any powerful man who awakens to find a protesting man starving himself at the entrance to his home. Let us call them Mr Power and Mr Protest. Power's first alternative is simple and substantial: it is to give Protest whatever he claims. The second alternative darkens the air like a flock of carrion crows, makes us glance superstitiously over our left shoulder, smell the presence of occult forces, supernatural powers, even that necromancy which betokens communication with the dead. For Power's second alternative is to start a counter-fast — that is, in Daniel Binchy's words, resist by 'counter-magic' and let the final victory go to whichever of the two men is the more favoured by ...well, you-know-who. Power's third alternative is supernal: to let

[2]Philippe Ariès, *The Hour of Our Death,* trans. Helen Weaver (Allen Lane, 1981); *Western Attitudes towards Death from the Middle Ages to the Present,* trans. Patricia Ranum (Calder, 1976): *Mourir Autrefois: Attitudes Collectives devant la Morte,* presented by Michel Vovelle (Gallimard, 1974).

the man on his doorstep starve himself to death. But Power can only do this at the risk of finding his home, and presumably himself, 'polluted' for ever after by the ghost of the unhappy Protest's cadaver. In which event which of the two has won? Ariès's word for 'pollution' is 'profanation'. This thanatologist also reminds us that funeral rites and their allied vocabulary interweave the idea of profanation (*pro-fanum,* outside the temple or fane) and de-profanation, since *funus* can mean either a body or a funeral, *funestus* means profanation, and in modern French *funeste* conveys the idea of sinister, ill-omened, fatal. Such a Hunger Strike could be fatal to both parties.

However, one may, thank goodness, always say of civilisation: *E pur si muove.* After the passage of many centuries, things began to change so much for the better that by the early Middle Ages the duel had been reduced, probably under the influence of Christianity, to a symbolic sunrise-to-sunset fast by both parties, who thereafter proceeded to operate another already ripened custom, though already, no doubt, as much honoured in the breach as in the observance: the Law. Not, as we know, that the coercive fast, with all its trail of dark associations, died suddenly or completely. This may be how things happen in hagiographies. In real life what happened was that those primitive Irish wrestling matches between Living and Dying, after first assuming, and long retaining, the form of black magic, met another and more powerful magician in Christ and proceeded to direct their attentions towards God. There are, in fact, several legends about Irish saints fasting against God, including one about the chief of them all, St Patrick, which presents him as refusing to descend from his now famous mountain, Croagh Patrick, until God had agreed to all his admirable demands on behalf of his beloved Irish converts. After that, one fasted *for* God, and perhaps prayed against one's neighbour. But if the Hunger Strike appears to have finished finally and completely by about the year 1000, our first 20th-century re-encounter with it — Gandhi in India, suffragettes in England — must make us feel that it disappears only as a stream that vanishes underground to resurface elsewhere.

Why did not all or any of this happen to the English, Welsh or Scottish ways of life next door? The answer is that the Irish are a very, very old people, and their life-way remained that way because they, like the people of India, are at one of the two peripheries of the Indo-European world. Linguists will corroborate that in this western island and that eastern peninsular subcontinent words are found, in Irish and in Sanskrit, with no equivalent elsewhere. We were for centuries secluded by what is now called the Irish Sea; they by the Himalayas. So true is this in Ireland's case that when, at this point, we look back at 'fasting' to see how it may have fared overground or underground during the late Middle Ages, or the period of the Renaissance, we find that we are looking at a country that had no Middle Ages at all in the European sense. Thus there are only two medieval cathedrals in Ireland, both in Dublin, 12th and 13th-century, the one founded by Christianised Danes, the other by Norman-Irish. Ruins abound, mostly of Norman castles, shelters now for wandering cattle and what we used to call wandering tinkers but must now politely call itinerants; though here and there we come on small, endearing remnants of earlier Romanesque, maybe crumbled away to a single arch of carved heads. What can any Irishman conclude, thinking of the medieval wealth of Europe, but that the old, native cultural well must have run dry some time after the Norman invasion of Ireland in the 12th century? Time was not to fulfil the promise of a life-exploring, all-embracing, ever-developing culture held out by earlier achievements: by the old Celtic sagas, shot through by lightning and purple flame, filled with supernatural powers, gods and goddesses who replace only to glorify actual fighting men, and fighting women, or by the monks' lovely, intricate illuminated manuscripts, or by the old high crosses with their often abstract, hieratic Byzantine designs. All these prove to be the first promising rays of a sunrise upthrown from below its horizon but halted there.

One reason at least for what Arnold Toynbee called this aborted Celtic civilisation must have been social. All our life-ways remained for far too long based on social structures dependent on the primitive idea of the local Ruler, while Europe was developing the more powerful concept of the centralised State.[3] Those structures lasted stubbornly to the brink of the 17th century. They finally collapsed before the death-ways of the Elizabethan armies. Their last bastion was Ulster, which in 1610 was parcelled out, six counties of it, to Scottish and English adventurers some, or perhaps many, or even most, of whose descendants hold it to this day.

---

[3] See *The Celtic Peoples and Renaissance Europe* by David Mathew, or my own *The Great O'Neill,* now published in paperback by Mercier Press, Dublin and Cork. O'Neill was the last native 'tribal ruler' and an Ulsterman.

Between 1610 and 1921 (the date of the founding of the Irish Free State, later called the Irish Republic), we Irish lived as a conquered race, down-beaten, for long virtually outlawed, never quite defeated.

One would expect a conquered people to change. We did. Very slowly. As one might guess, we laughed more. The last weapon of slaves. The blacks did it, to please, to deceive, to get by, to forget actuality. Still, one might also hazard a greater sense of reality in general, a coming to terms with life sternly, pushing all idle fancies aside. There one would be wrong. The Irish of those three centuries went on telling fanciful fireside stories of legendary heroes like Fionn and Usheen (Oisin, Ossian), tales of magic, of giants, ghosts, wizards, fairies. I open a collection of folk-tales that my wife made years ago and the very illustrations evoke a world of the weirdest imagination. From such folklore and folktales one hears true laughter. In the 18th century, the remnants of the old, pampered and feared poetic caste, now reduced mostly to near-beggary, invented a visionary myth of a Second Coming by some secular saviour (by then he would be a Stuart) who would come from over the sea to release their shackled queen. This Vision Poetry was written in various forms over and over again. But the two main changes of mentality in this later Ireland were its attitudes to Dying and to Thinking.

Death they always treated decorously, with dignity, with full feeling, as various 18th and 19th-century poems show, but they did not let it defeat their spirits. The Irish wake or late-night vigil in the home of a corpse is famous as a celebration both of death and of life made to seem all the richer by its loss. Death and Life waltz in one another's arms at a wake. In some remote mountainy country we approach a lighted cottage, with no other habitation, seemingly, within a mile. It consists of two storeys: downstairs, the kitchen and 'the' room, always so called; upstairs, two rooms for sleeping. Up there on the big white bed peacefully smoothed out lies the corpse arranged with crossed hands between four calm candles — the light we saw from across the heather-covered valley. Downstairs, the kitchen is full of his happy friends, chatting cheerfully, smoking, drinking, snuff-taking, reminiscing tirelessly. As each new visitor enters the kitchen and is led upstairs by the welcoming widow, the chatter falls for a moment, rises when he is out of sight, falls at his return until he has been plied with tobacco or drink, merges into the wake and everybody is in high spirits

again, including, to some degree, or so it is hoped, the widow: for
why are we all there but to cheer him on his voyage into the night-
sky and her on hers through life again? If the priest comes, they will
all sink on a knee, with others outside in the darkness, and pray in a
solemn murmur, after which good cheer will return once more. The
'Hades' episode in *Ulysses* — Paddy Dignam's funeral at Glasnevin
Cemetery, in Dublin — is an urban version of this blend of Living
and Dying. It also underlines that Irish post-conquest humour will,
even in that cottage in the mountainy west, carry many an
undertone of satire, can be sharp, double-meaning, mocking,
outrageously blend warm feeling and cold eye.

The intellectual change took longest to come. 'Cast a cold eye on
life, on death' were Yeats's last words to us, carved by his
command on his gravestone in Drumcliff churchyard. Time was
when we had not the cold thinking to match the cold looking. The
simplest illustration of the more modern Irish mind is the new
school of Irish historians, cool, judicious and discerning. Inside the
last thirty years or so, a generation of scholarly young men and
women have moved a thousand and more years away from that
great scholar Rudolph Thurneysen's observation when examining
some early law tracts that they revealed the total inability of the
Irish mind to form a concept. 'What,' the tract would ask, 'is
Justice?', and unable to universalise, would enumerate: 'There are
13 different kinds of Justice.' 'What is Indiscipline?' Answer:
'There are 15 kinds of Indiscipline.' This was not a comprehensive
intellect at work — rather, a divisive one. For so long as it persisted
the political-social mind would be in accord. One of our most
revered nationalist rebels, John Mitchel, may illustrate. Born about
a hundred years ago, a freedom-fighter, transported to Van
Diemen's Land, escaped to America, he was honoured there until
he was found to be in favour of black slavery. So, from the paper
called the *Citizen* (New York): 'We deny that it is a crime...to keep
slaves to do their work by flogging or other needful coercion...We,
for our part, wish we had a plantation well stocked with healthy
Negroes in Alabama.'[4] One cannot think that the man who wrote
like this was a political thinker. Perhaps our first real political
thinker was Edmund Burke. His earliest book, written when in his

---

[4] On asking a younger Irish historian whether this is a fact, I have been told that the
charge has been made against Mitchel more than once. The defence is that his mind
was, sadly, affected by his prison experiences. Very well. The equally sad fact is that
during the American Civil War Irish soldiers fought on both sides of the divide.

twenties, was a world away from the personal, the particular, the segregating. It was *A Philosophical Inquiry into the Origin of our Ideas of the Sublime and Beautiful*. He was to become one of the most large-minded political thinkers these islands have known. It is true that no Irish nationalist would consider him a patriot.

Yes... Well... We seem to have come to it. Nationalism. Not, observe, patriotism, which is a natural instinct. The word itself derives from a familial source, *pater,* parent, father, grandparents, back, I would hazard, to some Aryan (Sanskrit) root such as PA 'whose wish and care a few paternal acres bound'. Inside any inherited space, a few hectares in Calabria, a Dublin street, an English village, a youth will grow to knowledge of self, kin, country, finally enlarge to the extent of the world whose distant occupants may well seem to his patriotic mind a congeries of eccentrics who have yet to learn the full sweetness of *his* native air. By contrast, nationalism is not private, personal or natural. It is collective, impersonal and organised. It encloses vast masses of people who are not real persons because nationalism bewilders them all by reducing each to a numbered unit who will still be confusingly termed an individual — 'confusingly' because he will have lost all his individuality in the process. We who have experienced Hitler's Nazism, Mussolini's Fascism, Stalin's Communism know only too well how myths and mystiques can mesmerise, and make no wonder of Arnold Toynbee's declaration that nationalism 'has been... embraced by more people more intensely than any other modern religion' since the birth of Christianity, in whose name every known atrocity has been justified. Naturally our imaginary Irish nationalist would think Burke no patriot: thereby revealing his own incapacity to distinguish between a concept and a word; revealing also a sad lack of humour. Burke was a political philosopher.

We should not blame the nationalist for his rushes of blood to the head. It could happen to a bishop. It happens from time to time to the most intelligent amongst us, or so some at least of my countrymen believe, if we may trust a typically mordant Dublin anecdote about that great Celtic scholar Eoin MacNeill whom I have already mentioned. When the Irish Free State was founded in 1921, the precise limits of the deplorable boundary between North and South not being yet precisely defined, a small Boundary Commission consisting of three people was set up. They were a Britisher, an Ulster Unionist and Eoin MacNeill, all three of whom would travel North and, so to speak, fight the matter out peacefully along the Border. Since the North was supposed to contain the undiscovered tomb of the amazon-queen Medb (Maeve) who is the central figure of the oldest Celtic saga, the gleefully malicious Dublin prophecy at once began to circulate that MacNeill would, on entering the North, at once get a nationalist rush of blood to the head, find the tomb of Queen Medb and lose the Boundary. What the Dublin wits were onto, of course, was that old curse and bore of modernising Ireland, our revered, unforgettable, indestructible, irretrievable Past. Frank O'Connor held that all Gaelic poetry was infected by the Backward Look. I have here called it the Underground Stream that keeps on vanishing and reappearing. I do not believe that it will ever dry up. Only this morning the newspaper informs me that one of our highly respected citizens, a lawyer by profession, a shrewd businessman by avocation, has sworn to 'fast against' the Minister responsible for Broadcasting to force him to establish a separate daily TV programme in Irish for that part of the west of Ireland where, some 1500 years ago, St Patrick fasted against Almighty God to extract from Him such other special benefits as that on the Day of General Judgment nobody but St Patrick himself would judge the people of Ireland.

How beautiful, as Chekhov said of his Russia, life in Ireland will be two hundred years from now! It all takes time and thinking and in the end the result is, of the nature of things, patchy. After all, 18th-century England was beautiful and noble in many ways, but it saw the ruthless Enclosures, and more than half the slaves taken across the Atlantic were transported in the holds of English ships.

Accountability

Harold Lever

The debate on the proposed changes in the constitution of the Labour Party has been conducted without sufficient consideration of the policies which gave the proposals birth. These policies constitute an explicit commitment to produce rapid, comprehensive and irreversible changes in our economy and our society. The broad aims of such policies are by no means novel. What *is* novel is the Left's intention to drive them rapidly through Parliament, and their frank recognition that this is not compatible with our present Parliamentary and constitutional practices.

The essence of these is that the party in power is bound to subject its proposals to full Parliamentary scrutiny. This in turn produces wider public discussion, echoing through television, radio and press down to the shopfloor, pubs and clubs. As public opinion forms and clarifies, it is able to express itself on policies and the consequences flowing from them. Only by this means does the power of public opinion, and of the electorate, become effective, not only at election times, but throughout the life of a Parliament. This right of the electorate to enforce meaningful accountability upon those entrusted with their mandate is protected by all the subtle conventions, habits and inhibitions of our processes of parliamentary democracy. These, however, are to a negligible extent based upon formal law. Even the most fundamental, such as the one which restricts the right of Parliament to extend its own life or those which ensure that the electorate is given full opportunity to absorb, digest and react to major changes, are wholly dependent on the general respect for certain conventions and traditions. At the centre of this process are the MPs, who accept their continuous accountability to their constituencies and to the country. Of course, parliamentary democracy requires that representatives should be open to pressures, organised and unorganised. But all organised pressure groups are controlled by minority interests. The rights of the unorganised majority are protected only by each Member of Parliament's ultimate accountability to the electorate in the exercise of his judgment.

Our customary Parlimentary processes are therefore profoundly incompatible with the aspirations of those who want rapid,

70

wholesale and irreversible transformations. To accomplish wholesale change quickly necessarily involves a curtailment of these processes. So far, governments, parties and our people have not been willing to accept such curtailments and extremists have been repeatedly disappointed in their expectations. That is why all Labour governments have inevitably rejected many of the policies pressed upon them by the Left, even when such policies have been backed by repeated Conference decisions. The Conference speaks for the Party. Parliament speaks for the people. The Party proposes. Parliament disposes. And Conference, respectful of the role of Parliament, has had no difficulty in giving standing ovations to the leaders who have overridden its wishes. It saw its MPs and their leaders, not as traitors, cynics or cowards, but as firmly wedded to the principles of parliamentary democracy, which Conference itself accepted and which compel a respectful accountability to the electors. The political parties have always been by far the most effective of the pressure groups, but the electorate's sovereignty was protected by the respect which these parties themselves have always given to the processes of parliamentary democracy and by their voluntary acceptance of limitations to their control of MPs. Recent years have seen encroachments. But none have remotely approached the direct degree of control over the actions of governments and MPs which is now proposed.

The crucial ideological division in the Labour Party has always been between those who are respectful of the processes of parliamentary democracy, and who accept the restraints they impose, and those who are impatient of them and who seek to achieve purposes incompatible with them. Most, but by no means all, of the Left have come to recognise that, unless they can control what has hitherto been a confident majority of Parliamentary gradualists, their programmes cannot be implemented.

Personal ambitions and a false conception of what can properly be achieved by way of rapid change have in recent years led the Left to seek and accept allies who make no secret of their contempt for Parliament and for those who respect it. And with these allies they have manoeuvred to bring the Parliamentary Party under their control. They would radically change our conception of Parliamentary sovereignty without offering any compensating checks and balances. What has been argued for as mere changes in the Labour Party constitution is in fact designed to achieve fundamental changes in the British constitution itself.

The strategy of the Left has been based upon four proposals: 1. To bring sufficient continuous pressure upon Members of Parliament to make them directly accountable to their local party caucus. 2. To control the election of the Party Leader so as to ensure the election of one likely to prove compliant with their purposes. 3. To dictate the terms of the election manifesto in such a way as to make it binding on the Parliamentary Party and its leader. 4. To close down the House of Lords as a focus for the free expression of informed opinion (the demand to abolish its powers is fraudulent since they are already negligible).

In order to secure the acceptance of these proposals, the Left encouraged the admission into the Labour Party of extreme left-wing groups hitherto banned from membership. Favourable to their purpose was the growing recognition among a number of extremist groupings in recent years that their wilder dreams had little or no prospect of fulfilment in this country, and that the best means of achieving their purposes was to encourage their members to work in an organised way within the Labour Party and trade-union branches while at the same time retaining their separate organisations. Lord Underhill has reported on the effectiveness of this infiltration. Obsessive devotion to their cause and the carefully organised manner of their work readily gained them an influence within local Labour Parties quite disproportionate to their numbers. All this has constituted a major difficulty for the gradualist Labour Members of Parliament who have been their main targets.

At the centre of the Left's campaign is the cry for direct accountability of MPs to their local party caucus. Let the local parties have a say. Let the grass roots have a say. Why should a candidate once elected be able to sit in Parliament for ever and ignore his local party? But the local party committee, in addition to the right to nominate the candidate, has always enjoyed considerable influence on an MP's actions. If it was dissatisfied with him, there have always been careful, and by no means protracted, procedures for removing him. But local parties have in the past voluntarily restricted their power out of respect for Parliamentary conventions and have always allowed a wide measure of political judgment to Members. There is all the difference in the world between procedures which enable a party in exceptional circumstances to remove the nomination from its Member and the present procedures, which are designed to place a continuous threat over every Member to induce his conformity to the detailed wishes of his local committee. Before, they could argue but the Member decided. Now he must toe the line or be thrown out. It is very damaging that the Left and its new allies have succeeded in destroying among many management committees the convention which requires respect for the free judgment of an MP. The effects of this change are already apparent.

Several respected Members of Parliament have already come to understand that the reselection process will ensure their removal before the next election. Many others are under threat, and from now on all Labour MPs will speak and act in the knowledge that they are in peril. The Left majority of the NEC in effect acts to organise and guide the deployment of these constituency pressures. And, thus encouraged, the local Labour Party caucuses are becoming increasingly arrogant and aggressive in the deployment of their new powers. The range of pressure covers matters which it has never before been suggested were other than within the free judgment of the MP — including even such matters as the vote for the Parliamentary Leader. Many parties have contented themselves with badgering and menace. Others have demanded that the Member of Parliament should fill in the ballot form in the presence of his management committee. And this detailed harassing of MPs is in its infancy.

The spuriousness of the claim that this is an expression of grass-roots opinion is exposed by the fact that, whether in the reselection of MPs or in the proposed system for electing the leader of the party, the extremist caucuses have fought a vigorous battle to ensure that rank-and-file members should have no direct say. Of course, there will always be a minority of local Labour Parties who will continue to reject this attitude to their MPs. And there will always be a number of courageous and independent-minded Members who will continue, whatever the cost, in the traditional exercise of their duties. But over a period the majority will, either by coercion or replacement, become sufficiently respectful of their accountability to the local party caucus to transform the role of a British MP.

What is involved would become brutally plain if the Conservative Party were to imitate the actions of the Labour Party in respect of their MPs, and if the CBI and the Institute of Directors were given an affiliation and influence similar to that of the trade unions in the Labour Party. Instead of being important pressure groups, the main parties would come to enjoy effective control over Members of Parliament and governments. Parliament would become little more than the rubber stamp of policies of the majority party and the electorate would have suffered the gravest injury to its democratic powers. And if both parties were pledged to use their power to produce irreversible change, our democracy would not long survive.

There is a local back-up to the undermining of Members of Parliament which has received too little attention in the media. A similar process has been even more successfully and ruthlessly applied in the control of municipal offices. Hundreds of experienced Councillors of high quality have been ousted in favour of the nominees of this alliance of left-wingers and recently arrived extremists. Even more outrageous demands for control over Council members have been organised and to a large extent accomplished in all the great cities which enjoy large Labour representation — such as London, Manchester, Liverpool and Birmingham. The absence of these local figures further weakens the position of moderate MPs as well as dangerously undermining local democracy.

The Left have already succeeded to a large extent in the second of their objectives: namely, to control the appointment of the Parliamentary Party Leader. This campaign has been represented as a mere expression of the legitimate right of a party to appoint its own leader. The campaign has no such purpose. It seeks to impose by extra-parliamentary means the leader of the *Parliamentary Party*, who inevitably becomes the Prime Minister when that party is in a majority. Whatever its constituents, an extra-Parliamentary College deciding the leadership of a major Parliamentary Party outrages the fundamental principles and practices which have governed our parliamentary democracy. And this would be so even if proposals to allow one man, one vote were adopted in forming the College, though that would be less blatantly anti-democratic than what is now in prospect.

So far, the Left majority in the NEC have been thwarted of their desire to have exclusive control over the Manifesto. This is a limited victory for moderation, since their present role, backed by an increasing power to subordinate MPs, will ultimately prove to be sufficient to secure a broad achievement of their wishes. In the new situation, the Manifesto will have an unheard-of power of control over Members and governments. Measures and their timing will be enforced upon them in advance and unfolding realities will not be allowed to override the powerful purposes of a left-dominated NEC, who would become the true rulers of the country when there was a Labour majority.

The sum of all these changes, if they mature, would produce a parliamentary system quite different from our present one. There are sinister parallels where the forms of parliamentary democracy have been retained at least temporarily while the substance evaporated. Parliament's role in organising the accommodations and adjustments required by events would be largely curtailed. More important, its role of identifying and adjusting policies to have regard to the interests and purposes of the minority groups in Parliament and outside would almost cease to exist. And with it would disappear the preconditions for the tolerant pluralistic society our country has so far enjoyed.

It is also clear that, in the event of a Labour majority being elected in Parliament, it is intended that the mandate of a single election shall be used so as to face the nation with a *fait accompli* of irreversible changes, in the context, almost certainly, of a state of extreme political, economic and financial crisis, which would be likely to leave the electorate a minimum of freedom when it came to making their next choice.

What is so dismaying is that, almost without exception, the most experienced and respected leaders of the party know that the course that is being pursued is dangerously wrong. Some of the most gifted of them have been driven to leave the party. Many others will follow. Unless the whole programme is reversed, and this very soon, I believe that the public will come to the conclusion that it is wholly unsafe to elect a Labour majority. The Labour Party will be extensively abandoned, not only by moderate leaders but by moderate voters. It will become an extremist party, but one which has traditionally had the closest links with the trade union movement. This party, a rump of its former Parliamentary self, would recognise that the prospect of achieving its ends through Parliamentary means was virtually non-existent. It would be driven to attempt to organise acts of political irresponsibility and to seek to use its traditional ties with the trade union movement to link them with destructive acts of industrial irresponsibility.

If the Labour Party is to resume its former great role in developing our society within the framework of our parliamentary system, it will have to mobilise all the moderate democratic forces within it and within the trade union movement. The first and minimum step at the next Party Conference is not some irrelevant decision about the percentages of representation in an Electoral College, but the clear abandonment of this illegitimate proposal. The unrepresentative majority of the NEC must be corrected as a first step in restoring to Labour MPs and Councillors the democratic rights they have hitherto enjoyed as trustees for the electorate. Nomination and dismissal of candidates should be subjected to the vote of all constituency party members. The present Leader of the Labour Party knows well that the undermining of the independence of MPs, extra-Parliamentary appointment of the Parliamentary Party's leadership, and the demolition of local representation which has been taking place, are all wrong. He ought now to act unambiguously in support of his own known convictions.

Remaking the Centre

David Marquand

For more than a generation, what Europeans call social democracy and what Americans call liberalism has been the dominant political creed of the North Atlantic world. Its achievements have been enormous. As Ralf Dahrendorf points out in his important and persuasive pamphlet, 'After Social Democracy',[1] 'it has turned the empty promise of freedom of contract into effective citizenship rights; the welfare state lies at the heart of social democratic politics. It has proved the ability of open societies to change without revolution; the varieties of Fabianism are, among other things, a triumph of democracy. It has spread the belief in a rational society; human improvement by education, social improvement by the uses of science, decision-making by rational discourse are all a part of the prevailing creed.'

The welfare states of North-Western Europe and North America are not only richer than any previous societies have been. They are also freer, more equal and happier. For this, social democrats deserve most of the credit. In or out of office, they have drawn up the agenda of politics; until recently, their opponents on the right were much more anxious to claim the social democratic legacy for themselves than to challenge or dismantle it.

But no longer. In most of its old strongholds, social democracy is now unmistakably on the defensive. In Britain, Labour's social democratic right is a small minority of the party outside Parliament, and has only a bare majority even in the Parliamentary Party. The equivalent Conservative tradition — the tradition once exemplified by Harold Macmillan and Iain Macleod — is in eclipse. Outside formal politics, the intellectual running is increasingly being made by neo-Marxism on the left and by a curiously febrile neo-liberalism on the right. *Mutatis mutandis*, much the same is true of the United States. The old Roosevelt Coalition has collapsed; though the Democrats are still the majority party, their ideological centre of gravity has shifted from the social democracy of the New and Fair Deals towards a helpless, hand-ringing conservatism. Even in Scandinavia, the social

---

[1] Unservile State Papers No 25, Liberal Publication Department, 9 Poland St, London W1.

democratic hegemony of the last forty years seems to have been broken. Helmut Schmidt still reigns fairly securely in Bonn and Bruno Kreisky rather more securely in Vienna. Elsewhere, the social democratic lights are dimmed at best.

One reason, no doubt, is simply that politicians and intellectuals like novelty as much as anyone else. Yesterday's wisdom is always a little boring, even if it is true. The day before yesterday's can be made to sound smart, even if it is false. But there is more to the current eclipse of social democracy than a change of fashion. In two critically important respects, the social democracy of the last forty years — the social democracy of the New Deal in the United States or of the 'Attlee consensus' in this country — can no longer provide solutions to the most pressing problems of the day.

Almost by definition, it cannot provide solutions to the problems which it has itself created. Like all successful political movements, social democracy has been a victim of the law of unintended consequences. The slums have been cleared, but the tower blocks which replaced them have bred rootlessness and delinquency. Grammar schools have been abolished, but the independent schools have been strengthened and it is probably harder for bright working-class children to reach the top. Industries have been nationalised, but public monopolies have turned out to be as hard to control as private ones. Trade unions have been freed from judicial restrictions, but they have become less and less answerable to their members. Taxation has become more progressive, but the black economy has flourished. The savage, unregulated market of the 19th century has been tamed, but it has become increasingly clear that the tamers themselves now need taming.

The central discovery of the founding fathers of social democracy was that the Economic Man of the 19th century was a fiction; and that, because of this, the invisible hand of free competition would not always produce the greatest happiness of the greatest number. Their solution was to call in the polity to redress the balance of the economy: to allocate more resources through the state and fewer through the market, and to give the state instruments with which the market could be rigged. This solution attracted them partly because it was convenient. The state was there, and no other agency was at hand. But that was only one of the reasons why they were attracted to it. Another was that, as good democrats, they assumed that a combination of universal suffrage and the traditional liberal freedoms would subject the state to the popular will. Though they were properly sceptical of the liberal doctrine that the market always does what the consumer wants, they were hopelessly naive about the corresponding doctrine that the Government always does what the voter wants. And so decisions made through the political process seemed to them both more efficient than, and morally superior to, decisions made by the market.

We know better now. The first and most obvious reason why social democracy is now on the defensive is that the political assumptions of 19th-century liberalism have turned out to be as fallacious as its economic assumptions. It has turned out that the polity cannot be relied upon to redress the balance of the economy, and that politicised decision-making is not inherently better than market decision-making. The unregulated market of the 19th century was capricious and cruel, but an unregulated state is likely to be even more so; and the state is much harder to regulate than the market ever was. But although social democracy has been extraordinarily fertile in expedients for regulating the market, it has shown little or no interest in regulating the state. As a result, one of its chief legacies is an overmighty state, which is also becoming, in the current jargon, 'overloaded'.

Not only can the social democracy of the last forty years offer no solution to the problem of 'overload': it also offers no solution to the complex of problems summed up in the notion of the 'limits to growth'. More than any other political creed, more even than 19th-century liberalism or Stalinist Communism, modern social democracy has put its faith in continuous economic growth. The second obvious reason why it is now on the defensive is that economic growth, even if it is still feasible, is clearly enormously more difficult than it was in the Fifties or Sixties. For if growth is more difficult, peaceful redistribution is also more difficult; and one of the central postulates of the social democracy of the last forty years is that peaceful redistribution is not only possible but easy.

Read against this background, Professor Galbraith's collection of book reviews, essays and travel pieces[2] is doubly disappointing. *Annals of an Abiding Liberal* is a classic example of vanity publishing. It has no message — except, perhaps, that Galbraith is an important man, with important friends in important places —

---

[2] John Kenneth Galbraith, *Annals of an Abiding Liberal* (André Deutsch. 1980).

and no unity. It contains a few economic essays, which repeat old themes more powerfully developed elsewhere. There are a few rather laboured humorous pieces, written with a heavy facetiousness, which presumably some find funny but which I found unbearably arch. There are several book reviews, one or two of which are mildly interesting. The only piece which seems to me to have been worth reprinting is a sympathetic and moving little essay on Thorstein Veblen. The rest would have been better left to oblivion.

Yet the book has a strange, back-handed kind of importance. Professor Galbraith is, after all, one of the gurus of the social democracy of the past forty years. If Crosland's *Future of Socialism* was the Old Testament for my generation of social democrats, Galbraith's *Affluent Society* has a good claim to be the New Testament. We used his now rather shop-soiled paradox — 'private affluence and public squalor' — to justify any increase in public spending, however wasteful, and any extension of the public sector, however mischievous. The object of a reforming politician, we told ourselves smugly, waving our Galbraiths aloft, was to increase the 'social wage': in other words, to take people's money away from them in order to give it to highly-paid bureaucrats to spend it on their behalf.

It was nonsense, of course. But fifteen years ago it was — at least, I hope and believe it was — forgivable nonsense. The public sector was, after all, much smaller than it is now. Though the Whitehall mandarinate was, if anything, even more secretive and unadventurous than it is now, it did not fight quite so flagrantly to defend its own privileges and extend its power. The scandal of local government reorganisation was still to come. The public-sector unions had not yet revealed their full potential for rapacious disregard of the public interest. Parliament had not yet revealed its hopeless inability to control, or even to monitor, the spending of public money. Above all, the recession had not yet started; and we were still strangers to the alarming new world in which the public sector is much better protected from squalor than the private.

Now that all these things have happened, however, one might have expected the world's leading champion of the old equation between social virtue and the social wage to notice that something has gone wrong — or, if that is asking too much, to notice that large numbers of people clearly think that something has gone wrong. Such expectations would have been vain. Professor

Galbraith emerges from these pages as the Bourbon of the social democratic Establishment who has learned nothing and forgotten nothing. His solution to the agonising new problems of the late Seventies and Eighties is to repeat the old social democratic slogans of the Fifties and Sixties. Public spending is good, and private spending is bad. The notion that taxpayers are in revolt against high public expenditure is a myth, put about by the *Wall Street Journal*. The solution to our current economic ills is to combine the old Keynesian remedies with an incomes policy.

As it happens, I think he is right to advocate an incomes policy. But incomes policies have, after all, been tried rather often in this country; so far, they have all collapsed in the face of trade-union hostility and public apathy. This is not to say that they should not be tried again: they *do* offer the only way of combining low inflation with low unemployment. But it is to say that advocates of an incomes policy should acknowledge the enormous political obstacles to success, and think hard about the best way to overcome them. Professor Galbraith merely tells us that incomes policies are good things, which is about as useful as telling an advanced alcoholic that he should never have started to drink.

Yet, by a strange paradox of intellectual myopia, Professor Galbraith's own theory offers, if not a solution, then at any rate the beginning of a diagnosis. The central theme of virtually all the economic essays in this book is the distinction between the 'market system' altogether; that, since the 'planning system' will remain with part of the economy where market forces still operate in the old textbook fashion, and the part where giant firms and giant unions can bend the market to their will. This distinction is a crucial one, and the books in which Professor Galbraith first drew our attention to it are of enduring value.

For the 'planning system' is, of course, the source of most of our troubles. It generates the wage-cost pressures which make incomes policies necessary; it gives union leaders the muscle with which incomes policies can be destroyed. It, moreover, frustrates all three of the most widely-advocated solutions to the present crisis. The traditional social democratic solution, tried by George Brown and Harold Wilson in the Sixties and by Michael Foot and Jim Callaghan in the Seventies, is the 'social contract' — a private deal between the Government and the unions, by which the unions trade wage restraint in return for extensions of their organisational power. As the last Government showed, such a deal can bring inflation down, but only at the cost of progressive industrial 'sclerosis. The neo-liberal solution, currently being applied by the present Government, is, in effect, to act as though the 'planning system' did not exist. Not surprisingly, this simply makes the crisis worse. The neo-Marxist solution, peddled by Tony Benn and Stuart Holland, is to take over the planning system by huge extensions of public ownership. That would poduce even faster industrial sclerosis than we have already, and make the state even mightier and more overloaded.

It is silly to pretend that there is an obvious way out. The one undoubted lesson of the past fifteen years is that obvious solutions do not work. But two things do seem fairly clear. The first is that, since the 'planning system' is the source of the problem, we ought to do all we can to strengthen the 'market system' at its expense — by helping small firms, by encouraging worker co-operatives, by giving incentives to self-employment, by penalising energy-intensive technologies and fostering labour-intensive ones, by working with the social forces which are steadily enlarging the 'black economy' instead of against them. The second, however, is that such measures cannot conceivably eliminate the 'planning system' altogether; that, since the 'planning system' will remain with us for the foreseeable future, the problems to which it gives rise will remain with us also; and that, since these problems are political rather than strictly economic in character, the solutions will have to be political as well.

Professor Galbraith does not even recognise that these problems exist. Professor Dahrendorf does not solve them either, but he does at least see that they cannot be solved within traditional social democratic terms. As he puts it in his final paragraph,

at this point, there are no signs at all that a centre party based on the present right wing of the Labour Party will be any more forward-looking than the ruling Social Democratic parties on the Continent. The issue today is not how to be social democratic, much as this may agitate the victims of adversary politics. The issue is what comes after Social Democracy ... [It] will have to be an imaginative, unorthodox and distinctive liberalism which combines the common ground with the new horizons of the future of liberty.

Unlike Professor Dahrendorf, I do not believe that the 'imaginative, unorthodox and distinctive liberalism' he wants can be brought to bear on our politics unless the present party structure is smashed; and I do not believe that the present party structure can be smashed unless the social democrats of Labour's 'radical right' recognise that their attitudes have to be revised, that this cannot be done within the existing Labour Party, and that a new force of some kind is required. Whether that new force should be a new party, or an enlarged, and to some extent reconstituted, Liberal Party, is a subordinate question. What matters is that it should come into existence. Professor Dahrendorf's phrases sum up the direction in which it will have to move. We shall not escape from our present impasse until it does so.

War and Peace

A.J.P. Taylor

War has been throughout history the curse and inspiration of mankind. The sufferings and destruction that accompany it rival those caused by famine, plague and natural catastrophes. Yet in nearly every civilisation war has been the noblest of professions, and among the heroes of every age those distinguished in war have always ranked first, as a visit to St Paul's Cathedral will bear witness. In many civilisations, war has been a once-for-all affair: the conquest of neighbouring territory or the repulse of an invader. In some, however, war between contending states has gone on for generations — the Times of Trouble, in Toynbee's phrase. Ancient Greece experienced such a Time, and there followed one of the first attempts to limit the sufferings of war, as the Olympic Games indicate. But the Greek wars were not ended by moderation and wise agreement. They were ended by the Roman conquest, which provided one solution to the problem of war: the establishment of a single dominant power that subdued or eliminated all other contenders.

Europe, too, has known attempts at a single universal state from the early days of the Holy Roman Empire to the brief domination of Hitler's Nazi Germany. But broadly speaking European history has been a continual Time of Troubles, interrupted by occasional periods of armed peace. The realisation that war was here to stay produced a unique development in European thought: attempts to eliminate war altogether, or, if these failed, to lessen its horrific consequences. The first type of attempt lay behind the medieval pursuit of 'the just war', a pursuit as elusive as that of the Holy Grail. For it is almost universally true that in war each side thinks itself in the right, and there is no arbiter except victory to decide between them. Until recently, most historians have endorsed this verdict by applauding the victory or blessing the cause of their own state. Thus English historians saw little to question in the plundering raids of Henry V or even of William the Conqueror. French historians saw little to question in the Empire of Napoleon. The *jus ad bellum* has proved a will o' the wisp, though still actively pursued by some. The lesser attempt to moderate or even to civilise war has been more rewarding. This *jus in bello* is the topic of

Geoffrey Best's fascinating book,[1] a volume replete with scholarship and brilliant presentation.

Moderate or civilised wars can only operate within certain limitations. They are almost impossible when there is a conflict of creeds as well as of state power. The wars of religion or the crusade against the Albigensians were as savage as the wars of ancient Rome. Even the most civilised powers observe the rules only when at war with another civilised power. The British did not observe the rules when they blew Indian mutineers from the mouths of cannon. The Americans did not observe the rules when at war with the Red Indians, and of course the Red Indians also did not observe them. In fact, the laws of war were until recently confined to Europe, though Best ends by chronicling the present-day attempts to extend them more widely.

In more precise terms, the laws of war began when the European states contended over their respective ambitions, not over their fundamental beliefs, religious or political. Vattel was their acknowledged father. He sought for laws that the antagonists could accept without forfeiting their chance of victory. Ideally, wars should be conducted between professional armies without injury or disturbance to the civil population. Rousseau carried this view to extremes when he wrote: 'War, then, is not a relationship between man and man, but between State and State, in which private persons are only enemies accidentally.' Most theorists were more moderate and recognised that the laws of war must sometimes bow to 'necessity'. Indeed, far from necessity knowing no law, it became itself part of the law. Thus the soldier should not loot or plunder but he cannot be required to respect hen roosts when he is hungry. The bombardment of a town is deplorable but may be necessary in order to enforce its surrender, though only the necessary minimum should be used. Despite these exceptions, the Enlightened 18th century did pretty well with the laws of war. Armies carried their commissariat train with them instead of living off the countryside. Destruction was not operated for its own sake. There was little attempt to shake the morale of the civilian population. Combatants wore recognised uniforms and did not prolong a hopeless resistance.

There was one curious flaw which exasperated continental Europeans. This was the problem of how far the rules of war

---

[1] *Humanity in Warfare: the Modern History of the International Law of Armed Conflicts* (Weidenfeld & Nicolson, 1980).

applied at sea. The continentals held that they should be applied unchanged. The British argued that the differing maritime circumstances fundamentally affected the laws of war. For instance, bombardments of towns were to be deplored but how else could the Royal Navy employ its strength against a land power?

Still graver was the problem of blockade. Continentals were clear as to the answer: neutral ships and neutral goods must be respected unless they were 'absolute' contraband. The British did not share this view. For them, blockade was a weapon with which to strangle an enemy and the rights of neutrals were of little account. This rigorous attitude weakened a little when Great Britain was faced with a powerful league of Armed Neutrality. But it was a hint of greater difficulties that were to arise in the future.

The French Revolution signalled the breakdown of Enlighten-ment in the laws of war as in other matters, though its original intention was the precise opposite. The early revolutionaries certainly aspired to spread their example abroad, but they imagined that the instruments of liberation would be Jacobin chants and floral wreaths rather than muskets and cannon. Even when forced to fight they insisted that their antagonists were few: 'war to the castles, peace to the cottages'. But who were to pay the liberators? Revolutionary France could not do so with its finances in chaos. The liberated peoples must pay. Soon the revolutionary armies were expected to work at a profit. Add to this the revolutionary strategy of speed, carried to its highest point by Napoleon. There was no time to waste on commissariat trains. The French armies lived off the country and often did very well out of it.

These revolutionary wars lessened and in time almost obliterated the distinction between soldiers and civilians. The Jacobins proclaimed 'the nation in arms'. How then could the civilian claim immunity? Things grew still more troublesome when civilians in the shape of partisans or guerrillas took up arms themselves. In Spain, for instance, the French attempted to treat all partisans as criminals, an action they repeated in Russia. The British took the same attitude in 1798 when they accorded to the French invaders of Ireland the honours of war and massacred the Irish rebels whom the French had come to liberate. Even those such as the British in Spain who were in alliance with partisans agreed afterwards that this was an episode better forgotten.

Neutrals came off as badly as civilians. Nelson's assault on Copenhagen in 1801 brought him almost as much honour as the battle of Trafalgar. Two years after his death the Danes had their fleet ruthlessly snatched away from them. During the French wars the British blockade gradually eroded the securities for neutral trade established during the 18th century. This culminated in the Anglo-American war of 1812-14, a war fought, ironically enough, after the British had conceded the main point at issue. Once more the British appealed to necessity: relying on maritime power, it was necessary for them to do things which land powers did not need to do — though Napoleon also disregarded neutral rights and imposed a fictitious blockade. By the end of the Napoleonic wars neutral rights had almost ceased to exist.

More fundamentally, the revolutionary and Napoleonic wars demonstrated that the laws of war demanded some basis of common principles if they were to operate successfully. The Jacobins despised their enemies as tyrants. The tyrants responded by treating the Jacobins as subverters of civilisation. Napoleon was given a half-hearted welcome as the restorer of law and order. But the victorious Powers showed their true opinion of Napoleon when they proclaimed him the enemy of mankind. Even so, it is surprising how much of the laws of war survived the impact of the French Revolution. Prisoners-of-war were still taken and were interned, usually under tolerable conditions. Flags of truce were generally respected and it was thought immoral to use them deceptively as a stratagem of war. The laws of blockade continued to provide matter for argument even if the British preferred maritime power to high principles. Enlightenment and Revolution produced conflicting impacts — a legacy that Geoffrey Best has analysed with admirable clarity and frankness.

For forty years after the Napoleonic wars the laws of war did not advance. Their renewal came with the Congress of Paris in 1856, perhaps because the Congress had nothing better to do. The Congress celebrated the end of a war predominantly on land by wrestling with the laws of war at sea, a topic where even the British representatives proved for once slightly conciliatory. From the Congress of Paris stemmed further international discussions culminating in the two Peace Conferences at The Hague. Despite this accumulation of pointless oratory and ingenious drafting, the greatest advance in the laws of war ever made was the achievement of one man, Henri Dunant, seconded by that impractical dreamer, Napoleon III. The Red Cross began with individual initiative and was continued by it. Great Powers did not sponsor the Red Cross:

they succumbed to it until it became as acceptable an element of international society as war itself. Further, the Red Cross did not grow out of the existing laws of war: it imposed itself upon them.

What was the cause of this universal acceptance? Did each Power see advantage for itself in the Red Cross? Did the principles of humanity and civilisation for once triumph? There is no easy answer. Certainly the triumph was not repeated elsewhere. Geoffrey Best again shows his powers of exposition as he traces the advance in the laws of war during the 19th century. Certainly there was a more conscious and official application to the subject than there had been earlier. During the Enlightenment, aloof philosophers enunciated general principles which each state and each soldier, almost, was expected to work out in practice for himself. The 19th century saw the arrival of the international lawyer, of whom the Russian Martens was the chief. Martens would have liked to formulate laws of war which should be at once wise and acceptable. In practice, this meant discovering laws that should have at least some humanity in them and that would despite this be tolerated by the military. The intellectual agility required to produce this was confined almost to Martens alone. The various conferences laboured productively. But there was always the shadow of 'necessity', sharply raised whenever the military saw some encroachment on their powers.

Broadly, the laws of war improved most in their application to actual fighting on land, which took on almost the medieval character of armed combat under chivalrous conditions. There was less advance over the problems that had arisen during the Napoleonic wars: requisitions, reprisals, partisans and the treatment of civilians. The practices of the Royal Navy suffered further encroachments, even though Fisher dismissed them as 'nonsense' which would be 'ditched' if war came. The European legalists averted their eyes from bombardment as practised by the British at Alexandria, and still more from the Union operations in the American Civil War, particularly Sherman's demonstration to the inhabitants of the South that War was Hell.

The laws of war improved more in appearance than in reality. For, as Geoffrey Best points out, there were two flourishing movements during the 19th century: the Peace Movement, which everyone noticed and commended, and the War Movement, which many people ignored and which yet proved more powerful. Best has found a wonderful quotation from Joseph Conrad, who described the Hague Tribunal as 'a solemnly official recognition of the Earth as a House of Strife'. Conrad continued: 'War has made peace altogether in its own image; a martial, overbearing, war-lord sort of peace...eloquent with allusions to glorious feats of arms'.

The 19th century formulated the laws of war; the 20th century was expected to apply them. Geoffrey Best discusses in his powerful concluding chapter how far this has proved true. The answers, drawn from both world wars, are contradictory. The laws have been best observed in fighting between regular land forces, particularly on the Western Front and in such 'professional' areas as North Africa. It seems that soldiers have higher standards when they are not being criticised and provoked by civilians. On the Eastern Front Soviet Russia observed the laws of war more nearly than did Nazi Germany, despite allegations to the contrary. The laws of war came off less happily at sea and in the air. This sprang partly from the British reversion to the ruthless application of blockade which she had developed in earlier wars. The deeper cause was the development of weapons of war which could not be covered by the existing laws.

The first of these, already effective in the First World War, was the submarine, which, as the Germans showed, had to sink its victims without warning if it were to operate successfully. The Germans pleaded that they were retaliating to the British blockade. The true situation was that the submarine had been projected as an additional navy weapon and that its role as a commerce-destroyer had not been foreseen. This was even truer of the Zeppelin, which first set the practice, however ineffectually, of indiscriminate bombardment. This problem was exacerbated with the arrival of bombing aircraft. Best makes two striking remarks about air experiences in the First World War. The first is that Trenchard enunciated the doctrine of indiscriminate bombardment, quite without practical experience. The second is that the Royal Navy Air Service developed precision bombing during its short life. This achievement was subsequently ignored, partly as impractical and partly as being not aggressive or terrifying enough.

Best continues the problems of air warfare when he reaches the Second World War. Here the Trenchard legacy came to fruition. It is often not appreciated that indiscriminate or area bombing was a British speciality. The American Air Force disliked it; the German Luftwaffe operated it sceptically and reluctantly. British obsession with area bombing was an extension of British reliance on blockade

— the weapon of a power reluctant to develop a great army. Best traces Sir Arthur Harris's persistent and unjustified defence of area bombardment, which culminated in the unnecessary attack on Dresden in 1945 — not that this attack was any more reprehensible than earlier attacks except that it came towards the end of the war. Air warfare as practised during the Second World War, and particularly with its last achievements at Hiroshima and Nagasaki, left two profound holes in the restraining laws of war: the first that indiscriminate destruction, however horrible, was a legitimate means of war; the second that with 'the nation at war' there was no longer any distinction between the military and the civilians and that therefore civilians were legitimate targets. The same moral was drawn from the extension of partisan warfare, which led to the conclusion that every civilian who was not a collaborator of the invaders was a concealed or potential partisan, a moral the partisan forces applied the other way round. The logical consequence was that every inhabitant of a conquered country should be massacred or at the very least dispatched to slave labour, as the Germans demonstrated.

And so Best arrives at the present day. There have been even more conferences and regulations. The profession of international lawyer is more active than ever. There are two black clouds. The first is air warfare, which with the development of nuclear weapons transgresses all the laws of war ever known. The second is the attempt to extend the laws of war to cover colonial revolts or social revolutions, an attempt further confused by the Marxist insistence that Marxist acts of violence are always right and resistance to these acts always wrong. Despite these portents, Best remains mildly optimistic. He welcomes the persistent discussion of the laws of war as evidence that there is some desire to limit and restrain armed conflicts. He even hints a hope that this desire may be fulfilled. To my mind, the experiences of the past eighty years are not encouraging. Fortunately, the past is not always a guide to the future.

The experts in the laws of war claimed to be practical men, resigned to the fact that war, somewhat humanised, would go on for a long time, if not for ever. The search for an end to war has been of more recent origin, being almost confined to Great Britain during the last hundred years, with some echoes in the United States. Martin Caedel[2] approaches this search with a sharp

[2]*Pacifism in Britain 1914-1945: the Defining of a Faith* (Oxford University Press, 1980).

distinction between pacificism (a word which he claims to have borrowed from me and which I gladly lend him) and pacifism. Pacificists are those who favour peaceful foreign politics and who seek to develop international institutions for the promotion of peace. Pacifism in its pure form is a total rejection of war as an instrument of policy.

The distinction is clear to Caedel and will be clear to his readers. It has been less clear in the historical record. Pacifism is the older, in that there have always been a few men who refused to take part in war, but this was an individual gesture of abstention and not a contribution to solving the problem of war. The early Christians refused to serve in the Roman armies, but this sprang from their refusal to accord divine honours to the Emperor. Once they could serve under the sign of the Cross the Christians fought vigorously enough, not only against pagans and barbarians, but against each other.

Modern pacificism was part of the humanitarian outlook which characterised the philanthropists of the 19th century: peaceful aims went along with anti-slavery and prison reform. Quakers tended to take up a pacifist position, but this did not prevent their becoming advocates of a peaceful policy. A Quaker delegation visited Nicholas I at St Petersburg in an attempt to prevent the Crimean War. John Bright opposed that war in his greatest speeches, but he was clearly not a pacifist: he supported the armed suppression of the Indian Mutiny and applauded the Union victory in the American Civil War. With Great Britain not involved in a European war for nearly a century, the question for humanitarians was not, 'What do we do in the event of war?' but: 'How do we discourage or prevent war elsewhere?'

There was a further obstacle to the development of a clear-cut pacifism in Great Britain: even when at war, as in the Anglo-Boer war of 1899-1902, Great Britain fought with professional volunteer forces. The potential pacifist did not have to resolve what he would do if called upon to fight. On the contrary, his difficulty was to find outlets for his humanitarianism either by providing medical services or by conducting political agitation against the policy and operations of war. The pro-Boers were often stigmatised as pacifists, but it is clear that they were nothing of the kind, and Lloyd George, one of the most assertive pro-Boers, became later an outstanding war minister. Caedel is therefore right in taking the outbreak of war in August 1914 as the starting-point for his theme: pacifism in Britain. Even so, the emergence of pacifism remained obscure.

Caedel is pretty firm in dealing with those who opposed the First World War as being a mistaken policy or even as fought against the wrong enemy. The Union of Democratic Control was clearly not pacifist. But what about the Fellowship of Reconciliation, which Caedel specifies as 'quietest'? Even the No-Conscription Fellowship began as a political movement to oppose the legislative introduction of conscription, and continued on a practical basis after conscription operated. Conscription certainly made some people ask themselves whether they were pacifists or merely high-minded. There were few clear responses. Only 16,500 of those called up pleaded conscientious objection; only 6,000 of these refused to accept the tribunal's verdict, and only 1,298 of these resisted 'absolutely'. Nor were even the absolutists all of a kind. Some were religious pacifists; some were humanitarian pacifists. But a number were solely against the Great War which was raging: some as socialists, some as critics of British foreign policy, some as defenders of individual liberty. The experiences of war strengthened the confusion: conscientious objectors did not inquire into the theoretical basis on which the conviction of their comrades rested. All could be numbered as opponents of war, from the pure pacifist to the Marxist champion of war on the barricades.

The confusion which had developed during the Great War increased when the war was over. Many who had been combatants now regarded the war as mistaken in either its aims or its conduct or perhaps both together. Caedel analyses this confusion with admirable clarity. Perhaps he is a little too rigorous. The man who defines his convictions with absolute accuracy is very rare and rarest of all in the world of politics. Caedel tends to imply that all such confusions are foolish, and that pacifists and near-pacifists are peculiarly prone to them. Indeed, there is even a hint that those who reject the methods and arguments of pacifism are eminently sane — a strange view. How are we to describe the rulers of great states and their technical advisers who propose to defend civilisation by blowing the peoples and cities of the world to pieces? 'Sane' is not a word that would occur to me.

The 1920s were the heyday of pacificism and pacifism in a tangle. The former absolutists did not reproach those who had served in the war, and these latter for the most part did not reproach the absolutists. Many who had preached and even practised individual rejection felt that this was too self-centred and co-operated with others in the search for means of preventing war. The former conscientious objector might join the No More War Movement, but he recognised no contradiction in joining the League of Nations Union as well. Yet the basis of the League of Nations was 'collective security', which implied in the last resort military sanctions, or, as the American historian Harry Elmer Barnes expressed it, 'perpetual war for the sake of perpetual peace'. This was not a problem of any practical relevance when the prospect of another great war seemed remote.

The hard core of Caedel's book concerns the great transformation which began in the early Thirties with the realisation that perpetual peace would not come of itself or perhaps was not on offer at all. Some of the one-time pacifists decided that with the rapid approach of social revolution they were not pacifists after all. Since social revolution failed to arrive, this conversion had little practical application except to remove a rather disruptive element from the pacifist movement. Fascism, or, to be more precise, the appearance of Hitler, was a different matter. Comparatively few recognised Hitler's threat from the first. On the contrary, pacifists like nearly everyone else argued that the wisest as well as the most moral course was the redress of German grievances. It is curious to read of a time when former conscientious objectors applauded Neville Chamberlain.

The final years before the Second World War saw the rise of a pacifist movement that was political rather than ethical: the Peace Pledge Union. The Union was virtually the creation of one man, Canon Dick Sheppard, and a very erratic shepherd he proved. The origins of the Union went back, I think, to the spate of anti-war literature that characterised the end of the Twenties. Not surprisingly, the Union was an assembly of prima donnas, as Caedel entertainingly demonstrates. Perhaps there is nothing more absurd than gifted writers earnestly believing in some cause. Quite a number were members of the League of Nations as well as the Peace Pledge Union; many moved from one Union to the other and back again. Caedel does not fail to add that many were vegetarians while some had a high track record in plurality of wives. The Peace Pledge Union enlisted an impressive total of pledges against war. Comparatively few of these pledges were honoured when war actually arrived. Though there were many more conscientious objectors than in the First World War — 60,000 against 16,000 —

their impact was much less. Instead of being persecuted, they were tolerated or even admired. Some five thousand were sent to prison, more in sorrow than in anger: most of these took up some form of humanitarian work before the war was over. Only Christians — 'Christadelphians, Plymouth Brethren, Elimites, Particular People' — stuck to their belief. Caedel concludes that pacifism has been reduced to a religious belief, rather than a solution to the problems of war.

Though never a pacifist, I had more patience with the pacifists of that age than he has now. In my view, they were, though often foolish, a good deal more sensible than their opponents. Martin Caedel has a great future before him as an historian, particularly when he becomes more tolerant of human follies.

Isn't the news terrible?

Raymond Williams

'I see the news is bad again.' The banal phrase punctuates my memories of the late 1930s. I remember an adolescent anger that people would not name the things that were happening: the invasion of Austria; the cession of the Sudetenland; the invasions of Czechoslovakia and Albania — all packaged as 'the news'. While in London it no doubt seemed ridiculous that Chamberlain referred to Czechoslovakia as a far-off country of which we knew little or nothing, I could see, there in Wales, that what he said was true for these railwaymen and farmers, whose gravity and abstraction, at this level of affairs, puzzled and irritated me.

This situation is still, in general, too little understood. The banal phrase of our current years is a rhetorical question: 'Isn't the news terrible?' I still sometimes make the mistake of trying to answer it, since when I have taken off the packaging some of it is not at all terrible to me; indeed, some of the most officially outraging events are positively welcome. Yet the structural problem persists, and has become more acute. In the late Thirties, after all, the wireless news of these European convulsions came only after a steady reading of the fat-stock prices. Now the bumptious arresting music, the spinning images of the world, the celebrity reader, induce new forms of attention and of stress which are often justified, though the signals occur whether there is anything of substance to follow them or not. And then what we can observe, past the apparent sophistications, is a lack of human fit between exposure to reports of world-wide events and either effective knowledge, through which to try to assess them, or any effective possibility of response — some action even if it is as occasional as a vote: anything practicable, that is, beyond either spectacle or worry.

The official answer to this problem is at once easy and beside the point. It is factually true that some of these reported events could signal, through a chain of relationships, the most immediate effects, from a nuclear war through the more imaginable scales of disaster, disturbance and nuisance. Thus the public must be informed. If they do not know these connections, they must be made aware of them, or have them pointed out by our diplomatic, defence or industrial correspondents.

But this is an abstraction less forgivable than the more mundane blocking of all events as 'the news'. Those railwaymen and farmers did not need to be told that distant events could end in their own bodies. Some of them, including my father, still carried in their flesh the wounds of the wanton metal that had attended the last demonstration of relationships and consequences. It was not, then as now, the gravity of generalised attention that was lacking. Instead, now as then, the news was received, accurately if too simply, as alien: not just because it was coming from places and peoples of which there was no direct knowledge, beyond these isolated reports, but also because its mode of communication was not that of people talking, questioning, moving across to talk or listen to others, as in everyday practice and knowledge, but was this authoritative transmission — an authority without rivals and beyond effective challenge, imposing itself professionally, in every signal, accent and tone, upon the near and the far.

Let us face it then: the news has been very bad lately. But it is very difficult to be sure how much of this badness has been in the events themselves, and how much in their intense and relentless interpretation by the authorities: a one-sided polemic which I cannot remember being at this pitch since the late Forties. Some of us, at least, must be ready to appreciate the verbal joke by the Glasgow University Media Group, whose *Bad News* and now *More Bad News*[1] indicate the faults of news presentation rather than the import of the actual events.

To be sure, we cannot draw any firm line between events and their presentation. A very large number of the events now presented are in fact interpretations, by a small group of highly privileged voices, directly transmitted or read out by the hired celebrities. The privilege of such voices would matter less if it were not also, in the leading cases, the privilege of command of men and resources. Such privilege, now quaintly known as a 'mandate', even where it refers to unforeseen events on which no wider opinions have been canvassed, has to be distinguished, of course, from that of the voice alone. But then it is a very long time, in British broadcasting especially, since we heard any voice of this kind that sounded as if it were speaking quite for itself, from its own knowledge and experience. An institutional definition encloses

---

[1]Glasgow University Media Group, *More Bad News* (Routledge & Kegan Paul, 1980).

this absence. Discussion and argument occur elsewhere, but meanwhile, here is the news.

It is, then, a major intellectual gain, in recent years, to have found ways of seeing the news as a cultural product. There is still a central difficulty. On the one hand, it is true that in some respects we have to read the news as if we were reading a novel. Until the early 18th century the word 'novel' carried two senses — of a tale and of what we now call the news. Spenser had written, in a sense that we might now echo, observing the arranged features of a news-reader: 'You promise in your clear aspect, some novel.' 'Novelist', in the 18th century, meant a newsmonger as well as a writer of prose fiction. But a distinction was forming between 'fiction' and 'fact' , and this had serious effects, both ways, on what appear at first sight two distinct kinds of narrative. At its most confident, this assigned all novels to 'fiction' in the sense that the events had not occurred, but had been imagined or created: a definition that not only makes for many difficulties with the reading of certain novels of the past, from *Romola* to *War and Peace*, but is now in trouble with the arrival of the important contemporary form of the 'novel based on a real-life event', or 'faction'.

Yet the worst effects were at the other end of the scale. The fact that certain events have undoubtedly occurred — have happened to people, have been observed, have been reliably reported, have been tested from the evidence of participants and witnesses — has been used to conceal or to override the equally evident fact that as they now move from events to news they are being narrated, and that certain long-standing problems of narration — the identity of the narrator, his authority, his point of view, his assumed relationship to his readers or hearers, his possible wider purposes in selecting and narrating these events in this way — come inevitably into question. Most experienced adults get used to having to ask these questions, however politely or tacitly, when they hear stories and reports in everyday talk. Yet it seems that we have only to ask them about a broadcasting service or a newspaper to produce outraged cries about an assault on professional competence and independence, or to provoke dark hints, which at least sometimes are surely projections, about a conspiracy to interfere with freedom of news and indeed to manipulate or censor it.

Thus it would be reassuring to know that the minute of a high-level discussion in the BBC (quoted in the *Leveller* of January 1978) was inaccurate: the Director-General 'said there would be no sense in attacking *Bad News* in detail...he thought however that the ideology of sociologists was a subject which would repay a little study and hoped that it would be possible for a programme like *Analysis* to tackle it.' What *Analysis* or some other programme might equally have tackled, down to that level of detail which is one of the surest means of testing accuracy, was the body of evidence about actual news presentations which *Bad News* had presented. The 'ideology' (ideologies) of sociologists would have been a wholly proper matter to include, not least because it would have helped to promote a genuinely critical attitude to sociological 'findings', which in other, happier cases — this or that poll or survey — make their unproblematic way into the news. Moreover, once discussion had begun, the problem of the 'facts', and the related problems of selection and interpretation, could have been rationally addressed over the whole range, in and out of university and newsroom.

There are at least two reasons why this has not happened. The first, undoubtedly, is that this kind of independent criticism is taken, almost instinctively, as a challenge to authority, of a piece with all those other challenges to authority which sociologists (by those who do not know them, but have heard the ugly word) are supposed in recent years to have been making and inciting. Yet I do not find this response, however hasty or muddled, unreasonable. What is at stake is indeed authority at its deepest level: that deep sense of propriety and legitimacy which has assigned both authority and responsibility to certain public sources of news and interpretation. These qualities are tested over the years, and over a range of events are proved to have certain reliabilities. It is then easy to move from that kind of public record to an assumption of more general authority, in which the institution comes to see itself, and to be widely seen, as an organ of the 'national interest', a warrant of independence and fairness, standing above the mere ideologies which this or that minority might indulge. Anyone questioning this identity, backed as it is by a centralised and very powerful technology, and by the symbols, rhythms and timed regular occasions of public address, can rather readily be seen as a small boy throwing stones. And if he has written a fat book, full of tables and referenced details, he does not cease to be an unruly small boy: it is only that he has provided himself, for his own questionable purposes, with even more stones.

The second reason, an outraged professionalism, needs to be

carefully considered. It is true that the same kind of defence is rather often rejected, by news-gatherers, when it is made by other professions. 'What evidence do you have for saying that?' 'Don't other experts disagree with you?' 'Doesn't this go against what most of us believe?' These are the regular and admirable questions of the most persistent reporters, and at their best they are asked of the most as well as the least privileged. It seems then reasonable that they should be asked, with the same persistence, of reporters, correspondents and editors themselves. And indeed it is noticeable that when a reporter has delivered a certain kind of story — when he has, say, interviewed a representative of the IRA, or a Welsh republican, or has what he takes to be secret or confidential information about some national body — he is often quite sharply interrogated, within his profession and in other ways. These are indicators of situations in which reporters have broken the consensus of 'responsible' news-gathering. The professional defence, of the right to establish and publish the facts, is then qualified or overridden by other criteria.

Yet what this situation most illuminates is the underlying structure of communicative relationships, within a particular social order. For there is no normal space in which news reports can be examined and interrogated, unless the consensus has been broken and other social forces move through and take it into a public, administrative or legal domain. In the ordinary rush of news reports, within the consensus, this does not often happen, though the need is as great for events within the consensus as outside it.

It is at this point that the 'sociologists' announce themselves. The growth in media studies and cultural studies has been remarkable, in the last twenty years. A space which does not exist, to any effect, within the major news-and-opinion institutions is carved out in other institutions, mainly educational. Hence books like *Bad News* and *More Bad News*. But it is then obvious that the conditions under which such work is done are radically different from those in which the work being studied is and in most cases has to be done. It is understandable that reporters and editors, who work under considerable pressure, especially of time, are impatient when confronted by analyses of their work made by researchers who seem to have all the time in the world. I remember a related exchange between a gifted analyst of television and a gifted producer. The analyst had indicated a particular effect through a particular use of shot. 'Tell me that,' said the producer, 'next time

I'm filming in the rain on Liverpool Docks at five in the morning.' But then neither position, as it stands, can be quite accepted. The effect, after all, was there, and so were the real and difficult conditions of practice. When Annan found that editors and reporters were 'bewildered' by the findings of *Bad News*, it should not have been the end of the matter. The point is to investigate the social conditions of such bewilderment.

It is just because of the immediate pressures, the difficult moment on Liverpool Docks, that a detached analysis of methods and conventions is necessary. What we do, under pressure, and especially what we do as professionals, is what we have been trained to do, what we have got used to doing, what at deep levels we can take for granted so that we can get on with an immediate job. And there is no profession which can fail to learn from someone making explicit just the training, the usage, the taking for granted, that underlie all practice. These can then be consciously affirmed, or consciously amended. This is how all rigorous professions work.

The special problem of communications is not only the relative absence of fundamental as distinct from on-the-job training. It is also that the fundamental analyses of method — for example, the quite new problems of *visual* presentation — are being carried out in one place, and the practice in another. Yet nothing can be understood if it is not recognised that both these real levels exist. I do not see what more the *Bad News* group could have done to show the intricate practical problems (highlighted, of course, by the many practical failures) of the 'objectivity' and 'balance' which the professional broadcasters claim. The greater relative monopoly of broadcast news has at least this advantage: that the greater relative diversity of the press (for all its own tendencies to monopoly and shrinkage) provides accessible evidence to test 'objectivity'. This is well demonstrated in the reporting of the Price Commission's calculations of the contribution of wage-rises to inflation (*More Bad News*, pp. 19-22), where, in complicated ways (professionally traced by the *Financial Times*), an estimated 20% contribution became, through various hands, a 'between 60 and 75 pence in the pound' contribution in a BBC news item. Given the importance of such issues, and the genuine difficulties of interpreting such statistics, within different theoretical frameworks, there is really no case at all for saying that the exigencies of practice must override fundamental questions of method. Thus, on so contentious and professional an issue, there is no defensible practical reason for leaving interpretation to the single voice of 'our correspondent' or to the demotic skills of a particular news-writer. Why could there not be two 'correspondents', deliberately chosen for their theoretical differences? Because that would be discussion? But the whole problem is the selection of one interpretation as *news*.

Are we then asking for the impossible, a neutral news service? The *Bad News* team argue that neutrality is impossible and undesirable; indeed, that it is the claim of the existing organisations that what they offer is 'neutral, unbiased, impartial and balanced' which is at the heart of the problem, since what happens in practice is a demonstrably ideological presentation, at many levels, which at once presumes and helps to form an effective consensus of news and other values. There can be little doubt that they have, in general, made out their case, yet where, theoretically and practically, do we go from there?

It is a further effect of the institutional division of labour that professional researchers follow the rules of their own profession, presenting and commenting on evidence, but not otherwise, except implicitly, declaring themselves. I do not blame the *Bad News* team for this, but I notice the contrast with, say, Todd Gitlin's *The whole world is watching*,[2] where a comparable but more committed analysis is made of the American media on a specific set of issues. There the focus is on the definition and characterisation of the American New Left, and the fact that it is written by one who actively participated in the events reported, and saw not only their slanting by the media but the complex results within the movement itself, adds a welcome sharpness. I think we do have ultimately to say that the practices in question are matters of fundamental social and political conflict, though this should not prevent us from also saying that it has been an achievement of certain kinds of society, and of certain institutions and professionals, to create *some* space in which, over and above the conflict, the integrity of information and the actual diversity of opinion can be reasonably assured, and that we should all be looking for ways to enlarge that space to its still distant limits.

One notable opportunity for such enlargement now exists in the new communications technology, especially in the common-carrier and interactive versions of teletext. It may well not be taken, given

---

[2]Todd Gitlin, *The whole world is watching* (University of California Press, 1980).

the pressure to adapt the technology to current forms of news and marketing. But there would be immediate gain if broadcast news could be, in effect, footnoted, given the developing teletext services which can both handle and recall complicated information and necessary context. Moreover, here as more generally, an enlarged space requires that diversity of channels and voices which all existing systems and their ideologies seem determined to limit, in the name of their own irreplaceable excellence. This looks like being a very long struggle, but it is worth saying, finally, that a considerable amount of that 'terrible news' — the events, not the reports — occurs and will continue to occur because too few people are speaking to and for too many, in conditions in which, increasingly, they nevertheless cannot prevent others from acting and failing to act. That, more than anything, is now the welcome and terrible news.

Gielgud's Achievements

Alan Bennett

Sir John Gielgud is 75. To hear him talk or watch him on the stage he seems much younger, whereas his recollections of the lions of the Edwardian theatre ought to put him well past his century. It's an elastic life because baby Gielgud was so quick off the mark, the famous nose soon round the edge of the pram observing the odd behaviour of his Terry uncles and aunts. He had instantaneous success as a young actor and put his popularity with audiences to good effect, bringing Shakespeare and Chekhov to the West End. As an actor manager between the wars he ran what was virtually a national theatre on Shaftesbury Avenue. In the Fifties new directions in the theatre led him to flounder for a while, but in the last ten years he has found his place again. Adjectives like 'spry' and 'vigorous', indicating the subject is past it, are here inappropriate. His powers show no sign of diminishing, nor his enterprise. He has come a long way. As a juvenile his 'ambition was to be frightfully smart and West End, wear beautifully-cut suits lounging on sofas in French-window comedies'. Fifty years later 'I was asked to put suppositories up my bottom under the bedclothes and play a scene in the lavatory which I confess I found somewhat intimate.' Knighthoods nothing: actors should be decorated for gallantry.

This book[1] has been put together from conversations recorded by John Miller and John Powell for the BBC. They were delightful broadcasts: talking off the cuff, Gielgud rambled backwards and forwards over his life; he rarely paused and then needed only the gentlest nudge to set him off again, bowling down the years. Cut together into a book, the talks come much closer to his tone of voice than previous writings, the only thing one misses is the sound of his laughter: in the broadcasts, a narrative would begin seriously enough, then he would start to snuffle, the snuffle became a giggle and the whole episode would end in a snort of laughter, the object of the joke as often as not himself. It's a winning characteristic , and an artless one; few public figures can be less concerned with the presentation of self, less calculating of the effect produced. Hence the famous gaffes.

[1] John Gielgud, *An Actor and his Time* (Sidgwick & Jackson, 1979).

The foot went into the mouth quite early. At a first night of *Romeo and Juliet* in 1919, Ellen Terry's last professional appearance, the Terry family were out in force. Gielgud's grandmother Kate Terry and her sister Marion were both given rounds of applause as they made their separate entrances into the auditorium. 'In the interval I said in a loud voice to Marion, "Grandmother had a wonderful reception," and Marion replied: "Yes, dear. I expect they thought it was me."' To compare even implicitly the popularity of two actresses (let alone in a 'loud voice') is to invite disaster, but the joy of the story is that even 60 years afterwards Gielgud doesn't seem to realise that his aunt wasn't just being witty but that he had put his foot in it.

There were still giants to be glimpsed in the streets of Edwardian London. He saw Sir Squire Bancroft walking every morning to his bank 'where he would demand a slip with the amount of his current balance, which he would diligently examine before proceeding to lunch at the Garrick'. Bancroft was scrupulous about attending funerals and memorial services 'and was heard to remark on his return from a cremation service, in those days something of a novelty: "A most impressive occasion. And afterwards the relatives were kind enough to ask me to go behind."' Gielgud's language still retains a flavour of those days. He can talk of 'bounders', of someone being 'out of the picture' or 'caddish' even. 'She was jolly and red-faced,' he says of a costume designer, 'like an admiral's daughter.'

In his own person he retains a visible characteristic of that less inhibited generation in his 'Terry tears'. He has ready access to his emotions and like Churchill he weeps with unaffected ease. On the stage he will produce a wonderfully effective tear seconds after telling some ribald story in the wings, and in full flood his tears are a remarkable phenomenon. I saw him once giving an address at a memorial service, one of those gatherings that seem to occur more frequently in the theatrical profession than any other, generally in the Covent Garden area. This was a service for the old Bensonian actress, Nora Nicholson. Nora had had a happy life and was 81 when she died, so the service was by no means a gloomy one. Sybil Thorndyke, herself 92 and crippled by arthritis, sat enthroned in the front pew surrounded by a posse of ladies who were scarcely younger. At a given moment, these attendants slid along the pew, got their frail shoulders under Dame Sybil and slowly hunched her into a standing position, remaining massed behind her like an aged rugger scrum while she recited the 23rd Psalm in wonderful ringing tones. The contrast between Dame Sybil's physical incapacity and the undimmed beauty of her voice set Gielgud off crying. By the time he stood up for his memorial address he could scarcely speak, the tears splashing on the chancel steps in a display of grief which, if it was disproportionate, was not inappropriate. It was a sight both moving and funny, and much appreciated by the congregation.

Gielgud is dispassionate about his own talents, and generous about those of others. The publishers are said to have had a hard time preparing this book, with the gentle knight anxious to tone down any remark that might offend. None do, but the anxiety is typical and so is the hard time, as he's notorious for changing his mind. In fact, the only person who does get any stick is young Mr Gielgud. 'I had little idea at that time of playing a part with any originality,' he says, and dismisses many of his youthful efforts as just 'showing off'. There have been many failures, particularly as a director. 'I am feather-headed,' he says, 'not really thorough.' True, but he is also conscientious in hidden and unexpected ways. Like many actors from time to time, he tapes books for the blind. It's a one-off job which most actors do without much thought. I once in his dressing-room picked up a book which he was due to record: he had scored and stressed and underlined it as if for a Command Performance.

Methodical, however, he is not, particularly as a director. His production of *Don Giovanni* which opened the newly-restored Coliseum in 1968 was a disaster (though that's not surprising as opening productions generally are — why anybody ever consents to open a theatre I do not understand). At the last dress rehearsal some members of the chorus had still not been placed. A final dress rehearsal in the theatre is done properly, behind closed doors. Opera dress rehearsals seem slightly busier than the first night, grand and populous with all the members of the board on view. There are titled patrons and their ladies, and crowds of discreet functionaries discreetly function in an atmosphere of hushed reverence. This is Art with a capital S. The opera was well under way when Gielgud suddenly noticed the hitherto undirected members of the chorus uneasily wandering about the stage. He rose from his seat, rushed down to the front of the stalls to call a halt while he told them what to do. But operas are not so easily stopped as plays and the orchestra ploughed on relentlessly, with Gielgud trying to make himself heard. Suddenly his voice rose above the din in an anguished wail: 'Oh, do stop that awful *music*.'

His has been a fabled and fabulous life and the book is a stream of anecdotes and vignettes. 'I am Mrs Sabawala,' an Indian admirer announces. 'My house on Malabar Hill is a sermon in stone. Lunch with me tomorrow.'

He takes part in a gala at the Foreign Office to celebrate the visit of the French President in March 1939: 'It was a tremendous affair, the last of its kind before the war and I could not help referring to it afterwards as the Duchess of Richmond's Ball.' Sacha Guitry was to appear with Seymour Hicks in a not very funny sketch they had written, adorned but not improved by Guitry's latest wife, Genevieve Sereville, an extremely pretty girl. 'At rehearsal Mlle Sereville was dressed in a very short skirt and her stockings were rolled below her knees like a footballer's, showing a considerable expanse of thigh.' Sounding unaccountably like Ralph Lynn in an Aldwych farce, Gielgud ventured to remark to Hicks: 'I say, sir, that's a remarkably attractive girl with M Guitry, don't you think,' and was rewarded with the trenchant comment: 'Try acting with her old boy. It's the cabman's goodbye.'

In one respect, however, this anecdotal style does him less than justice. One would not gather from these pages the nature of the role Gielgud played in the theatre between the wars, nor the extent to which he has been a pioneer. 'It was not until the Thirties,' he writes, 'that by a lucky chance I was able to bring Shakespeare back to the West End as a commercial success.' This 'lucky chance' occurred in a period of theatrical history vividly re-created by Irving Wardle in his biography of George Devine. Devine brought Gielgud to Oxford to direct the OUDS production of *Romeo and Juliet* in 1932. He had never directed before, though he had played Romeo at the Old Vic. Gielgud has always been interested in stage design; he had at one time considered going into the theatre in that capacity and it was at his suggestion that three unknown designers were brought in to do the costumes. These were Elizabeth Montgomery and her two partners Margaret and Sophia Harris, the Motleys, who specialised in producing stunning effects with the cheapest materials. The OUDS *Romeo and Juliet* entranced all who saw it and was the trial run for the triumphant version Gielgud directed at the New Theatre in 1935, when he and Olivier alternated Romeo and Mercutio. In this and his other productions in the Thirties, Gielgud was able to put into practice some of the lessons he had learned from Harcourt Williams at the Old Vic, and through Harcourt Williams from Granville Barker. These were simple productions with continuity of action and unity of design, and were entirely modern in feeling. Wardle quotes Tyrone Guthrie as saying that Gielgud's production of *The Merchant of Venice* at the Old Vic 'made Maugham and Coward seem like two Nonconformist parsons from the Midlands'.

It must have been an exciting time to be in the theatre and some of Wardle's best pages are about the early days of Motley. They had taken as a studio Chippendale's old workshop behind St Martin's Lane, where a gang of actors, led by Gielgud, could generally be found sitting around, gossiping, discussing productions and having tea. With a tea bill that sometimes came to £100 a week, it sounds cosy, cliquey and not the stuff of theatrical revolution, and this is the way Gielgud tells it — casually, with lots of anecdotes about Komisarjevsky and Michel St Denis, both of whom he backed. What he does not say is that to design and direct productions in this way brought a gust of fresh air into the English theatre. He made Shakespeare a commercial success 20 years before the Royal Shakespeare Company. Through Komisarjevsky and St Denis he put the English theatre in touch with a European tradition 20 years before the Royal Court. It cannot have been easy to bear that when the Court's day did come his pioneering work had been forgotten. Out of sympathy with Beckett and Brecht, he missed the bus to Sloane Square and it was a long time before another one came along. But when he did begin to take part in modern plays again it should be remembered that it was a return, not a departure.

Gielgud's greatest success in the Fifties was his one-man show *The Ages of Man,* adapted from George Rylands' anthology. It was a *tour de force*, a showcase for his talents and also a copy-book exercise in which he could demonstrate as no one else how Shakespeare should be spoken. He did it superlatively well and he did it everywhere. It was something he could fall back on to earn money and to wipe out the memory of less successful enterprises, of which in the Fifties and Sixties there were quite a few. But if *Ages of Man* was a *tour de force* it was also a *cul de sac*. It typed him in the eyes of younger theatregoers as grand, solemn and remote. He was the Voice Beautiful. Not to mention the Voice Imitable. And it was not theatre: 'I toured it for so many years I feared I would be out of practice when it came to acting again with other people. Also eight performances a week all by myself and sitting alone in a dressing-room between the acts was a very lonely and depressing business.'

I had always assumed that this fairly bleak period in his life came to an end with his portrayal of Lord Raglan in Tony Richardson's *Charge of the Light Brigade* in 1967, and then his success in *Forty Years On* the following year. It was certainly clear from Richardson's film that Gielgud was beginning to act in a different way. Indeed, he was hardly acting at all, allowing much more of his own personality to be seen. In many ways he was like Raglan, absent-minded, impulsive, out of touch. The headmaster in *Forty Years On* was the same sort of man and I had thought it was the succession of the two parts that broke the mould. But this is to forget Peter Brook's National Theatre production of *Oedipus,* which intervened between the film and my play. Gielgud had had a glorious season at Stratford in 1950 in which he had done *Measure for Measure* with Brook. But this was Brook 'when he was still young and approachable and jolly', not the legend he had since become. On *Oedipus* he would walk into the rehearsal room and bark: 'No newspapers.' Deprived of his beloved crossword, Sir John was made to do exercises. 'It was rather like being in the army and I dreaded it; but at the same time I knew I wanted to be part of such an experiment.' Brook even tried to alter his voice: 'I had to go into the voice and manner of the blinded Oedipus, trying to produce my voice in a strange, strangled tone which Peter had invented at rehearsal with endless experiment. Technically one of the most difficult things I had ever done in my life...very good, I suppose, for my ego.' That 'I suppose' hides the doubts, the sense of humour suspended, the abject subjection and the outlawing of common sense that working with Brook now seems to entail. If the experiment comes off, as it did with his production of *Midsummer Night's Dream*, the result is magical. If it doesn't (and it didn't with *Oedipus*), it is just embarrassing.

Stories abound. The cast were dressed in sweaters and slacks in a tasteful shade of tan. They looked like a Bulgarian table-tennis team. Some, representing plague-stricken Thebans, were tethered to pillars in the auditorium where they were frequently asked for programmes by the latecomers. One of the exercises in rehearsal required each member of the cast to come down to the front of the stage and shout out at the top of his voice the worst thing he could think of. 'We open in three days!' bellowed one bold spirit. But such jokes were not encouraged, and Gielgud was systematically battered down to lowest ebb, shorn of experience and expertise. 'You can't do that,' Brook would tell him. 'It's awfully false and

theatrical.' But though Brook might strangle his voice and strip
him of his manner, he could not eradicate the iron streak of tinsel
that runs through Gielgud's character. This, after all, was a man
who first saw his name in lights in 1928, in a farce called *Holding
Out the Apple*. He had one immortal line: 'You've got a way of
holding out the apple that positively gives me the pip.' Dissolve to
Oedipus 40 years later. Irene Worth playing Jocasta has to impale
herself on a small portable projection that was brought onto the
stage. 'I can't find my plinth,' she moaned at one rehearsal.
'Really,' said the veteran of *Holding Out the Apple*: 'Do you mean
Plinth Philip or Plinth Charles?'

But I would guess now that it was *Oedipus*, though rated a
failure with Gielgud somewhat out of place in it, that gave him a
new lease of life. He has always been a self-conscious man, his
shyness masked by a bubbling stream of anecdote. Brook had
somehow inoculated him against embarrassment and in his
subsequent career, at a time of life when most men would be
standing on their dignity, he threw his away entirely and to splendid
effect.

There were plenty of terrible jokes in *Forty Years On*, and maybe
it was those which commended it to him. It still surprises me that he
agreed to do it and I'm sure there were times, particularly on tour
in Manchester, when he thought he had backed a wrong horse. If
so, he never showed it.

'You won't fill this place,' said the stage doorman as Gielgud
came into the Palace, Manchester. 'Nobody fills this place. Ken
Dodd doesn't fill this place.' He was quite right, and we played
sometimes to 30 people. The performances seemed like rehearsals,
the more so since Gielgud had only a very shaky hold on the text
and, as always when he is nervous, kept coming up with suggestions
for radical alterations:

'I wonder, should the boys come in singing a hymn? It's very dismal. It
makes it seem just like school.'
  'But it's supposed to be school.'
  'Oh, yes, so it is.'

He had to speak directly to the audience, something he was
initially reluctant to do, thinking it vulgar and against all his
training. When he eventually plucked up courage to do it and
found that it worked, there was no stopping him. He has always

been a great counter of the house, able to tell you within five minutes of curtain-up exactly who is in the stalls. Now he could do it legitimately: he would lean far out over the footlights, shading his eyes with his mortar-board, supposedly trying to catch the eye of his sister, Nancy, a woman of easily outraged sensibilities. In reality, he was spotting friends, sometimes even waving. His dressing-room was always crammed with visitors, including a fair quota of the great and famous. I would be summoned in to meet them while Mac, his 80-year-old dresser, who had dressed Martin Harvey and Fred Terry before him, would be struggling to put on the knightly trousers (something old-fashioned dressers take pride in doing, though why I don't know: to be helped into one's trousers is no help at all). We had been so close to disaster on tour that it took time for him to register that audiences actually loved him; that this was not respect, which he was used to, but affection.

How narrow an escape we had had with *Forty Years On* I only appreciated when I saw what happened to Charles Wood's play *Veterans* in 1972. This was a play about the making of a film, loosely based on *Charge of the Light Brigade*, so that Gielgud virtually played himself playing Lord Raglan. It was a very funny piece, with a memorable image of Gielgud hoisted in the air astride a headless wooden horse, doing simulated riding. It was also mildly scatological. Due to go on at the Royal Court after a short provincial tour, it suffered a rough passage. At Nottingham pennies were thrown onto the stage and Gielgud was bombarded with abusive letters saying: 'You have been sold a pup.' When the play reached Brighton the audience left in droves, something audiences in Brighton are very prone to do. Indeed, having toured there several times myself, I am convinced that one of the chief pleasures in going to the theatre in Brighton is leaving it. The sleek Sussex matrons sit poised in the stalls like greyhounds in the slips. The first 'fuck' and they're a mile down the sea front, streaking for Hove. Once *Veterans* got to the Court, where the occasional oath is part of the house style, it was a great success and would have transferred to the West End. But the reception on tour had so convinced Gielgud of its ultimate failure that he had meanwhile signed to do a Hollywood remake of *Lost Horizon*.

The public is a problem. Actors of Gielgud's generation had a strong sense of what an audience expected and what it should be given. In the Fifties and Sixties it was this sense of 'my public', as much as a shortage of opportunities, that kept him trundling out

Ages of Man. In the last ten years he has shed his public and found another. But then so has everybody else, though not as painfully. Few actors now have this sense of 'my public'. One or two actresses perhaps, but that's all. It is not hard to see why. There is no such thing in the West End now as 'the public'. It survived until quite recently; it was there as late as five years ago, surviving, even strengthened by, the tidal wave of Americans that swept up Shaftesbury Avenue every summer. The Americans were at any rate English-speaking even if they were not always English-joking. Now they too have been submerged. In season and out of season, audiences are now so polyglot they no longer constitute an entity and even playing of the highest quality does not weld them into one. The sense does not carry. The actor is a spectacle, and someone from Taiwan goes to see Gielgud or Guinness in the same spirit as he takes in the Changing of the Guard, which he marginally prefers if only because he is allowed to film it.

The public which goes to the theatre to see Gielgud goes to see Great Acting. These days what the public calls Great Acting is often not even good acting. It's acting with a line round it, acting in inverted commas, acting which shows. The popular idea of Great Acting is a rhetorical performance (award-winning for choice) at the extremes, preferably the extremes of degradation and despair. Such a performance seems to the public to require all an actor has got. Actors know that this is a false assessment. The limit of an actor's ability is a spacious and fairly comfortable place to be: such parts require energy rather than judgment. Anything goes. Gielgud's farting, swearing role in *Providence*, while it was riveting to watch, was a feat of courage, not great acting. It's much harder in artistic terms to keep a delicate balance, as he did with Spooner in Pinter's *No Man's Land*. And even more so as Harry in David Storey's *Home*, the latter an understated part of immense technical difficulty. Extremes are not edges and the edge is where he excels; the edge of comedy, the edge of respectability, the edge of despair. If he continues to amaze and delight, his powers not to stale, it is because at his best nowadays he does not seem to be acting at all. The skill lies in letting it seem that there is no skill. He has broken his staff, but he has kept his magic.

A Blizzard of Tiny Kisses

Clive James

To be a really lousy writer takes energy. The average novelist remains unread not because he is bad but because he is flat. On the evidence of *Princess Daisy*,[1] Judith Krantz deserves her high place in the best-seller lists. This is the second time she has been up there. The first time was for a book called *Scruples*, which I will probably never get around to reading. But I don't resent the time I have put into reading *Princess Daisy*. As a work of art it has the same status as a long conversation between two not very bright drunks, but as best-sellers go it argues for a reassuringly robust connection between fiction and the reading public. If cheap dreams get no worse than this, there will not be much for the cultural analyst to complain about. *Princess Daisy* is a terrible book only in the sense that it is almost totally inept. Frightening it isn't.

In fact, it wouldn't even be particularly boring if only Mrs Krantz could quell her artistic urge. 'Above all,' said Conrad, 'to make you see.' Mrs Krantz strains every nerve to make you see. She pops her valves in the unrelenting effort to bring it all alive. Unfortunately she has the opposite of a pictorial talent. The more detail she piles on, the less clear things become. Take the meeting of Stash and Francesca. Mrs Krantz defines Prince Alexander Vassilivitch Valensky, alias Stash, as 'the great war hero and incomparable polo-player'. Stash is Daisy's father. Francesca Vernon, a film star, is her mother. Francesca possesses 'a combination of tranquillity and pure sensuality in the composition of the essential triangle of eyes and mouth'. Not just essential but well-nigh indispensable, one would have thought. Or perhaps that's what she means.

This, however, is to quibble, because before Stash and Francesca can generate Daisy they first have to meet, and theirs is a meeting of transfigurative force, as of Apollo catching up with Daphne. The scene is Deauville, 1952. Francesca the film star, she of the pure sensuality, is a reluctant spectator at a polo game — reluctant, that is, until she claps eyes on Stash. Here is a description of her eyes, together with the remaining component of the essential triangle, namely her mouth. 'Her black eyes were long and widely

[1] Judith Krantz, *Princess Daisy* (Sidgwick & Jackson, 1980).

spaced, her mouth, even in repose, was made meaningful by the grace of its shape: the gentle arc of her upper lip dipped in the centre to meet the lovely pillow of her lower lip in a line that had the power of an embrace.'

And this is Stash, the great war hero and incomparable polo-player: 'Valensky had the physical presence of a great athlete who has punished his body without pity throughout his life and the watchful, fighting eyes of a natural predator. His glance was bold and his thick brows were many shades darker than his blonde hair, cropped short and as coarse as the coat of a hastily brushed dog...His nose, broken many times, gave him the air of a roughneck...Not only did Valensky never employ unnecessary force on the bit and reins but he had been born, as some men are, with an instinct for establishing a communication between himself and his pony which made it seem as if the animal was merely an extension of his mind, rather than a beast with a will of its own.'

Dog-haired, horse-brained and with a bashed conk, Stash is too much for Francesca's equilibrium. Her hat flies off.

'Oh no!' she exclaimed in dismay, but as she spoke, Stash Valensky leaned down from his pony and scooped her up in one arm. Holding her easily, across his chest, he urged his mount after the wayward hat. It had come to rest two hundred yards away, and Valensky, leaving Francesca mounted, jumped down from his saddle, picked the hat up by its ribbons and carefully replaced it on her head. The stands rang with laughter and applause.

Francesca heard nothing of the noise the spectators made. Time, as she knew it, had stopped. By instinct, she remained silent and waiting, passive against Stash's soaking-wet polo shirt. She could smell his sweat and it confounded her with desire. Her mouth filled with saliva. She wanted to sink her teeth into his tan neck, to bite him until she could taste his blood, to lick up the rivulets of sweat which ran down to his open collar. She wanted him to fall to the ground with her in his arms, just as he was, flushed, steaming, still breathing heavily from the game, and grind himself into her.

But this is the first of many points at which Mrs Krantz's minus capability for evocation leaves you puzzled. How did Stash get the hat back on Francesca's head? Did he remount, or is he just very tall? If he did remount, couldn't that have been specified? Mrs Krantz gives you all the details you don't need to form a mental picture, while carefully withholding those you do. Half the trick of pictorial writing is to give only the indispensable points and let the reader's imagination do the rest. Writers who not only give the indispensable points but supply all the concrete details as well can leave you feeling bored with their brilliance — Wyndham Lewis is an outstanding example. But a writer who supplies the concrete details and leaves out the indispensible points can only exhaust you. Mrs Krantz is right to pride herself on the accuracy of her research into every department of the high life. What she says is rarely inaccurate, as far as I can tell. It is, however, almost invariably irrelevant.

Anyway, the book starts with a picture of Daisy ('Her dark eyes, not quite black, but the colour of the innermost heart of a giant purple pansy, caught the late afternoon light and held it fast...') and then goes on to describe the meeting of her parents. It then goes on to tell you a lot about what her parents got up to before they met. Then it goes on to tell you about *their* parents. The book is continually going backwards instead of forwards, a canny insurance against the reader's impulse to skip. At one stage I tried skipping a chapter and missed out on about a century. From the upper West Side of New York I was suddenly in the Russian Revolution. That's where Stash gets his fiery temperament from — Russia.

'At Chez Mahu they found that they were able only to talk of unimportant things. Stash tried to explain polo to Francesca but she scarcely listened, mesmerised as she was with the abrupt movements of his tanned hands on which light blonde hair grew, the hands of a great male animal.' A bison? Typically, Mrs Krantz has failed to be specific at the exact moment when specificity would be a virtue. Perhaps Stash is like a horse not just in brain but in body. This would account for his tendency to view Francesca as a creature of equine provenance. 'Francesca listened to Valensky's low voice, which had traces of an English accent, a brutal man's voice which seemed to vibrate with an underlying tenderness, as if he were talking to a newborn foal...'

There is a lot more about Stash and Francesca before the reader can get to Daisy. Indeed, the writer herself might never have got to Daisy if she (i.e. Mrs Krantz) had not first wiped out Stash and Francesca. But before they can be killed, Mrs Krantz must expend about a hundred and fifty pages on various desperate attempts to bring them alive. In World War Two the incomparable polo-player becomes the great war hero. Those keen to see Stash crash, however, are doomed to disappointment, since before Stash can win medals in his Hurricane we must hear about his first love affair. Stash is 14 years old and the Marquise Claire de Champery is a sex-pot of a certain age. 'She felt the congestion of blood rushing between her primly pressed together thighs, proof positive that she had been right to provoke the boy.' Stash, meanwhile, shows his customary tendency to metamorphose into an indeterminate life-form. 'He took her hand and put it on his penis. The hot sticky organ was already beginning to rise and fill. It moved under her touch like an animal.' A field mouse? A boa constrictor?

Receiving the benefit of Stash's extensive sexual education, Francesca conceives twins. One of the twins turns out to be Daisy and the other her retarded sister, Danielle. But first Stash has to get to the clinic. 'As soon as the doctor telephoned, Stash raced to the clinic at 95 miles an hour.' Miserly as always with the essentials, Mrs Krantz trusts the reader to supply the information that Stash is attaining this speed by some form of motorised transport.

Stash rejects Danielle, Francesca flees with Danielle and Daisy. Stash consoles himself with his collection of jet aircraft. Mrs Krantz has done a lot of research in this area but it is transparently research, which is not the same thing as knowledge. Calling a Junkers 88 a Junker 88 might be a misprint, but her rhapsody about Stash's prize purchase of 1953 is a dead giveaway. 'He tracked down and bought the most recent model available of the Lockheed XP-80, known as the Shooting Star, a jet which for many years could out-manoeuvre and outperform almost every other aircraft in the world.' USAF fighter aircraft carried 'X' numbers only before being accepted for service. By 1953 the Shooting Star was known as the F-80, had been in service for years, and was practically the slowest thing of its type in the sky. But Mrs Krantz is too fascinated by that 'X' to let it go. She deserves marks, however, for her determination to catch up on the arcane nomenclature of boys' toys.

Stash finally buys a farm during a flying display in 1967. An old Spitfire packs up on him. 'The undercarriage of the 27-year-old plane stuck and the landing gear could not be released.' Undercarriage and landing gear are the same thing — her vocabularies have collided over the Atlantic. Also an airworthy 27-year-old Spitfire in 1967 would have been a very rare bird indeed: no wonder the undercarriage got in the road of the landing gear. But Mrs Krantz goes some way towards capturing the excitement of machines and should not be mocked for her efforts. Francesca, incidentally, dies in a car crash, with the make of car unspecified.

One trusts that Mrs Krantz's documentation of less particularly masculine activities is as meticulous as it is undoubtedly exhaustive, although even in such straightforward matters as food and drink she can sometimes be caught making the elementary mistake of piling on the fatal few details too many. Before Stash gets killed he takes Daisy to lunch every Sunday at the Connaught. After he gets killed he is forced to give up this practice, although there is no real reason why he should not have continued, since he is no more animated before his prang than after. Mrs Krantz has researched the Connaught so heavily that she must have made herself part of the furniture. It is duly noted that the menu has a brown and gold border. It is unduly noted that the menu has the date printed at the bottom. Admittedly such a thing would not happen at the nearest branch of the Golden Egg, but it is not necessarily the mark of a great restaurant. Mrs Krantz would probably hate to hear it said, but she gives the impression of having been included late amongst the exclusiveness she so admires. There is nothing wrong with gusto, but when easy familiarity is what you are trying to convey, gush is to be avoided.

Full of grand meals served and consumed at chapter length, *Princess Daisy* reads like *Buddenbrooks* without the talent. Food is important to Mrs Krantz: so important that her characters keep turning into it, when they are not turning into animals. Daisy has a half-brother called Ram, who rapes her, arouses her sexually, beats her up, rapes her again, and does his best to wreck her life because she rejects his love. His passion is understandable, when you consider Daisy's high nutritional value. 'He gave up the struggle and devoured her lips with his own, kissing her as if he were dying of thirst and her mouth were a moist fruit.' A mango? Daisy fears Ram but goes for what he dishes out. 'Deep within her something sounded, as if the string of a great cello had been plucked, a note of remote, mysterious but unmistakable warning.' Boing.

Daisy heeds the warning and lights out for the USA, where she becomes a producer of television commercials in order to pay Danielle's hospital bills. She pals up with a patrician girl called Kiki, whose breasts quiver in indignation — the first breasts to have done that for a long, long time. At such moments one is reminded of Mrs Krantz's true literary ancestry, which stretches all the way

back to Elinor Glyn, E.M. Hull and Gertrude Atherton. She is
wasting a lot of her time and too much of ours trying to be John
O'Hara. At the slightest surge of congested blood between her
primly pressed together thighs, all Mrs Krantz's carefully garnered
social detail gives way to eyes like twin dark stars, mouths like
moist fruit and breasts quivering with indignation.

There is also the warm curve of Daisy's neck where the jaw joins
the throat. Inheriting this topographical feature from her mother,
Daisy carries it around throughout the novel waiting for the right
man to kiss it *tutto tremante*. Ram will definitely not do. A
disconsolate rapist, he searches hopelessly among the eligible young
English ladies — Jane Bonham-Carter and Sabrina Guinness are
both considered — before choosing the almost inconceivably well-
connected Sarah Fane. Having violated Sarah in his by now
standard manner, Ram is left with nothing to do except blow
Daisy's secret and commit suicide. As Ram bites the dust, the world
learns that the famous Princess Daisy, star of a multi-million-dollar
perfume promotion, has a retarded sister. Will this put the kibosh
on the promotion, not to mention Daisy's love for the man in
charge, the wheeler-dealer head of Supracorp, Pat Shannon ('larky
bandit', 'freebooter' etc)?

Daisy's libido, dimmed at first by Ram's rape, has already been
reawakened by the director of her commercials, a ruthless but
prodigiously creative character referred to as North. Yet North
finally lacks what it takes to reach the warm curve of Daisy's neck.
Success in that area is reserved for Shannon. He it is who undoes all
the damage and fully arouses her hot blood. 'It seemed a long time
before Shannon began to imprint a blizzard of tiny kisses at the
point where Daisy's jaw joined her throat, that particularly warm
curve, spendthrift with beauty, that he had not allowed himself to
realise had haunted him for weeks. Daisy felt fragile and warm to
Shannon, as if he'd trapped a young unicorn [horses again —
C.J.], some strange, mythological creature. Her hair was the most
intense source of light in the room, since it reflected the moonlight
creeping through the windows, and by its light he saw her eyes,
open, rapt and glowing; twin dark stars.'

Shannon thinks he's holding some kind of horse, but as far as
Daisy's concerned she's a species of cetacean. 'It was she who guided
his hands down the length of her body, she who touched him wherever
she could reach, as playfully as a dolphin, until he realised that her
fragility was strength, and that she wanted him without reserve.'

Daisy is so moved by this belated but shatteringly complete experience that she can be forgiven for what she does next. 'Afterward, as they lay together, half asleep, but unwilling to drift apart into unconsciousness, Daisy farted, in a tiny series of absolutely irrepressible little pops that seemed to her to go on for a minute.' It takes bad art to teach us how good art gets done. Knowing that the dithyrambs have gone on long enough, Mrs Krantz has tried to undercut them with something earthy. Her tone goes wrong, but her intention is worthy of respect. It is like one of those clumsy attempts at naturalism in a late-medieval painting — less pathetic than portentous, since it adumbrates the great age to come. Mrs Krantz will never be much of an artist but she has more than a touch of the artist's ambition.

Princess Daisy is not to be despised. Nor should it be deplored for its concern with aristocracy, glamour, status, success and things like that. On the evidence of her prose, Mrs Krantz has not enough humour to write tongue-in-cheek, but other people are perfectly capable of reading that way. People don't get their morality from their reading matter: they bring their morality to it. The assumption that ordinary people's lives could be controlled and limited by what entertained them was always too condescending to be anything but fatuous.

Mrs Krantz, having dined at Mark's Club, insists that it is exclusive. There would not have been much point to her dining there if she did not think that. A bigger snob than she is might point out that the best reason for not dining at Mark's Club is the chance of finding Mrs Krantz there. It takes only common sense, though, to tell you that on those terms exclusiveness is not just chimerical but plain tedious. You would keep better company eating Kentucky Fried Chicken in a launderette. But if some of this book's readers find themselves day-dreaming of the high life, let us be grateful that Mrs Krantz exists to help give their vague aspirations a local habitation and a name. They would dream anyway, and without Mrs Krantz they would dream unaided.

To pour abuse on a book like this makes no more sense than to kick a powder-puff. *Princess Daisy* is not even reprehensible for the three million dollars its author was paid for it in advance. It would probably have made most of the money back without a dime spent on publicity. The only bad thing is the effect on Mrs Krantz's personality. Until lately she was a nice Jewish lady harbouring the usual bourgeois fancies about the aristocracy. But now she gives interviews extolling her own hard head. 'Like so many of us,' she told the *Daily Mail* on 28 April, 'I happen to believe that being young, beautiful and rich is more desirable than being old, ugly and destitute.' Mrs Krantz is 50 years old, but to judge from the photograph on the back of the book she is engaged in a series of hard-fought delaying actions against time. This, I believe, is one dream that intelligent people ought not to connive at, since the inevitable result of any attempt to prolong youth is a graceless old age.

Joan Didion's Style

Martin Amis

Joan Didion is the poet of the Great Californian Emptiness. She sings of a land where it is easier to Dial-A-Devotion than to buy a book, where the freeway sniper feels 'real bad' about picking off a family of five, where kids in High Kindergarten are given LSD and peyote by their parents, where young hustlers get lethally carried away while rolling elderly filmstars, where six-foot-two drag queens shop for fishnet bikinis, where a 26-year-old woman can consign her five-year-old daughter to the centre divider of Interstate 5: when her fingers were prised loose from the fence 12 hours later, the child pointed out that she had run after the car containing her family for 'a long time'.

All of us are excited by what we most deplore — 'especially', as Miss Didion says in another context, 'if we are writers'. Miss Didion used to be excited by human stupidity and viciousness. *Slouching towards Bethlehem* (1968), her previous collection of journalism and essays, begins with a piece about a murder in the San Bernadino Valley — Mormon country. On 7 October 1964, Lucille Miller took her depressive and generally below-par husband, Cork, out for a moonlight drive in their Volkswagen. After a visit to a nearby supermarket, Mrs Miller stopped the car in the middle of the road, poured a can of petrol over her husband, set fire to him, and then attempted to propel the VW over a four-foot drop. As it happened, the car got stuck on the ledge; Mrs Miller seemed to have a change of heart at this point, and spent the next 75 minutes trying to save her husband by poking at him with a stick ('I just thought if I had a stick, I'd push him out'); but by now, anyway, Cork was 'just black'. The trial was surprisingly protracted, considering that the tirelessly hysterical Mrs Miller had a boyfriend and $120,000 coming to her in the event of Cork's accidental death. 'It wasn't a very interesting murder as murders go,' Miss Didion quotes the DA as saying 'laconically', intending a gentle laugh on him. Actually the DA was right. It wasn't a very interesting murder. But it was certainly very stupid and vicious, and Miss Didion used to be excited by that kind of thing.

She isn't any more. No longer can Miss Didion regard the neurotic waywardness and vulgar infamies of California as simply 'good material'. *The White Album*[1] deals with the late Sixties and early Seventies. During these menacing years Miss Didion lived with her husband and daughter in a large house in Hollywood, at the heart of what a friend described as a 'senseless-killing neighbourhood'. Across the street, the one-time Japanese Consulate had become a group-therapy squat for unrelated adults. Scientologists used to pop by and explain to Miss Didion about E-meters and how to become a Clear. High-minded narcotic dealers would call her on the telephone ('what we're talking about, basically, is applying the Zen philosophy to money and business, dig?'). Pentecostalist Brother Theobald informed her that there were bound to be more earthquakes these days, what with the end of time being just round the corner. One night a baby-sitter remarked that she saw death in Miss Didion's aura; in response, Miss Didion slept downstairs on the sofa, with the windows open. Then it happened — not to Joan Didion, but to Jay Sebring, Abigail Folger, Voytek Frykowski, Steven Parent, Rosemary and Leno LaBianca, and Sharon Tate:

On August 9, 1969, I was sitting in the shallow end of my sister-in-law's swimming pool in Beverly Hills when she received a telephone call from a friend who had just heard about the murders at Sharon Tate Polanski's house on Cielo Drive. The phone rang many times during the next hour. These early reports were garbled and contradictory. One caller would say hoods, the next would say chains. There were twenty dead, no, twelve, ten, eighteen. Black masses were imagined, and bad trips blamed. I remember all of the day's misinformation very clearly, and I also remember this, and wish I did not: *I remember that no one was surprised.*

And, at a stroke, the Sixties ended — 'the paranoia was fulfilled.'

Miss Didion reached her own breaking-point almost exactly a year before Charles Manson reached his. Alerted by an attack of nausea and vertigo (and such an attack 'does not now seem to [her] an inappropriate response to the summer of 1968'), Miss Didion enrolled as a private outpatient of the psychiatric clinic at St John's Hospital in Santa Monica, where she underwent the Rorschach Test, the Thematic Apperception Test, the Sentence Completion Test and the Minnesota Multiphasic Personality Index. Miss Didion quotes at italicised length from the ensuing psychiatric report: *'a personality in process of deterioration ... regressive,*

---

[1] Joan Didion, *The White Album* (Weidenfeld & Nicolson, 1980).

*libidinal preoccupations ... fundamentally pessimistic, fatalistic
... feels deeply that all human effort is foredoomed to failure ...'*
Following a series of periodic visual disturbances, she then submits
to three electroencephalograms, two sets of skull and neck X-rays,
one five-hour glucose-tolerance test, two electromyelograms,
a variety of chemical tests and consultations with two opthalmo-
logists, one internist and three neurologists. Damage to the
central nervous system is diagnosed and given a nasty name by
the sinister doctors. 'The startling fact was this,' writes Miss
Didion: 'my body was offering a precise physiological equivalent to what had been going on in my mind.' At that moment she
had a sharp apprehension 'of what it was like to open the door
to the stranger and find that the stranger did indeed have the knife.'
Charles Manson had come calling, but under the name of Multiple
Sclerosis. 'Lead a simple life,' the neurologist concluded: 'Not that
it makes any difference we know about.'

In her relatively self-effacing preface to *Slouching towards
Bethlehem* Miss Didion admitted: 'whatever I write reflects,
sometimes gratuitously, how I feel.' Ten years on, the emphasis has
changed; you might even say, after 200 pages of these high-profile
musings, that whatever Miss Didion feels reflects how she writes.
'Gratuitous' hardly comes into it any more — and this doesn't
apply only to the essays specifically addressed to her migraines,
marital problems, book-promotion activities, and so on. 'I am
talking here about being a child of my time,' begins one essay. 'I
had better tell you where I am, and why,' begins another. Having
told us where she is and why (Honolulu, to save her marriage), Miss
Didion proceeds: 'I tell you this not as aimless revelation but
because I want you to know, as you read me, precisely who I am
and where I am and what is on my mind. I want you to understand
exactly what you are getting: you are getting a woman who for
some time now has felt radically separated from most of the ideas
that seem to interest other people. You are getting a woman who...'

Only someone fairly assured about certain of her bearings would
presume to address her readers in this (in fact) markedly high-
handed style. The style bespeaks celebrity, a concerned and captive
following; it is inconceivable, for instance, that any beginner would
risk such a take-me-or-leave-me tone. It occurs to you that Miss
Didion's reasons for disliking Woody Allen's *Manhattan,* and for
attacking it at length in the *New York Review,* are perhaps largely
defensive in origin. What is objectionable about *Manhattan* is not

that it is knowing, cute, 'in', as Miss Didion claimed. What is objectionable about *Manhattan,* and *Annie Hall,* is that Woody Allen is publicly analysing a past love affair, *with* his past lover, *on screen* (Woody Allen used to be with Diane Keaton, as is well-known; as is also well-known, Diane is now with Warren Beatty, or was at the time of writing). Such self-advertisement feels cheap and, for all its coy alienations, looks thick-skinned. Miss Didion would dismiss the comparison as footling when compared to the inescapability of her new-found emotional rawness. She feels that she is responding accurately to some extremity in the observed life — in the great and desperate human action she reads about in the newspapers, listens to on the radio, and fragmentarily witnesses. Yet it remains true that writing, unlike living, is artificial, disinterested: it is not just another facet of reality, however clamorous and incorrigible that reality may sometimes feel.

Miss Didion, however, has come out. She stands revealed, in *The White Album*, as a human being who has managed to gouge another book out of herself, rather than as a writer who gets her living done on the side, or between the lines. The result is a volatile, occasionally brilliant, distinctly female contribution to the new New Journalism, diffident and imperious by turns, intimate yet categorical, self-effacingly listless and at the same time often subtly self-serving. She can still find her own perfect pitch for long stretches, and she has an almost embarrassingly sharp ear and unblinking eye for the Californian inanity. Seemingly obedient, though, to the verdicts of her psychiatric report, Miss Didion writes about everything with the same doom-conscious yet faintly abstract intensity of interest, whether remarking on the dress sense of one of Manson's henchwomen, or indulging her curious obsession with Californian waterworks. In these pieces, Miss Didion's writing does not 'reflect' her moods so much as dramatise them. 'How she feels' has become, for the time being, how it is.

The effect on her style is everywhere apparent. In the middle of a piece about the design of shopping-centres, Miss Didion abruptly announces: 'If I had a center I would have monkeys, and Chinese restaurants, and Mylar kites and bands of small girls playing tambourine.' That sentence could have been written by Richard Brautigan; it is a peculiarly Californian style, a schlepping style. Bouts of wooziness affect the judgment too. After a wearily lucid analysis of the Women's Movement and a precise appraisal of Doris Lessing, Miss Didion moves on to a bizarre hymn to Georgia

O'Keeffe, the veteran American painter. Miss Didion makes the mistake, at the outset, of taking along her seven-year-old daughter to see a Chicago retrospective of the painter's work:

One of the vast O'Keeffe 'Sky Above Clouds' canvasses floated over the back stairs in the Chicago Art Institute that day, dominating what seemed to be several stories of empty light, and my daughter looked at it once, ran to the landing, and kept on looking. 'Who drew it,' she whispered after a while. I told her. 'I need to talk to her,' she said finally.

My daughter was making, that day in Chicago, an entirely unconscious but quite basic assumption about people and the work they do. She was assuming that the glory she saw in the work reflected a glory in its maker...that every choice one made alone...betrayed one's character. *Style is character.*

It is easy to see here how quickly sentimentality proceeds to nonsense. The extent to which style isn't character can be gauged by (for example) reading a literary biography, or by trying to imagine a genuinely fruitful discussion between Georgia O'Keeffe and Miss Didion's seven-year-old daughter: a scene of painful mawkishness springs unavoidably to mind. When the child whispered, 'I need to talk to her,' Miss Didion should have whispered back, 'Quiet, I'm working,' and got on with her job. As it is, Miss Didion gives us a tremulous pep-talk on O'Keeffe's career, fondly stressing the 'crustiness' and 'pepperiness' of 'this hard woman', 'this angelic rattlesnake'. She sums up:

In Texas there was only the horizon she craved. In Texas she had her sister Claudia with her for a while, and in the late afternoons they would walk away from town and toward the horizon and watch the evening star come out. 'That evening star fascinated me,' she wrote... 'My sister had a gun, and as we walked she would throw bottles into the air and shoot them. I had nothing but to walk into nowhere and the wide sunset space with the star. Ten watercolors were made from that star.' In a way one's interest is compelled as much by the sister Claudia with the gun as by the painter Georgia with the star, but only the painter left us this shining record. Ten water-colors were made from that star.

A tribute to 'hardness', from one tough performer to another, becomes a husky gasp of shared prostration.

'Style is character.' Or, as Miss Didion puts it: *Style is character.* If style were character, everyone would write as self-revealingly as Miss Didion. Not everyone does. Miss Didion's style relishes emphasis, repetition, re-emphasis. Her style likes looking at the same things from different angles. Her style likes starting and finishing successive sentences with identical phrases. Take these two little strophes, separated by a hundred-odd pages in the present book:

In the years after World War I my mother had put pennies for Grace [Episcopal Cathedral] in her mite box but Grace would never be finished. In the years after World War II I would put pennies for Grace in my mite box but Grace would never be finished.

And:

In 1973 the five pillboxes on Makapuu Head had seemed to James Jones exactly as he had left them in 1942. In 1973 the Royal Hawaiian Hotel had seemed to James Jones less formidably rich than he had left it in 1942...

Both passages evoke the passing of time with the same reflexive cross-hatching. Equally, you know when to ready yourself for some uplift, because each sentence — like the one about Miss Didion's shopping centre — contains more 'and's' than a song by Leonard Cohen: 'I thought about barrack rats and I thought about Prewitt and Maggio and I thought about Army hatred and it seemed to me that night in Honolulu...' That night in Honolulu, that day in Chicago. It is a style that has become set in its own modulations, proclaiming its individuality by means of a few recurrent quirks and lilts. In other words, it has become mannered.

It could be argued that the same thing happened to Miss Didion's fiction. *Run, River* (1963) is an exemplarily solid first novel, mildly ambitious in construction and restrained in delivery and scope — contentedly minor, above all. It is set in rural California during and after the Second War, and examines familial and community power-balances in relaxed, elegant, clichéless prose. Miss Didion's somewhat top-heavy interest in madness and stupefaction — the vanished knack of 'making things matter' — puts in an early appearance here, but it is at least placed against a background where not everything is mad and stupefied. The trouble starts with *Play it as it lays* (1970). This is when the Californian emptiness arrives and Miss Didion attempts to evolve a style, or a manner, to answer to it. Here come divorces, breakdowns, suicide bids, spliced-up paragraphs, 40-word chapters, and italicised wedges of prose that used to be called 'fractured'. The 'bad' characters are movie people who drink and take drugs to excess, sleep with one

another a lot, and don't go crazy. The 'good' characters are movie
people who drink and take drugs to excess, sleep with one another a
lot, and do go crazy. The bad characters are shallow pragmatists.
The good characters are (between ourselves) shallow nihilists. We
are meant to think that BZ, the ruefully degenerate producer, is
acting with perversely heroic decorum when he kills himself with
vodka and Seconal at the end of the book ('Don't start faking me
now...Take my hand'). And we are meant to think that Marie, the
ruefully degenerate actress, is actually trumping BZ in the nihilism
stakes by the shrewd expedient of *not* killing herself. The book
closes:

I know what 'nothing' means, and keep on playing.
Why, BZ would say.
Why not, I say.

Her italics.
   The area occupied by *A Book of Common Prayer* (1977) might
be called the aftermath of breakdown. Told by one woman about
another, the novel's catalogue of lost husbands, lost children and
lost lucidity — its endless 'revisions and erasures' — is glimpsed
through a mesh of distortion and dislocation. From the outset, the
prose tangles with a good deal of counterpoint, elision and
italicisation, and gets more hectic as the novel proceeds. Towards
the end, such is the indirection on display, Miss Didion seems
incapable of starting a new subordinate clause without splintering
off into a new paragraph.

In fact she had.
Told Leonard what she was going to do.
She was going to stay.
Not 'stay' precisely.
'Not leave' is more like it.

and

I am told, and so she said.
I heard later.
According to her passport. It was reported.
Apparently.

are examples. I find this kind of writing as resonant as a pop-gun.
The most poetic thing about Miss Didion's prose in this novel is

that it doesn't go all the way across the page.

However much she would resist the idea, Miss Didion's talent is primarily discursive in tendency. As is the case with Gore Vidal, the essays are far more interesting than the fiction. The novels get taken up, with the enthusiasm, the unanimity, the relief which American critics and readers often show when they discover a new and distinctly OK writer. Miss Didion is already being called 'major', a judgment that some might think premature, to say the least: but she is far more rewarding than many writers similarly saluted. In particular, the candour of her femaleness is highly arresting and original. She doesn't try for the virile virtues of robustness and infallibility; she tries to find a female way of being serious. Nevertheless, there are hollow places in even her best writing, a thinness, a sense of things missing.

There are two main things that aren't there. The first is a social dimension. At no point in *The White Album* does Miss Didion think about the sort of people she would never normally have cause to come across: the 'cunning Okie' who doesn't actually commit the crime and hit the headlines, the quietly crazy mother who never gets round to leaving her daugher on the centre divider of Interstate 5, the male-prostitute flop who will never have the chance to roll and murder a Ramon Novarro and win a place in Miss Didion's clippings file. Lucille Miller was alive and ill and living in San Bernadino Valley long before she tried to burn her husband to death. Miss Didion sensed this, in *Slouching towards Bethlehem*, and had the energy to follow it up: but in *The White Album* her imaginative withdrawal seems pretty well complete. It must be easier to get like this in California than anywhere else on earth. Even the black revolutionaries Miss Didion goes to see chat about their BUPA schemes and the royalties on their memoirs. It is interesting, though, that Miss Didion fails to identify a strong element in the 'motives' behind the Manson killings: the revenge of the insignificant on the affluent. What frightened Miss Didion's friends was the idea that wealth and celebrity might be considered sufficient provocation to murder. But Miss Didion never looks at things from this point of view. It is a pity. If you are rich and neurotic it is salutary in all kinds of ways to think hard about people who are poor and neurotic: i.e. people who have more to be neurotic about. If you don't, and especially if you are a writer, then it is not merely therapy you miss out on.

The other main thing that isn't there is any kind of literary spaciousness or solidity. Miss Didion has excellent sport with the culturelessness of her fellow Californians: 'As a matter of fact I hear that no man is an island once or twice a week, quite often from people who think they are quoting Ernest Hemingway.' Or again, writing about Hollywood: 'A book or a story is a "property" only until the deal; after that it is "the basic material", as in "I haven't read the basic material on *Gatsby*."' Miss Didion has read the basic material on *Gatsby*; she has even read *The Last Tycoon*. But what else has she read, and how recently? A few texts from her Berkeley days like *Madame Bovary* and *Heart of Darkness* get a mention. Lionel Trilling gets two. And while holidaying in Colombia she takes the opportunity to quote from *One Hundred Years of Solitude* ('by the Colombian novelist Gabriel Garcia Marquez') and Robert Lowell's 'Caracas'. Yet at no point does Miss Didion give a sense of being someone who uses literature as a constant model or ideal, something shored up against the randomness and babble that is fundamental to her distress. When Miss Didion herself attempts an erudite modulation we tend to get phrases like 'there would ever be world enough and time' or 'the improvement of marriages would not a revolution make' or 'all the ignorant armies jostling in the night' — which might be gems from a creative-writing correspondence course.

'Slouching towards Bethlehem' is, of course, a literary reference itself. As Miss Didion dramatically points out in her Preface: 'This book is called *Slouching towards Bethlehem* because for several years now certain lines from the Yeats poem which appears two pages back have reverberated in my inner ear as if they were surgically implanted there.' The whole of 'The Second Coming' is indeed printed a few pages back, along with a deflationary extract from the sayings of Miss Peggy Lee ('I learned courage from Buddha, Jesus, Lincoln, Einstein, and Cary Grant'). The title essay duly begins: 'The centre wasn't holding.' It doesn't seem to have occurred to her with the necessary force that 'The Second Coming' was written half a century ago. The centre hasn't been holding for some time now; actually the centre was never holding, and never will hold. Probably all writers are at some point briefly under the impression that they are in the forefront of disintegration and chaos, that they are among the first to live and work after things fell apart. The continuity such an impression ignores is a literary continuity. It routinely assimilates and domesticates more pressing burdens than Miss Didion's particular share of vivid, ephemeral terrors.

Colette

Angela Carter

Colette is possibly the only well-known woman writer of modern
times who is universally referred to simply by her surname, *tout
court*. Woolf hasn't made it. even after all these years; Rhys
without the Jean is incognito: Nin without the Anais looks like a
typo. Colette, Madam Colette, remains, in this as much else,
unique.

Colette did not acquire this distinction because she terrorised
respect language out of her peers, alas: by a happy accident, her
father's name doubles as a girlish handle — and a very ducky one,
too. One could posit 'Bonny' or 'Rosie' as English equivalents. It
was by a probably perfectly unconscious sleight-of-hand that
Colette appropriated for herself the form of address of both
masculine respect and masculine intimacy of her period — a fact
that, in a small way, reflects the message of her whole career. This
is: if you can't win, change the rules of the game.

Her career was a profoundly strange one and necessarily full of
contradictions, of which her uncompromising zeal for self-
exploitation is one. Madame Colette, though never quite Madame
Colette de l'Académie Française — one game she couldn't crack —
was accorded a state funeral by the French government: this was
the woman who was dismissed by her second husband's aristocratic
family as a cunning little striptease artist over-eager for the title of
baroness. As Madame Colette, she first appeared on pin-up
pictures: 'Our pretty actresses: Madame Colette of the Olympia'.
And, in these pictures, taken in her late thirties, she is very
beautiful and sexy indeed; she looks out at you with all the
invitation of the stripper: '*You* can call me Colette.'

The artificial creation of a sense of intimacy with Colette herself
is one of the qualities that gives her writing its seductiveness. She
certainly wasn't on the halls all those years for nothing, although
the extent to which a wilful exhibitionism kept her on the boards
(against the advice of the majority of her critics) well into her fifties
may be connected with a capacity to embarrass which often frays
the edges of her writing.

'*You* can call me Colette' isn't a statement of the same order as
'Call me Ishmael.' The social limitations to experience in a

woman's life still preclude the unself-conscious picaresque adventuring that formed the artistic apprenticeships of Melville, Lowry, Conrad, while other socio-economic factors mean that those women who see most of the beastly backside of the world — prostitutes — are least in a position to utilise this invaluable experience as art. Norman Mailer has said that there won't be a *really* great woman writer — one, you understand, *con cojones* and everything — until the first call-girl tells her story. Though it's reasonable to assume that, when she does, Mailer won't like it at all, the unpleasant truth in this put-down is that most women don't have exposure to the breadth of experience that, when digested, produces great fiction. (Okay, so what about the Brontës? Well, as vicar's daughters in a rural slum parish, peripatetic international governesses and terminal consumptives, they *did* have such a variety of experience. So.) But the life of Colette was as picaresque as a woman's may be without putting herself in a state of hazard.

Her first novels, *Claudine at School* and its sequels, appeared with the husband's name on the title-page. The peculiar Willy, one of the best-publicised bohemians of the Belle Epoque, ensured that the little Burgundian village girl, Colette's favourite disguise, encountered at an impressionable age not only numerous whores of both sexes but also *everybody* — Proust, Debussy, Ravel, you name them. When Willy left her, his wife found herself in the unusual position of having written a number of best-sellers for which she was unable to take any financial or artistic credit. To earn a living in the years before the First World War, she felt she had no alternative but to go on the halls. As she could neither sing nor dance, she performed as a sex-object and subject of scandal — and not a particularly up-market sex-object, either. Since Willy had enjoyed sexually humiliating her, no doubt there was a special pleasure in exploiting her sexuality whilst herself secure and unavailable. After Willy, she took refuge in the bosom of the lesbian establishment of the period. Our pretty actress had an aristocratic protector, the Marquise de Mornay — nothing unusual about this, not even the sex of the Marquise, in those permissive times. Then came a Cinderella-esque marriage to (Baron) Henry de Jouvenal, editor of *Le Matin,* later a politician of considerable distinction. One thing about Colette interests me: when did she stop lying about her age? The voluptuous dancer was pushing 40 when she married De Jouvenal: 'But the registry office has to know your age,' she complained to a friend. There comes a time when a woman freely publicises her age so that people can say: 'How young you look!' It seems to have come later than most to Colette, but when it did, she gloried in it.

In tandem with this characteristically, if rather Hollywood, Edwardian career, two writers are growing within her. One writes, in 1910, *La Vagabonde*, a novel which is still one of the most truthful expositions of the dilemma of a free woman in a male-dominated society. Perhaps because Colette, having the triumphant myopia of a vain woman, refused to acknowledge her society as male-dominated, she sees no dilemma: there is no real choice: one *is* free. In the same year, the other writer, the one more nearly related to our pretty actress, began work as a journalist for *Le Matin*, which is how she met its editor. Renée Néré, music-hall artiste, prefers to go it alone in *La Vagabonde*, but Colette, Colette married and married well. Her marriage also sealed her fate as a journalist, which in turn sealed her fate as a novelist.

Colette became literary editor of *Le Matin* in 1919, and thereafter was to work almost continuously in newspapers in one way and another, whilst also writing fiction, and acting from time to time. In 1924, after her divorce from De Jouvenal, she started signing her work neither 'Colette Willy' nor 'Colette de Jouvenal' but simply 'Colette'. Her third marriage, some ten years later, never made her dwindle into Colette Goudeket, even though Colette was not her own but her father's name. You can't subvert patriarchy *that* easily, after all, even if your father's name is roughly analogous to 'Darling' and he so weak and feckless that you have acquired only the haziest grasp of patriarchal power.

As a writer of both journalism and fiction, she exploits the intimacy of the stripper with her reader quite remorselessly. She trades on the assumption that you are going to care about Maman because this is the unique Colette's unique Maman. The details of her Burgundian childhood, endlessly recapitulated and, one suspects, endlessly elaborated over the years, are purveyed with such a child-like sense of self-importance, such a naive expectation that the smallest details of the Colette family diet and customs are worth recounting, that it seems churlish to ask: 'What is the point of all this?' It is not so much that all her fiction tends to draw on childhood, on the music hall, on the sad truths distilled from unhappy marriages, as that whole short novels — *Chance Aquaintances, Break of Day* — and many short stories are recounted in the first person of a Colette very precisely realised as subject and object at the same time. In the collection that Penguin publish under the title *The Rainy Moon* most of the stories feature Colette herself, not always as a major character but never as passive narrator. She always gives herself a part, it is as though she could not bear to leave herself out, must always be on stage.

She stopped writing fiction altogether after *Gigi*, in 1942 — a Belle Epoque fable of the apparent triumph of innocence, which would be nauseating were it not so cynical. Her later work, until her death in 1954, is mostly a series of extended autobiographical reveries, among them *The Blue Lantern* and *The Evening Star*. These and the autobiographical journalism that preceded them — *My Mother's House* (given this curious Biblical title in English, in French, it's *La Maison de Claudine*), *Sido*, *My Apprenticeships*, *Music Hall Sidelights* — are a peculiar kind of literary striptease: a self-exploitation that greedily utilises every scrap of past experience in an almost unmediated form.

There is no sense of the confessional about this endless flow of memory. Colette never tells you about herself. Instead, she describes herself. Few writers have described their own physicality so often: 'savage' child, with the long, blond plaits; bride with the 'splash of red carnations on the bodice of her white wedding gown'; in dinner jacket and monocle; pregnant, looking like 'a rat dragging a stolen egg'. And so on. But she gives the impression of telling all, in a literary form unclassifiable except as a version of what television has accustomed us to call 'fictionalised documentary'. Robert Phelps was able to construct a perfectly coherent autobiography from Colette's scattered reminiscences, and present *The Early Paradise* as if it were, not an imaginative parallel to her life, but the real thing. All Colette's biographers, even Michèle Sarde in her recent, exhaustive, life,[1] rely heavily on the sources she herself provides, as if Colette could be trusted not to keep her fingers crossed when she was talking about herself, even when remembering events across a great gulf of years. It is as if her sincerity *mattered*. Such is the sense of intimacy Colette creates: you feel you know her, because she has said, '*You* can call me Colette,' although she says this to everybody who pays.

And yet those memories, this experience, is organised with such conscious art, such lack of spontaneity! She must have acquired from Balzac her taste for presenting those she loved best and

---

[1] *Colette: A Biography* (Morrow, 1980).

admired most, including herself, as actors in *tableaux vivants*, beings complete in themselves, as if unmodified by the eyes of an observer who is herself part of the tableau; she describes finished objects in a perfect perspective, almost *trompe l'oeil*, stuck in the lucid amber of her prose. Her portrait of her friend, the poet Renée Vivian, in *The Pure and the Impure*, has the finite quality of 19th-century fiction. 'I remember Renée's gay laughter, her liveliness, the faint halo of light trembling in her golden hair all combined to sadden me, as does the happiness of blind children who laugh and play without the help of light.' All that Colette has left out of this portrait is the possibility of some kind of inner life beyond Colette's imagining which belongs to Renée Vivian alone. This holds true for all the dazzling galaxy of heterogeneous humanity in her fictionalised documentaries. The apparent objectivity of her prose is a device to seal these people in her own narrative subjectivity.

The portraits, of Renée Vivian, of actresses like La Belle Otéro and Polaire, even of Willy and, later, of her own daughter, are exemplary because of their precision, and troubling because of their detachment. Even in the accounts of her beloved mother, Colette's prose implicitly invites the reader to admire both the quality of the observation and the skill with which a different time and place are re-created; then, with a shock, you realise you have been seduced into applauding, not so much a remarkable woman, as the quality of Colette's love for her. Colette's prose is itself narcissistic. Her apparently total lack of reticence tells us, in the end, nothing about her real relationships, and her self-absorption comes to seem more and more a come-on, a device like a mask behind which an absolute privacy might be maintained. Her obsessive love of make-up, of the stage, of disguises, suggests a desire, if not to conceal, then to mystify. The daughter of Captain Jules-Joseph Colette of the Zouaves could die happy in the notion she had never been on first-name terms with anyone outside her immediate family — not even, least of all, with any of her three husbands.

Since she appears to have been a profoundly disingenuous woman, there seems no reason to think she did *not* die happy in this respect. The best lie is the truth, after all. Colette was indeed her name. Her childhood *was* spent in rural Burgundy, does seem to have been happy, even if one sister later killed herself and a brother burned all of Colette's two thousand letters to her mother after that

mother's death: he would not give them back to Colette — perhaps
to ensure that some things, at least, would remain sacrosanct from
her guzzling, inordinate rapacity for material. This rapacity would
grow and grow, would make Colette ransack her own past again
and again; once a journalist has established the power-base of a
cult of personality, he or she is positively encouraged to trot
out their own opinions and anecdotes over and over again.

Colette's novels are of a different order of reality from her
autobiographical pieces. Her novels are fiction and hence truth; the
rest is journalism and so may bear only the most peripheral
relationship to the truth — the relationship utterly modified by the
eye of the beholder. In Colette's first novel, *Claudine at School*,
she kills off Claudine's mother before the action begins; Claudine
is her alter ego. This is a far more interesting fact than all the
obsessive gush about Colette's allegedly real mother that spills out
later in *La Maison de Claudine, Sido* and *Break of Day*. *Break of
Day* does not have the fictional dimension even of the Claudine
novels; it sets itself up as a fictionalised documentary, using real
Provençale locations, 'Madame Colette' herself as heroine-
narrator and apart from one or two inventions a cast of perfectly
real people. *Break of Day* is also the apotheosis of Colette's dead
mother, whose spirit is invoked in every chapter and whose letters,
heavily edited by Colette, feature in the text. But Colette leaves out
altogether any hint that her third husband, Maurice Goudeket, is
happily ensconced by her side, even as she pens a rather moving
farewell to fleshly pleasures: 'I have paid for my folly, shut away
the heady young wine that intoxicated me, and folded up my big,
floating heart...' The absence of Goudeket from *Break of Day* is as
interesting as the absence of the mother from *Claudine at School*,
though in a different way. *Break of Day* is a conscious decoy.

The extent to which Colette came to believe her own mythology
of herself is, of course, another question. Goudeket himself entered
into the spirit of the thing whole-heartedly. His memoir of her last
twenty years with him, *Close to Colette,* celebrates her peasant
wisdom, her childlike enthusiasm. To him we owe the anecdote of
her encounter with the cat in New York: 'At last someone who
speaks French!' Michèle Sarde repeats this unblushingly, as if it
told us something about the wit and wisdom of Colette. But
Michèle Sarde has swallowed the mythology whole, too. The
anecdote *does* tell us a good deal about Colette: it shows how wisely
she picked her last companion, her Boswell, her public-relations

officer faithful beyond the grave. Goudeket rhapsodises: 'There were so many arts which she had not lost. With her the art of living came before the art of writing. She knew a receipt for everything, whether it was for furniture polish, vinegar, orange-wine or quince-water, for cooking truffles or preserving linen and materials.' French, he says — she was French to her fingertips, and provincial to boot, even after sixty years' total immersion in the heady whirlpool of Paris artistic life. French and provincial as Elizabeth David's *French Country Cooking* — and just as much intended for publication. This ineradicable quality of the fraud, the fake, of the unrepentant self-publicist, is one of the things about Colette I respect most, indeed, revere. Michèle Sarde's biography, however besotted, however uncritical, however willing to draw illegitimate parallels between art and life, nevertheless demonstrates how it was the passionate integrity of Colette's narcissism that rendered her indestructible.

It's possible to see her entire career as a writer, instigated as it was by Willy, who robbed her of the first fruits of her labours, as an act of vengeance on him. A certain kind of woman, a vain woman — that is to say, a woman with self-respect — is spurred on by spite. Had the Rev. Brontë supported and encouraged his daughters' ambitions, what would the poor things have done then? I don't think Leonard Woolf did his wife a favour by mothering her. After Colette met kind, sweet, intelligent, loving Goudeket, she wrote very little major fiction.

In Simone de Beauvoir's memoirs, there's a description of a dinner party De Beauvoir attended with Sartre, at which Colette, already the frizzed and sacred cow of French letters, babbling away to *les gars* about dogs, cats, knitting, *le bon vin, les bons fromages* and so on, offered De Beauvoir only the meagre attention of an occasional, piercing stare. De Beauvoir thought Colette disliked women. Possibly Colette, never one to be bouleversé by a great mind, and perhaps privately relishing boring a great mind into the ground with nuggets of earthy Burgundian wisdom, was only contemplating the question every thinking woman in the Western World must have posed herself one time or other: why is a nice girl like Simone wasting her time sucking up to a boring old fart like J-P? Her memoirs will be mostly about him; he will scarcely speak of her.

Of course, Colette could no more have written *The Second Sex* than De Beauvoir could have danced naked on a public stage —

which precisely defines the limitations of both these great ladies. However, it is hard to imagine Colette, had she attended the Sorbonne, getting any kind of buzz out of coming second to Sartre in her final examinations — or, indeed, out of coming second to anybody. After all these years, De Beauvoir still appears to be proud that only Sartre achieved higher marks in those first exams than she. What would have happened, one wonders, if she had come top? What would it have done to Sartre? Merely to think of it makes the mind reel. Only love can make you proud to be an also-ran.

But Colette simply did not believe that women *were* the second sex. One of Goudeket's anecdotes from her declining years is very revealing. He carried her in her wheelchair into a holiday hotel: the lobby filled with applauding, cheering fans — she was a national institution in France, after all. Colette appeared to be touched. 'They've remembered me from last year.' This isn't modesty, though Goudeket pretends to think so. It's irony, I hope, because, if it isn't irony, then what is it? What monstrous vanity would think it was perfectly natural for a little old lady to receive a tumultuous welcome from her hotel staff? Of course she didn't believe she was really famous, towards the end. She knew she wasn't famous *enough*. These are not the passions of a woman who knows her place.

Nevertheless, to believe women are not the second sex is to deny a whole area of social reality, however inspiriting the toughness and resilience of Colette and most of her heroines may be, especially after the revival of the wet and spineless woman-as-hero which graced the Seventies. (The zomboid creatures in Joan Didion's novels, for example; the resurrected dippy dames of Jean Rhys, so many of whom might have had pathetic walk-on parts in Colette's stories of Paris in the Twenties.) Colette celebrated the status quo of femininity, not only its physical glamour but its capacity to subvert and withstand the boredom of patriarchy. This makes her an ambivalent ally to the Women's Movement.

Her fiction, as opposed to her journalism, is dedicated to the proposition of the battle of the sexes: 'love, the bread and butter of my pen,' she observes in a revealing phrase. But, in Colette's battles, the results are fixed: men can never win, unless, as in the story 'The Képi', the woman is foolish enough to believe that a declaration of love is tantamount to a cessation of hostilities. In the brief, fragile, ironic novels that are Colette's claim to artistic seriousness — *Ripening Seed, The Vagabond, Chéri* and *The Last of Chéri* — the men are decorative but useless. The delicious adolescent, Phil, in *Ripening Seed*, lolls at ease on the beach while little Vinca arranges their picnic: her role is to serve, but this role makes him a parasite. The beautiful (and, like so many of Colette's heroines, economically self-sufficient) lady who seduces him, whom he calls his 'master', is not really Vinca's rival at all, but her fellow conspirator in the ugly plot to 'make a man' of Phil, with all that implies of futility and arrogance and complacency. Renée Néré, the vagabond, tenderly consigns her rich suitor to the condition of a fragrant, unfulfilled memory, since that is the only way she can continue to think kindly of him. She knows quite well that the truth of the fairy-tale is: kiss Prince Charming and he instantly turns into a frog. Léa simply grows out of Chéri, which is tough on Chéri.

The two 'Chéri' novellas probably form Colette's masterpiece, although they are now so 'period' in atmosphere that the luxurious Edwardian décor currently blurs their hard core of emotional truth. As they recede into history, the décor will disappear, and we will be left with something not unlike *Les Liaisons Dangereuses*. They are her masterpieces because they transcend the notion of the battle between the sexes by concentrating on an exceptionally rigorous analysis of the rules of war. Léa's financial independence is, of course, taken for granted: otherwise, in Colette's terms, there would be no possibility of a real relationship. *Julie de Carneilhan*, a brief novel about upper-class alimony published in 1941, is interesting in this respect because it deals specifically with a woman as an economically contingent being. I suspect this is what Colette meant when she said it was as close a reckoning with the elements of her second marriage as she ever allowed herself: De Jouvenal was theoretically in control of their joint finances for the duration of their relationship. Without financial resources of her own, Julie is duped and stripped of self-respect, finally taking refuge with her brother and father — an obvious fantasy ending to which the shadow of approaching war promises an appropriately patriarchal resolution. Curiously enough, another war, the First World War, provides the watershed between the two 'Chéri' novellas; released from the maternal embrace of Léa, anyone but Colette would have thought the trenches would make a *real* man of Chéri. But she knew it wasn't as simple as that.

The Chéri novels are about the power-politics of love, and Léa and Chéri could be almost any permutation of ages or of sexes. It is not in the least like *Der Rosenkavalier*, although we first meet Léa in her graceful late forties, some twenty-five years older than her boy lover. They could both as well be men; or both women. Psychologically, Chéri could just as well be Chérie and Léa Leo, except that we are socially acclimatised to the sexual vanity of middle-aged men; a handsome, successful, rich 50-year-old Léo might well feel that, after an affair of six years, Chérie, at 25, was getting a touch long in the tooth for his tastes. But even the age difference is not the point of the stories; the point is that Léa holds the reins of power. The only person who could film these novels with a sufficiently cold and dialectical eye is Fassbinder and he is the contemporary artist whom, at her very best, Colette most resembles. Not that she was a political person at all, in the Fassbinder sense.

Given the thrust towards an idealised past of the major part of Colette's work, it is disconcerting to find that the moral of the Chéri novellas is: memory kills. When Chéri goes to see his aging mistress after the war and an absence of seven years, he finds, not the faded, touching ghost of love and beauty — no Miss Havisham, she — but, a fat, jolly altogether unrecognisable old lady, quite unprepared to forgive him for once having flinched from her wrinkles. No tender scene of a visit to Juliet's tomb ensues, but a brisk invitation to grow up and forget, which Chéri is temperamentally incapable of accepting. A bullet in the brain is the only way out for Chéri. Léa was forced to reconstruct herself as a human being in order to survive the pain of Chéri's first rejection of her; the reconstructed Léa destroys Chéri by its very existence. Colette's 'personal' voice is altogether absent from this parable. All the leading characters are either whores or the children of whores. They are all rich. If Colette set in motion the entire Colette industry in order to create for herself the artistic freedom and privacy to construct this chilling account of libido and false consciousness, it was all abundantly worthwhile.

Penguin continue to reissue translations of most of Colette by a variety of hands, some of them, especially Antonia White's (the Claudine books), conspicuously handier than others. These slim volumes are currently dressed up in melting pinks, tones of mauve and almond green not unlike the colours of Léa's knicker drawer. The exquisite period photographs on the covers often turn out to depict Colette's own foxy mask, done up in a variety of disguises: a sailor suit for *Gigi*; full drag for *The Pure and the Impure*. The Women's Press put a charcoal drawing of the geriatric Colette, foxier than ever, on their edition of *Break of Day*. The cult of the personality of Colette, to which Michèle Sarde's biography is a votive tribute, continues apace, although it detracts attention from the artist in her and turns her more and more into a figure of historic significance: the woman who *did*, who occupied a key position in a transitional period of social history, from 1873 to 1954, and noted most of what happened to her down. Her achievement as a whole was extraordinary, though — apart from the Chéri novels and one or two others — not in a literary sense; she forged a career out of the kind of narcissistic self-obsession which is supposed, in a woman, to lead to the peaks. Good for her. I've got a god-daughter named after her. Or rather, such are the contradictions inherent in all this, named after Captain Jules-Joseph Colette, one-legged tax-gatherer and bankrupt.

The Earthenware Head

Ted Hughes

Who modelled the head of terracotta?
An American friend. Life-size, the lips half-pursed,
Raw-edged with crusty tooling — a naturalistic attempt
At a likeness that just failed. You did not like it.
I did not like it. Comments magnetised it
For a perverse ritual. What possessed us
To take it with us, in your red bucket-bag?
November fendamp haze, the river unfurling
Dark whorls, ferrying slender willow yellows.
The pollard willows wore comfortless antlers,
Leafless switch-horns. Just past where the field
Broadens and the path strays up to the right
To lose the river, and puzzle for Grantchester,
A chosen willow leaned towards the water.
Above head-height, a twiggy crotch, the socket
Of a healed bole-wound, nearly an owl's porch,
Made a mythic shrine for your double.
I fitted it firm. And a willow tree
Was a Herm, with your head, watching East
Through those tool-stabbed pupils. We left it
To live the world's life and weather forever.

You ransacked Thesaurus in your poem about it,
Veiling its mirror, rhyming yourself into safety
From its orphaned fate. But it
Would not leave you. Weeks later
We could not seem to hit on the tree. We did not
Look too hard — just in passing. Already
We did not want to fear, if it had gone,
What witchcraft might nurse it. You never
Said much about it.

What happened?
Maybe nothing happened. Perhaps it's still
Representing you to the sunrise, happy
In its cold pastoral, lips pursed slightly
As if my touch had only just left it.
Or did boys find it? (And shatter it?) Or
Did the tree too kneel finally?

Surely the river got it. Surely
The river is its chapel. And keeps it. Surely
Your head, made in a furnace, kisses God —
Mudded at the bottom of the Cam,
Beyond recognition or rescue,
All our fears washed from it, and perfect,
Under the stained mournful flow, saluted
Only in summer briefly by the slender
Punt-loads of shadows flitting towards their honey
And the stopped clock.
                              Evil.
That was what you called the head. Evil.

Scotland

Frederick Seidel

A stag lifts his nostrils to the morning
In the crosshairs of the scope of love,
And smells what the gun calls Scotland and falls.
The meat of geology raw is Scotland: Stone
Age hours of stalking, passionate aim for the heart,
Bleak dazzling weather of the bare and green.
Old men in kilts, their beards are lobster-red.
Red pubic hair of virgins white as cows.
Omega under Alpha, rock hymen, fog penis —
The unshaved glow of her underarms is the sky
Of prehistory or after the sun expands.

The sun will expand a billion years from now
And burn away the mist of Caithness — till then,
There in the Thurso phone book is Robin Thurso.
But he is leaving for his other castle.
'Yes, I'm just leaving — what a pity! I can't
Remember, do you shoot?' Dukes hunt stags,
While Scotsmen hunt for jobs and emigrate,
Or else start seeing red spots on a moor
That flows to the horizon like a migraine.
Sheep dot the moor, bubblebaths of unshorn
Curls somehow red, unshepherded, unshorn.

Gone are the student mobs chanting the *Little Red
Book* of Mao at their Marxist dons.
The universities in the south woke,
Now they are going back to the land of dreams —
Tour buses clog the roads that take them there.
Gone, the rebel psychoanalysts.
Scotland trained more than its share of brilliant ones.
Pocked faces, lean as wolves, they really ran
To untrain and be famous in London, doing wild
Analysis, vegetarians brewing
Herbal tea for anorexic girls.

Let them eat haggis. The heart, lungs and liver
Of a sheep minced with cereal and suet,
Seasoned with onions, and boiled in the sheep's stomach.
That's what the gillie eats, not venison,
Or salmon, or grouse served rare, not for the gillie
That privilege, or the other one which is
Mushed vegetables moulded to resemble a steak.
Let them come to Scotland and eat blood
Pud from a food stall out in the open air,
In the square in Portree. Though there is nothing
Better in the world than a grouse cooked right.

They make a malt in Wick that tastes as smooth
As Mouton when you drink enough of it.
McEwen adored both, suffered a partial stroke,
Switched to champagne and died. A single piper
Drones a file of mourners through a moor,
The sweet prodigal being piped to his early grave.
A friend of his arriving by helicopter
Spies the procession from a mile away,
The black speck of the coffin trailing a thread,
Lost in the savage green, an ocean of thawed
Endlessness and a spermatozoon.

A vehement bullet comes from the gun of love.
On the island of Raasay across from Skye,
The dead walk with the living hand in hand
Over to Hallaig in the evening light.
Girls and boys of every generation,
MacLeans and MacLeods, as they were before they were
Mothers and clansmen, still in their innocence,
Walk beside the islanders, their descendants.
They hold their small hands up to be held by the living.
Their love is too much, the freezing shock-alive
Of rubbing alcohol that leads to sleep.

Althusser's Fate

Douglas Johnson

'Is it easy to be a Marxist?' Louis Althusser put this question to a crowded audience at the University of Picardy in 1975. Is it possible to be an Althusserian? The question has to be asked now. Althusserian Marxism has always been under threat, but since the tragic events of last November we are obliged to wonder whether the ruin of Althusser's own life and career, as he faces a future necessarily bounded by the mental hospital, will also encompass the definitive destruction of his philosophical work. If so, Althusser's story has a very real relevance to the history of the French Left.

The fact that Althusser is not likely to face any charge for the murder of his wife, since he is, in English parlance, 'unfit to plead', only underlines the deep tragedy of this affair. The suggestion that he is now also suffering from a physical ailment which affects his respiration, so that having, according to his own statement, strangled his wife, he can now be said to be strangling himself, adds a further, intense sadness to the story, which will be deeply felt by all those who knew this gentle, reflective and withdrawn man. It was, of course, inevitable that popular newspapers should have sought to add scandal to sensation as soon as the news was known. It was claimed that when he summoned the doctor of the Ecole Normale Supérieure (where he lived) on the morning of Sunday, 16 November and, in a state of great distress, announced that his wife was dead and that he had killed her, he was immediately rushed to the mental hospital of Saint-Anne in order that he should escape being arrested and interrogated by the police. Such allegations are only to be expected when an eminent Communist is involved: newspapers are always eager to show that there is no sense of equality or justice among Communists, that they have no difficulty in accepting the idea of élitism (the word springs to mind as soon as the Ecole Normale is mentioned). But it was not inevitable that this terrible and astonishing event should have been used as a means of attacking both Althusser's role as a philosopher and his brand of Marxism. Weekly papers such as *L'Express* asked whether, if he was so ill and had such a long history of mental depression, he should have been allowed to function for more than thirty years as the chief philosophy teacher at the Ecole Normale, where he also held the official title of Secretary. An eminent Academician was outraged that a mentally-disturbed person should have been allowed to corrupt French youth by teaching them Marxism. *Le Nouvel Observateur*, after a sympathetic account of *'la tragédie de Louis Althusser'* (reprinted in *New Left Review*), went on to point out that he had never written the thesis which is the traditional means by which a French *universitaire* achieves his position; and the more conservative *Le Point* wrote of Althusser pursuing his researches *'dans un isolement qu'il ne désirait pas'*. His disciples had left him and, supreme irony, this Marxist was now left alone with his own conscience. Rumours grew of disagreements within the Althusser ménage and this intellectual who had consistently played down the value of individual human endeavour had, it seemed, committed a crime of passion. Somehow, what happened to the Althussers, whether described as a tragedy or, more tellingly, as a *fait divers,* has been turned into an instance of the inadequacy of Marxism in general and of Althusserian Marxism in particular. And this is not only a French phenomenon, something to be explained by the hot-house atmosphere of Parisian intellectual life: some of those British and American academics who discussed and criticised Althusser in the past now shrug their shoulders as if to say (when they don't actually say it) that they always knew he was mad.

It is true that Althusser had always suffered from some form of depressive illness. I first met him in 1947 when I became a student at the Ecole Normale Supérieure. By chance, on my first day there, we happened to eat at the same table in the refectory and we continued to eat together for the rest of the academic year. He described himself as being *'très fatigué'*, the result, he said, of a long period as a prisoner of war in Germany. He had passed the competitive examination for entrance to the Ecole in 1939, having prepared the *concours* in the *khâgne* at Lyons, where he had been the student of Jean Lacroix (who has recently retired as the philosophy correspondent of *Le Monde* and who described Althusser to subsequent generations as *'la plus grande intelligence métaphysique'* that he had ever taught). He returned to the Rue d'Ulm at the Liberation and was given a permanent room in the Infirmerie. This was not a sign of deep or disturbing illness, since it was the ambition of every *normalien* to have *'une thurne à l'infirmerie'*, and thus to enjoy some privacy and a little comfort in an institution which was much more spartan (and less bourgeois) than it is now. After the New Year, in 1948, I was suffering from a minor ailment and was moved into the Infirmerie, where I stayed for longer than illness required. For a time Althusser and I were the only students there, and it was then that I met Hélène Legotien (this was the name she had used in the Resistance movement), later to become his wife. He explained that she had greatly helped him to recover from the experience of being a prisoner of war.

It was then, too, that I realised to what extent Althusser had set himself apart from others. He was very much a detached observer, looking on his fellow students, who were usually much younger than he was, in a kindly manner, indulging in gentle irony at their expense, amusing himself by noting their weaknesses. (It is cruel to recall that when Foucault, then a second-year student, first went to the Saint-Anne hospital to begin his research into madness, he inquired whether there was not a danger of his being kept there.) It was difficult to know what would interest Althusser. When the historian Jacques Le Goff, then a fellow *normalien,* came back from Prague and spoke about the Communist takeover, Althusser did not stop to listen, yet he wished endlessly to discuss British policy in Palestine with me. There was always something unpredictable about his reactions.

He seemed able to do his work without much trouble and it was no surprise when he was received first at the notoriously difficult *agrégation de philosophie* in the summer of 1948. He remained at the Rue d'Ulm and became tutor in philosphy to those students who were preparing the same examination. He soon had a reputation for looking after them, like *une mère poule,* as one professor put it, and was very constant in his personal loyalty to them (he always spoke well of former students, even when he disapproved of their activities: I have heard him praise Jean-Marie Benoist, although he had become a Giscardien, and Paul Victor, although 'he was helping Sartre to write bad books').

But he remained apart. He rarely spoke about himself, and few people knew anything about him. Some said that he was Belgian by origin. In fact, he was born in Algeria and educated at the Lycée Saint-Charles at Marseilles (where he was greatly admired by another future Communist, Raymond Jean) before going on to Lyons. It was rumoured both that he was from a very rich and from a very poor family. In fact, his father was in banking in a modest way. It was rumoured that he was well advanced in writing some enormous work on Hume. But if he was, no one has ever seen it.

He indulged in the ritual wit and the *canulars* of the Rue d'Ulm, but avoided serious discussions, and this, combined with the way Hélène Legotien kept him under her special care, maintained the air of aloofness and mystery. There were lapses of memory, periods of fatigue and depression when complete rest was required. These lapses of memory were accompanied by bizarreries. When he claimed that he could not remember having known someone, or having taught on some topic, or — most bizarre of all — when he stopped someone in the corridor in order to confide in them that he had lost all sense of his own identity, it was as if the vagueness and forgetfulness were accompanied by a certain alertness, watchfulness, even calculation, as if Althusser were more interested in observing people's reactions than in explaining his own personal predicament.

This way of life was to become part of a method. Within the Ecole Normale, there were important and tempestuous meetings which he never attended (such as the one at which the Director suspended all student study groups because he feared there would be a clash between the Gaullists and the Communists, who had invited André Marty to speak to them on the same evening as the Gaullists had invited Jacques Soustelle), but he would turn up unexpectedly at others and dominate the discussion. The porter would be instructed to tell all callers that *'Monsieur Althusser n'est pas là,'* and then, without countermanding these instructions, Althusser would emerge from his room or suddenly expect people to call on him. Similarly, in more public matters, long periods of silence and apparent withdrawal would be followed by sudden and, at times, spectacular interventions and by periods of intense activity.

It was in the autumn of 1948 that he joined the Communist Party, but it is not clear exactly what his activities were, except that they were spasmodic and, generally speaking, rather prudent. In 1978, he apparently discovered for the first time some of the elementary principles of political campaigning. Many of his friends were surprised by his naivety. He explained, for example, that because of the shift system, if one went to distribute leaflets at the factory gates only in the early morning, one would miss a whole section of the work-force. It seems unlikely that he did much work at grass-roots level. He was to criticise this period in his political life as he was to criticise the way intellectuals then gave their time to political and ideological conflict, blaming the tendency among

French Communists for intellectuals of petty bourgeois origin to feel obliged to repay by activity the imaginary debt they had contracted by not being proletarians.

In 1959 Althusser took more decisive action. He brought together a group of philosophers, in the Salle des Actes of the Ecole Normale, and proposed a collective work on Marx. His project was for a long and exhaustive analysis of the principal Marxist texts, an analysis which would be both philosophical and linguistic. To his annoyance, the majority of the philosophers with whom he had been associated up to then (such as Desanti and Maurice Caveing) refused to join him in this work, and he found himself surrounded by a group of young people. It was the seminars arising from this project which made him famous, and after a number of articles had been published in reviews without attracting much attention, the near-simultaneous publication in 1965 of *Pour Marx* and *Lire le Capital* aroused intense interest. They placed Althusser in what Perry Anderson has described as a unique position in the history of the Parti Communiste Français. The Party had, in Althusser's own words, suffered from a negative tradition, 'the French misery', a stubborn and profound absence of theoretical culture. He had searched in vain for a French equivalent of Labriola, or Gramsci, or Rosa Luxemburg, and explained their absence both by the distrust which the French worker movement naturally felt for an intellectual class which had so easily been assimilated to a supposedly revolutionary bourgeoisie and by the general and long-standing poverty of all 'official' philosophy.

It is certainly true that the French Communist Party had always been backward in purely doctrinal terms. It had emerged from the Socialist Congress of Tours in 1920, not as the result of a difference in belief (such as had caused the many splits in 19th-century French socialism), but as the result of differing assessments of the international scene. The 'class against class' policies of the 1920s, the adherence to the Popular Front in the 1930s, the policies at the time of the Liberation in the 1940s, were all results of strategic rather than theoretical analysis. There was a tendency to regard each situation as special and particular, and it was because of this, according to Althusser, that the party had made endless mistakes. Above all, it had failed to respond to recent events: the Liberation, the Cold War, Khrushchev's denunciation of Stalin in 1956 and the advent of de Gaulle's Republic in 1958 (which Maurice Thorez had in fact denounced as the precursor of a fascist state). It was as if the

Party had ceased to exist. 1959 was, therefore, both symbolically and in historical terms, the appropriate moment for Althusser to act and to bring the Party to a true Marxist doctrine. His publications were part of a series, entitled *Théorie*, which sought to bring together the concepts of Marxism and developments in other fields of knowledge: the political and doctrinal opportunism of French Communism was to be replaced by an orthodoxy of doctrine and belief.

It is not surprising that the enterprise was not consistently appreciated by the leadership of the French Communist Party. There was, to begin with, a lack of interest, as there was a lack of discussion. In the early Sixties Althusser remarked ironically that from time to time he slipped an article (*'je fais glisser un article'*) into one of the Party periodicals but it aroused no comment because it was not understood. Jean Kanapa, the closest adviser to Georges Marchais, then the rising star of the Party administration, had denounced the intellectuals who had left the Party after the Soviet invasion of Hungary in 1956, with the words, 'just as there are abstract painters, so there are abstract thinkers,' and there was a whole tradition of Party hostility to the type of analysis and exposition with which Althusser was concerned. When, in 1966 for the first time in thirty years, a meeting of the Central Committee was devoted entirely to intellectual questions and to the role of philosophy, a number of speeches, and the final resolution itself, served to remind philosophers such as Althusser that it was the Party as a whole, and its leaders in particular, who had the responsibility of deciding the Party's philosophy. Lucien Sève, a former pupil of Althusser's and soon to become the Party's official philosopher, warned Althusser of the dangers of *gauchisme* and of behaving towards the Party in the manner of Sartre.

The fact was, as the Secretary-General of the Party, Waldeck-Rochet, pointed out in his report to this special meeting (which was held at Argenteuil), that philosophy was a science closely associated with day-to-day politics. In 1966 the day-to-day politics of the Party were complex. In 1958 opposition to the Fifth Republic was total: but the desire for peace in Algeria came to modify that total opposition, and the institution of a Presidential election by universal suffrage, which took place for the first time in 1965, raised the problem of the working class as voters, and seemed to require the Communist Party to insert itself into a system to which it was intransigently opposed. Doctrinally, the cult of the young

Marx, and the belief that his early writings showed a kind of liberal-humanism, seemed to offer a certain latitude in Party tactics and made it possible to think in terms of a practical collaboration with social democrats. In effect, the Party was in the process of becoming more opportunistic, not less, and this was the case both before and after the death of Thorez in 1964 and under his successors, Waldeck-Rochet (until, in practice, 1970) and Georges Marchais. The meeting at Argenteuil may well have been held, not to settle questions of Party philosophy, but to bring the intellectuals into line, in what R.W. Johnson, in his new book,[1] has picturesquely called 'the long march of the French Left', culminating in the Communist-Socialist alliance which hoped to win the legislative elections of 1978 but failed to do so.

R.W. Johnson is the sort of writer who does not hesitate to put history in the wrong. For example, in 1961 two would-be reformers of the Party, Marcel Servin and Laurent Casanova, were expelled: this, he says, was the turning-point where the Party failed to turn. De-Stalinisation, democratic liberalisation, Eurocommunism: all these options should have been chosen. The only difficulty for Johnson is the question of how Thorez's lieutenants would have managed to direct such a transformed party and to co-operate with Servin and Casanova. His account of this episode, like most of his book, is caustic about the French Communist Party: what was good enough for the Kremlin, he writes, was good enough to put the PCF in two minds. It was said that Thorez, in opposing Casanova, was at the same time opposing Khrushchev, whom he suspected of wishing to see Casanova at the head of the French Party, but Johnson doesn't go into this; nor does he mention the further allegation that Khrushchev eventually sacrificed Casanova in return for Thorez promising to support him against Peking. One would have thought these interpretations would have pleased him.

It has been claimed that Althusser, though placing himself on a totally different level, shared the uncertainty and hesitations of the rest of the Party. Simon Clarke,[2] in a bitterly hostile account of Althusserian Marxism, recounts what he chooses to call its 'sordid history'. He suggests that when Althusser undertook the important and radical task of counterposing Marx's authority to that of the

---

[1] *The Long March of the French Left* (Macmillan, 1980).

[2] Simon Clarke, Terry Lovell and others, *One-Dimensional Marxism* (Allison & Busby, 1980).

Party organisation, he came under pressure from the Party. In fact, the first time he came under pressure from the Party was on the matter of student agitation when the Party was worried that Communist students were claiming a similar theoretical autonomy. In 1963 he delivered a lecture in which he spoke very much as a professor, warning the students not to go too far in their revolutionary aspirations, defending certain university institutions (such as the *agrégation*) and criticising the students for their failure to recognise the integrity of the science to which they claimed to appeal. Then, at the time of the Congrès d'Argenteuil, Althusser began to modify the texts of his 1965 publications and, using prefaces for foreign translations and for new editions, embarked on the process of self-criticism which Clarke and others have seen as a retraction, the equivalent to a confession of the failure of his grand enterprise.

It is only fair to Althusser to point out that the suggestion that the Party hierarchy brought pressure to bear on him is not necessarily true. It is derived from a dissident 'Althusserian' and may well be mistaken in emphasis. Hesitations and uncertainties came naturally to Althusser and were undoubtedly part of his personality. He was prudent, he shrank from demagoguery, and he was deeply attached to his students and anxious not to lead them up a blind alley. He genuinely feared that they would succumb to technocratic temptations if they acted independently, and it was more honest for him to stand with the more authoritarian Left than to preach, as Casanova had done in 1960, the cause of '*un humanisme nouveau*' or proclaim that '*le romantisme révolutionnaire se pare de couleurs nouvelles.*' It is, of course, true that it is difficult for a successful *normalien* to reject the system, *agrégation* included. It is also true, as he told me, that he was very touched by the personal kindness shown to him at Argenteuil by Roland Leroy (who was then the chief Party spokesman on cultural and intellectual matters); and he was evidently impressed by Waldeck-Rochet's conversation with him in which the Party leader expressed his fear that the intellectuals might desert the Communist Party altogether. But there can be no question of Althusser having become an official spokesman. When the Editions Sociales, the Party publishers, began to examine the project of producing a paperback edition of Marx's *Capital*, the idea of approaching Althusser was rejected.

The dramatic events of 1968 saw Althusser conforming to the

pattern of his life at the Ecole Normale. When it seemed natural that he should speak out, he did not do so. Hence the slogan on the walls of the Latin Quarter, *'A quoi sert Althusser?'* As *Le Nouvel Observateur* put it, he was one of the most mysterious and least public figures in the world. When a famous caricaturist made a drawing of the leading structuralists, showing Barthes, Lacan, Lévi-Strauss and Foucault, someone asked why Althusser had not been included, since it was thought that he shared their scienticity, their anti-humanism and anti-historicism. The answer was that no one knew what he looked like. Paris bookshops sought to get a photograph of him to put beside the other *maîtres à penser,* but in vain.

His next intervention was typically unexpected. In 1972, the English Marxist John Lewis published an article in *Marxism Today* (which was a response to a lecture by Graham Locke, an English friend of Althusser's). Althusser's reply was surprisingly full and detailed, and it is ironical that the *Réponse à John Lewis* should have occasioned widespread discussion among so many people who did not know anything about John Lewis. Ironical, but typical of Althusser.

In the *Réponse à John Lewis,* he analysed Stalinism, not from the point of view of fashionable liberalism, but from that of Marxist doctrine. In this sense, Stalinism was a bourgeois deviation, a concession to bourgeois ideology, in that it led to a concentration on the forces of production, rather than to an understanding of the class struggle and of the social relations created by productive forces. The point here, perhaps better understood in England than in France, was whether the errors of Stalin and of Stalinism were to be corrected by still greater concentration on 'humanism' and 'economism'. It is noticeable that in 1974, the year after the publication of the *Réponse à John Lewis,* Althusser took the (for him) rare step of writing to *L'Humanité* in preparation for the 21st Party Congress. What he wrote was an appeal for the union of the Left (the Common Programme between Communists and Socialists had been agreed upon in 1972) to avoid the pitfalls of such concocted alliances — 'electoral cretinism', 'utopian idealism', 'the spontaneity of history' and the danger of reforms which hindered revolution (this was the definition of 'reformism'). Once again, opportunism was seen as the danger, and 'the base of the Party' as the necessary centre of initiative.

R.W. Johnson rightly points out that the October 1974 Congress was an answer to the Socialist 'Assises' which were held at Nantes and which celebrated both the revival of the Socialists as the largest party of the Left and the fact that the Socialist Mitterrand had so narrowly failed to beat Giscard d'Estaing that he could fairly claim to stand for one half of the French population. But Johnson fails to see that the Communists were not simply faced with the problem of an accommodation between those who were supposedly liberal (led by Marchais) and those who were supposedly hard-liners (led by Roland Leroy). He writes of the autumn of 1975 as seeing an abatement of the anti-liberal current: it would be more accurate to say that the Party was forced to face up to the twin exigencies of its situation, an obligation which was inescapable whether one was a supposed liberal or a supposed hard-liner. Roland Leroy put it simply: *'Ménager à la fois l'action indépendante de notre parti et développer l'action commune pour la victoire du Programme commun.'*

It was with the 22nd Congress of 1976 and the electoral defeat of 1978 that Althusser's activities became known to a wide public. Marchais announced well in advance that this Congress would delete from the Party constitution its historic commitment to the dictatorship of the proletariat. This was to be the sign of a break with the past, it would herald a new, national Communism, *'un socialisme aux couleurs de la France'*, and usher in the possibility of a sharing of power between Communists and Socialists (Johnson does not hesitate to talk about 'the reality of the appetite for power of the post-Thorez generation'). For some, it was the manner in which Marchais had proceeded that caused offence. Jean Elleinstein, the historian, was quite ready to wash his hands of such doctrinal burdens as the dictatorship of the proletariat, but he objected to learning about Party decisions from Marchais's television appearances. (Elleinstein has since become a full supporter of François Mitterrand.)

Althusser, speaking at the 'Fête de *l'Humanité*' in September 1974, had insisted upon the need to bring about changes in the Party from within, in opposition to a number of individuals who had left the Party. In December 1976, he responded unexpectedly to an invitation from the Cercle de Philosophie de l'Union des Etudiants Communistes. He sent the typescript of his lecture to Party headquarters, and suggested that it be published in one of the Party's periodicals. For a time there was no response. Then, suddenly, he was summoned before Marchais and Chambaz, then in charge of intellectual affairs. A long discussion ensued. It was not, as was popularly rumoured, an occasion when the Party leadership endeavoured to call Althusser to order. On the contrary, Marchais saw no reason why Althusser's criticisms should not be published by the Party press (although, in the end, Althusser himself preferred to publish it in his own series, *Théorie*). Nor was the discussion about whether the doctrine of the dictatorship of the proletariat should or should not have been abandoned. The question was the same as before. *'Un concept ne s'abandonne pas comme un chien,'* Althusser had said at the Semaine de la Pensée Marxiste in April 1976. While various positions could or could not be adopted in the light of political happenings, questions of theory or of principle, in so far as they were linked to matters of Marxist knowledge and science, could not simply be abandoned. They would be discovered once again, whenever the problems of socialism, or a socialist state, or a socialist ideology, were brought up. Either the Communist Party was condemned to stay with such concepts, or it would cease to be a Communist Party. There was no struggle for influence in the Party: there were those who feared for the continued existence of the Party within its established identity, and Althusser's belief that the apparatus of the bourgeois state controlled the expressions and assumptions of ideology, in a way that was far from innocent, spelt danger to the idea that the Party should happily contemplate participation in power.

Johnson believes that Althusser's position was somehow false, because he held these ideas before the elections of 1978, but he seems totally to have misunderstood the situation, since he refers to an Italian Communist 'leaking' these ideas in *Il Manifesto* when Althusser had already published them in his *22ème Congrès*; and he misunderstands Althusser completely when he writes as if there was, in these ideas, a nostalgia for the old ghetto in which the Party had languished for so many years. It is true that the articles which Althusser published in *Le Monde* towards the end of April 1978, attacking Marchais and the leadership of the Party, were particularly devastating, and that they included a denunciation of Stalinism in post-Stalinist Russia which was more daring than anything Althusser had said before. But what is called 'his outburst' was in line with everything Althusser had undertaken since 1959. The Party had never been more opportunistic than it was in its bid for middle-class votes and its assumption that it would be right for it to share power with the bourgeoisie. Althusser denounced this opportunism, and demanded the elucidation of a Marxist theory of the state.

It is curious that Johnson should feel that Elleinstein's opposition was more significant than Althusser's, since Elleinstein thought only in terms of tactics. A pity, too, that he suggests that Althusser had 'shot his bolt' by April 1978, as if everything Althusser wanted might have been accomplished by a change in the composition of the Political Bureau or some resolution of the Central Committee. And the phrase 'the great man himself dropped from sight' is undeservedly sarcastic. The interview which Althusser gave to Fanti, of *Paese Sera,* in May 1978 is notable, not for its attempt to persuade the 'dissidents' to remain within the Party, but for pointing out that the situation which the Communists were discovering after the elections of 1978 was endemic in the signing of the Programme Commun in 1972.

In June 1978 I published an article in the *New Statesman* on the French Communists after the elections. Much to my surprise, Althusser got in touch with me and suggested that he should come to London and speak to my seminar. This he did. In the course of the seminar, he was asked why it was that he had not attacked the leadership of the Party in such an open and direct way before. Why had he not spoken out earlier (a reproach which Elleinstein was also to make)? Althusser's reply was quite typical. The question, he claimed, was not whether he had spoken too late, but whether he had not spoken too soon. His criticisms and arguments had been lost in the welter of reckoning and bewilderment which had followed defeat in the elections. For him, this was a secondary matter: by attempting to ally democracy to Marxism he sought to shape the destiny of the Party in a longer perspective. Marchais could only too easily dispose of Althusser by referring to 'the intellectual seated at his desk' and Roland Leroy could avoid the issue by confessing that he too might have been wrong in not publishing Althusser in *L'Humanité.*

Althusser had great hopes of future activity. He thought that he would operate from two centres, from Leyden and from London. He had many plans. It was illness rather than events which obscured them. But by December 1978 *La Pensée* devoted a special number to the existence or non-existence of Marxist philosophy, as if Althusser had never written, and in the course of 1979 *L'Humanité* took the title of Althusser's articles in *Le Monde,* which had been called *'Ce qui ne peut plus durer dans le parti communiste français'*, and adapted it to an article of their own: *'Ce qui ne peut plus durer dans le parti socialiste français'*.

His English commentators are not enthusiastic. Simon Clarke and his associates argue that Althusser's Marxism was subversive. They object to his attacks on humanism, on empiricism and on historicism. They object to his silences on sexual politics and on cultural production. Maurice Cornforth,[3] while admiring his modesty and sharing his aim of wanting to find a way whereby social life can be lived to the profit of all men, cannot follow him in schematic ventures into would-be Marxist theory. Jack Lindsay[4] believes that Althusser's use of structuralism caused him to read into Marx what Marx did not write, and caused him to reject the unity of theory and practice. R.S. Neale, in a wide-ranging and stimulating examination of the ways in which historians have used the concepts of class and class-consciousness,[5] considers E.P. Thompson's attack on Althusser in *The Poverty of Theory* and concludes that the Althusserian revolution, far from being in the mainstream of Marxism, had placed itself outside it.

It can, of course, be argued that Althusser himself did away with Althusserianism when he claimed it was the ignorant rather than scholars who understood Marxism, since they knew exploitation: it was the very substance of their lives. It can be argued that with such a remark Althusser recognised the poverty of theory. This is not the place to discuss the logical flaws in Althusser's work, nor its incompleteness, which is now likely to remain. There is a greater drama in failure than there can ever be in success. But the inadequacies of the intuitive Marxism which seems to be successful, and the weaknesses of Marxism as a critical method rather than a philosophical system, only highlight 'the French misery' to which Althusser alluded in *Pour Marx*. Better the poverty of theory than the misery of opportunism.

---

[3] *Communism and Philosophy* (Lawrence and Wishart, 1980).

[4] *The Crisis of Marxism* (Moonraker, 1980).

[5] *Class in English History 1680-1850* (Basil Blackwell, 1980).

Did Darwin get it right?

John Maynard Smith

I think I can see what is breaking down in evolutionary theory — the strict construction of the modern synthesis with its belief in pervasive adaptation, gradualism and extrapolation by smooth continuity from causes of change in local populations to major trends and transitions in the history of life.

A new and general evolutionary theory will embody this notion of hierarchy and stress a variety of themes either ignored or explicitly rejected by the modern synthesis.

These quotations come from a recent paper in *Palaeobiology* by Stephen Jay Gould. What is the new theory? Is it indeed likely to replace the currently orthodox 'neo-Darwinian' view? Proponents of the new view make a minimum and a maximum claim. The minimum claim is an empirical one concerning the nature of the fossil record. It is that species, once they come into existence, persist with little or no change, often for millions of years ('stasis'), and that evolutionary change is concentrated into relatively brief periods ('punctuation'), these punctuational changes occurring at the moment when a single species splits into two. The maximal claim is a deduction from this, together with arguments drawn from the study of development: it is that evolutionary change, when it does occur, is not caused by natural selection operating on the genetic differences between members of populations, as Darwin argued and as most contemporary evolutionists would agree, but by some other process. I will discuss these claims in turn; as will be apparent, it would be possible to accept the first without being driven to accept the second.

The claim of stasis and punctuation will ultimately be settled by a study of the fossil record. I am not a palaeontologist, and it might therefore be wiser if I were to say merely that some palaeontologists assert that it is true, and others are vehemently denying it. There is something, however, that an outsider can say. It is that the matter can be settled only by a statistical analysis of measurements of fossil populations from different levels in the rocks, and not by an analysis of the lengths of time for which particular named species or genera persist in the fossil record. The trouble with the latter method is that one does not know whether one is studying the rates of evolution of real organisms, or merely the habits of the

157

taxonomists who gave the names to the fossils. Suppose that in some lineage evolutionary change took place at a more or less steady rate, to such an extent that the earliest and latest forms are sufficiently different to warrant their being placed in different species. If there is at some point a gap in the record, because suitable deposits were not being laid down or have since been eroded, then there will be a gap in the sequence of forms, and taxonomists will give fossils before the gap one name and after it another. It follows that an analysis of named forms tells us little: measurements of populations, on the other hand, would reveal whether change was or was not occurring before and after the gap.

My reason for making this rather obvious point is that the only extended presentation of the punctuationist view — Stanley's book, *Macroevolution* — rests almost entirely on an analysis of the durations of named species and genera. When he does present population measurements, they tend to support the view that changes are gradual rather than sudden. I think that at least some of the changes he presents as examples of sudden change will turn out on analysis to point the other way. I was unable to find any evidence in the book which supported, let alone established, the punctuationist view.

Of course, that is not to say that the punctuationist view is not correct. One study, based on a proper statistical analysis, which does support the minimal claim, but not the maximal one, is Williamson's study of the freshwater molluscs (snails and bivalves) of the Lake Turkana region of Africa over the last five million years. Of the 21 species studied, most showed no substantial evolutionary change during the whole period: 'stasis' was a reality. The remaining six species were more interesting. They also showed little change for most of the period. There was, however, a time when the water table fell and the lake was isolated from the rest of the rift valley. When this occurred, these six species changed rather rapidly. Through a depth of deposit of about one metre, corresponding roughly to 50,000 years, successive populations show changes of shape great enough to justify placing the later forms in different species. Later, when the lake was again connected to the rest of the rift valley, these new forms disappear suddenly, and are replaced by the original forms, which presumably re-entered the lake from outside, where they had persisted unchanged.

This is a clear example of stasis and punctuation. However, it offers no support for the view that changes, when they do occur, are not the result of selection acting within populations. Williamson does have intermediate populations, so we know that the change did not depend on the occurrence of a 'hopeful monster' (see below), or on the existence of an isolated population small enough to permit random changes to outweigh natural selection. The example is also interesting in showing how we may be misled if we study the fossil record only in one place. Suppose that, when the water table rose again, the new form had replaced the original one in the rest of the rift valley, instead of the other way round. Then, if we had examined the fossil record anywhere else but in Lake Turkana, we would have concluded, wrongly, that an effectively instantaneous evolutionary change had occurred.

Williamson's study suggests an easy resolution of the debate. Both sides are right, and the disagreement is purely semantic. A change taking 50,000 years is sudden to a palaeontologist but gradual to a population geneticist. My own guess is that there is not much more to the argument than that. However, the debate shows no signs of going away.

One question that arises is how far the new ideas are actually new. Much less so, I think, than their proponents would have us believe. They speak and write as if the orthodox view is that evolution occurs at a rate which is not only 'gradual' but uniform. Yet George Gaylord Simpson, one of the main architects of the 'modern synthesis' now under attack, wrote a book, *Tempo and Mode in Evolution*, devoted to emphasising the great variability of evolutionary rates. It has never been part of the modern synthesis that evolutionary rates are uniform.

Yet there is a real point at issue. If it turns out to be the case that all, or most, evolutionary change is concentrated into brief periods, and associated with the splitting of lineages, that would require some serious rethinking. Oddly enough, it is not so much the sudden changes which would raise difficulties, but the intervening stasis. Why should a species remain unchanged for millions of years? The explanation favoured by most punctuationists is that there are 'developmental constraints' which must be overcome before a species can change. The suggestion is that the members of a given species share a developmental pathway which can be modified so as to produce some kinds of change in adult structure rather easily, and other kinds of change only with great difficulty, or not at all. I do not doubt that this is true: indeed, in my book

The Theory of Evolution, published in 1958 and intended as a popular account of the modern synthesis, I spent some time emphasising that 'the pattern of development of a given species is such that there are only a limited number of ways in which it can be altered without causing complete breakdown.' Neo-Darwinists have never supposed that genetic mutation is equally likely to produce changes in adult structure in any direction: all that is assumed is that mutations do not, as a general rule, adapt organisms to withstand the agents which caused them. What is at issue, then, is not whether there are developmental constraints, because clearly there are, but whether such constraints can account for stasis in evolution.

I find it hard to accept such an explanation for stasis, for two reasons. The first is that artificial selection can and does produce dramatic morphological change: one has only to look at the breeds of dogs to appreciate that. The second is that species are not uniform in space. Most species with a wide geographical range show differences between regions. Often these differences are so great that one does not know whether the extreme forms would behave as a single species if they met. Occasionally we know that they would not. This requires that a ring of forms should arise, with the terminal links overlapping. The Herring Gull and Lesser Black-Backed Gull afford a familiar example. In Britain and Scandinavia they behave as distinct species, without hybridising, but they are linked by a series of forms encircling the Arctic.

Stasis in time is, therefore, a puzzle, since it seems not to occur in space. The simplest explanation is that species remain constant in time if their environments remain constant. It is also worth remembering that the hard parts of marine invertebrates, on which most arguments for stasis are based, tell us relatively little about the animals within. There are on our beaches two species of periwinkle whose shells are indistinguishable, but which do not interbreed and of which one lays eggs and the other bears live young.

The question of stasis and punctuation will be settled by a statistical analysis of the fossil record. But what of the wider issues? Is mutation plus natural selection within populations sufficient to explain evolution on a large scale, or must new mechanisms be proposed?

It is helpful to start by asking why Darwin himself was a believer in gradual change. The reason lies, I believe, in the nature of the problem he was trying to solve. For Darwin, the outstanding characteristic of living organisms which called for an explanation was the detailed way in which they are adapted to their forms of life. He knew that 'sports' — structural novelties of large extent — did arise from time to time, but felt that fine adaptation could not be explained by large changes of this kind: it would be like trying to perform a surgical operation with a mechanically-controlled scalpel which could only be moved a foot at a time. Gruber has suggested that Darwin's equating of gradual with natural and of sudden with supernatural was a permanent feature of his thinking, which predated his evolutionary views and his loss of religious faith. It may have originated with Archbishop Sumner's argument (on which Darwin made notes when a student at Cambridge) that Christ must have been a divine rather than a human teacher because of the suddenness with which his teachings were accepted. Darwin seems to have retained the conviction that sudden changes are supernatural long after he had rejected Sumner's application of the idea.

Whatever the source of Darwin's conviction, I think he was correct both in his emphasis on detailed adaptation as the phenomenon to be explained, and in his conviction that to achieve such adaptation requires large numbers of selective events. It does not, however, follow that all the steps had to be small. I have always had a soft spot for 'hopeful monsters': new types arising by genetic mutation, strikingly different in some respects from their parents, and taking a first step in the direction of some new adaptation, which could then be perfected by further smaller changes. We know that mutations of large effect occur: our only problem is whether they are ever incorporated during evolution, or are always eliminated by selection. I see no *a priori* reason why such large steps should not occasionally happen in evolution. What genetic evidence we have points the other way, however. On the relatively few occasions when related species differing in some morphological feature have been analysed genetically, it has turned out, as Darwin would have expected had he known of the possibility, that the difference is caused by a number of genes, each of small effect.

As I see it, a hopeful monster would still stand or fall by the test of natural selection. There is nothing here to call for radical re-thinking. Perhaps the greatest weakness of the punctuationists is their failure to suggest a plausible alternative mechanism. The nearest they have come is the hypothesis of 'species selection'. The idea is that when a new species arises, it differs from its ancestral species in ways which are random relative to any long-term evolutionary trends. Species will differ, however, in their likelihood of going extinct, and of splitting again to form new species. Thus selection will operate between species, favouring those characteristics which make extinction unlikely and splitting likely. In 'species selection', as compared to classical individual organism, extinction replaces death, the splitting of species into two replaces birth, and mutation is replaced by punctuational changes at the time of splitting.

Some such process must take place. I have argued elsewhere that it may have been a relevant force in maintaining sexual reproduction in higher animals. It is, however, a weak force compared to typical Darwinian between-individual selection, basically because the origin and extinction of species are rare events compared to the birth and death of individuals. Some critics of Darwinism have argued that the perfection of adaptation is too great to be accounted for by the selection of random mutations. I think, on quantitative grounds, that they are mistaken. If, however, they were to use the same argument to refute species selection as the major cause of evolutionary trends, they might well be right. For punctuationists, one way out of the difficulty would be to argue that adaptation is in fact less precise than biologists have supposed. Gould has recently tried this road. As it happens, I think he is right to complain of some of the more fanciful adaptive explanations that have been offered, but I also think that he will find that the residue of genuine adaptive fit between structure and function is orders of magnitude too great to be explained by species selection.

One other extension of the punctuationist argument is worth discussing. As explained above, stasis has been explained by developmental constraints. This amounts to saying that the developmental processes are such that only certain kinds of animal are possible and viable. The extension is to apply the same idea to explain the existence of the major patterns of organisation, or 'bauplans', observable in the natural world. The existence of such bauplans is not at issue. For example, all vertebrates, whether swimming, flying, creeping or burrowing, have the same basic pattern of an internal jointed backbone with a hollow nerve cord above it and segmented body muscles either side of it, and the vast majority have two pairs of fins, or of legs which are derived from fins (although a few have lost one or both pairs of appendages). Why should this be so?

Darwin's opinion is worth quoting. In *The Origin of Species*, he wrote:

It is generally acknowledged that all organic beings have been formed on two laws — Unity of Type, and the Conditions of Existence. By unity of type is meant that fundamental agreement in structure which we see in organic beings of the same class, and which is quite independent of their habits of life. On my theory, unity of type is explained by unity of descent. The expression of conditions of existence, so often insisted on by the illustrious Cuvier, is fully embraced by the principle of natural selection. For natural selection acts by either now adapting the varying parts of each being to its organic and inorganic conditions of life; or by having adapted them during the long-past periods of time...Hence, in fact, the law of Conditions of Existence is the higher law; as it includes, through the inheritance of former adaptations, that of Unity of Type.

That is, we have two pairs of limbs because our remote ancestors had two pairs of fins, and they had two pairs of fins because that is an efficient number for a swimming animal to have.

I fully share Darwin's opinion. The basic vertebrate pattern arose in the first place as an adaptation for sinusoidal swimming. Early fish have two pairs of fins for the same reason that most early aeroplanes had wings and tail-plane: two pairs of fins is the smallest number that can produce an upward or downward force through any point in the body. In the same vein, insects (which are descended from animals with many legs) have six legs because that is the smallest number which permits an insect to take half its legs off the ground and not fall over.

The alternative view would be that there are (as yet unknown) laws of form or development which permit only certain kinds of organisms to exist — for example, organisms with internal skeletons, dorsal nerve cords and four legs, or with external skeletons, ventral nerve cords and six legs — and which forbid all others, in the same way that the laws of physics permit only elliptical planetary orbits, or the laws of chemistry permit only certain compounds. This view is a manifestation of the 'physics envy' which still infects some biologists. I believe it to be mistaken. In some cases it is demonstrably false. For example, some of the earliest vertebrates had more than two pairs of fins (just as some early aeroplanes had a noseplane as well as a tailplane). Hence there is no general law forbidding such organisms.

What I have said about bauplans does not rule out the possibility that there may be a limited number of kinds of unit developmental process which occur, and which are linked together in various ways to produce adult structures. The discovery of such processes would be of profound importance for biology, and would no doubt influence our views about evolution.

One last word needs to be said about bauplans. They may, as Darwin thought, have arisen in the first place as adaptations to particular ways of life, but, once having arisen, they have proved to be far more conservative in evolution than the way of life which gave them birth. Apparently it has been easier for organisms to adapt to new ways of life by modifying existing structures than by scrapping them and starting afresh. It is for this reason that comparative anatomy is a good guide to relationship.

Punctuationist views will, I believe, prove to be a ripple rather than a revolution in the history of ideas about evolution. Their most positive achievement may be to persuade more people to study populations of fossils with adequate statistical methods. In the meanwhile, those who would like to believe that Darwin is dead, whether because they are creationists, or because they dislike the apparently Thatcherite conclusions which have been drawn from his theory, or find the mathematics of population genetics too hard for them, would be well advised to be cautious: the reports of his death have been exaggerated.

Sexuality and Solitude

Michel Foucault and Richard Sennett

Richard Sennett: A few years ago, Michel Foucault and I discovered we were interested in the same problem, in very different periods of history. The problem is why sexuality has become so important to people as a definition of themselves. Sex is as basic as eating or sleeping, to be sure, but it is treated in modern society as something more. It is the medium through which people seek to define their personalities, their tastes. Above all, sexuality is the means by which people seek to be conscious of themselves. It is that relationship between self-consciousness, or subjectivity, and sexuality that we want to explore. Few people today would subscribe to Brillat-Savarin's 'Tell me what you eat, and I will tell you who you are,' but a translation of this dictum to the field of sex does command assent: know how you love, and you will know who you are.

Michel Foucault and I are working, as I say, on two very different historical periods in which this theme of self-consciousness via sexuality appears. He focuses on how Christianity in its early phases, from the third to the sixth century, assigned a new value to sexuality, and redefined sexuality itself. I focus on the late 18th and 19th centuries, and within that period on how medical doctors, educators and judges took a new interest in sexuality. When it became apparent to us that we are asking rather similar questions about our two periods, we decided to set up a seminar to see what connections we could make. We hope to get some rough, tentative ideas about the continuing influence of Christianity on modern culture.

I myself did not set out to study sexuality at all. I set out to study the history of solitude in modern society. I wanted to understand the evolution of experiences of solitude because it seemed to be a good way to study a vast but amorphous subject, the development of subjectivity in modern culture. How has the concept of 'I' changed in the last two centuries? To tame this very general subject, I sought to understand the changing circumstances in which people felt alone with themselves, the conditions of family, work and political life which prompted people to consider themselves to be alone. Originally I had focused on such tangible

165

matters as how people felt alone in the midst of city crowds (an incomprehensible notion to someone of the mid-17th century), and how factory conditions changed so that people felt more or less isolated from each other. This history of the circumstances in which people felt alone appeared to me after a while, however, to be inadequate to the subject. In particular, it did not account for the mental tools people use to think about themselves when they are alone. In the last century, one tool of self-definition which has grown ever more important is the perception of one's own sexuality. For instance, by the end of the 19th century, there existed the notion that when one left the family and went out into the crowd, one was free to have all kinds of sexual experiences which one would have been ashamed to admit one could desire, thinking of oneself as a member of a family. There thus appeared two kinds of desire — one for the anonymous man, one for the family man.

Let me now say something about what the word 'solitude' means. We know three solitudes in society. We know a solitude imposed by power. This is the solitude of isolation, the solitude of *anomie*. We know a solitude which arouses fear on the part of those who are powerful. This is the solitude of the dreamer, of the *homme révolté,* the solitude of rebellion. And finally, there is a solitude which transcends the terms of power. It is a solitude based on the idea of Epictetus that there is a difference between being lonely and being alone. This third solitude is the sense of being one among many, of having an inner life which is more than a reflection of the lives of others. It is the solitude of difference.

Each of these solitudes has a history. In the ancient world, the solitude imposed by power was exile; in 17th-century France, the solitude imposed by power was banishment to the countryside. In a modern office, the solitude created by power is a sense of loneliness in the midst of the mass. In the ancient world, the detached dreamer whom the powerful feared was a Socrates, one who set against the laws of the state a discourse of superior law, an ideal against an established order of power. The modern *homme révolté*, an Artaud or a Genet, sets against the order of power the truth of lawlessness. The solitude of difference, of an inner life more than the reflections of other lives, is similarly historical.

In most of the writings on this subject, the emphasis is put on the first two solitudes: people in isolation perceived either as victims or as rebels. Emile Durkheim is probably the greatest spokesman for the solitary as a victim, Jean-Paul Sartre for the solitary as a rebel.

The sense of apartness, of difference, is more neglected, and for a good reason. This is an immensely confused experience in modern society, and one reason for the confusion is that our ideas of sexuality as an index of self-consciousness make it hard for us to understand how we stand apart from other individuals in society. It is this third solitude upon which M. Foucault and I have focused.

Confusion about standing apart because of one's sexuality is partly bred of fear. The first modern researchers on sexuality believed they were opening up a terrifying Pandora's box of unrestrained lust, perversion and destructiveness in looking at the sexual desires of people alone without the civilising restraints of society. When we come to analyse the texts of Tissot and others about masturbation, I hope some sense of this terror will become apparent. A person alone with his or her sexuality appeared to be a person alone with a very dangerous force. In our seminar we have sought to understand these late Enlightenment and Victorian fears of the Pandora's box within a person to be not simply blind prejudices, or aberrations of scientific inquiry. These fears expressed ideas about the relation between mind and body, speech and desire, of which the Victorian doctors were themselves unaware. Their attitudes are buried in fundamental Christian formulas about the relationship between desire, discourse and political domination. What is inherited blindly is likely to be passed on blindly. Victorian morality provides not simply the moral foundation of the sort of right-wing clamour for social repression which appeared in the last American election: it is also the foundation of the belief, in more benign circles, that contemplation of one's sexuality is the contemplation of 'a problem', of mysteries inside oneself which can do one great damage in the course of giving one pleasure. This highly-charged psychological value put on sexuality is a legacy of Victorian wisdom, even though we flatter ourselves that we no longer share their repressive prejudices. The idea of having an identity composed of one's sexuality puts a tremendous burden on one's erotic feelings, a burden that for someone in the 18th century would be very hard to understand.

The second way in which our seminar has focused on the disorientations of sexual self-awareness concerns the act of relating the mind to the body. We have used in the seminar the phrase 'the technology of the self' to describe how sexuality is used to measure human character. Part of the modern technology of the self consists in using bodily desire to measure whether or not a person is being truthful. 'Do you really mean it?' 'Are you being honest with yourself?' These are questions people have come to answer through trying to chart what the body desires: if your body doesn't desire it, then you aren't being honest with yourself. Subjectivity has become yoked to sexuality: the truth of subjective self-consciousness is conceived in terms of measured bodily stimulation. The notion in American speech of asking whether 'you really feel what I am saying,' that idea of using the word 'feeling' as a measure of the truth between people, is a consequence of this yoking of sexuality to subjectivity, and carries with it the connotation that if something isn't felt it isn't true. The origins of telling the truth through bodily desire have been traced back in our seminar work, again, to Christian sources. The modern consequence is that the wayward course of sexual desire has acted like acid on the confidence in one's own self-consciouness: as bodily desires change, people have to keep telling themselves new or different or contradictory truths about themselves. Faith in oneself, in the integrity of self-consciousness, is eroded as the truth of one's self is yoked to the standard of the body.

Sexuality, then, has introduced elements of both fear and self-doubt into the experience of this third solitude, the condition of knowing oneself as a distinct, separate human being. It's a psychological truism that what's feared or ambiguous becomes urgent to a person. The very uncertainties which sexuality creates for subjectivity magnify the importance of the experience: that is to say, as sexuality becomes more problematical it becomes more important to us in defining ourselves. I think the rhetorical and political view M. Foucault and I share is that sexuality has become too important, that it has become charged with tasks of self-definition and self-knowledge it can't and shouldn't perform.

Let me add a final introductory note. One logical response to this problem of sexuality and solitude is to maintain: 'Forget it. Enjoy the sex and stop thinking about yourself.' I'd like to say why I don't think the issue of solitude can be disposed of in this way.

There is a direct relationship between solitude and sociability: unless a human being can be comfortable alone, he or she cannot be comfortable with others. There is a rhythm between the solitude of difference and sociability which ought to obtain in society, and it is a rhythm we do not feel because, in part, the experience of being alone with ourselves is so troubled. I should also like to say that this rhythm is possible for us to experience in a way that it was not in the past, because an immense opportunity has opened up in Western bourgeois society. It is the opportunity to live in a fragmented society.

There exists today an opportunity to escape the organic bonds of religion, family, work and community which have held many societies together before — if not completely in fact, at least as a common ideal. The love of the organic is a love we can begin to do without. Large bureaucracies are not held together by principles of organic solidarity, as Durkheim was the first to point out; the family and the work-place are no longer joined, even physically in the same household, as they were in the 18th-century city or in the countryside. Religion no longer plays the integrating role it played in traditional Catholic or Jewish life. Rather than bewailing these changes as signs of decline in society, I think we have to accept them and try to see what good they serve. The good I see them serving is to create a new opportunity both for solitude and for sociability.

The loosening of organic bonds means that social relations could become more and more matters of choice. The less social relations appear embedded in a scheme of nature, of divine law, of organic necessity, the more people should be able to imagine themselves as creatures with a life apart from their social roles. When we choose to enter into social relations, the more they matter. But that sense of choosing or not choosing whom a person cares about in a fragmented society depends on knowing how to see oneself as a separate, distinct human being in one's own right. The inflation of sexuality to be a measure of psychological truth has come to disorient this kind of self-knowledge.

Michel Foucault: In a work consecrated to the moral treatment of madness and published in 1840, a French psychiatrist, Louren, tells of the manner in which he treated one of his patients — treated and of course, as you may imagine, cured. One morning he placed Mr A., his patient, in a shower-room. He makes him recount in detail his delirium. 'But all that,' said the doctor, 'is nothing but madness. Promise me not to believe in it any more.' The patient hesitates, then promises. 'That is not enough,' replies the doctor. 'You have already made me similar promises and you haven't kept them.' And he turns on the cold shower above the patient's head. 'Yes, yes! I am mad!' the patient cries. The shower is turned off; the interrogation is resumed. 'Yes. I recognise that I am mad,' the patient repeats. 'But,' he adds, 'I recognise it because you are forcing me to do so.' Another shower. 'Well, well,' says Mr A., 'I admit it. I am mad, and all that was nothing but madness.'

To make somebody suffering from mental illness recognise that he is mad is a very ancient procedure in traditional therapy. In the works of the 17th and 18th centuries, one finds many examples of what one might call truth therapies. But the technique used by Louren is altogether different. Louren is not trying to persuade his patient that his ideas are false or unreasonable. What happens in the head of Mr A. is a matter of perfect indifference to Louren. The doctor wishes to obtain a precise act, the explicit affirmation: 'I am mad.' Since I first read this passage of Louren, about twenty years ago, I kept in mind the project of analysing the form and the history of such a bizarre practice. Louren is satisfied when and only when his patient says, 'I am mad,' or: 'That was madness.' Louren's assumption is that madness as a reality disappears when the patient asserts the truth and says he is mad.

We have, then, the reverse of the performative speech act. The affirmation destroys in the speaking subject the reality which made the same affirmation true. What conception of truth of discourse and of subjectivity is taken for granted in this strange and yet widespread practice? In order to justify the attention I am giving to what is seemingly so specialised a subject, let me take a step back for a moment. In the years that preceded the Second World War, and even more so after the war, philosophy in continental Europe and in France was dominated by the philosophy of subject. I mean that philosophy took as its task *par excellence* the foundations of all knowledge and the principle of all signification as stemming from the meaningful subject. The importance given to this question was due to the impact of Husserl, but the centrality of the subject was also tied to an institutional context, for the French university, since philosophy began with Descartes, could only advance in a Cartesian manner. But we must also take into account the political conjunct. Given the absurdity of wars, slaughters and despotism, it seemed to be up to the individual subject to give meaning to his existential choices. With the leisure and distance that came after the war, this emphasis on the philosophy of subject no longer seemed so self-evident. Hitherto-hidden theoretical paradoxes could no longer be avoided. This philosophy of consciousness had paradoxically failed to found a philosophy of knowledge, and especially of scientific knowledge. Also, this philosophy of meaning had failed to take into account the formative mechanisms of signification and the structure of systems of meaning.

With the all too easy clarity of hindsight — of what Americans call the Monday-morning quarterback — let me say that there were two possible paths that led beyond this philosophy of subject. The first of these was the theory of objective knowledge as an analysis of systems of meaning, as semiology. This was the path of logical positivism. The second was that of a certain school of linguistics, psychoanalysis and anthropology — all grouped under the rubric of structuralism. These were not the directions I took. Let me announce once and for all that I am not a structuralist, and I confess, with the appropriate chagrin, that I am not an analytic philosopher. Nobody is perfect. But I have tried to get out from the philosophy of the subject, through a genealogy of the modern subject as a historical and cultural reality. That means as something which can eventually change, which is of course politically important. One can proceed with this general project in two ways. In dealing with modern theoretical constructions, we are concerned with the subject in general. In this way, I have tried to analyse the theories of the subject as a speaking, living, working being in the 17th and 18th century. One can also deal with the more practical understanding found in those institutions where certain subjects became objects of knowledge and of domination: asylums, prisons and so on.

I wished to study those forms of understanding which the subject creates about himself. But since I started with this last type of problem, I have been obliged to change my mind on several points. Let me introduce a kind of auto-critique. It seems, according to some suggestions of Habermas, that one can distinguish three major types of technique: the techniques which permit one to produce, to transform, to manipulate things; the techniques which permit one to use sign systems; and finally the techniques which permit one to determine the conduct of individuals, to impose certain ends or objectives. That is to say, techniques of production, techniques of signification or communication, and techniques of domination. But I became more and more aware that in all societies there is another type of technique: techniques which permit individuals to effect, by their own means, a certain number of operations on their own bodies, their own souls, their own thoughts, their own conduct, and this in a manner so as to transform themselves, modify themselves, and to attain a certain state of perfection, happiness, purity, supernatural power. Let's call these techniques technologies of the self.

If one wants to analyse the genealogy of subject in Western civilisation, one has to take into account, not only techniques of domination, but also techniques of the self. One has to show the interaction between these types of technique. When I was studying asylums, prisons and so on, I perhaps insisted too much on the techniques of domination. What we call discipline is something really important in this kind of institution. But it is only one aspect of the art of governing people in our societies. Having studied the field of power relations taking techniques of domination as a point of departure, I would like, in the years to come, to study power relations starting from the techniques of the self. In every culture, I think, this self technology implies a set of truth obligations: discovering the truth, being enlightened by truth, telling the truth. All these are considered important either for the constitution or for the transformation of the self.

Now, what about truth as a duty in our Christian societies? As everybody knows, Christianity is a confession. This means that Christianity belongs to a very special type of religion — those which impose obligations of truth on those who practise them. Such obligations in Christianity are numerous. For instance, there is the obligation to hold as truth a set of propositions which constitute dogma, the obligation to hold certain books as a permanent source of truth and obligations to accept the decisions of certain authorities in matters of truth. But Christianity requires another form of truth obligation. Everyone in Christianity has the duty to explore who he is, what is happening within himself, the faults he may have committed, the temptations to which he is exposed. Moreover everyone is obliged to tell these things to other people, and hence to bear witness against himself.

These two ensembles of obligation — those regarding the faith, the book, the dogma, and those regarding the self, the soul and the heart — are linked together. A Christian needs the light of faith when he wants to explore himself. Conversely, his access to the truth can't be conceived of without the purification of the soul. The Buddhist also has to go to the light and discover the truth about himself. But the relation between these two obligations is quite different in Buddhism and in Christianity. In Buddhism, it is the same type of enlightenment which leads you to discover what you are and what is the truth. In this simultaneous enlightenment of yourself and the truth, you discover that your self was only an illusion. I would like to underline that the Christian discovery of the self does not reveal the self as an illusion. It gives place to a task which can't be anything else but undefined. This task has two objectives. First, there is the task of clearing up all the illusions, temptations and seductions which can occur in the mind, and discovering the reality of what is going on within ourselves. Secondly, one has to get free from any attachment to this self, not because the self is an illusion, but because the self is much too real. The more we discover the truth about ourselves, the more we have to renounce ourselves; and the more we want to renounce ourselves, the more we need to bring to light the reality of ourselves. That is what we could call the spiral of truth formulation and reality renouncement which is at the heart of Christian techniques of the self.

Recently, Professor Peter Brown stated to me that what we have to understand is why it is that sexuality became, in Christian cultures, the seismograph of our subjectivity. It is a fact, a mysterious fact, that in this indefinite spiral of truth and reality in the self sexuality has been of major importance since the first centuries of our era. It has become more and more important. Why is there such a fundamental connection between sexuality, subjectivity and truth obligation? This is the point at which I met Richard Sennett's work.

Our point of departure in the seminar has been a passage of St François de Sales. Here is the text in a translation made at the beginning of the 17th century:

I will tell you a point of the elephant's honesty. An elephant never changes his mate. He loves her tenderly. With her he couples not, but from three years to three years. And that only for five days, and so secretly that he is never seen in the act. But the sixth day, he shows himself abroad again, and the first thing he does is to go directly to some river and wash his body, not willing to return to his troupe of companions till he be purified. Be not these goodly and honest qualities in a beast by which he teaches married folk not to be given too much to sensual and carnal pleasures?

Everybody may recognise here the pattern of decent sexual behaviour: monogamy, faithfulness and procreation as the main, or maybe the single, justification of sexual acts — sexual acts which remain, even in such conditions, intrinsically impure. Most of us are inclined, I think, to attribute this pattern either to Christianity or to modern Christian society as it developed under the influence of capitalist or so-called bourgeois morality. But what struck me when I started studying this pattern is the fact that one can find it also in Latin and even Hellenistic literature. One finds the same ideas, the same words, and eventually the same reference to the elephant. It is a fact that the pagan philosophers in the centuries before and after the death of Christ proposed a sexual ethics which was partly new but which was very similar to the alleged Christian ethics. In our seminar, it was very convincingly stressed that this philosophical pattern of sexual behaviour, this elephant pattern, was not at that time the only one to be known and put into practice. It was in competition with several others. But this pattern soon became predominant, because it was related to a social transformation involving the disintegration of city-states, the development of the imperial bureaucracy, and the increasing influence of the provincial middle class.

During this period we may witness an evolution towards the nuclear family, real monogamy, faithfulness between married people and distress about sexual acts. The philosophical campaign in favour of the elephant pattern was both an effect and an adjunct of this transformation. If these assumptions are correct, we have to concede that Christianity did not invent this code of sexual behaviour. Christianity accepted it, reinforced it, and gave to it a much larger and more widespread strength that it had before. But the so-called Christian morality is nothing more than a piece of pagan ethics inserted into Christianity. Shall we say then that Christianity did not change the state of things? Early Christians introduced important changes, if not in the sexual code itself, at least in the relationships everyone has to his own sexual activity. Christianity proposed a new type of experience of oneself as a sexual being.

To make things clearer, I will compare two texts. One was written by Artemidorus, a pagan philosopher of the third century, and the other is the well-known 14th book of *The City of God* by Augustine. Artemidorus wrote a book about the interpretation of dreams in the third century after the death of Christ, but he was a pagan. Three chapters of this book are devoted to sexual dreams. What is the meaning, or, more precisely, what is the prognostic value, of a sexual dream? It is significant that Artemidorus interpreted dreams in a way contrary to Freud, and gives an interpretation of sexual dreams in terms of economics, social relations, success and reverses in political activity and everyday life. For instance, if you dream that you have sex with your mother, that means that you will succeed as a magistrate, since your mother is obviously the symbol of your city or country.

It is also significant that the social value of the dream does not depend on the nature of the sexual act, but mainly on the social status of the partners. For instance, for Artemidorus it is not important in your dream whether you had sex with a girl or with a boy. The problem is to know if the partner was rich or poor, young or old, slave or free, married or not. Of course, Artemidorus takes into account the question of the sexual act, but he sees it only from the point of view of the male. The only act he knows or recognises as sexual is penetration. Penetration is for him not only a sexual act, but is part of the social role of a man in a city. I would say that for Artemidorus sexuality is relational, and that sexual relations cannot be dissociated from social relations.

Now let's turn to Augustine's text, whose meaning is the point at which we want to arrive in our analysis. In *The City of God*, and later on in the *Contra Julian*, Augustine gives a rather horrifying description of the sexual act. He sees the sexual act as a kind of spasm. All the body, says Augustine, is shaken by terrible jerks. One entirely loses control of oneself. 'This sexual act takes such a complete and passionate possession of the whole man, both physically and emotionally, that what results is the keenest of all pleasures on the level of sensations, and at the crisis of excitement it practically paralyses all power of deliberate thought.' It is worthwhile to note that this description is not an invention of Augustine: you can find the same in the medical and pagan literature of the previous century. Moreover Augustine's text is almost the exact transcription of a passage written by the pagan philosopher, Cicero in Otensius.

The surprising point is not that Augustine would give such a classical description of the sexual act, but the fact that, having made such a horrible description, he then admits that sexual relations could have taken place in Paradise before the Fall. This is all the more remarkable since Augustine is one of the first Christian Fathers to admit the possibility. Of course, sex in Paradise could not have the epileptic form which we unfortunately know now. Before the Fall, Adam's body, every part of it, was perfectly obedient to the soul and the will. If Adam wanted to procreate in Paradise, he could do it in the same way and with the same control as he could, for instance, sow seeds in the earth. He was not involuntarily excited. Every part of his body was like the fingers, which one can control in all their gestures. Sex was a kind of hand gently sowing the seed. But what happened in the Fall? Adam rose up against God with the first sin. Adam tried to escape God's will and to acquire a will of his own, ignoring the fact that the existence of his own will depended entirely on the will of God. As a punishment of this revolt and as a consequence of this will to will independently from God, Adam lost control of himself. He wanted to acquire an autonomous will, and lost the ontological support for that will. That then became mixed in an indissociable way with involuntary movements, and this weakening of Adam's will had a disastrous effect. His body, and parts of his body, stopped obeying his commands, revolted against him, and the sexual parts of his body were the first to rise up in this disobedience. The famous gesture of Adam covering his genitals with a fig leaf is, according to Augustine, not due to the simple fact that Adam was ashamed of their presence, but to the fact that his sexual organs were moving by themselves without his consent. Sex in erection is the image of man revolted against God. The arrogance of sex is the punishment and consequences of the arrogance of man. His uncontrolled sex is exactly the same as what he himself has been towards God — a rebel.

Why have I insisted so much on what may be nothing more than one of those exegetic fantasies of which Christian literature has been so prodigal? I think this text bears witness to the new type of relationship which Christianity established between sex and subjectivity. Augustine's conception is still dominated by the theme and form of male sexuality. But the main question is not, as it was in Artemidorus, the problem of penetration: it is the problem of erection. As a result, it is not the problem of the relationship to other people, but the problem of the relationship of oneself to oneself, or, more precisely, the relationship between one's will and involuntary assertions.

The principle of autonomous movements of sexual organs is called libido by Augustine. The problem of libido, of its strength, origin and effect, thus becomes the main issue of one's will. It is not an external obstacle to the will. It is a part, an internal component, of the will. And it is not the manifestation of petty desires. Libido is the result of one's will when it goes beyond the limits God originally set for it. As a consequence, the means of the spiritual struggle against libido do not consist, as with Plato, in turning our eyes upwards and memorising the reality we have previously known and forgotten The spiritual struggle consists, on the contrary, in turning our eyes continuously downwards or inwards in order to decipher, among the movements of the soul, which ones come from the libido. The task is at first indefinite, since libido and will can never be substantially dissociated from one another. And this task is not only an issue of mastership but also a question of the diagnosis of truth and illusion. It requires a permanent hermeneutics of oneself.

In such a perspective, sexual ethics imply very strict truth obligations. These do not only consist in learning the rules of a moral sexual behaviour, but also in constantly scrutinising ourselves as libidinal beings. Shall we say that after Augustine we experience our sex in the head? Let's say at least that in Augustine's analysis we witness a real libidinisation of sex. Augustine's moral theology is, to a certain extent, a systematisation of a lot of previous speculation, but it is also an ensemble of spiritual techniques.

When one reads the ascetic and monastic literature of the fourth and fifth centuries, one cannot but be struck by the fact that these techniques are not directly concerned with the effective control of sexual behaviour. There is little mention of homosexual relations, in spite of the fact that most ascetics lived in permanent and numerous communities. The techniques were mainly concerned with the stream of thoughts flowing in consciousness, disturbing, by their multiplicity, the necessary unity of contemplation, and secretly conveying images or suggestions from Satan. The monk's task was not the philosopher's task: to acquire mastership over oneself by the definitive victory of the will. It was perpetually to control one's thoughts, examining them to see if they were pure, whether something dangerous was not hiding in or behind them, if they were not conveying something other than what primarily appeared, if they were not a form of illusion and seduction. Such data have always to be considered with suspicion; they need to be scrutinised and tested. According to Cassian, for instance, one has to be towards oneself as a money-changer who has to try the coins he receives. Real purity is not acquired when one can lie down with a young and beautiful boy without even touching him, as Socrates did with Alcibiades. A monk was really chaste when no impure image occured in his mind, even during the night, even during dreams. The criterion of purity does not consist of keeping control of oneself even in the presence of the most desirable people: it consists in discovering the truth in myself and defeating the illusions in myself, in cutting out the images and thoughts my mind continuously produces. Hence the axis of the spiritual struggle against impurity. The main question of sexual ethics has moved from relations to people, and from the penetration model to the relation to oneself and to the erection problem: I mean to the set of internal movements which develop from the first and nearly imperceptible thought to the final but still solitary pollution. However different and eventually contradictory they were, a common effect was elicited: sexuality, subjectivity and truth were strongly linked together. This, I think, is the religious framework in which the masturbation problem — which was nearly ignored or at least neglected by the Greeks, who considered that masturbation was a thing for slaves and for satyrs, but not for free citizens — appeared as one of the main issues of the sexual life.

Richard Sennett: In concluding, I wish to show how certain Christian ideas of confronting oneself through confronting one's sexuality have reappeared in modern society. I shall do this by tracing some of the history of ideas about masturbation from the middle of the 18th to the end of the 19th century.

In setting out this theme, I use the word 'reappear' on purpose. At the opening of the 18th century, auto-eroticism was not of much interest to medical and educational authorities. Of course, onanism was a sin, but there was a gap between the Christian rule and the medical diagnosis of it. Auto-eroticism was simply grouped as one of a number of disorders which would occur if a person was sexually over-indulgent. In Boerhaave's *Institutes of Medicine*, published in 1708, the general diagnosis of sexual over-indulgence is given as follows: 'The semen discharged too lavishly occasions a weariness, weakness, indisposition of motion, convulsions, leanness, dryness, heat and pains in the membranes of the brain, with a dullness of the senses, more especially of the sight, a *tabes dorsalis*, foolishness and disorders of the like kind.' By the time of Krafft-Ebing's *Psychopathology of Sexuality* in 1887, these symptoms are confined to masturbation. Moreover the cause of these symptoms is no longer 'too lavish a performance of the sexual act', but sexual desire. Sexual desire, when experienced alone and continually, will lead to masturbation, thence to homosexuality, finally to madness. From the time of Boerhaave to Krafft-Ebing, sexuality is displaced from how a person behaves to how he or she feels.

Perhaps the single most critical medical document in this shift is the work of the French-Swiss physician Samuel Tissot: *Onania, or a Treatise upon the Disorders Produced by Masturbation,* published in Lausanne in 1758. Tissot's was not the first book on this subject in the 18th century: that dubious honour belonged to the anonymous Englishman who published a work also called *Onania* in 1716. The Englishman asserted, for the first time, that masturbation was a special disease with a special clinical profile, but his assertions were made in so lurid and loose a way that, while the book had a success among collectors of erotica, it was not taken seriously by the scientific public. Tissot's book, however, was: he set out to explain why, physiologically, masturbation should lead to insanity.

Tissot asserted that masturbation was the most powerful sexual experience a person could have physiologically. More than any other sexual act, it pumped blood to the brain. 'This increase of blood,' he wrote, 'explains how these excesses produce insanity ... The quantity of blood distending the nerves weakens them; and they are less able to resist impressions, whereby they are enfeebled.' Given the theories of blood/nerve relations current at the time, this seemed perfectly logical. What was new, shocking, and seemingly scientifically certified by Tissot's theory, was that the pleasure a person can give himself or herself is more erotically powerful than the pleasure he or she can derive from intercourse with a member of the opposite sex. Without social restraints, left alone to follow the purest dictates of pleasure, everyone was in danger of being consumed by auto-eroticism and so eventually driven insane.

In his text, Tissot argues against the clinical profile established a half-century earlier by Boerhaave. Tissot adduces eight reasons why masturbation is more dangerous than sexual excesses committed with women. The last and strongest is psychological. The masturbator is overcome with 'shame and shocking remorse' as no Don Juan is. This inner psychological recognition pumps so much blood to the brain that a veritable flood of the nerves occurs. Again the physiological explanation made sense to his contemporaries, and the shocking fact it seemed to prove was that the psyche can literally drive itself mad through unrestrained desire.

The notion of being driven mad by oneself as an internal process is something that appears with Tissot. A wholly inner system of desire, recognition and destruction is set up; Tissot defined the boundaries of a terrifying enclosed inner erotic life. More passionate, more important, more dangerous than any other form of erotic experience: We must rescue man, Tissot says, from this solitude.

It is significant in Tissot's text that he applies his Calvinist puritanism to this particular sexual phenomenon. He makes a distinction between the dispassionate, scientific attitude the doctors must have about other forms of sexual disease, like over-indulgence, and the moral attitude the doctor must take toward masturbation. Masturbation is a 'crime' which 'more justly entitles' the masturbator to 'the contempt than pity of his fellow creatures'. Boerhaave fought to establish a scientific discourse about sexuality free of Christian morality. Tissot brings it back in, but selectively: only auto-eroticism is worthy — if that is the right word — of Christian censure.

Tissot set in motion three attitudes about auto-eroticism that profoundly influenced medical and educational opinion later in the 18th and throughout the 19th century: sexuality in solitude is, first, profoundly arousing; auto-eroticism is, secondly, the condition in which a person is most aware of him or herself. To be both sexually aroused and self-aware, alone, is, thirdly, dangerous: the body is on the road to madness and the soul on the road to perdition. What is important about Tissot's legacy, and about the phenomenon of auto-eroticism generally in the 19th century, is that through the prism of auto-eroticism authorities attempted to understand eroticism itself. Armed with these three assumptions, researchers set out to try to understand sexuality. Rather than considering people making love together as constituting a domain of knowledge about which the doctor would learn, the notion was to separate the individual and to study him by himself, because it was in isolation that the person felt his sexuality most strongly. It was an application to the study of sex of other forms of 19th-century individualism, this assumption that a person was to be considered as an isolated individual.

The Tissot approach to auto-eroticism became a method of conceiving of sexuality itself during the 19th century in the following ways. First, because of their beliefs about auto-eroticism, doctors and educators became accustomed to think that sexual desire existed prior to, and was separable from, sexual attraction. Desire was thought to be normally experienced as a secret. That is, if desire belongs to the body in and of itself, it's something prior to desiring anyone else, and is strongest when kept a secret. This sexual desire belongs to the individual: it is satisfied rather than created by the attraction to another human being. The problem for the doctor or teacher was to find out about this desire, since it was hidden within the individual. We are all aware of the bizarre symptoms Victorian medicine had to invent for the masturbator: hair suddenly growing on the palms of the masturbating hand, the tongue swelling up, the eyes distending, or, in the case of women, the radically distended clitoris. Victorian doctors had a reason for inventing these symptoms: since sexual desire itself was secret, hidden within the individual, the doctor or other authority could get control over the individual only by creating symptoms which would give sexual desire away. The extreme of this fantasy-invention appeared in 1876 in a text by Pouillet on female masturbation, one of the first texts in the medical literature on the subject. The diagnosis of female masturbation was peevishness, surliness towards strangers, and lying. These are the invariable signs that a woman has been masturbating. Finally, says Pouillet, 'there is a certain aspect, a *je ne sais quoi*, easier to recognise than to express in words.' Tissot had maintained that auto-eroticism drew the offender into an inner, self-contained world. By the time of Pouillet, the very idea of sexual desire had become privately enclosed. Someone else can get power over this desire only by finding signs on the body which betray its presence. It has to be something perceptible if that power relation is to be exercised.

The second way auto-eroticism became a prism for understanding eroticism concerns the relation between sexual desire and the imagination. It will be recalled that Tissot believed auto-erotic experience to be the most powerful sexual experience a person could have. In the 19th century, this was extended to the sexual imagination. In isolation, it was believed that a person's sexual desires went wild. In solitude, writes Lallemand in 1842, a person invents an erotic life the world can never sufficiently fulfil. The doctor must tamp down the fires of sexual desire by externally repressive measures. According to Lallemand, marital sex was seen as the great chastiser of desire. What is aimed at in these external, social technologies of control is the counteracting of the influence of imagination. There is a basic antagonism between fantasy and social order.

Finally and crucially, the lesson of auto-eroticism was that sexuality itself could be a barometer for measuring human character. In the course of the 19th century, the physiological view of Tissot fell by the wayside, but his connection of auto-eroticism to the moral character of an individual grew even stronger. Here is how a popular 'sex hygiene' guide for young people put the matter in 1917 (it is Robert Willson's *The Education of the Young in Sex Hygiene*): 'The boy who can look his father and mother fully and laughingly in the eye, who can throw his shoulders back and breathe deep, that boy who regards his father as his comrade and his mother as his best friend, does not masturbate.' The boy can look his parents fully and laughingly in the eye because he has nothing to hide: he has no private, solitary secret about sex. It is this way of thinking which becomes more general. Truthfulness with other people will depend on how a person has managed his or her own sexuality. What makes this management difficult is that sexuality has come to be seen as an inner-drawing, powerful, enclosed experience of desire. The problem in telling the truth about sex thus becomes enmeshed in telling the truth about a self that resists revelation.

Augustine believed that the definition of sexuality revolved around the question of feeling, rather than, as Artemidorus believed, questions of action or social position. That is also the case here. Sexuality is the architecture of the whole realm of inner desire. And the notion is shared in the medical and Christian texts that confronting what one desires rather than what one does is what really constitutes self-knowledge.

There is a power relationship implicated in this knot of truthfulness, sexuality and personal self-knowledge. The knot is tied in so complicated a way that an outside authority is necessary for the person to unravel it: the Christian confesses to the priest, we go to the doctor. It was not in its advocacy of sexual repression that Victorian medicine returned to the Christian roots of the culture, but in the psychological importance assigned to knowledge of oneself through the counsel and control of another, more knowing human being.

This analysis of Tissot's legacy may be related to the issue of difference which I raised at the outset. Sexuality is something every human being experiences, yet our inheritance from the medical and educational theories of the last century is that by understanding our sexuality we believe we will understand what is distinctive and individual about ourselves. The universal is used to define the particular. If there is one element in the Victorian heritage which makes this process confusing, it is the definition of sexuality in terms of desire rather than activity. 'Everyone makes love,' said one of Krafft-Ebings's subjects, 'but each person is thinking of something special when they do.' It is in point of fact difficult, if not impossible, to deduce from private sexual desires a person's capacity for loyalty, courage, or truthfulness with others. That these thoughts, these desires, these fantasies should be seen as privileged, as of importance in defining the whole of an individual personality, is what creates such a mystery about individual difference. The privilege accorded to desire is a Christian heritage. We are today far from being able to cope with what we have inherited.

Witty Ticcy Ray

Oliver Sacks

In 1884-5 Gilles de la Tourette, a pupil of Charcot, described the astonishing syndrome which now bears his name. 'Tourette's syndrome', as it was immediately dubbed, is characterised by an excess of nervous energy, and a great production and extravagance of strange motions and notions: tics, jerks, mannerisms, grimaces, noises, curses, involuntary imitations and compulsions of all sorts, with an odd elfin humour and a tendency to antic and outlandish kinds of play. In its 'highest' forms, Tourette's syndrome involves every aspect of the affective, the instinctual and the imaginative life; in its 'lower', and perhaps commoner, forms, there may be little more than abnormal movements and impulsivity, though even here there is an element of strangeness. It was well recognised and extensively reported in the closing years of the last century, for these were years of a spacious neurology which did not hesitate to conjoin the organic and the psychic. It was clear to Tourette, and his peers, that this syndrome was a sort of possession by primitive impulses and urges: but also that it was a possession with an organic base — a very definite (if undiscovered) neurological disorder.

In the years that immediately followed the publication of Tourette's original papers many hundreds of cases of this syndrome were described — no two cases ever being quite the same. It became clear that there were forms which were mild and benign, and others of quite terrible grotesqueness and violence. Equally, it was clear that some people could 'take' Tourette's, and accommodate it within a commodious personality, even gaining advantage from the swiftness of thought and association and invention which went with it, while others might indeed be 'possessed' and scarcely able to achieve real identity amid the tremendous pressure and chaos of Tourettic impulses. There was always, as Luria remarked of his 'mnemonist', a fight between an 'It' and an 'I'.

Charcot and his pupils, who included Freud and Babinski as well as Tourette, were among the last of their profession with a combined vision of body and soul, 'It' and 'I', neurology and psychiatry. By the turn of the century, a split had occurred, into a soulless neurology and a bodiless psychology, and with this any understanding of Tourette's disappeared. In fact, Tourette's syndrome itself seemed to have disappeared, and was scarcely at all reported in the first half of this century. Some physicians, indeed, regarded it as 'mythical', a product of Tourette's colourful imagination; most had never heard of it. It was as forgotten as the great sleepy-sickness epidemic of the 1920s.

The forgetting of sleepy-sickness (*encephalitis lethargica*) and the forgetting of Tourette's have much in common. Both disorders were extraordinary, and strange beyond belief — at least, the beliefs of a contracted medicine. They could not be accommodated in the conventional frameworks of medicine, and therefore they were forgotten and mysteriously 'disappeared'. But there is a much more intimate connection, which was hinted at in the 1920s, in the hyperkinetic or frenzied forms which the sleepy-sickness sometimes took: these patients tended, at the beginning of their illness, to show a mounting excitement of mind and body, violent movements, tics, compulsions of all kinds. Some time afterwards, they were overtaken by an opposite fate, an all-enveloping trance-like 'sleep' — in which I found them forty years later.

In 1969, I gave these sleepy-sickness or post-encephalitic patients L-DOPA, a precursor of the transmitter dopamine, which was greatly lowered in their brains. They were transformed by it. First they were 'awakened' from stupor to health: then they were driven towards the other pole — of tics and frenzy. This was my first experience of Tourette-like syndromes: wild excitements, violent impulses, often combined with a weird, antic humour. I started to speak of 'Tourettism', although I had never seen a patient with Tourette's.

Early in 1971, the *New York Times*, which had taken an interest in the 'awakening' of my post-encephalitic patients, asked me how they were getting on. I replied, 'They are ticcing,' which prompted them to publish an article on 'Tics'. After the publication of this article, I received countless letters, the majority of which I passed on to my colleagues. But there was one patient I did consent to see — Ray.

The day after seeing Ray, it seemed to me that I noticed three Touretters in the street in downtown New York. I was confounded, for Tourette's syndrome was said to be excessively rare. It had an incidence, I had read, of one in a million, yet I had apparently seen three examples in an hour. I was thrown into a turmoil of bewilderment and wonder: was it possible that I had been over-looking this all the time, either not seeing such patients or vaguely dismissing them as 'nervous', 'cracked', 'twitchy'? Was it possible that everyone had been overlooking them? Was it possible that Tourette's was not a rarity, but rather common — a thousand times more common, say, than previously supposed? The next day, without specially looking, I saw another two in the street. At this point I conceived a whimsical fantasy or private joke: suppose (I said to myself) that Tourette's is very common but fails to be recognised until it is recognised (and, thereafter, is easily and constantly seen). Suppose one such Touretter recognises another, and these two a third, and these three a fourth, until, by incrementing recognition, a whole band of them is found: brothers and sisters in pathology, a new species in our midst, joined together by mutual recognition and concern? Could there not come together, by such spontaneous aggregation, a whole association of New Yorkers with Tourette's?

Three years later, in 1974, I found that my fantasy had become a reality: that there had indeed come into being a Tourette's Syndrome Association. It had fifty members then: now, seven years later, it has a few thousand. This astounding increase must be ascribed to the efforts of the TSA itself, even though it consists only of patients, their relatives and physicians. The association has been endlessly resourceful in its attempts to make known (or, in the best sense, 'publicise') the Touretter's plight. It has aroused responsible interest and concern in place of the repugnance, or dismissal, which had so often been the Touretter's lot, and it has encouraged research of all kinds, from the physiological to the sociological: research into the biochemistry of the Tourettic brain; on genetic and other factors which may co-determine Tourette's; on the abnormally rapid and indiscriminate associations and reactions which characterise it. Instinctual and behavioural structures, of a developmentally and even phylogenetically primitive kind, have been revealed. There has been research on the body-language and grammar and linguistic structure of tics; there have been unexpected insights into the nature of cursing and joking (which are also characteristic of some other neurological disorders); and, not least, there have been studies of the 'interaction' of Touretters with their family and others, and of the strange mishaps which may attend these relationships. The TSA's remarkably successful endeavours are an integral part of the history of Tourette's, and, as such, unprecedented: never before have patients led the way to understanding, become the active and enterprising agents of their own comprehension and cure.

What has emerged in these last ten years — largely under the aegis and stimulus of the TSA — is a clear confirmation of Gilles de la Tourette's intuition that this syndrome indeed has an organic neurological basis. The 'It' in Tourette's, like the 'It' in Parkinsonism and chorea, reflects what Pavlov called 'the blind force of the subcortex', a disturbance of those primitive parts of the brain which govern 'go' and 'drive'. In Parkinsonism, which affects motion but not action as such, the disturbance lies in the midbrain and its connections. In chorea — which is a chaos of fragmentary quasi-actions — the disorder lies in higher levels of the basal ganglia. In Tourette's, where there is excitement of the emotions and the passions, a disorder of the primal, instinctual bases of behaviour, the disturbance seems to lie in the very highest parts of the 'old brain': the thalamus, hypothalamus, limbic system and amygdala, where the basic affective and instinctual determinants of personality are lodged. Thus Tourette's — pathologically no less than clinically — constitutes a sort of 'missing link' between body and mind, and lies, so to speak, between chorea and mania. As in the rare, hyperkinetic forms of *encephalitis lethargica,* and in all post-encephalitic patients over-excited by L-DOPA, patients with Tourette's syndrome, or 'Tourettism' from any other cause (strokes, cerebral tumours, intoxications or infections), seem to have an excess of excitor transmitters in the brain, especially the transmitter dopamine. And as lethargic Parkinsonian patients need more dopamine to arouse them, as my post-encephalitic patients were 'awakened' by the dopamine-precursor L-DOPA, so frenetic and Tourettic patients must have their dopamine lowered by a dopamine-antagonist, such as the drug haloperidol ('haldol').

On the other hand, there is not *just* a surfeit of dopamine in the Touretter's brain, as there is not *just* a deficiency of it in the Parkinsonian brain. There are also much subtler and more widespread changes, as one would expect in a disorder which may alter personality: there are countless subtle paths of abnormality which differ from patient to patient, and from day to day in any one patient. Haldol can be an answer to Tourette's, but neither it nor any other drug can be *the* answer, any more than L-DOPA is *the* answer to Parkinsonism. Complementary to any purely medicinal, or medical, approach there must also be an 'existential' approach: in particular, a sensitive understanding of action, art and play as being in essence healthy and free, and thus antagonistic to crude drives and impulsions, to 'the blind force of the subcortex' from which these patients suffer. The motionless Parkinsonian can sing and dance, and when he does so is completely free from his Parkinsonism; and when the galvanised Touretter sings, plays or acts, he in turn is completely liberated from his Tourette's. Here the 'I' vanquishes and reigns over the 'It'.

Between 1973 and his death in 1977, I enjoyed the privilege of corresponding with the great neuropsychologist A.R. Luria, and often sent him observations, and tapes, on Tourette's. In one of his last letters, he wrote to me: 'This is truly of tremendous importance. Any understanding of such a syndrome must vastly broaden our understanding of human nature in general...I know of no other syndrome of comparable interest.'

When I first saw Ray he was 24 years old, and almost incapacitated by multiple tics of extreme violence coming in volleys every few seconds. He had been subject to these since the age of four and severely stigmatised by the attention they aroused, though his high intelligence, his wit, his strength of character and sense of reality, enabled him to pass successfully through school and college, and to be valued and loved by a few friends and his wife. Since leaving college, however, he had been fired from a dozen jobs — always because of tics, never for incompetence — was continually in crises of one sort and another, usually caused by his impatience, his pugnacity, and his coarse, brilliant 'chutzpah' , and had found his marriage threatened by involuntary cries of 'Fuck me!' 'Shit!', and so on, which would burst from him at times of sexual excitement. He was (like many Touretters) remarkably musical, and could scarcely have survived — emotionally or economically — had he not been a weekend jazz drummer of real virtuosity, famous for his sudden and wild extemporisations, which would arise from a tic or a compulsive hitting of a drum and would instantly be made the nucleus of a wild and wonderful improvisation, so that the 'sudden intruder' would be turned to brilliant advantage. His Tourette's was also of advantage in various games, especially ping-pong, at which he excelled, partly in consequence of his abnormal quickness of reflex and reaction, but especially, again, because of 'improvisations', 'very sudden, nervous, *frivolous* shots' (in his own words), which were so unexpected and startling as to be virtually unanswerable. The only time he was free from tics was in post-coital quiescence or in sleep; or when he swam or sang or worked, evenly and rhythmically, and found 'a kinetic melody', a play, which was tension-free, tic-free and free.

Under an ebullient, eruptive, clownish surface, he was a deeply serious man — and a man in despair. He had never heard of the TSA (which, indeed, scarcely existed at the time), nor had he heard of haldol. He had diagnosed himself as having Tourette's after reading the article on 'Tics' in the *New York Times*. When I confirmed the diagnosis, and spoke of using haldol, he was excited but cautious. I made a test of haldol by injection, and he proved extraordinarily sensitive to it, becoming virtually tic-free for a period of two hours after I had administered no more than one-eighth of a milligram. After this auspicious trial, I started him on haldol, prescribing a dose of a quarter of a milligram three times a day.

He came back, the following week, with a black eye and a broken nose and said: 'So much for your fucking haldol'. Even this minute dose, he said, had thrown him off balance, interfered with his speed, his timing, his preternaturally quick reflexes. Like many Touretters, he was attracted to spinning things, and to revolving doors in particular, which he would dodge in and out of like lightning: he had lost this knack on the haldol, had mistimed his movements, and had been bashed on the nose. Further, many of his tics, far from disappearing, had simply become slow, and enormously extended: he might get 'transfixed in mid-tic', as he put it, and find himself in almost catatonic postures (Ferenczi once called catatonia the opposite of tics — and suggested these be called 'cataclonia'). He presented a picture, even on this minute dose, of marked Parkinsonism, dystonia, catatonia and psychomotor 'block': a reaction which seemed inauspicious in the extreme, suggesting, not insensitivity, but such over-sensitivity, such pathological sensitivity, that perhaps he could only be thrown from one extreme to another — from acceleration and Tourettism to catatonia and Parkinsonism, with no possibility of any happy medium.

He was understandably discouraged by this experience — and this thought — and also by another thought which he now expressed. 'Suppose you *could* take away the tics,' he said. 'What would be left? I consist of tics — there'd be nothing left.' He seemed, at least jokingly, to have little sense of his identity except as a ticqueur: he called himself 'the ticcer of Little Neck Parkway', and spoke of himself, in the third person, as 'witty ticcy Ray', adding that he was so prone to 'ticcy witticisms and witty ticcicisms' that he scarcely knew whether it was a gift or a curse. He said he could not imagine life without Tourette's, nor was he sure he would care for it.

I was strongly reminded, at this point, of what I had encountered in some of my post-encephalitic patients, who were inordinately sensitive to L-DOPA. I had nevertheless observed in their case that such extreme physiological sensitivities and instabilities might be transcended if it were possible for the patient to lead a rich and full life: that the 'existential' balance, or poise, of such a life might overcome a severe physiological imbalance. Feeling that Ray also had such possibilities in him, that, despite his own words, he was not incorrigibly centred on his own disease, in an exhibitionistic or narcissistic way, as is the case, alas, with a number of severe Touretters, who become 'professional patients' and lacerated, demonic exhibitionists of their disease, I suggested that we meet weekly for a period of three months. During this time we would try to imagine life without Tourette's; we would explore (if only in thought and feeling) how much life could offer, could offer *him*, without the perverse attractions and attentions of Tourette's; we would examine the role and economic importance of Tourette's to him, and he how he might get on without these. We would explore all this for three months — and then make another trial of haldol.

There followed three months of deep and patient exploration, in which (often against much resistance and spite and lack of faith in self and life) all sorts of healthy and human potentials came to light: potentials which had somehow survived twenty years of severe Tourette's and 'Touretty' life, hidden in the deepest and strongest core of the personality. This deep exploration was exciting and encouraging in itself and gave us, at least, a limited hope. What in fact happened exceeded all our expectations and showed itself to be no mere flash in the pan, but an enduring and permanent transformation of reactivity. For when I again tried Ray on haldol, in the same minute dose as before, he now found himself tic-free, but without significant ill-effects — and he has remained this way for the past nine years.

The effects of haldol, here, were 'miraculous' — but only became so when a miracle was allowed. Its initial effects were close to catastrophic: partly, no doubt, on a physiological basis; but also because any 'cure', or relinquishing of Tourette's, at this time would have been premature and economically impossible. Having had Tourette's since the age of four, Ray had no experience of any normal life: he was heavily dependent on his exotic disease and, not unnaturally, employed and exploited it in various ways. He had not been ready to give up his Tourette's and (I cannot help thinking) might never have been ready without those three months of intense preparation, of tremendously hard and concentrated deep analysis and thought.

The past nine years, on the whole, have been happy ones for Ray — a liberation beyond any possible expectation. After twenty years of being confined by Tourette's, and compelled to this and that by its crude physiology, he enjoys a spaciousness and freedom he would never have thought possible (or, at most during our analysis, only theoretically possible). His marriage is tender and stable — and he is now a father as well; he has many good friends, who love and value him as a person — and not simply as an accomplished Tourettic clown; he plays an important part in his local community; and he holds a responsible position in 'the City'. Yet problems remain: problems perhaps inseparable from having Tourette's — and haldol.

During his working hours, and working week, on Wall Street, Ray remains 'sober, solid, square' on haldol — this is how he describes his 'haldol self'. He is slow and deliberate in his movements and judgments, with none of the impatience, the impetuosity, he showed before haldol, but equally, none of the wild improvisations and inspirations. Even his dreams are different in quality: 'straight wish-fulfilment,' he says, 'with none of the elaborations, the extravaganzas, of Tourette's'. He is less sharp, less quick in repartee, no longer bubbling with witty tics or ticcy wit. He no longer enjoys or excels at ping-pong or other games; he no longer feels 'that urgent killer instinct, the instinct to win, to beat the other man'; he is less competitive, then, and also less playful; and he has lost the impulse, or the knack, of sudden 'frivolous' moves which take everyone by surprise. He has lost his obscenities, his coarse chutzpah, his spunk. He has come to feel, increasingly, that something is missing.

Most important, and disabling, because this was vital for him — as a means both of support and self-expression — he found that on haldol he was musically 'dull', average, competent, but lacking energy, enthusiasm, extravagance and joy. He no longer had tics or compulsive hitting of the drums — but he no longer had wild and creative surges.

As this pattern became clear to him, and after discussing it with me, Ray made a momentous decision: he would take haldol 'dutifully' throughout the working week, but would take himself off it, and 'let fly', at weekends. This he has done for the past three years. So now, there are two Rays — on and off haldol. There is the sober citizen, the calm deliberator, from Monday to Friday; and there is 'witty ticcy Ray', frivolous, frenetic, inspired, at weekends. It is a strange situation, as Ray is the first to admit:

Having Tourette's is wild, like being drunk all the while. Being on haldol is dull, makes one square and sober, and neither state is really free...You 'normals', who have the right transmitters in the right places at the right times in your brains, have all feelings, all styles, available all the time — gravity, levity, whatever is appropriate. We Touretters don't: we are forced into levity by our Tourette's and forced into gravity when we take haldol. *You* are free, you have a natural balance: we must make the best of an artificial balance.

Ray does make the best of it, and has a full life, despite Tourette's, despite haldol, despite the 'unfreedom' and the 'artifice', despite being deprived of that birthright of natural freedom which most of us enjoy. But he has been taught by his sickness and, in a way, he has transcended it. He would say, with Nietzsche: 'I have traversed many kinds of health, and keep traversing them...And as for sickness: are we not almost tempted to ask whether we could get along without it? Only great pain is the ultimate liberator of the spirit.' Paradoxically, Ray — deprived of natural, animal physiological health — has found a new health, a new freedom, through the vicissitudes he is subject to. He has achieved what Nietzsche liked to call 'The Great Health' — rare humour, valour, and resilience of spirit: despite being, or because he is, afflicted with Tourette's.

Ryle Remembered

Bernard Williams

Gilbert Ryle, who died in 1976, was for many years a professor of philosophy in Oxford. He was a man of genially military appearance, with a knobbly, cubic head; rather soldierly in speech and manner, he punctuated his sentences with an abrupt half-cough, highly characteristic of him and much imitated. He was an exceptionally nice man, friendly, generous, uncondescending, unpretentious, and, for a well-known professional philosopher, startlingly free from vanity. He affected an amiable philistinism, which to some degree was also genuine: 'no ear for tunes,' he was disposed to say, if music was mentioned. He was often amusing. He once said of a philosophically-disposed senior Tory politician that he stood like a light out to sea, firmly beckoning ships on to the rocks.

He gave very sensible advice, telling his pupils, for instance, not to do a PhD unless they had to, since it was 'better to write a short good book later than a bad long book earlier'. He also gave excellent advice in philosophy, and communicated some good philosophical habits. His example was borne along on a certain anti-theoretical breeziness, but he showed philosophy to be a serious subject, and he conveyed a sound contempt for 'isms', schools, and mechanical party loyalties. He told a story, which he claimed to be true — and he was a truthful man — to the effect that when he had lectured in Germany after the war, a young man came up and said: 'Doctor Ryle, I admired your lecture, and should like to join your school: unfortunately I am a Kantian.'

I first encountered Ryle myself as a student, around the time that he published his major book *The Concept of Mind* in 1950. The book had considerable influence, creating both a style and a focus of discussion. It was a professedly anti-Cartesian tract, aimed at 'the ghost in the machine', and against theories which represented the mental life as a hidden immaterial process duplicating or paralleling observable doings (as Ryle was disposed to put it). In pushing against such models, it inclined, to put it mildly, in a behaviourist direction. It seemed to suggest that there was no conscious inner life at all. This impression was not intended by Ryle, and was denied by him, but it was encouraged both by the general style of the argument and by the briskly commonsensical tone in which the mental life was treated. Along with the philosophical aim of reducing, so far as possible, the hidden inner to the obvious outer, Ryle seemed to have a more general project of replacing the less workaday with the more workaday.

Ryle had started out, in the late 1920s, with an interest in Phenomenology. He even wrote a quite favourable review of Heidegger's *Sein und Zeit* when it first appeared. There are historical connections between these interests and some features of *The Concept of Mind,* but by the time he wrote that book his methods had become 'linguistic', and his style one of those that constituted what has been called 'linguistic philosophy'. He dealt in uses of words, and his arguments rested heavily on considerations of what did and did not make sense. Since he wrote in English, it was a question of what did and did not make sense in English, but he always dissociated himself from the minute interest in fine points of usage which some of his colleagues displayed. He claimed that any sound argument of the kind that he used reached below the level of a particular natural language, and could be translated. *The Concept of Mind* has indeed experienced, and perhaps survived, translation into other languages, most recently — very recently — into French.

The idea that the results transcended any local language was expressed in *The Concept of Mind* in terms of a notion of *categories,* which allowed Ryle to say that certain terms stood for dispositions, or processes, or occurrences, and so forth; and he thought that the errors underlying the dualistic view of mind stemmed in good part from what he called 'category mistakes' — in particular, from a tendency to interpret as a hidden or inner occurrence something that was correctly understood as an overt or behavioural disposition. Many of Ryle's results took the form of allocations of concepts to categories, a style of conclusion memorably parodied by a student at the time in the dictum: 'shop-lifting is not a feat of strength.'

In later years, Ryle became suspicious of the category machinery, feeling, as he was disposed to feel with any technical machinery, that it created its own problems. By the time he wrote the pieces collected in this volume,[1] he had largely given it up. This book gathers together seven papers and one review all concerned with the

---

[1] *On Thinking,* edited by Konstantin Kolenda (Basil Blackwell, 1979).

topic of thinking, and also a fragment about another philosopher's views of Wittgenstein. Three of the papers have not been published before; all the papers form part of the work Ryle had done for a book on thinking which he was planning when he died.

The central question, variously and often obliquely approached, is one that he felt that he had left unsolved in *The Concept of Mind*: how to characterise that sort of thinking which consists in silent meditation or reflection, the activity, as Ryle constantly puts it, of Rodin's *Penseur*. *The Concept of Mind* had effectively attacked any idea that mental activity typically takes such a form, or that intelligent action is action monitored by such an internal process. The book gave no account, however, of what that activity itself might be, and indeed left little room for its existence. In pursuit of this question, Ryle takes up such subjects as talking to oneself, teaching oneself, and thinking as soliloquy.

The apparatus of categories did earlier provide some rationale, if an obscure and insecure one, for the linguistic arguments. If one thinks that there is a basic, universal framework of categories, then it is a sensible procedure, by examining language, to try to relate various concepts to that framework. In the absence of that apparatus, however, Ryle's linguistic arguments are scarcely tied to anything, and it is a persistent failing of these essays that it is quite unclear why given linguistic considerations are supposed to count for particular philosophical conclusions. Many of the arguments here fail, because they rest on no coherent conception of the relation between mental phenomena and the language that describes them.

Thus, supporting a conclusion of Zeno Vendler's (a conclusion contrary to a long philosophical tradition) that knowledge is not a kind of belief — for example, true and well-founded belief — Ryle cites the fact that one can know what..., where..., whether...etc, but one cannot believe what...etc. But this does not prove anything at all. Leaving aside the important area of practical knowledge — and the tradition has not supposed that practical knowledge is a species of belief — the answer to Ryle's point will simply be that if someone knows, for instance, who stole the jewels, then he knows of some person that that person stole the jewels: that is to say, he *knows that* something, and this knowledge may indeed be a species of belief. The grammars of 'know' and 'believe' are indeed different, but more than that is needed to lead one to this sort of conclusion about knowledge and belief.

Other arguments in the book are just too blunt and brisk. One of the more startling conclusions that Ryle claims is that it makes no sense to assert or deny that someone thinks *in* English, say, or French — or *in* words, come to that. If that is a truth, it is a surprising one. But the only argument Ryle offers, so far as I can see, is that an orator considering words for a speech, or a translator for a translation, does not think 'in' the words he is considering for his purpose, but thinks about them. No general conclusion can follow from that: he may think about those words *in* other words. There is probably a truth lurking in what Ryle says, but his considerations do not bring it to light.

Ryle believed in arguments in philosophy. The tiny fragment about Wittgenstein interestingly, and convincingly, makes out that Wittgenstein also did so, though it has been said that in his later work he did not (Wittgenstein seems sometimes to say it himself). Ryle shared also with Wittgenstein, and no doubt in part derived from him, certain other things. One was the important belief that the philosophy of mind had to get beyond both dualism and behaviourism: in these essays Ryle can be seen explicitly trying to do that, as he had not successfully done in *The Concept of Mind*.

Another thing he shared was a hatred, not of argument, but of philosophical theory. This distrust of theory was typical of much linguistic philosophy of the 1950s; with it there went a rejection of the idea that philosophy could be continuous with theoretical interests of the sciences. Ryle was open to many new philosophical ideas, but these limiting conceptions he sustained into a later time. When he found a disposition to theorise joined to an admiration for Cartesian notions of innate knowledge, every hackle was raised, and the only intemperate piece here is that in which, disagreeing now with Vendler, he attacks Chomsky for his well-known view that a child's acquisition of language can be explained only by postulating a determinate innate mechanism for acquiring it, a mechanism which, Chomsky thinks, it is appropriate to call innate knowledge. It is a deep idea, and a powerful and illuminating debate has occurred about it. It is sad to find Ryle bluffly dismissing the whole business with a philistine diagnosis, clearly wrong, of why Chomsky thought that there was anything in it.

Ryle had a very distinctive style, marked by long lists of words, particularly adverbs, and by an epigrammatic turn. He seems to have developed the style without reflection, but he became very conscious of himself as a stylist, and the mannerisms eventually took over, and carried him at times beyond the bounds of self-parody. The most exaggerated example here is probably the first piece, in which he writes, for instance:

If *Le Penseur* is trying to compose a melody, then he is very likely to be humming notes and sequences of notes, aloud, under his breath or in his head — not just humming them, of course, but humming them experimentally, suspiciously, cancellingly, rehearsingly, recapitulatingly, and so on. These very notes and note sequences that he hums composingly, he might, by chance, have hummed gramophonically and with his mind on something else. Or if *Le Penseur* is trying to render an English poem into French, while he is unlikely to be humming notes and note-sequences, he is likely instead to be murmuring under his breath or in his head, French words or phrases, murmuring them, of course, experimentally, suspiciously, cancellingly, rehearsingly, recapitulatingly...

The mannerisms seem to have provided a substitute for the theoretical backing which he was so reluctant to give his arguments. He taught his pupils, in the most honourable and impressive way, to sift argument from rhetoric, but his own philosophy came increasingly to depend on an idiosyncratic rhetoric. Having given up the only account he had of the relations between linguistic observation and philosophical subject-matter, he was left only with common-sense and the resources of a style: a style which, to some extent, in its consciously dry jokes, expressed him, but which, under pressure of what it had to provide, was driven at the extreme to a kind of compulsive incantation which was far from the nature of this clipped, controlled man.

I knew Gilbert Ryle quite well, and liked him very much. As many others do, I owe him a lot, both personally and intellectually. I am afraid that those who did not know him, although they will get an overpowering sense of a certain style, will not find the real quality of his intellectual presence in these mannered, empty and unconvincing essays. They are late work, and he left better and perhaps more lasting material in pages of *The Concept of Mind* and in earlier papers. But it may be that, more generally, it was the activity rather than the product that mattered. I do not think that that would have surprised or upset him.

Kripke versus Kant

Richard Rorty

When these lectures[1] were first published eight years ago (in a collection), they stood analytic philosophy on its ear. Everybody was either furious, or exhilarated, or thoroughly perplexed. No one was indifferent. This welcome republication in a separate volume (with a helpful new preface, but no substantive changes) provides a chance to look back at a modern classic, and to say something about why it was found so shocking and liberating.

Since Kant, philosophers have prided themselves on transcending the 'naive realism' of Aristotle and of common sense. On this naive view, there is a right way of describing things, corresponding to how they are in themselves, to their real essences. Scientists, philosophers like to say, are especially prone to adopt this unreflective view. They think they are discovering the secrets of nature, but philosophers know that they are really constituting objects by synthesising the manifold of intuition, or predicting the occurrence of sensations, or wielding instruments to cope with the flux of experience, or something equally pragmatic and anthropocentric. This condescending attitude towards common sense, Aristotle and science has been shared by people as far apart as Russell and Bergson, Whitehead and Husserl, James and Nietzsche, Carnap and Cassirer.

Until Kripke came along, almost the only exceptions to this consensus were the Catholics and the Marxists. Between the two Vatican Councils, neo-Thomists tried to explain that the 'naive' Aristotelian view was the sound intuitive belief of the common man, and that Cartesian subjectivism, Kantian transcendental idealism and positivistic empiricism were successively more virulent forms of a mad modern heresy. But nobody listened, and after the *aggiornamento* the neo-Thomists pretty well gave up. Old-time Marxists, who had cut their teeth on Lenin's *Materialism and Empirio-Criticism*, used to argue that Russell was just the latest English version of the 'bourgeois formalism' which Hegel had diagnosed in Kant. But nobody listened to them either, and after the discovery of the young, humanist, pragmatist Marx they, too,

---

[1] Saul Kripke, *Naming and Necessity* (Basil Blackwell, 1980).

gave up. Just when it seemed that the dialectic which Kant began had culminated in universal acceptance of the relaxed pragmatism of Wittgenstein and Quine, Kripke exploded his bomb.

In a hundred pages of sinewy colloquial prose, Kripke offered a realistic, anti-Kantian, anti-pragmatist way of treating the concepts of 'meaning', 'reference' and 'truth' which Frege and Russell had treated in a Kantian way. The Kantian picture is that we decide what counts as an 'object' by putting ideas together. We build a world inside our minds by tying concepts together so as to package sensations more conveniently. Frege and Russell updated this picture by handing the mind over, with a shrug, to empirical psychology and putting the point in terms of language — talking about words instead of ideas. In Russell's view, names are shorthand for descriptions — lists of the qualities which we have decided to use to identify occasions on which we shall use a name. Russell took his cue from Frege's distinction between a term's meaning and its reference, a distinction between such a list of qualities and the portions of the world to which the term is correctly applied. Meaning, Frege claimed, determines reference. This claim is uncontroversial if you think of the world as an undifferentiated manifold waiting for us to structure it. But, as Marxists and neo-Thomists insist, such a view smacks of idealism. It leads fairly quickly to the pragmatist view that science, and human inquiry generally, makes truth rather than finds it — that we did not discover sub-atomic particles, but rather discovered that it was helpful to package the flux under such labels as 'positron'.

Philosophers raised on Frege and Russell are so habituated to this Kantian way of thinking that the very idea that some properties of a thing are necessary ones — properties a thing could not lack while remaining the same thing — has seemed merely a Gothic curiosity, the last enchantment of the Middle Ages. It has seemed clear that if you describe Aristotle as 'the author of the *Metaphysics*', then it is essential to him that he was literate and accidental that he was male, whereas if you describe him as the father of Nicomachus the converse will be true. Essentiality and necessity had seemed obviously relative to one's choice of description, rather than a matter of what some particular hunk of space-time *had* to be like. There is something giddy and intoxicating about this Kantian freedom to redescribe, and thus to create new essences, new necessities, new structures. Philosophers of language in the Frege-Russell-Quine tradition share with Fichte

the thought that we make worlds as we make poems and pictures —
a thought which finds full expression in Nelson Goodman's recent
Ways of Worldmaking.

Kripke tries to sober us up by denying that meaning determines
reference. Rather, we name things by confronting them and
baptising them, not by creating them out of a list of qualities.
Names are not, *pace* Russell, shorthand for such lists. They are not
abbreviations for descriptions, but (in Kripke's coinage) 'rigid
designators' — that is, they would name the same things in any
possible world, including worlds in which their bearers did not have
the properties we, in this world, use to identify them. The non-
philosopher can hardly imagine how shocking these Kripkean
claims sounded. Analytic philosophers had been brought up to
believe that semantics was constituted as 'first philosophy' (and
had thus become the glory of our century) precisely by accepting
Frege's and Russell's way of looking at things — just as
metaphysics had once been constituted as 'first philosophy' by
accepting Aristotle's (and had thus become the putative glory of the
13th century). To have the brightest young philosopher of language
denounce not merely the details of Russell's Theory of Descriptions
but the Kantian world-view which that theory articulated was like
having a newly-elected Pope denounce the Incarnation. The whole
idea of what it was to be an analytic philosopher, what it was to be
sophisticated about the relation of thought to the world, began to
totter. For a moment, nobody could quite believe that a leading
modal logician should seriously commend the Aristotelian way of
looking at things. Perhaps it was merely affected Gothicising?

Kripke was, however, entirely serious. *Naming and Necessity*
lays out a way of thinking about the relation between language and
the world which permits just as formal and rigorous a treatment of
notions like 'meaning', 'truth' and 'reference' as had Russell's and
Frege's. Nobody would have believed that the neatness — what
Kripke calls 'the marvellous internal coherence' — of Frege-Russell
semantics could be duplicated after everything was turned upside
down. But Kripke showed how to do it, and now philosophers are
busily rewriting all of semantics (and a good deal of epistemology)
in Kripkean terms. The basic idea which Kripke develops is that we
pick out the bearers for proper names like 'Aristotle' and
'Brezhnev', or common names like 'gold' or 'positron', by saying
'We'll call *that* "X",' rather than by saying: 'We'll call something
"X" if it meets the following criteria...' The coarseness and

brutality of this sort of semantics can only be appreciated by those who have lived in lotus-land, exulting in their Kantian-Goodmanian freedom to create worlds. Kripke showed that one could be coarse about how language works while being delicate and polished in the theory that spells out the details.

It would be impossible, in this space, to exhibit just how *Naming and Necessity* did this. Instead, it might be well to ask: now that we know that Arsitotle as well as Kant can be successfully updated, how are we supposed to decide between them? How do we choose between the attractions of the Gothic and the modern, between naive realism and quasi-idealism? Sometimes Kripke suggests that there are simple arguments which show he is right — as when he urges that no Russell-like account can pick out a unique bearer for a proper name. But his opponents could easily give up Russell's claim that *uniqueness* is required, and urge that a Russellian account in terms of descriptions need merely pick out a (possibly non-unique) referent which can be agreed on for present conversational purposes. This pragmatical cop-out would leave the argument up in the air. Kripke's usual strategy, however, is not to look for knock-down arguments. Instead, he appeals to the greater 'intuitive' appeal of his view. He asks his reader to cleave to untutored intuition and resist the false sophistication of the schools.

It has even been suggested in the literature, that though a notion of necessity may have some sort of intuition behind it...this notion (of a distinction between necessary and contingent properties) is just a doctrine made up by some bad philosopher, who (I guess) didn't realise that there are several ways of referring to the same thing...It is very far from being true that this idea [that a property can meaningfully be held to be essential or accidental to an object independently of its description] is a notion which has no intuitive content, which means nothing to the ordinary man. Suppose that someone said, pointing to Nixon. 'That's the guy who might have lost.' Someone else says 'Oh no, if you describe him as the winner, then it's not true that he might have lost.' Now which one is being the philosopher here, the unintuitive man? It seems to me obviously to be the second. The second man has a philosophical theory. The first man would say, and with great conviction. 'Well, of course, the winner of the election *might have been someone else*...So, such terms as ''the winner'' or ''the loser'' don't designate the same objects in all possible worlds. On the other hand, the term ''Nixon'' is just the *name* of *this man*.'

But do ordinary men really have views about what they would call by what name in counterfactual situations — situations in which the various qualities are shifted about the various space-time points in all sorts of funny ways? Do they have 'a direct intuition of the rigidity of names, exhibited in our understanding of the truth conditions of particular sentences' (page 14)? Suppose 'Aristotle' was the name of an unreflective scribe who copied out the various treatises making up what we call 'the Aristotelian corpus', each treatise having been composed by a different member of a committee, only one of whom was also named 'Aristotle'. What, intuitive reader, are the truth-conditions of 'Aristotle was less religious than Plato'? Philosophers of language have to supply truth-conditions in such puzzle-cases; it is their job. But it is not clear that the man in the street is going to be of much help to either side in the controversy.

Still, even if we have no intuitions about truth-conditions in weird counterfactual situations, maybe we do have intuitions about realism v. idealism, Aristotle v. Kant? Or is this a matter for the cultivated taste of those who have savoured both? Is the success of Kant among practically everybody from Schiller to Goodman a matter of his seductive appeal to our more irresponsible impulses? Or does Kant have some sturdy intuitions on his side too? If semantics really is (as Michael Dummett has claimed) 'first philosophy', should we try desperately to make the right decision between Russell and Kripke, so as to know whether it will be necessary to reconstruct the rest of philosophy and culture? Modern thought on everything from politics to literature to religion is, after all, shot through with Kantian assumptions. Maybe a thorough house-cleaning is in order? Can we just shrug the quarrel between Kripke and the Frege-Russell-Quine tradition off as a 'technical' issue, or is there more to it?

On the narrow 'technical' ground of how to explicate concepts like 'meaning' and 'reference', the Russell-Kripke issue is probably a stand-off. One can play it either way, and develop a system from either starting-point with equal completeness and elegance. In either case, the budget of paradoxes will be about equally long, though much will depend upon what one has been brought up to find paradoxical. On the slightly larger ground of reflection on the nature of science, and of inquiry generally, it is hard to see that the new possibilities within semantics change the traditional stand-off between the pragmatist who says, 'Talking about positrons gets us what we want,' and the realist who says: 'There *really are* positrons.' The same goes for the more sophisticated stand-off between the pragmatist claim that 'are really there' just *means* 'talk about it gets us what we want' and those who think that there is more to reality than that. On still larger questions, it is very doubtful indeed that the Kantian ideas which are taken for granted in our culture are going to be *refuted* by anything that philosophy professors do. The senses in which philosophy is 'queen of sciences' and in which semantics is 'first philosophy' are not strong enough to permit any straightforward deductions from new semantical theories to consequences for culture as a whole.

Nor, of course, need Kripke claim that such deductions are possible. It is enough for his purposes in this book to have pointed semantics in a new direction. Still, the connection between traditional Russell-Frege semantics and the larger world-picture it adumbrates leads one to reflect on the relation of developments in 'technical' philosophy to philosophy's larger role. Such reflection suggests that Kripke may have demoted philosophy of language in the course of revolutionising it. As long as we took for granted Kant's notion that we structure the world by representing it, the study of the nature of representation (of Mind in the 19th century, of Language in this century) took pride of place. For in studying the activity of representation philosophy takes itself to discover 'formal', 'conceptual', 'structural' truths — truths higher and purer than those produced by science. If we lose our grip on the Kantian picture, this structure-content distinction begins to evaporate. So does the notion of philosophy as the armchair study of the nature of representation. So, *a fortiori*, does semantics as the study of how language relates to the world. By rediscovering (or, as disgruntled Kantians would say, by reinventing) 'metaphysical necessity', as opposed to Kant-Russell description-relative 'epistemic necessity', Kripke has revoked the charter of modern philosophy.

Further, by showing that semantics need not be committed to Kant — that one can have a philosophy of language which plays it the other way — he has made it easier to dismiss the question of which way to play it as 'merely technical'. This attitude is encouraged if one reads the attempts in the philosophical journals to resolve conundrums such as the one about Aristotle set out above — attempts which make irresistible the epithet 'decadent scholasticism'. A similar insouciance is encouraged by neo-Quinean philosophers of language like Donald Davidson, who object to 'building-block' approaches of either the Russellian or the

Kripkean sort. Davidsonian 'holistic' semantics, which may emerge as *tertius gaudens,* presents itself as an empirical theory of linguistic behaviour, not as a successor subject to Kantian epistemology. It eschews theories of how language either structures *or* copies the world. Given all these ways in which the old consensus is breaking up, 'philosophy of language' is losing the ideological overtones it once shared with 'linguistic philosophy'. It may become the sort of academic speciality which neither wants nor needs links with, or readers in, the larger world.

Perhaps, however, such speculations are premature. At the moment, everybody is waiting for Kripke to drop the other shoe, to fill us in on his new way of seeing things, beyond the few tantalising details revealed in *Naming and Necessity*. That work resembles Wittgenstein's *Tractatus* in hinting at a larger context and higher motives. Since Kripke changed the tone of analytic philosophy with ideas formulated before his 25th year (see page 3), he may well have surprises in store.

Educating the Planet

Frank Kermode

It is a commonplace that among I.A. Richards's first achievements was a modern defence of poetry. In the years following the Great War, he saw the world as entering an unprecedented historical crisis. He believed that the collapse of the old 'Magical View' of the world had left us in a condition of bewilderment, of deep privation, of affective destitution. People (I think he supposed them to be a minority) who were not content to 'live by warmth, food, fighting, drink and sex alone' must 'require other satisfactions': but the sources of such satisfactions had been stopped by the advance of knowledge. As throughout his life, he saw in trouble and disorder an immediate invitation to action, though, as at first conceived, this action was of a subtle kind, hardly to be distinguished from contemplation. 'A sense of desolation, of uncertainty, of futility, of the groundlessness of aspirations, of the vanity of endeavour, and a thirst for a life-giving water which seems suddenly to have failed, are the signs in consciousness of this necessary reorganisation of our lives.' What distinguishes this sentence from similar exclamations of dismay, which would not be hard to find in the literature of the period, is that it ends with the affirmation of a need to act. The rest of it owes most to Eliot's *Waste Land*, as Richards acknowledged in a footnote. He valued the poem, not only as an exhibition of disorder and desolation, but as affording us means to contemplate them in a valuable way; it was modern, belonging to a world that had outlived the Magical View; but it offered what must take the place of that view if our psychological privations were to be ended.

In this poem, Eliot had achieved 'a complete severance between his poetry and all belief' and that is what modern poetry must do. Eliot mildly objected to this statement, but I doubt if Richards was much bothered. He confided in poems rather than poets, as we see from his version of Shelley's pronouncement: '*Poems* are the unacknowledged legis*lation* of mankind.' But in the second edition of *Science and Poetry* he took the opportunity of explaining himself, and extended that already famous footnote. *The Waste Land,* he claimed, 'realised what might otherwise have remained a speculative possibility ... by finding a new order through the contemplation and exhibition of disorder'. The poem was a simultaneous image of both — a typical Richards formula, for he liked to hold antinomies in a single thought, to speak, for example, of the 'interinanimation' of separate words, and of what he came later to call 'complementarities'. But the immediate point is that this difficult modern poem was recommended as an example of the 'necessary reorganisation'.

Thus did Richards help to establish Eliot's poem as the *livre de chevet* of a generation of educated readers. He did more: for when he extended the note, Richards added to it some lines, now but not then very familiar, from Conrad's *Lord Jim*. 'The way is to the destructive element submit yourself... So if you ask me how to be? In the destructive element immerse ... that was the way.' This is an instance of his uncanny aptness in quotation: the way to read *The Waste Land*, and the way to live in the new, more hostile world, is not to try to climb out, but to let the deep, deep sea keep you up. The second edition of *Science and Poetry* had not been out a year before Stephen Spender entitled his book on modern writers and belief (or unbelief) *The Destructive Element*, describing Richards's note as 'a focal point from which diverge rays towards past and future'. Certainly Conrad's words give some insight into Richards's future dealings with the destructive world.

When he wrote this longer footnote, he had been engaged on his modern defence of poetry for more than a decade. His ideas, widely circulated, did not go unopposed. Eliot himself, reviewing *Science and Poetry*, noted 'a certain discrepancy between the size of [the author's] problems and the size of his solutions'. 'Mr Richards,' he said, 'is apt to ask a supra-scientific question and to give a merely scientific answer.' This is an objection often made, in one form or another, to Richards's procedures, and I believe it to be, in the end, false. The response of the young was less critical. Christopher Isherwood went as an undergraduate to Richards's lectures and hailed him as 'the prophet we have been waiting for ... To us, he was infinitely more than a brilliantly new literary critic; he was our guide, our evangelist, who revealed to us, in a succession of astounding lightning flashes, the entire expanse of the modern world.' For all its extravagance, that strikes me as a truer response. Richards was much more a prophet than a scientist.

The immediate, but by no means the only, consequence of the early prophecies had been to entrust to poets and their readers an

unexpectedly central responsibility for dealing with the world crisis.
A great borrower, Richards took from the neurologist Henry Head
the notion of 'vigilance' — 'what happens in a given stimulus
situation varies with the vigilance of the appropriate portion of the
nervous system' — and explained the extraordinary availability of
experience to the poet, and his power to organise that experience,
as the consequences of his superior vigilance. The notion is, in
literary terms, Romantic, and was stated in other language by
Wordsworth and Coleridge. What Richards added to it was his
conviction that only in such poetic vigilance could we find a means
to construct a new world, difficult but inhabitable. And like
Hölderlin he called upon the people (or the best of them) to assist
the poet in this work. He is again in the native Romantic tradition
when he insists that the poet is possessed of 'normality'. 'To be
normal is to be a standard, but not, as things are and are likely to
remain, an average.' The object of his new methods of teaching
poetry was simply to make others as vigilant as poets, so that the
gap between the average and the standard might be progressively
closed. The whole plan was conceived as rational, and as supported
by modern psychology and physiology.

That is why he could be accused of going in for science and so
giving comfort to an enemy. And of course it was always part of his
plan that a new poetry and a new criticism should benefit by the
very expansion of knowledge that had helped to bring about the
world crisis. Just as he had intended, when he decided to be a
psychoanalyst, to take a medical degree, so he prepared himself for
the task he actually undertook by immersing himself in psychology,
physiology and philosophy. In doing so, he drew copiously on
the resources of Cambridge at that time. That does not mean
he agreed with everything he was told. With G.E. Moore, for
example, he had what he might later have called a relationship
of complementarity: 'I feel like an obverse of him. Where there's
a hole in him there's a bulge in me.' 'Moore was vocally convinced that few indeed could possibly *mean* what they *said*; I was
silently persuaded that they could not possibly *say* what they
mean.' He held Wittgenstein in only moderate awe. Russell he
dismissed in a brisk appendix to *The Meaning of Meaning,* though
he had from time to time to repeat and revise his reasons for doing
so.

However, mention of *The Meaning of Meaning* is a reminder
that in his first and seminal book (for *The Meaning of Meaning*

really is the foundation of nearly all Richards's later work) he had as collaborator C.K. Ogden, a walking encyclopedia of philosophy and science. The union of prophet and polymath was not only extremely productive, but, as Richards often remarked, great fun. Never was a book of such gravity written in such high spirits. The opinions of the great go down like skittles. 'There's something insipid about agreeing with an author,' said Richards long afterwards, 'especially when you're young. You feel it's your business to be *other*.' He could give a precise and interesting date for the conception of the book: Armistice Day, 11 November 1918. That day he had watched drunken medical students sacking Ogden's shop in King's Parade; they met in the evening to see if they could identify any of the marauders. In the small hours they had a long conversation on the stairs under the flare of an aged bat-wing gas-jet. This was either outside Richards's room in Free School Lane or outside Ogden's attic above Mac Fisheries in Petty Cury: in two different accounts Richards specifies both places. By the time they parted they had roughed out *The Meaning of Meaning,* Ogden was at the time editing a weekly paper, *The Cambridge Magazine.* Its circulation rose to 25,000 and the only way he could solve the paper shortage was to buy books in bulk and pulp them — not, however, before he had looked through them.

Ogden believed in being reasonable if he could find a reasonable auditor ('Will you change your mind if I convince you?' he would ask). Richards found in him 'a central clarifying insistence, a flame of curiosity and impatience, a disdain for the acquiescence of sloth, a trust in mind' which spoke to the same qualities, differently but complementarily compounded, in himself. The collaboration seems to have been very intimate, 'It's a most extraordinary experience, finding you can agree with someone,' said Richards years afterwards. 'Decades later it wasn't the case that we could understand one another *at all*.' The book they called *The Beadig of Beadig* because of the heavy colds they suffered during its composition was, for all its laborious and combative argumentation, an entertainment. Ogden, in fact, seems to have regarded it as a way of relaxing from his work on the translation of Wittgenstein's *Tractatus* and Vaihinger's *Philosophy of 'As If'.* But it was an indispensable prelude to the subsequent careers of both authors; and it belonged firmly to the Cambridge of the immediate post-war years.

And indeed at this time Cambridge was virtually the whole

world. Some day, I hope, we shall be told more about the intellectual horizons of the early Richards — not only about the precise nature of his collaboration with Ogden, and his beneficent mutual misunderstanding with Moore, but also about his dealings with the psychologists and with Cornford. The four remarkable books of the Twenties were all very Cambridge books. Nevertheless they were read everywhere, and changed attitudes to poetry and criticism throughout the English-speaking world.

It is a curious fact that they were also misunderstood everywhere. W.H.N. Hotopf, author of the most serious book yet written on Richards, notes with astonishment that of all the eminent philosophers and critics who have written on Richards there are very few who 'do not betray some fairly important misunderstanding' of his position.[1] What happened in the world at large, I think, was that some notion of the *Principles* got through, but with much loss of detail and some general distortion. The reasons are doubtless many: careless reading, impatience with the psychology and linguistics, a tendency also on the part of the writer to say too many things in too many ways, and to say them, sometimes, obscurely. But to demand minute consistency and a slow clear progress of argument is to ask the wrong gift of Richards, and to misunderstand his prophetic role. What mattered was the prior conviction of the value of poetry and the importance of language, and of the teachability of right reading. The utilitarian-psychologistic theories were instruments that lay to hand.

It was his fate, then, to be both influential and misunderstood, in Cambridge as elsewhere. Though he was a don for most of his life, Richards was not, I think, a very academic man, and the partial institutionalisation of his method in the English Tripos could not have satisfied him. His unease is demonstrated in the continual recurrence of his worry about correctness in interpretation. As is well-known, he was committed to new and heretical views about meaning in poetry, discounting the simple intentionalist position and placing a high value on ambiguity. Where the conventional pedant found in poetry instances of 'incorrectness' or lack of clarity, Richards saw 'interinanimation,' 'a movement among meanings'. All discourse, he maintained, is 'over-determined', and ambiguity is 'the indispensable means of most of our important utterances.' Professor Kittredge, for example, believed that good

---

[1] *Language, Thought and Comprehension: A Case of the Writings of I.A. Richards* (Routledge & Kegan Paul, 1965).

writing was writing that left the reader with no need to go in for 'inference and guesswork': Professor Richards asked what interpretation could be if it *wasn't* inference and guesswork.

But he was very clear that this didn't mean you could say anything you liked about a poem. It is possible to be wrong. Hence the list, in *Practical Criticism*, of the ten 'chief difficulties' (more properly, causes of error) in criticism; hence the denunciation, in the Clark Lectures he gave almost half a century later, of what he vehemently labelled 'omnipossibilism'. And in between he had often returned to the topic. 'Whatever accounts are offered to a reader must leave him — in a very deep sense — free to choose... This is not ... any general licence to readers to differ as they please... For this deep freedom in reading is made possible only by the widest surface conformities.' I think he was troubled, in later years, by demands for a freedom that defied such a consensus. While he and Ogden were at work on *The Meaning of Meaning*, they looked at Saussure's *Cours de Linguistique Générale*, which had appeared only a few years before, but dismissed it in a page or two. *La langue,* they argued, was a useless abstraction; the project for a semiology, though 'a very notable attempt in the right direction', makes a fatal division between signs and what signs stand for: thus it 'was from the beginning cut off from any contact with scientific methods of verification'. At about the same time, the Russian Formalists were active: but they were soon suppressed, and perhaps news of them did not reach Cambridge.

In the Sixties, however, both Saussure and the Formalists made a long-delayed and rather spectacular reappearance on the scene, and the consequences have been many, and often omnipossibilistic. Richards gave a characteristically warm though not unqualified welcome to Jakobson's experiments in poetic analysis, but the new libertarian semiologists of France and America cannot have pleased him. He believed steadfastly that there were such things as wrong readings. And of course he also believed that one could progressively acquire competence in reading, that error could be corrected. The question arises: who shall distinguish right from wrong? And his answer, inevitably, was: those who have acquired competence, the teachers. Thus the belief in the possibility of corrigible error heads directly to a belief in the need for institutions of criticism.

Yet it seems clear that he did not greatly care for such institutions. Of the English School he has few good words to say.

'It's hard on the poets to make everybody study them like this . . . As far as I can see, making it into an academic subject has not increased the amount of *enjoyment* taken in the poems.' The senior members of the critical institution, participants in the consensual establishment of right reading, must perforce be scholars. And although he had a great respect for scholarship, Richards was dismayed by its side-effects. It prevents us 'from supplying our greatest need — teachers able to help humanity to remain humane'.

In the early Thirties, times were changing, and so was Richards, but this need did not change, and the defence of poetry continued. One of the doctrines of *Principles* is that the effect of good readings, of equilibrated impulses, achieved poise, is cumulative: we are talking not about discrete, self-sufficient Paterian moments, but about provision for the future, in the form of what he later called 'feedforward'. Certainly his own experience confirmed the doctrine: directions changed, horizons widened, Richards would 'cross the tracks' into educational enterprises improper to Cambridge. But in a sense he did not change, only built on his past. *Coleridge on Imagination*, published in 1934 when his wider enterprises were already well started, shows no diminution in his hopes for a central and humane criticism of poetry. It is in the 'searchings for meanings of a certain sort', he says, that the being of a poem consists; and that search is the best response to the vast alterations in consciousness that beset us, our only way of recovering 'a less relaxed, a less adventitious order for the mind'. It is the point of *Science and Poetry*, reinforced by an understanding of Coleridge as the herald of the revolution in consciousness. To attack science, he says, is a futile error, a 'myth reflecting our unease'. The point is to match and master the new human world, as science does the physical world. And the task still falls to the poet. When all knowledge is either myth or without meaning, he becomes responsible for the very principle of human order. The writing and reading of the necessary new poetry is arduous, but it must be done.

It is here, near the end of his first defence of poetry, that Richards comes closest to Shelley. 'Poetry acts in a diviner manner,' says Shelley. 'It awakens and enlarges the mind itself by rendering it the receptacle of a thousand unapprehended combinations of thought.' And Richards: 'Because the universe as it is known to us is a fabric whose forms, as we alone can know them, have arisen through and in reflection; and because that reflection, whether made by the intellect in science or by "the whole soul of man" in poetry, has developed through language ... the study of the modes of language becomes ... the most fundamental and exhaustive of all inquiries. It is no preliminary or preparation for other profounder studies ... The very formation of the objects which these studies propose to examine takes place through the processes ... by which the words they use acquire meanings.'

These words look back to work already done, and forward to a different future. But we may hear in them a note of exaltation that will sound strange to anyone who thinks about the teaching of poetry in modern universities. Perhaps we have lost confidence in the poets, as Richards himself partly did. Certainly most of us are not convinced that he was right when he said, in *Coleridge*, that 'critics in the future must have a theoretical equipment of a kind which has not been felt to be necessary in the past.' In the Thirties, there was an automatic reflex of opposition to the New Criticism, of which he was the chief patron; and any other *nouvelle critique* must expect a largely contemptuous and unexamined rejection now. Richards saw it happening. Like the Old Testament prophets he liked to quote in his epigraphs — on the whole a disappointed body of men — he found us duller of apprehension and more apt to backslide than he had hoped. Interpretation was teachable: but the institution, with its narrowly conceived and conservative view of scholarship, came between the teacher and the taught.

That was doubtless one reason for 'crossing the tracks'. The approaching war was another. That poetry could arduously satisfy human needs no longer met by religion and ignored by science was a position tenable only, perhaps, by an élite capable of strenuously and courageously sitting still. It was already under threat, not only from the retreat to primitivism Richards deplored in Yeats and Lawrence, but also from history itself — from Spain most immediately. 'Today the struggle.' Julian Bell, whom Richards knew, died there, but not before he had diagnosed the disturbed visions of civilised discontent he found in Freud and Richards as 'mild troubles'. Poetry seemed unlikely to save us after all.

But even before Spain made a cruder form of action seem urgent, Richards had been considering the problem of right reading on a larger scale, as a problem of universal communication. Of course he always supported Basic English as a general solution, but his Chinese book, *Mencius on the Mind*, which appeared in 1932, first revealed his new direction. It is an anti-institutional book, for Richards thought it more important to be bold than to be academically cautious. *Mencius* uses Chinese, a language 'not governed by an explicit logic', to explore the principles of 'Multiple Definition' and extend our consciousness of what we do with language. He wrote it at Harvard, while lecturing on Joyce and Dostoevsky, but the manuscript was stolen, and abandoned by the thief on a Chinese rooftop. Back in Cambridge, England he wrote it again. Then the first version was recovered from the roof. One version was affected by Richards's determination to avoid 'the intellectual currencies of the Harvard scene'; the other by his equal determination not to get caught up in 'the local logical game' at Cambridge. Which one we got I don't know: perhaps a blend of both.

All this seems characteristic of the independence and the plunging boldness of his approach. He liked best to start a book and then, writing with great speed, find out what the book wanted to be — an admirable method, I think. He was aware of the risks: what justified them was the possibility (repeatedly but not obtrusively mentioned in the prefaces to many books) that the enterprise might be of benefit to humanity. He looks to Mencius, not for information about the truth, but for what, in his view, all philosophy ought to provide: 'the opportunity of considering modes of meaning carried to their revealing limits'. And he asks us to read his books in the same way, as steps on the road to 'a single comprehensive view of comprehending'. That his linguistic equipment might be fallible didn't matter. 'The detail of my commentary may be a tissue of misconceptions and yet the trouble I share with my readers will be justified' by the importance of the problems. I have spoken of his 'uncanny aptness' in quotation. His epigraphs are also witty. The one to *Mencius* is from *Troilus and Criseyde*, where Pandarus is explaining to Troilus that even if his own record as a lover is bad he can still be useful as an example: 'Thus ofte wyse men ben war by folis,' he says. 'By his contrarie is every thing declared.'

And we shall never, I think, have a true sense of the man unless we understand this gay calculated audacity. He rushes forward, as if some gap had opened on the future. He wrote *Interpretation in Teaching*, a difficult book of over four hundred pages, in six weeks, and in the leisure time of those same six weeks turned out the none too simple *Philosophy of Rhetoric*. To bring that off you

cannot afford to make a cautious survey of the path before you
dash down it. All you can hope for is that you are well enough
programmed, or 'taped', as he used to say — that you have
adequate 'feed-forward'. And you must be very inventive. From
The Meaning of Meaning on, Richards prodigally invented new
terms; some, like the 'Canon of Actuality' and the 'Utraquist error'
of *Meaning*, died young; others, like the 'stock response' of
Practical Criticism and the Tenor-Vehicle distinction of *The
Philosophy of Rhetoric,* have stuck. All were expendable; what
mattered was the forward movement. One thinks of the lines,
addressed to Mrs Richards, which recall the descent of a glacier, the
scrambling across innumerable half-hidden crevasses before being
overtaken by darkness on the abrupt edge:

> At the stiff-frozen dawn
> When time had ceased to flow,
> — The glacier our unmade bed —
> I hear you through your yawn:
> 'Leaping crevasses in the dark,
> That's how to live!' you said.
> No room in that to hedge;
> A razor's edge of a remark.

And so he did not hedge, but wrote precipitately, and
precipitately he crossed the tracks. If one looked outside the
university, where highly educated people made such a hash of one's
protocols, and equally highly educated people regarded 'English' as
a joke or a soft option, one saw vaster problems of interpretation,
life-and-death problems calling for immediate action and new
methods. In the Richards of the Twenties there is a certain not fully
conscious élitism — a few would find their salvation in poetry,
most of them probably in Cambridge. But the world as a whole
needed order, and order could be taught. The world was largely
analphabetic; it lacked the means to communicate between
different cultures; it lacked the knowledge to resist systematic
corruption by fraudulent manipulators of language. Basic English
was meant to take care of some of these problems, to help order the
world. *Basic English and its Uses*, published in 1943, begins: 'This
is a reconstruction book. It looks to the future and assumes that the
reader enjoys a moderate faith in man.' Very characteristic; and so
is the assumption that the corruption of communications is the
source of all modern disasters, including war. Working with

language, one fought fire with fire; and one used all forms of modern communication in order to combat their harmful effects. In 1976, he was still saying that 'TV or satellite-distributed sentence-situation-depiction games are going to be the way to educate the planet.'

Educating the planet was the larger enterprise he took on after he stopped educating Cambridge. In retrospect, he saw *Interpretation in Teaching*, published in 1938, as 'the grand hinge' of his career. However salvific poetry might be for some, the world at large urgently needed instruction in the reading of prose. In came the new prose protocols, and in commenting upon them Richards hoped to found a new discipline. As knowledge, information monitored by feed-forward, had grown towards superior organisation in his own mind, so he hoped that there might be, in this matter of imparting knowledge, a useful and ordered accumulation. He saw *Interpretation in Teaching* as 'the beginning of a vast collective *clinical* study of the aberrations of average intelligence', and wondered why *Practical Criticism*, a work of much more limited ambition, should have prospered while this one, 'though offering a deeper examination of concerns nearer to everyman's essential capacities, was comparatively little studied'. But of course he did not regret the effort. 'I had to do something about the general condition of incompetence I had uncovered. I felt (and still feel) it to be too threatening to the human prospect to be left uncured.' So he wrote in the second edition of *Interpretation*, 35 years after the first. *Interpretation* had looked back to Coleridge, having as its aim the increase of 'organic inter-inanimation of meanings, the biological growth of the mind in the individual and in a social inheritance maintaining the human advance': but it looked forward, also, to years of ingenious and indefatigable labour in those causes.

In short, the diagnosis of grosser diseases than those of the academic intellect now absorbed most of his attention. Reviewing Eliot's *Notes towards a Definition of Culture* in 1948, he agreed with the author that 'a high degree of culture (or Education) in an equalitarian society can only be attained if the great majority of men can be raised to a level, and kept at a level, which has never been remotely approached in the past.' But the truth of this did not, for him, entail the closing down of unnecessary schools and universities. 'High things are hard,' he wrote. 'And I do not see how this greatest of human efforts is to be made wholeheartedly unless the salvation we are seeking is for all.'

Salvation for all! Richards believed that because it was necessary to change everybody, everybody could, given the right, continuous application of intellectual energy on the part of the clerisy, be changed. From the time of *The Meaning of Meaning* on, he had been sure that atavistic assumptions about language and meaning made ordinary men vulnerable to people who manipulated them for base ends: he particularly feared the application, in times of peace, of methods of manipulation devised for war.

Later, as I've mentioned, he tried to use television and radio against themselves, against their venal use. He did not succeed, and he came to think, like many apocalyptic spirits before him, that the times must get worse before the world will be ready to make so great an effort. 'Much can be done if things get *bad* enough,' he said in 1968. 'Things are going to get bad rather soon, and so I'm hopeful.' The theory and the method were ready and waiting. Unlike some prophets, Richards believed in theory. Having bad theories makes people misinterpret things: good theories are at least prophylactic. 'The duties of good critical theory . . . are analogous to those of a good police in a society as nearly anarchic as possible.' He was speaking then of a theory that would protect poets, but good theory would protect ordinary citizens as well. For the poet is normal; there is no difference in kind, only in the measure of sensibility or vigilance, between him and the ordinary man whom the language-manipulators cheat and stupefy. That is part of the theory, and it is also part of the prophecy: the gap between the citizen and the poet must and will be closed.

Richards has been called a mystic, and there is at least a little justice in the description. Behind all his work there is a vision (a poet's vision, but a vision available to every man) of inter-inanimation, of opposites reconciled, of peace, as when Isaiah spoke of wolf and lamb feeding together. And there is also that confidence in a participation beyond the ordinary range of sense, the transmission of poetic experience, a sort of fruitful silence beyond the movement of meaning. His tireless forward thrusting, as if to press through a gap into the future, sometimes seems to have that silence as its ultimate goal.

> If ever in the windings of the dance,
> *To-be-said* and *saying* in perfection fit,
> Another silence listens . . .

And if he was a mystic, he was not the only one we know of who exhibited from day to day an intense practicality. If you want to affirm a principle of order you must work in chaos, and understand the ills besetting 'the poor loveless, ever-anxious crowd'. Basil Willey called Richards 'the Coleridge of our time', and one can imagine the fervour with which Richards read those lines:

> Ah! from the soul itself must issue forth
> A light, a glory, a fair luminous cloud
> Enveloping the Earth —
> And from the soul itself must there be sent
> A sweet and potent voice, of its own birth,
> Of all sweet sounds the life and element!

For interinanimation, and the complementarity of opposites, and the apprehension of the world as a single organism, are creative acts of the human mind, of human language 'carried to its revealing limit'.

It has indeed been argued that Richards, the enemy of Word Magic, was himself a word-magician. Like Russell and Whorf and Wittgenstein, in their different ways, he thought that the purgation of error from language could lead us into magical peace, a silence beyond all this fiddle. 'This conception,' says Dr Hotopf, 'is magical because they attribute such great power to language, and write as though their mere insight had already given them that power.' To hold that since language mirrors the structure of reality, we can made the structure of reality *our* structure is sympathetic magic. So says Dr Hotopf. It may be so: but Richards is a rational magician. As a prophet, he sees the prospect of order; and the image of that order, that interinanimated whole, is language. Within it we may move in our own minds, to a human peace. When *to-be-said* and *saying* are one, so are being and becoming.

Language is our programme for that journey into silence. And not ours alone, not just the programme of those already educated: 'the salvation we are seeking is for all.' It is hard to conceive of a nobler magic; and Richards never abjured it.

In Theory

Christopher Ricks

Is there an honourable, thoughtful alternative to literary theory? Literary theory at present dishonourably pretends that there is not. So the case against literary theory begins with its overbearing insistence that there is no genuine case for anything else. The advocates of theory often declare that we are all theorists whether we realise it and acknowledge it or not. This stratagem is an easy extension of the announcement that we all have an ideology whether we realise it or not — an announcement which has had too easy a ride, since the choice of the word 'ideology' is itself the reflection of an ideology. To choose another word — 'faith', for instance — and to announce that everyone has a faith whether realising it or not, would be to tilt the implications away from the political incitement to which the word 'ideology' ministers.

The theory-missionaries who find it convenient to practise baptism with a hose are clearly running a risk, since in theory they are running another argument: that these days we urgently need more literary theorists. For if everybody really utters theory, as everybody talks prose, there never could be more theorists than we already have or are. Still, the risks of inviting this retort are thought worth taking, because there are three advantages to the political insistence that the only distinction is between those who acknowledge that they are theorists and those who, deceived or devious, deny that they are.

First, this shifts attention away from the demerits and merits of theory in general and of any theory in particular; second, it sheerly attributes good faith to one party and bad faith to the other; and third, it erases even the possibility of any other distinction, such as that between an allegiance to theory and an allegiance to principles. These three polemical advantages are a matter of tactics. (Not of strategy, though this is the word so loved of armchair generalising critics just now — a recent vade-mecum is called *Textual Strategies*.) An attendant disadvantage, though, is the manifest arrogance of the claim, since it arrogates to itself, not only intellectual strenuousness and advancement of thought (as if the alternative to 'advanced thought' were retarded thought), but also all good faith.

Geoffrey Hartman of Yale, whose advocacy of literary theory (rather, of one rampancy of it) is impassioned and learned, is not personally an arrogant man. But the enterprise arrogates so handsomely that his nature is subdued to what it works in. So it is not surprising, though it is shocking, to find that in *Criticism in the Wilderness*[1] Hartman musters the theorist's arrogations. On bad faith and the inescapability of theorising: 'Leavis's refusal to acknowledge that he was a theoretician *malgré lui* showed how strongly fixed the aversion to theorising had become.' On principles: 'There were English stirrings of theory, nevertheless: in Richards's work especially, even if "principles" sounded more modest and practicable than laws, methods, etc.'

Hartman gives no evidence at all that Leavis was refusing to acknowledge something. Indeed, since Hartman refuses to acknowledge that there are such things as principles and that they differ from theory (and not just from 'laws, methods, etc'), he feels himself under no obligation even to imagine what might count as evidence for his assertion against Leavis. The tactic, throughout the book, is to divide all criticism into two camps: theory, and practical criticism. If it is acknowledged, just for once, that someone used the word 'principles', he is merely being English and sly, and availing himself of the fact that the word 'principles' sounds modest and practicable. Hartman, who rebukes Matthew Arnold for deprecating French thought, says sternly that 'concepts of national character are dangerous or comic,' but proceeds immediately to ignore the danger and the comedy: 'but this Anglo-American conservatism...' In fact, he has all along proceeded by using concepts of national character (no harm in that, unless you announce there is harm in that), as when he suggests that T.S. Eliot's 'dissociation of sensibility' really shows 'that social and intellectual issues have gotten confused in a characteristic English way.'

Annulling even the possibility of a principled alternative to theory — namely, principles — Hartman slides into the politicised falsity which pretends that the alternative to one's own programme is vacancy or chaos. 'We have as yet no principled, or theoretically founded, way of dismissing the question of critical style.' A treacherous 'or' there, since the two are not offered sincerely as alternatives: 'theoretically founded' is being equated with

---

[1]Geoffrey Hartman, *Criticism in the Wilderness* (Yale University Press, 1980).

'principled', and principles find themselves glossed away. It is tacitly urged that theory is our only hope, as when we are told either to try to understand other cultures or else to 'find a theory (and not just a prejudice) that allows us to overlook their existence'. The use of 'prejudice' there is prejudicial, since converts can gullibly be won to the cause of theory if the only alternative to theory is prejudice.

Yet an alternative exists, and a dedication not to literary theory but to literary principles is neither a self-deception nor a subterfuge but a grounded choice. Theory is characterised by its degree of elaboration, concatenation, completeness, abstraction, self-consciousness, and technicality risked. None of these is unique to theory, and since matters of degree are involved, there will always be disputed instances. But to deny that theory is characterised by something — indeed, by some such things — is simply to eviscerate the argument. The word 'theory' points towards philosophy, which is why Hartman can speak repeatedly of theoretical or philosophical criticism, or of 'the philosophy or theory'. It would be as debilitating to claim that all men who think are philosophers as it would be to claim that there is on every occasion a clear-cut distinction of kind. T.S. Eliot, who could have held down a job in the philosophy department of Harvard but fortunately found even better things to do, said that 'to theorise demands vast ingenuity, and to avoid theorising requires vast honesty.' In his vast honesty, Dr Johnson stands as the greatest of English critics, and his greatness is not distinct from his sustained and rational opposition to philosophy and to theory.

'The task of criticism' was, for Johnson, to 'establish principles', and he everywhere made clear that his refusal to elaborate and concatenate the needed concepts beyond a certain point (a point reached early) was not a refusal to continue to think, but a decision to think thereafter about the application of the principles rather than to elaborate principle into theory. His comprehension of *Areopagitica*, 'a speech of Mr John Milton, for the liberty of unlicensed printing', is profound in the immediacy with which it arrives at the principles at issue:

The danger of such unbounded liberty, and the danger of bounding it, have produced a problem in the science of government, which human understanding seems, hitherto, unable to solve. If nothing may be published but what civil authority shall have previously approved, power must always be the standard of truth; if every dreamer of innovations may propagate his projects, there can be no settlement; if every murmurer at government may diffuse discontent, there can be no peace; and if every skeptic in theology may teach his follies, there can be no religion.

Johnson was given to growling 'And there's an end on't,' but here is not the end on't — only the end of thinking in the abstract or in theory about the matter. Hartman approvingly quotes John Crowe Ransom: 'The good critic cannot stop with studying poetry, he must also study poetics. If he thinks he must puritanically abstain from all indulgence in the theory, the good critic may have to be a good little critic.' But abstaining from theory and committing himself to principles made the good critic Johnson not a good little critic but a great big critic.

The distinction between theory and principles is not just a terminological matter. (In any case, those who study literature should not grant that there is such a thing as a terminological matter.) To head an examination paper with the words 'The History and Theory of Literary Criticism' is to incite an understanding which is partial in both senses. The strength of William Empson's criticism has always been its commitment to principles and not to theory. and this strength is clear in one of his apophthegms, itself a principle about principles: 'Life involves maintaining oneself between contradictions which can't be solved by analysis.' A fully-fledged theory is a philosophy; a fully-compacted principle is a proverb. Theory is hostile to contradictions; proverbs admit contradictions, and leave us only (only!) to decide which of two contradictory proverbs applies on any particular occasion. Principles, like proverbs, suppose that difficulties are more worth our attention than are problems; theory, like philosophy, is sure that once you have said, 'What you must do is to admit that a problem exists,' then what you must do is attend to the problem. But it does not follow that you must attend to that problem. The contrast is between an exchange in *Measure for Measure* —

ISABELLA: Yet show some pity.
ANGELO: I show it most of all, when I show justice,
For then I pity those I do not know —

and John Rawl's *A Theory of Justice*. Angelo utters a thought — thought as principle — which is not less serious and searching than are Rawls's concatenated and elaborated thoughts — thoughts as theory. Not less serious, and more often appropriate to the study of literature.

'One sees that what is at stake is still "an anti-self-consciousness principle",' complains Hartman. But theory must not arrogate to itself all self-consciousness. Angelo's words lack self-knowledge but not a due self-consciousness. Anyway, there is, as the very wobble within the word 'self-conscious' attests, some reason for opposition to the mere maximising of self-consciousness, and insofar as theory works for this maximising, theory may legitimately be resisted. Hartman's concessions are meant to witness to his mind's not being bolted and barred, but they open up these matters more than is prudent. 'The practical critic may be blind to what he is doing and the hermeneuticist too aware, but...' Remember that for Hartman every non-hermeneuticist is a practical critic, and wonder if Dr Johnson and T.S. Eliot were blind to what they were doing; and then ask what it would be, within Hartman's world of discourse, for the hermeneuticist to be 'too aware'. The entire book is blind to, or deafeningly silent about, these dangers of too much awareness of what one is doing, but from the silence it does sound as if there may, after all, be limits to the value of self-consciousness. They are limits of which principles are more aware than is theory. 'There are some good reasons underlying the resistance to theory: here I wish to signal only the bad ones.' Fine, but what is this 'here' business? Here, there and everywhere, Hartman signals only the bad reasons for resisting theory. Or rather, he offers just this once a small footnote: 'For some good reasons, see R.P. Blackmur' — these then not at all being good reasons for resisting theory, so much so as to make one suspect that Hartman has selected them to show that even the good reasons aren't much good. 'Neither afraid of theory nor overestimating it': but the book has no terms with which to conceive of the overestimation of theory.

The antagonism of theory to principles turns on the value of a high degree of elaborated concatenation. It is analogous to the argument about exactness and cogency on which Aristotle is to be believed: 'It is the mark of an educated mind to expect that amount of exactness in each kind which the nature of the particular subject admits. It is equally unreasonable to accept merely probable conclusions from a mathematician and to demand strict demonstration from an orator.' What is true of exactness and cogency here is as true of elaborations and recedings of a philosophical nature. The death of D.H. Lawrence in 1930 moved E.M. Forster 'to say straight out that he was the greatest imaginative novelist of our generation.' Whereupon T.S. Eliot's philosophical proclivities notoriously encouraged him to speak in a certain way: 'The virtue of speaking out is somewhat diminished if what one speaks is not sense. And unless we know exactly what Mr Forster means by *greatest, imaginative* and *novelist*, I submit that this judgment is meaningless.' But the philosophical incitement was disabling, not enabling, and Forster did well to resist it and to turn the tables on it: 'Mr T.S. Eliot duly entangles me in his web. He asks what exactly I mean by "greatest", "imaginative" and "novelist", and I cannot say. Worse still, I cannot even say what "exactly" means — only that there are occasions when I would rather feel like a fly than a spider, and that the death of D.H. Lawrence is one of them.' For the resistance to the philosophical web was no less adroit than dignified. Once you insist on recessive elaboration, not one of your own terms is stable.

Keats's 'negative capability' is twice smiled upon by Hartman in passing, but it is not heeded. Nor could it be, given the disposition of the book, for Keats's paragraph is not only an exemplary principle but is itself a defence of principle against any irritable reaching after something more:

I had not a dispute but a disquisition with Dilke, on various subjects; several things dovetailed in my mind, & at once it struck me, what quality went to form a Man of Achievement especially in Literature & which Shakespeare posessed so enormously — I mean *Negative Capability*, that is when man is capable of being in uncertainties, Mysteries, doubts, without any irritable reaching after fact & reason. Coleridge, for instance, would let go by a fine isolated verisimilitude caught from the Penetralium of mystery, from being incapable of remaining content with half knowledge. This pursued through Volumes would perhaps take us no further than this, that with a great poet the sense of Beauty overcomes every other consideration, or rather obliterates all consideration.

What is compelling in Keats's own achievement here is the even-handedness by which it warns against 'any irritable reaching after fact & reason', seeing so clearly that literature has both to acknowledge and to resist the claims of history or science (fact) and of philosophy or science (reason). Coleridge was 'incapable of remaining content with half knowledge', the word 'knowledge' encompassing both factual exactness and philosophical stringency. Keats's word 'perhaps' is then itself evidence of this invaluable 'negative capability', in the moment when he imagines the needless elaborations of his own principle into a theory of the matter. 'This pursued through Volumes would perhaps take us no further than this...' It is the mark of those critics who have given their allegiance not to theory but to principles that they decline to pursue things through volumes. The work of Donald Davie, for instance (the best critic of the post Eliot-Leavis-Empson world), neither practises nor advocates literary theory; its hard thinking is resolutely unelaborated beyond the exposition and application of principles. Hartman praises highly *Purity of Diction in English Verse*, as well he might but as he may not, given his inability to allow for the high value of any such enterprise as Davie's.

There is theory and theory, though, and the current advocacy of theory is distinguished by some urgings which are not endemic in theory itself but are the present clamourers for prime time. Hartman's book has many merits and demerits which have nothing to do with theory: notably, the merits of agility of mind and of adept erudition, and the demerits of travestying its opponents and of verbal affectation. 'That hyphen-hymen persephonates Emily': except for the word 'that', every word of this sentence is insulting to Emily Dickinson, and to Persephone come to that. Similarly there is a good deal of the twinkling play with names which has been gravely deplored when committed by those outside the hermeneutical circle, but which is esteemed when practised by the insiders. Derrida is loved for his Hegel/*aigle*, and Hartman likes the thought of himself as 'art-man'. But these demerits are peripheral: what is at the heart of the book is the insistence that 'we' too much divide creation from criticism. ('We' in Hartman, as in much else of this 'We-tend-to' school of criticism, often means You guys: 'We like to consume our literature. We like to think of critics as service stations that keep readers fuelled for their more important business, refreshing them and speeding them on.') Sometimes Hartman speaks as if there isn't really such a division between creation and criticism at all; on other occasions, as if there is but we shouldn't overstate it. The latter is more plausible and is better substantiated by Hartman, but it is the duller claim, so he needs to enliven things by occasionally enunciating the more extreme doctrine — more extreme but also more the done (or said) thing these days. 'Refusing the subterfuge of a passive or restrictive role, he [the reader] becomes at once reader and writer.' Where does this leave the reader who is not a critic or hermeneuticist? In the same place.

The betraying moment comes when Hartman juxtaposes real reading with what passes for it in the real world: 'We have talked for a long time, and unself-consciously, of the *work of art*; we may come to talk as naturally of the *work of reading*...I would suggest that as in work generally there is something provocative of or even *against nature* in reading: something which develops but also spoils our (more idle) enjoyment of literature. Hence the tone of weariness and the famous acedia that characterise the professional reader even when he has the force to recycle his readings as writing.' How anybody can enjoy literature, even idly, other than by reading it: this remains unattended-to (as does the sudden use of 'unself-consciously' in an approbatory way, happily equivalent to 'naturally'), because what matters is the supersession of readers by professional readers. There is, naturally, nothing wrong with the admission that a critic is a professional reader: but there is something very wrong with saying that non-professional reading isn't really reading at all, and is the 'more idle' 'enjoyment of literature'. It is this double impulse — to occlude non-professional reading, and, complementarily, to occlude the fact that writing is something done by writers prior to critics — which animates not literary theory in general but the reigning upsurpers. It is then a short step to the abolition of much else. Hartman speaks with level derangement of the 'illusion that genius exists.' No, he doesn't mean the illusion that there are geniuses around now, he means what he blankly says: the illusion that there is such a thing as genius.

Geoffrey Hartman is not a theorist himself, not even a theorist *malgré lui,* but an advocate of theory. Stanley Fish is both advocate and theorist. The blurb to *Is there a text in this class?*[2] dubs him 'one of America's most stimulating literary theorists'; the advertisements have upped this to 'one of the world's most stimulating literary theorists'. The blurb alone could occupy a hermeneuticist for some time, especially with its saying that Fish 'offers a stunning proposal for a new way of thinking about the way we read'. Not since Nureyev was described on the BBC as 'a staggering dancer' has there been so soft a sell as this stunning of

[2]Stanley Fish, *Is there a text in this class?* (Harvard University Press, 1980).

our thinking. But Fish, who is very lively, does not stun critical thought, though his theory would, if acted upon, lobotomise it.

His procedure is to reprint a series of his works. Like Fish, I don't think that the practice of literary criticism is something one must apologise for, but if Fish's claims were true, then no apology by academic critics — to authors and to readers — could ever be adequate. Dr Strangelove nukes them out of existence.

The attack on not just the authority of authors but their very existence is inseparable from the attack on intention in literature. Fish is very persuasive on the inescapability of interpretation, and he shows that if you seem to meet an utterance which doesn't have to be interpreted, that is because you have interpreted it already. But it is a fundamental objection to the extreme of hermeneuticism today that, in its adept slighting of authorial intention, it leaves itself no way of establishing the text of a text. To put it gracelessly like this is to bring out that some of the convenience of the word 'text' for the current theorists is its pre-emptive strike against the word 'text' as involving the establishing of the words of a text and their emending if need be. For on Fish's principles, need could never be. There are no facts independent of interpretation: moreover every interpretative strategy can make — cannot but make — perfect sense, according to its lights, of every detail of every text.

To put it at its simplest, Fish's theory has no way of dealing with misprints. His book happens to be full of misprints. I acknowledge that I call them misprints only by an act of interpretation: that is, I judge that Fish's enterprise in *Is there a text in this class?*, unlike Joyce's in *Finnegans Wake*, makes it so unlikely that he intended to call the word 'pleasurably' an 'adverb' that I'd feel bound — if I were his executor and he dead — to change it, to correct it, for the next printing. Of course, he *could* want the word 'abverb' (as in 'pleasur*ably*'), but I so much doubt it that I'd bet on it. In other words, we may legitimately judge that we should here read another word ('adverb'), in the most fundamental sense of what it is we should read. The result of my interpreting it as a misprint would be the emendation of the text of this text, and would be the removal thereafter from interpretability at all of the word 'adverb' once so interpreted. Fish didn't mean 'abverb', and so it doesn't make sense to ask what he meant by it. I'd do the same with other misprints here, all of which *could* be in lively creative relation with other words in their vicinity but all of which I am confident are merely misprints: 'distinterested', which might be distantly dis-interested, but isn't; 'defintion', which lacks clear definition; 'ambguity', which has one type of it; 'Ftting together', which doesn't; 'innaccurate', which is so (like an Errata-slip which I once saw, headed 'Erata', and which the hermeneuticist might offer as a meta-Errata-slip); 'exhilirating'; and — best of all — 'paristic on everyday usage', which would do very nicely as meaning 'parasitic on Paris' yet which is probably not a revealing pun but a misprint such as reveals nothing except that Harvard University Press lacks good proof readers. Nothing except that Fish, like other extremists of interpretation, is committed to an inordinate and unworkable sacrosanctity for the text of any text. His theory forbids him to emend, since there isn't anything which he *could* emend, there being no text independent of interpretation, and all interpretation being, on his explicit and detailed account, perfectly self-fulfilling. 'Interpretation creates intention,' so you could not posit an intention, outside your interpretation; and since interpretations always work perfectly upon whatever they are given, you can't use intention to emend a misprint.

Yet I don't believe that when Fish refers to Christina Brooke Rose, he is referring to a hitherto-neglected near-namesake of Christine Brooke-Rose, or somehow subtly intimating something about Christine Brook-Rose by 'subverting' her into a Brooke-Rose by any other name. I think Christina should be interpreted as a mistake or a misprint, and so should be tacitly or physically emended away, out of harm's (hermeneuticism's) way. The same goes for all the other people who are here misnomers: Macauley, and Mark Kinkead-Weakes, and Frederic Jameson, and Philip Hosbaum. These phantoms have in common only that they appear in Fish's book and should be emended into disappearance, as should a non-existent poem by Wallace Stevens twice called 'Anecdote of a Jar'. At least, I hope that Fish wouldn't claim that this mistitling has called the poem into existence, along the lines of his conclusion to 'Interpreting "Interpreting the *Variorum*"': 'I was once asked whether there are really such things as self-consuming artifacts, and I replied: "There are now." In that answer you will find both the arrogance and the modesty of my claims.'

The case of the poem which perhaps didn't exist is there in Fish's telling how he left up on the blackboard the list of names from a previous class on linguistics:

    Jacobs-Rosenbaum
        Levin
        Thorne
        Hayes
        Ohman(?)

Then, having drawn a frame round it and added a fictitious page-reference, Fish told the incoming class (students of 17th-century religious poetry) that this was a poem. They then exercised their critical faculties on it, and said much that was ghoulishly plausible and imaginative. For Fish, this odious experiment proves that 'skilled reading...is a matter of knowing how to *produce* what can thereafter be said to be there. Interpretation is not the art of construing but the art of constructing. Interpreters do not decode poems; they make them.' But his demonstration is flawed in three crucial ways. The first concerns his claim that 'my students did not proceed from the noting of distinguishing features to the recognition that they were confronted by a poem; rather, it was the act of recognition that came first — they knew in advance that they were dealing with a poem — and the distinguishing features then followed.' But when the students came in, Fish 'told them that what they saw on the blackboard was a religious poem,' and therefore to speak of their 'recognition' of it as a poem is to ignore too much about the experiment (and about its replacing of authors' authority by pedagogues' authority and sanctions). Second, Fish cannot himself describe the names on the blackboard without just such a removing of the matter from contestable interpretation as his theory forbids:

Ohmann's name was spelled as you see it here ['Ohman(?)'] because I could not remember whether it contained one or two n's. In other words, the question-mark in parenthesis signified nothing more than a faulty memory and a desire on my part to appear scrupulous. The fact that the names appeared in a list that was arranged vertically, and that Levin, Thorne and Hayes formed a column that was more or less centered in relation to the paired names of Jacobs and Rosenbaum, was similarly accidental and was evidence only of a certain compulsiveness if, indeed, it was evidence of anything at all.

But the insistence, confident of its own stability, that something in a text 'signified nothing more than' what its writer now declares; the belief that something, several things, in a text can be attributed to accident ('similarly accidental'), and that we can rest assured that something 'was evidence only of a certain compulsiveness if, indeed, it was evidence of anything at all': these are admissions as to accident and as to evidence which are incompatible with Fish's theory of interpretation. For Fish, there is no such thing as evidence distinct from interpretation, and from interpretation's self-fulfilling perfection. Yet he needs here to say that something in a text may not just be explained but may be explained away (away from the need to be interpreted as signifying something); he says that something in a text might be evidence of nothing at all. How could it, on his terms? Or (it comes to the same thing) how could it *not* be, since on Fish's terms all evidence is evidence *of* nothing at all? In other words (see how he uses 'In other words' there), he can make his classroom experiment real to us, and establish its interest, only be declaring what the listed names really were, really accidental or partly so. Yet for him the idea 'really were' is a delusion, a vacancy. Then at the very end of this essay, he says: 'That text might be a poem, as it was in the case of those who first "saw" "Jacobs-Rosenbaum Levin Hayes Thorne Ohman(?)" … but whatever it is, the shape and meaning it appears immediately to have will be the "ongoing accomplishment" of those who agree to produce it.' But there are two questions still. First, what can it mean for Fish to put the word 'saw' in inverted commas since on his terms there could not possibly be a difference between seeing and 'seeing'? Second, why is the order given here for the names different from that on the blackboard as Fish has several times given it ('Thorne' before 'Hayes' not after)? Perhaps, as with the old radio programme and its 'this week's deliberate mistake', Fish is a pedagogue to the last, keeping us on our toes with a last-minute trick. But I doubt it. The difference is not to be interpreted except by being interpreted away (removed from the sphere of interpretation thereafter) as 'accidental' — that is, interpreted as a slip not needing to be further interpreted. But for Fish to acknowledge any such error or accident or misprint, any possibility of wise emendation, would be for him to acknowledge something independent of interpretation, even if it were only the fact that he had meant to give the list once more in the real and authorised version.

Cornelius Gallus Lives: A Lost Latin Poet

Peter Parsons

Waste-paper is rubbish; ancient waste-paper is scholarship. Most of Greek and Latin literature disappeared without trace in the Dark Ages; what survived in manuscript was printed and so perpetuated at the Renaissance; since then the texts remain constant, while the commentaries multiply. But there is one source that produces new material rather than novel opinions; and that is the salvage of the Egyptian Greeks. The dry sand of Egypt preserves a mass of litter, the books and papers of Greek-speaking settlers and their Roman masters; these fragments, deciphered and published by papyrologists, make their special contribution to the *immortalité mouvante* of the classics. Each year turns up surprises on papyrus: Archilochus and his Lolita, the prosy Jocasta of Stesichorus, Menander's love-lorn mercenary, the rococo exercise in rustic chic which Callimachus created from the story of Heracles and the Nemean Lion. This year's surprise is more surprising than most: a snippet from the most glamorous missing link in Latin literature.

The find itself is remarkable enough. The rock-fortress of Primis (now Qasr Ibrîm) lies at the back of beyond, 750 miles south of Cairo and 150 miles south of Aswan. It was a key point in the frontier zone between Egypt and Nubia, dominating the east bank of the Nile; it has been garrisoned by successive empires, Egyptian, Roman, Nubian and Ottoman, and its waste-paper covers three and a half millennia, from the hieroglyphs of the New Kingdom to the Turkish of the 18th-century mercenaries. The Egypt Exploration Society of London has dug the site since 1963. Last year the team began to clear a narrow alley which runs between the south bastion of the fortress and the girdle-wall surrounding it. The alley turned out to be choked with refuse thrown down from the bastion above — sacking, clothes and sandals, lamps and pottery, some of distinctively Roman type. The Romans are known to have captured the fortress in 25 BC: here apparently is a legionary rubbish-tip. Among the detritus there was also written material, mostly in Greek: scrappy private letters (one dated 22/1 BC) belong to the correspondence of two army trumpeters. But on 11 March 1978 the excavator, Robert Anderson, found himself looking at

something quite different: five tattered scraps, with elegant Latin
capitals. Individual words stood out:

CAESAR

was interesting.

LYCORI

was sensational. Only one Lycoris occurs in Latin literature: she
was the mistress, in life and in verse, of C. Cornelius Gallus, friend
of Virgil, political suicide and literary ancestor of the European
love sonnet.

There is much to be said for being lost. Of Gallus's poetry we
possessed — until now — one solitary line; but his reputation has
stood very high. The drama of his life has dazzled most critics. He
was born to provincial obscurity, about 70 BC, near Fréjus; at 20
he was a famous poet, at 40 Viceroy of Egypt; three years later, in
26 BC, disgrace and death. The poets themselves celebrate his
career in poetry: in Virgil's Sixth Eclogue, Gallus is shown
receiving his inspiration from the Muses; in the Tenth Eclogue,
Gallus is at the centre, dying of love for the faithless Lycoris; for
Propertius, Gallus is the latest exemplar for love poets; for Ovid,
Gallus begins the apostolic succession of the amorous — Gallus,
Tibullus, Propertius, Ovid. Historians and monuments record the
political career: in 30 BC Octavian advanced into Egypt, eliminated
Antony and Cleopatra, and became sole ruler of the Roman world;
Gallus led an army in this campaign, and immortalised his title of
Imperial Adjutant on the obelisk which now stands outside St
Peter's; in 29 he was made Prefect of the new province, the most

glamorous and (so long as Rome depended on Egyptian corn) the most politically sensitive in the Empire. Octavian no doubt expected loyalty and discretion from the man he had made. But Gallus could not resist acting the pharaoh. He drank, and spoke imprudently of the Emperor; he welcomed a man of letters whom the Emperor had exiled; he filled Egypt with his own statues and his own inscriptions (one of these, which still survives at Philae, naively recounts how Gallus marched far to the south, 'to a point where neither Roman nor Egyptian had ever ventured'). The Emperor publicly and formally broke off their friendship. Private accusers swarmed in to dismember the fallen favourite. The senate condemned him to confiscation and exile. He killed himself. But poets remained loyal to his memory; and so, as it now turns out, did one reader in the Roman garrison at Qasr Ibrîm.

Gallus's literary achievement had two sides, to judge from ancient allusions. Apparently he wrote 'subjective elegy' (that is, he described his own experiences, if not in his own person, at least in his own persona); and devoted a whole cycle of poems (four books, according to the commentator Servius) to his relationship with one woman — as Propertius and Ovid did later, and Petrarch and Shakespeare after them. Apparently he wrote mythological narratives, in imitation of the Hellenistic poet Euphorion (whose surviving works combine obscure myth, recondite vocabulary and crossword-puzzle allusiveness in crabbed donnish diversions which later found favour with the special tastes of the Emperor Tiberius). The textbooks therefore write him up as a transition and a synthesis: a transition between the age of Catullus and the age of Propertius; a synthesis between personal passion and Alexandrian artifice. The difficulty has been to put flesh on this tidy skeleton; we lack words and details. The one surviving line is quoted only for its geographical content, and is notable only for its crude verbal neatness. Beyond that, we have some lines in the Tenth Eclogue, which Servius (in the fourth century) alleged to be 'taken over' from Gallus; and some lines in the Sixth Eclogue, which Skutsch (in 1906) guessed to be summaries of Gallan poems. The vacuum invites filling. Pomponius Gauricus published the works of Gallus in 1501: but they turned out to be by the Christian poet Maximian. Aldus Manutius the Younger discovered the works of Gallus in 1590: but they turned out to be his own. Caspar von Barth in 1607 attributed to Gallus the anonymous poem 'Ciris', and so have others since: but no one ever believes it for long. The moderns have generally been more subtle in the quest for Gallus. The Roman literary world was as small as Bloomsbury; Gallus must have had great influence in it; if there are coincidences between the poems of Gallus's admirers, should we not see their origin in poems of Gallus? And so Gallus becomes omnipresent, like God or phlogiston, invisible but deducible.

The new papyrus comes as a breeze in the hot-house.[1] It is in itself a romantic object, this splendidly elegant book: it is probably the oldest Latin manuscript to survive, so old indeed that it could have been in the hands of Virgil, could have been copied in the lifetime of Gallus. It had a romantic fate: when the Romans came to Qasr Ibrîm, Gallus had been dead a year or more; but some officer carried his ex-commander's poems to the far south, well beyond the point his ex-commander had boasted of reaching, and it was in this exotic spot that they were finally consigned to the garbage. The content is less romantic but more interesting: nine lines of the real Cornelius Gallus.

The first is the end of a poem, addressed to Lycoris: 'my life made miserable by your misbehaviour'. This is what we expected.

There follows a four line epigram: 'Caesar, my fate will be sweet to me, when you are the greatest part of Roman history and when I read how the temples of many gods are enriched with the spoils you place there.' Caesar makes history, the poet reads it: stock flattery. But which Caesar is it? And from which war is he returning full of booty? A major war, if the compliment is rational (but you need not expect rationality from a poet on the make); the major wars of Gallus's career are early and late — the Parthian war of Julius Caesar (44 BC, aborted by his murder), the Egyptian war of Octavian (30 BC) or the Parthian war which was expected to follow. R.G.M. Nisbet opts for the early date, on the ground that by the Twenties Gallus was too grand to write verse, and Lycoris too old to be written about (one might doubt the first argument, and indeed the second: Lycoris, like Propertius's Cynthia, may have remained a symbol long after she ceased to be a siren). In that case, the great man is Julius, not Octavian; the compliment is an early rung on the ladder to the top.

The third poem is another epigram: 'Now at last the Muses have made me poems that I can speak as worthy of my mistress. I at least

---

[1] The Gallus papyrus has been published in the *Journal of Roman Studies,* Vol. LXIX.

have no fear...when you, Viscus, or you, Cato, are the judge.' These are the critics: Viscus, one of two brothers whose judgment Horace respected; Valerius Cato, poet, scholar, critic and guru to the avant-garde poets of Catullus's generation. Perhaps Gallus claimed their approval for his new poetry, perhaps he dismissed them as irrelevant, once Lycoris approved (the text is damaged). Certainly the Mistress is central: the first clear use of the word in European literature.

Lycoris, Caesar, Viscus and Cato: love, power, poetry: these three poems cover systematically chief themes, and dominating personalities, of Gallus's career. The themes themselves interlock: Lycoris's infidelity makes him sad; Caesar's triumph relieves the sadness; new inspiration will win Lycoris back. But the style of the lines, and the shape of the whole, are equally puzzling. We expected a sequence of love elegies: we have a series of epigrams. We expected Grecising elegance and mythological ornament: we have plain flat diction, foursquare and even lumpish metric, and one prosodic feature that the next generation would find strikingly old-fashioned. Nothing suggests the deutero-Euphorion, and almost nothing the proto-Propertius. Now of course the proprieties of epigram *may* be different from the proprieties of elegy; the lucky dip *may* have turned up the least typical, or the least successful, of Gallus's works. But reality ought to weigh more heavily than reputation. In the ancient world, Gallus had the advantage of friends and glamour: in the modern world, the encroaching charm of a missing link. Now that we have an actual sample before us, we recognise a more human Gallus: modest talent, of historical interest.

The Gallus-construction industry has reared gorgeous palaces from its few bricks; it will be interesting to see how it copes with the new breeze-block. Meanwhile there is the hope of more reality: the Egypt Exploration Society has been digging the same site again this Christmas.

The Flight in 'A Midsummer Night's Dream'

William Empson

This is the new Arden edition of *A Midsummer Night's Dream*,[1] and it is splendid to have the old series still coming out. Full information, and a proper apparatus at the foot of the page: where else would you find that? It has got a bit stiff in the joints; the Introduction is so long and so full of standard doctrine that it is hard to pick out the plums; but the sobriety itself is a comfort. One major new emendation is proposed — that Theseus said: 'Now is the mure rased between the two neighbours.' Professor Brooks admits that this is bad, and agrees that Shakespeare may have agreed to have it changed on the prompt-book, but is certain he wrote it at first, because of the rules invented by Dover Wilson for the misinterpretation of his handwriting. Surely anyone used to correcting proofs knows that all kinds of mistakes may occur, whereas this bit of pedantry would be quite out of key for Theseus. 'Mural down' (Pope) goes quite far enough.

As part of a general process of soothing, he speaks warmly of the merits of Bottom, but adds that 'he is quite unsusceptible to the romance of fairyland,' and will soon have forgotten his meeting with Titania. What on earth can the weasel-word 'romance' be doing here? As a Greek of the age of myth, he simply worships the goddess. As a man who is driven by his vanity, he finds her love for him immensely gratifying, but not really surprising, so that he can keep his cool. When we see him return to his friends he has urgent news: they must collect their theatrical props and go to the palace at once, but he is bursting to tell them his dream as soon as there is time. When Oberon remarks that he and the lovers will remember the night as 'but the fierce vexation of a dream', he is not giving an order, and some fierce dreams do get remembered long and vividly (or at least you can remember your reconstruction of them). The real feeling of Brooks, I submit, is: Thank God we don't have to watch a lady actually giving herself to a stinking hairy worker. 'Even a controlled suggestion of carnal bestiality is surely impossible,' he remarks.

---

[1] Edited by Harold Brooks (Methuen, 1980).

These cloudy but provocative phrases conceal a struggle which had better have been brought into the open. The opponent is Jan Kott, who wrote *Shakespeare Our Contemporary* (1967), and the Peter Brook production (1970) which dramatised his findings. I take my stand beside the other old buffers here. Kott is ridiculously indifferent to the letter of the play, and labours to befoul its spirit. And yet the Victorian attitude to it also feels oppressively false, and has a widespread influence. We need here to consider Madeline Bassett, who figures decisively in the plot of a number of stories by P.G. Wodehouse. This unfortunate girl, though rich, young, handsome and tolerably good-tempered, has a habit of saying, for example, that a dear little baby is born every time a wee fairy blows its nose. She never repeats herself but keeps steadily within this range. It excites nausea and horror in almost all the young men who have become entangled with her, and their only hope of escape without rudeness is to marry her to the sub-human Augustus Fink-Nottle. Such is the mainspring for a series of farces. However remotely, her fancies are clearly derived from Shakespeare's *Dream*, and Wodehouse was a very understanding, well-read man, with a thorough grasp of this general revulsion. Such is the strength of our opponents. It is no use for the present editor to complain in a footnote that the Brook production lacked 'charm': a too determined pursuit of charm was what spelt doom for poor Madeline Bassett.

What a production needs to do is to make clear that Oberon and Titania are global powers, impressive when in action. There is nothing to grumble about in the tenderness of the fairy scenes towards small wild flowers and young children, but it needs balancing. Many thinkers, summarised by Cornelius Agrippa, had believed in these Spirits of Nature, neither angels nor devils, in the first part of the 16th century, but Luther and Calvin denounced the belief, and the Counter-Reformation largely agreed, so further discussion in print was prevented by censorship. But ten of the Cambridge colleges, at the time of the play, had Agrippa's treatise in their libraries. So the dons were not hiding it from the children, and it gives you positively encouraging advice about how to raise nymphs from water-meadows. The New Astronomy was in the same position: learned books arguing in its favour could not get a licence, though a mere expression of agreement with it was not penalised. And Copernicus in his Introduction had actually claimed support from Hermes Trismegistus, who was considered the ancient source of the belief in Middle Spirits.

The fairy scenes here say a good deal about astronomy, though none of it further out than the Moon; and there are other reasons for thinking that the public had largely accepted the daily rotation of the Earth, but thought its yearly orbit to be supported by obscure arguments and probably dangerous.

If these spirits control Nature over the whole globe, they need to move about it at a tolerable speed. When the audience is first confronted by the magic wood, at the start of Act Two, a fairy tells Puck, 'I am going everywhere, faster than the moon's sphere,' because she has been given the job of putting the smell into the cowslips. As they all come out at about the same time, this requires enormously rapid movement, continually changing in direction. She should be found panting against a tree-trunk, having a short rest at human size, but when in action her body must be like a bullet. It seems tiresome to have human-sized spirits described as very tiny, but it is standard doctrine that they could make themselves so, and we find that they could also make themselves very heavy. It is an old textual crux that Puck speaks to Oberon of 'our stamp', but he should at once give a specimen of their magic stamp, which is echoed tersely by a deep-voiced drum under the stage. Thus we are prepared for Oberon and Titania to 'shake the ground' when they dance good fortune to the lovers: the drums now become a form of music, echoing each step (there is a faint repetition of it when they are dancing off-stage in the palace bedroom). Then, immediately after shaking the ground, they go up on the crane, apparently weightless. Oberon remarks:

We the globe can compass soon,
Swifter than the wandering moon.

He is thus recalling what the fairy said at the start. He does not say they will do it now, only that they can do what is needed with a comfortable margin, if they are to dance again in the palace soon after midnight.

At the end, after the fifth Act, in the palace, Puck says again that fairies prefer to live permanently in the dawn: they run

From the presence of the sun,
Following darkness like a dream.

At the equator they would need to go 1000 miles an hour, nearer a quarter than a third of a mile a second, but probably they stick to the latitude of Athens, at about 800 miles an hour. Titania, for one, does not seem a very athletic type, and the idea is more plausible if they merely rise above the air resistance, afterwards remaining at rest and observing the Earth as it parades beneath. For so long as they can be bothered, the lords of Nature hold a continual durbar.

To explain this might offend the censor or part of the audience, and anyhow would hardly fit the style. But the words assume it without any room for compromise. The distance to the Moon is about 60 times the radius of the Earth, as was already known in Classical times, and the Moon goes round the Earth in about 30 days, so the speed of the middle of the Moon's sphere, the part which carries the moon, is about twice the speed of the equator, which revolves in a day. So the working fairy does at least half a mile a second, probably two-thirds, and the cruising royalties can go as fast as her, if they need to. Puck claims to go at five miles a second, perhaps seven times what the working fairy does. This seems a likely social arrangement. But if all the stars go round the Earth every day, with the Moon and planets lagging only slightly behind, the speed of the Moon's sphere is about 60 times the speed of Oberon when he remains in the dawn, and the working fairy is going very much faster that the boast of Puck. I agree that the phrases are meant to sound rather mysterious — probably Shakespeare asked the advice of Hariot, who was certainly a friend of Marlowe — but they would not be meant to be sheer nonsense, as has for so long been assumed.

Coming now to the flights of Puck, I am sorry that I must just assert conclusions, but the argument is rather lengthy. Puck really did fly — that is, get jerked aside on a rope. This was easy in the hall of a mansion, where he could be caught by three strong men behind a curtain, but it was an achievement of the Globe Theatre to make him do it in public, flying into one of the upper lords' rooms. The trick was dangerous and impressive, and quite enough to prevent you from regarding the fairies as footling. Also it was a challenge to a third act of censorship, as would be obvious if this hush-up (unlike the other two) had not triumphed. Puck says he can go anywhere, as far as possible on the round earth, in 40 minutes. Now this is just the speed that Major Gagarin was going at, when he took the first trip in space round the world. Or rather, he took 42 or 43, but the accepted radius of the Earth then was too small by about a seventh, and this makes the answer a bit too small, but it is right if you let the astronaut get above the air — say, 30 miles high.

Hariot had arrived at this important result in 1592 or so, and was refused publication: probably it was the university dons rather than the clerical censorship who said (with some excuse) that his proof was riddled with ignorant fallacies. He was furious, and refused to print anything ever again, though warned that he was losing all his priorities. There must have been some major early incident to make him sulk like this, and his indignant supporters would need a slogan. Hariot would insist upon 'Forty for Half-Way' because the figure really was nearer 40 than 39 or 41, whereas to be correct one would have to say '79 to go all round' — a less ringing slogan. Shakespeare, of course, would not use it in a play unless a number of people in the audience would know what it meant, but perhaps he had used it first in a satirical piece to entertain Southampton, in 1592, and merely retained it in the greatly enlarged play for the wedding in 1596. A number of people in that distinguished audience would remember what it meant, though perhaps very few in the Globe of 1600. It is to the credit of Professor Brooks, by the way, that he does not copy out the note: '*Forty*: Used frequently as an indefinite number.' I should add that the idea of an astronaut with only enough power to start and stop would not trouble the mind of Hariot, or indeed of Puck. Opponents of the daily rotation always said that it would throw us off into space, as from a spinning top, and Copernicus had had no answer except that this movement was a natural one and would therefore do no harm. Hariot found the real answer: no one would be thrown off the Earth, even at the equator, unless the Earth went round 18 times faster than it does, which allows a comfortable margin. Five miles a second is the speed at which you have no weight, and if Puck had gone twice as fast he would be struggling all the time not to fly up to Heaven.

Professor Brooks quotes someone who remarked it was 'boyish' of Puck, before his second flight, to say:

I go, I go, look how I go!
Swifter than arrow from the Tartar's bow.

It is hardly a point of character: surely, if he had said this and then merely scampered off, the Globe audience would have hooted him. This is the strongest bit of evidence that he really flew. It looks as if the second flight was added for the Globe production: partly to give more length, partly because it seemed wasteful not to use the machinery twice, and partly to give each side of the theatre a good view of the trick. Puck is offended at being told he chose the wrong man, and insists that he can clear it up at his immense speed: but it does not really need using at all, to look round the wood. The third Act is now well over six hundred lines, far longer than the others, because to excuse the flight Shakespeare added there an extra complication for the lovers, which I have to feel makes them a bore, undeservedly. Several critics have felt this, and Professor Brooks does not really refute them by showing that the boys and girls argue according to the correct rules of rhetoric. It is a comfort to observe that Puck is so unshaken by his flight as to return after only eight lines: but they are solemn lines, restoring Demetrius to his true love, from whom he switched by no fault of the fairies. The grand smash of the second flight is followed by this priestlike behaviour from Oberon.

A different type of care is taken over the first flight. In Act Two, Scene One, as the audience first sees the magic wood, Puck meets the working fairy and shows how jolly he is in rhymed couplets. Then Titania and Oberon enter from the two sides and quarrel, and Puck says nothing. Then his master calls him up to receive orders, and he behaves like the traditional Scotch head-gardener, respectful but curt, plainly an expert. Of course he talks prose. He says only, 'I remember,' before he says: "I'll put a girdle about the earth in forty minutes.' He must be presumed to fly off at once, and Oberon, absorbed in passion, says: 'Having once this juice...' It is a rather lifelike feature that he presumes Puck to have talked blank verse, as *he* does. Then, when Puck comes back, impossibly quickly, he says:

OBERON: Hast thou the flower there? Welcome, wanderer.

PUCK: Ay, there it is.

For the last line of the scene, when Puck has learnt that the intention of the plot is to make Titania 'full of hateful fantasies', he is pleased, and rhymes with an approving leer as he leaves his master.

OBERON: And look thou meet me ere the first cock crow.
PUCK: Fear not, my lord, your servant shall do so.

He has got back to rhyming, but he has never once used blank verse
so far.

We have here a familiar type of textual problem. The first
Quarto inserts the word 'round', thus making the lines scan:

PUCK: I'll put a girdle round about the earth
    In forty minutes.
OBERON: Having once this juice...

As to the choice between five and ten miles a second, I doubt
whether the word 'round' makes much difference. The familiar
dressing-gown has a girdle held up on slots, and most of the time it
goes half-way round, with the ends hanging from the slots. Puck
has only in mind going to a far place, not going all round. But it
makes a great difference whether he is singing in opera or talking
like a Scotch gardener. The second Quarto is only a pirate edition,
but it is described by the *Riverside*, for example, as 'a reprint of
Q1, with a few added stage directions, and an occasional correction
of obvious errors'. The intrusive 'round' seems to me an obvious
error, which might well have been corrected on the text of Q1
available to the pirate. It is still excluded by the Folio, which is
admitted to have had further sources of evidence. Even so,
Professor Brooks might feel that Q1 is impregnable: but then, why
does he not print it? It gives the remark of Puck as prose, even
while adding the word which excuses printing it as verse. Both other
sources also give it as prose. Granting that he was determined to
print it as verse, his apparatus ought to have admitted that it always
comes in prose. But he was determined to make the fairy sound
'charming'.

As to whether it is 'bestiality' to love Bottom, many a young girl
on the sands at Margate has said to her donkey, unblamed: 'I kiss
thy fair large ears, my gentle joy.' If the genital action is in view,
nobody denies that the genitals of Bottom remained human. The
first audience would not have admired Bottom, and nor would I,
for letting the thing go so far if unwilling to respond. The sequence
is sadly short. After their first contact, she leads him to her bower,
and a scowling husband holds them up. They arrive, and he speaks
charmingly to a few babies, but then says: 'I have an exposition of
sleep come upon me.' He often gets words wrong, but you can
never be sure, and if he means a pretence of sleep it is greeted by
immediate connivance. Titania orders her fays to explode like
shrapnel ('be all ways away') and hugs him saying: 'how I dote on

thee.' He is still quiet and cautious, but this is the time for exploring fingers to inquire whether she is solid enough for the purpose, and also whether he is genuinely welcome. This groping process could be made obvious and entertaining, but then the lurking husband comes forward and performs an act of magic. Probably it sounded like a pistol going off, and the audience wondered whether he had killed them, but no, they are only in deep sleep. He at once speaks confidently to Puck, having got what he wanted and settled all the other troubles. Soon after he wakes his wife up, and they are ready to do their tremendous dance.

Kott says that the four lovers, or the six including Titania and Bottom, all wake up in an agony of shame, determined to forget what has happened, because they have had an orgy. It is a wild degree of misreading. No act of sex takes place on the fierce Night, and there is never anything to drink. Bottom really would have felt shame if he had heard what Titania said about him after she woke, but he has been carefully spared from it. He proposes to boast about the memory for the rest of his life. The others all wake up awed, rather exalted, wanting to explain themselves to each other, and we are soon told they had decided they had been teased by spirits. Professor Brooks says archly that of course Shakespeare would add any lie for a dramatic effect: but this only occurs to him because he does not believe in Middle Spirits at all. Among people who did, such as the lovers, it would only be a matter of checking up on the details.

The sex life of the spirits needs also to be considered, but this review is already too long. The book is an excellent one, and the points where it is too much within the tradition can easily be recognised.

To be continued

Brigid Brophy

The boldest way to supply the missing second half of *Edwin Drood* would be in the idiom of the present time. Such a course would nowadays come naturally or at any rate fashionably to an architect were he required to complete a building that had stopped short in 1870. But the mini-vogue among writers (or is it among publishers?) for endings to fictions that their authors left unfinished during the 19th century has not thrown up a single modern-dress production.

In this respect, the arts have swopped places. During most of Dickens's mature lifetime it was architecture that versed itself in pastiche and would scarcely venture out except under the veil and justification of some 'historical' style. The novelists, by contrast, had the nerve of the devil. On the strength of nothing less could they have committed themselves to serial publication in the nerve-stretching form it then took.

In his contract for *Drood* Dickens for the first time had a clause inserted providing for arbitration on how much of the up-front money (£7,500 to cover the first 25,000 copies) should be repaid 'if the said Charles Dickens shall die' or be otherwise incapacitated 'during the composition of the said work'. (Presumably nothing had, in fact, to be repaid, since John Forster recorded that 50,000 copies were sold 'while the author yet lived'.) The clause shows that Dickens knew he might be dying, but it is also witness to his splendid confidence that nothing short of death or a stroke could stop him composing the intended dozen monthly numbers.

The more pleasurable suspense that serial publication generated in the consumers (except Queen Victoria, who didn't take up Dickens's offer to disclose *Drood* to her earlier than to her subjects) has now passed to television, leaving to novelists the peace of mind and the diffidence that come from knowing that thousands of readers are *not* hanging on your next instalment.

In the event, Dickens wrote six numbers. The last was two pages short — the second time, during *Drood*, that he was failed by the as it were 'ring sense' he had by then reliably cultivated for writing to an exact length. Leon Garfield[1] has opted for the diffident method

---

[1] *The Mystery of Edwin Drood* concluded by Leon Garfield (André Deutsch, 1980).

of completion and has produced an honourable and, where style is concerned, mainly plausible fake. Perhaps at the dictate of publishing economics, he falls far shorter than Dickens did. To fulfil Dickens's design, he should have supplied the same amount of text (equal to six numbers) as Dickens did. But he runs (in the format of this edition) only to 122 pages, whereas Dickens occupies 201.

The outright blots in the Garfield text consist of two howlers in syntax: 'His thoughts were still partly with Rosa, and with she of whom Rosa was an ever-present reminder' and 'And Rosa, what of she?' Dickens was not an elegant syntactician, but I don't think he would have let his narrative do *that*. Elsewhere Mr Garfield's narrative, in contrast to his dialogue, which is on the awkward side, is a forgery good enough, I should guess, to deceive. Try these four in a blindfold test:

As though he had been called into existence, like a fabulous Familiar, by a magic spell which had failed when required to dismiss him, he stuck tight to Mr Grewgious's stool, although Mr Grewgious's comfort and convenience would manifestly have been advanced by dispossessing him.

Ordinarily this animal — the property of the watchman and known, for sufficient reason, as Snap — was of a voracious, biting disposition; but in Vacation time lapsed into a fly-blown apathy, like the law itself, as if all unlawful appetites were but a source of dreamy speculation.

Once in London, where, as usual, the summer is unseasonably warm, and leaden, as if everybody has breathed out and nobody wants to breathe in, she proceeds...

There has been rain this afternoon, and a wintry shudder goes among the little pools on the cracked, uneven flag-stones, and through the giant elm-trees as they shed a gust of tears.

Mr Garfield is better at the manner (his are the middle two quotations above, the first and the fourth being from Dickens's text) than at the plot. We know in advance, from Edward Blishen's Introduction, that he is not going to do anything outrageous. He has not taken space enough to do anything deeply complicated. Above all, he is under the great, restricting disability of the faker: he cannot do anything unDickensian. Dickens, of course, could and well might have done, it being his privilege that, the moment he did it, it would *become* Dickensian.

Diligently Mr Garfield extrapolates from the obvious clues in Dickens's text and from some of what Dickens disclosed to friend (Forster), family and illustrator. (Queen Victoria's incuriosity is a smaller loss than critics think. It is inconceivable that Dickens was offering to write her a précis of each number before he wrote the number itself. He can have been offering only to rush her an advance copy. Had she taken him up on it, we should be no better off.) The Garfield Drood *is* dead, and the murderer the obvious suspect, John (or, to Edwin, Jack) Jasper. Something is made of Helena Landless's aptitude for dressing up and something of 'that great black scarf' which, as Dickens's Jasper pulls it off and loops it round his arm, makes his face 'knitted and stern'. Mr Garfield invents an amusingly lightweight Datchery, who is *not* any of the other dramatis personae in disguise. But when the all-important ring is finally recovered (in the manner Forster said Dickens meant it to be), he has Mr Grewgious give it away to Datchery, which Dickens's Grewgious has invested far too much emotion in it ever to do.

Rightly, Mr Garfield makes nothing of the 'Sapsea Fragment', no doubt agreeing with Forster that it was designed for an early, not a later, part of the novel and then discarded by Dickens himself. He takes up Dickens's disclosure to Forster that the story was to end in the condemned cell, that the ring was to come uncorroded through the lime that destroys the corpse, that Helena was to marry Crisparkle and that Neville Landless was to perish, but he ignores Forster's recollection that Neville was to do so 'in assisting Tartar finally to unmask and seize the murderer'.

His is clearly meant to be a reading version, sparing readers the frustration of being left in mid-air, and also a *giving* version. With a shamelessness that is his most deeply Dickensian stroke, Mr Garfield wrenches his story to a conclusion on another, and happier, Christmas. Like many objects designed as Christmas presents, it falls at best flat and sometimes insultingly light. It scurries through the murder trial in a light comedy tone (and *did* judges actually *put on* the black cap?), managing not a touch of the grand grotesquerie that would have been forced from Dickens by his ambivalence towards both crime and punishment. Neither does the Christmas market discharge the publisher from scholarly obligations. The notorious misprint of 'tower' for 'town', twice over, which makes nonsense of Dickens's opening words, is repeated — a laziness that will merely direct buyers towards the

Penguin edition, which will leave them in mid-air but does give Dickens's text as it stands in his manuscript. Apart from the fact that they illustrate moments in the fake as well as the Dickens text and can therefore run all through the volume, Anthony Maitland's genteel illustrations have no advantages over the 12 (two to each number) plus frontispiece that Luke Fildes drew to Dickens's instructions, from which they anyway borrow the characters' clothes.

A satisfying completion of *Drood* will have to await a writer who can match Dickens's confidence by a confidence on his own part of having understood not just Dickens's style but Dickens's mind. The use of modern language might help, by forcing the writer to decide what he thinks structural and what decorative in Dickens's text. Pastiche can fudge it by using an idiom as ambiguous on that point as Dickens's own. The writer destiny has up its sleeve, who cannot be appointed but must messianically recognise himself, will be confident not only that he can provide a plausible solution to the mystery of Edwin Drood but that he has solved the deeper mystery of *The Mystery of Edwin Drood* — namely, what sort of book it was to be: merely, if magnificently, another Dickens novel or a true mystery in the genre classically established by Wilkie Collins with *The Moonstone*, which Dickens had published two years earlier in *All the Year Round?*

Either answer points to considerable complexity of plot in the second half. Forster's recollection that the story was to concern 'the murder of a nephew by his uncle' seems to leave no doubt that Edwin is killed. Yet Dickens's notes, skeletal and inconclusive though they are (and broken off at the same point in the story as his text), suggest more emphasis on the uncertainty of Drood's fate than he incorporated in the text before he left it. As well as inquiring 'Dead? Or alive?', his preliminary notes include 'The flight of Edwin Drood' and 'Edwin Drood in hiding'. Perhaps the second half was to revive and prolong the uncertainty or perhaps it was to disclose that Drood did in fact stay alive a little longer than the first half implies. His death need not coincide with his disappearance. Three days elapse before Crisparkle finds his watch in the weir. If Jasper's behaviour has alarmed him, he might pass them 'in hiding' and in 'flight'. And indeed, although Dickens reconciles Edwin and Rosa after they have agreed not to marry, his moralism might well keep Edwin alive long enough to visit on him some ironic remorse for having misprized Rosa.

Certainly, complexity in the second half is argued by Dickens's title for the chapter of the Christmas Eve meeting between Jasper, Neville and Edwin, after which Edwin disappears. I do not think he would have called it 'When shall these three meet again?' had he not planned that there should be a meeting again between Jasper, Neville and at least the corpse of Edwin — which may be what is depicted in the bottom centre vignette in the Fildes frontispiece.

Whether or not Dickens was writing a positive whodunit, he was prompted, I think, to experiment with narrative method by the dovetailed first-person narratives, the one filling in the ignorance and bafflement of the others, in *The Moonstone*. Perhaps he contemplated, though momentarily, a transplant of *The Moonstone* method, crude. The 'Sapsea Fragment' consists, like the narratives in *The Moonstone*, of a document written (by Mr Sapsea) in the first person. But what I suspect he was really after is a variation, less mechanical and more psychological, on Collins's ingenuity.

Rereading Dickens's text, I was astonished to notice that its first five chapters are in the present tense. They include Jasper's opening opium dream and his introduction to Deputy's job of stoning the drunken Durdles home. In Chapter Eight, where Neville and Edwin quarrel at the instigation of Jasper and Jasper's drink, the narrative is again in the historic present. So it is in Chapters Twelve (Jasper's night expedition to the tombs and Durdles's 'dream' of Jasper abstracting the key), Fourteen (the crucial 'When shall these three...?') and Nineteen (Jasper's declaration to Rosa). Chapter Twenty-Two opens in the past tense with a round-up of what has happened meanwhile, but quickly moves into the present tense and stays there for Jasper's opium session and Datchery's detection.

Something very near half of Dickens's text (ten chapters out of 22) is written in the historic present. Apart from Chapter Twenty-Two, which comes from a number where there was a mix-up, both in Dickens's notes and in some editions, about the numbering and the division of chapters, each of Dickens's chapters is either wholly in the past or wholly in the present tense. In other books, Dickens uses the present haphazardly, when it strikes him as apt. In *Drood* I think his switches of tense are systematic.

I cannot name an exact significance for each of the present-tense chapters (though I'd like an acknowledgment, please, if some other critic can), and in some cases the significance may be designed to emerge only in the second half. The effect of Wilkie Collins's systematic jigsaw of narratives is that, for instance, Rachel Verinder can actually see Franklin Blake steal the moonstone and yet, of course, really see no such thing, since not only is his motive non-thieving but he is unaware of his own actions, being, unknown to himself, drugged by opium. My hypothesis is that, by a refinement on Collins, Dickens used the present tense in *Drood* for chapters where something is seen to happen and can be vouched for in good faith by the narrative and yet is not what really happens.

It is obvious how this could come about in the present-tense chapters where Jasper is drugged and in those where Edwin, Neville and Durdles are, on their various occasions, drunk (and sometimes, conceivably, drugged as well, by Jasper). Moreover, some double vision of this sort on Jasper's part, a faculty for seeing what happens correctly yet not seeing what really happens, must, I think, be the interpretation of the most important but the most neglected of the clues Dickens gave Forster — namely, that 'the originality' of the story 'was to consist in the review of the murderer's career by himself at the close, when its temptations were to be dwelt upon as if, not he the culprit, but some other man, were the tempted'.

Thus the fears Jasper expresses, even before Edwin disappears, that Neville will do him violence are, I think, though not true to the facts, sincere: he is expressing his own temptation as Neville's. The same is true of his stated conviction, after Edwin's disappearance, that it is Neville who has murdered him. Jasper's double vision has, so to speak, mistaken Neville's infatuation with Rosa for his own, which, as he avows to Rosa, 'is so mad that, had the ties between me and my dear lost boy been one silken thread less strong, I might have swept even him from your side when you favoured him.'

Those silken ties between Jasper and his dear lost nephew are stronger than critics have allowed. The true and desperate madness in Jasper's love for Rosa seems to me to lie in his not being sure which of the betrothed pair, Rosa or Edwin, he is more in love with. Is he tempted to kill Edwin in order to take Rosa for himself, or tempted to keep Edwin for himself (or at least in the family) by killing Rosa — who is, quite rightly, scared of him to the point of running away to Mr Grewgious's custody? In choosing to kill Edwin, a deed he can plausibly see, through his double vision, as done by Neville, Jasper may even seem to himself to make the right choice, since he thereby suppresses the more culpable of his two sexual passions.

The discovery, which makes Jasper faint, of what Forster calls 'the utter needlessness of the murder for its object', since Rosa and Edwin were not going to marry in any case, perhaps reflects Dickens's sense of personal irony in having wounded his family and risked his respectability for the sake of a mistress with whom he was then not happy. The surname of Helena and Neville Landless is interpreted by Mr Garfield when he makes Helena exclaim: 'We are Landless; we are homeless!' Yet, apart perhaps from Honeythunder, the names in *Drood* (including Drood itself) are not of such Restoration Comedy transparency, and they have more to do with Dickens's feelings about the people concerned than with those people's natures. Drood is not a person to inspire either brooding or dread. Neither could one guess that Mr Grewgious, that amalgam of *greed, screw* and *egregious*, is, besides angular, good. Landless, which was changed in Dickens's notes from 'Heyridge or Heyfort', owes something, I suspect, to the unusual middle name of Dickens's mistress, Ellen Lawless Ternan, and the Lawless itself must, I think, have sounded in Dickens's thoughts as an indictment of his own behaviour on her account. Jasper attributes his own guilt to Neville Landless, whose surname signified for Dickens, I think, both the lawlessness and the outlandishness of Jasper's desires.

Dickens's narrative could never have *stated* Jasper's sexual love for Edwin, but it can and does *show* it even more explicitly than *Our Mutual Friend* shows the homosexuality of Eugene and Mortimer. Indeed, in *Drood* Dickens makes his point by deliberate contrasts. A disconsolate Neville, touched on the shoulder by Crisparkle, 'took the fortifying hand from his shoulder, and kissed it' — once, and in any case Neville is markedly not English. What Dickens expected of the English he makes clear when Crisparkle is re-united with his rescuer from drowning, Tartar: 'The two shook hands with the greatest heartiness, and then went the wonderful length — for Englishmen — of laying their hands each on the other's shoulders, and locking joyfully each into the other's face.'

Those exceptional incidents throw into conspicuity the very different conduct of the dinner Jasper gives Edwin in Chapter Two, which begins with Jasper watching Edwin arrive and take off his outer clothes with 'a look of hungry, exacting, watchful, and yet devoted affection' and continues with Edwin's flirtatiously bidding Jasper take him in to dinner, in pursuit of which 'the boy', as Edwin now significantly becomes, 'lays a hand on Jasper's shoulder, Jasper cordially and gaily lays a hand on *his* shoulder, and so Marseillaise-wise they go in to dinner' — in the course of which Jasper lays 'an affectionate and laughing touch on the boy's extended hand', presently suffers one of his glazed spells, after which Edwin 'gently and assiduously tends him', recovers and 'lays a tender hand upon his nephew's shoulder' and then astonishes Edwin by saying he hates his job, provoking Edwin first to bend 'forward in his chair to lay a sympathetic hand on Jasper's knee', next to the declaration 'you love and trust me, as I love and trust you' and thus to the demand 'Both hands, Jack,' which leads to uncle and nephew each standing 'looking into the other's eyes' and holding (both) hands through five exchanges of dialogue.

It is this chapter that is, I think, destined eventually, through the disclosures of the second half, to make clear to the reader, though not necessarily, given its present-tense narrative, to the participants, why the murder is inevitable. Rosa is one of the participants by proxy, by means of the much-looked-at amateur portrait of her by Edwin that hangs on Jasper's wall. Edwin elects himself victim by flirting with Jasper and yet not telling Jasper that his heart is not truly engaged to Rosa.

I think the same dinner discloses the method and the immediate occasion of the murder. Luke Fildes's recollection (in 1905) was that Dickens had told him the 'secret' that Jasper's 'double necktie' was an indispensable property because Jasper was to strangle Drood with it. So far as I can see, Fildes didn't draw a Jasper with a double necktie. No doubt commentators are right in thinking that Dickens replaced the necktie by 'that great black scarf' which Jasper takes to the crucial Christmas Eve meeting. All the same, Dickens's thoughts must have continued, in parallel, along the necktie groove. At his reconciliation with Rosa, Edwin explains to her: 'with me Jack is always impulsive and hurried, and, I may say, almost womanish.' In the next chapter, before he goes to the Christmas Eve meeting he reflects: 'Dear old Jack! If I were to make an extra crease in my neck-cloth, he would think it worth noticing!'

Both thoughts are foreshadowed at the Chapter Two dinner, where, while Edwin takes off his topcoat, hat and gloves, Jasper fusses: 'Your feet are not wet? Pull your boots off. Do pull your boots off.' Edwin replies: 'Don't moddley-coddley, there's a good fellow. I like anything better than being moddley-coddleyed.'

Whether the murder was to have taken place during the Christmas Eve storm or on one of the three ensuing winter nights, I am convinced in my literary bones that it was destined to begin as an act of protective tenderness. Originally, perhaps, Jasper was to tighten Edwin's necktie for him against the cold and Dickens replaced that by an indeed more plausible gesture where Jasper wound his own great black scarf round Edwin's throat. Edwin, I think, was to resist being moddley-coddleyed; and only then was Jasper to make an 'impulsive and hurried' decision (designed, however, to refute and suppress all imputations of the 'womanish') to kill him instead.

Jane Austen's Latest

Marilyn Butler

'There would be more genuine rejoicing at the discovery of a complete new novel by Jane Austen than any other literary discovery, short of a new play by Shakespeare, that one can imagine.' Brian Southam begins his Introduction to 'Grandison' by quoting the apparently prophetic observation of Margaret Drabble in 1974. Ever since she said it, there has been a run of near misses or all-buts, beginning with Another Lady's completion of Jane Austen's fragment 'Sanditon', and continuing with someone else's notion of 'The Watsons'. Then, in the autumn of 1977, there *was* an Austen discovery, not of a novel but not of a fragment either — a complete new play, apparently Jane Austen's version of a work she had admired from childhood, Samuel Richardson's *Sir Charles Grandison*.[1]

It was actually a discovery only in a manner of speaking, since the manuscript was never properly lost. It had been handed down among the descendants of Jane Austen's niece Anna Lefroy, born Anna Austen in 1793, the eldest child of Jane Austen's brother James. According to family tradition, the play, though written down by Jane Austen, was not her brainchild. Anna, who knew *Grandison* as familiarly in youth as her aunt did, was always understood to have devised the play as a child and to have dictated it to Jane Austen. Scholars knew of the existence of the manuscript, and were on the whole not moved to try to see it. But when 'Grandison' was offered for auction at Sotheby's in December 1977, it was examined closely, perhaps for the first time, and the experts apparently concurred in finding that the play was essentially by Jane Austen after all.

Brian Southam, in the Introduction to his edition, gives the line of reasoning:

'Grandison' is over fifty pages long. For all its lightness and absurdity, it bears the stamp of an adult mind. Can we really suppose that a child of seven, too young to write out the play for herself, who had to depend on her aunt as copyist, was capable not just of composing such a work but of composing it in her head? If 'Grandison' was written later than 1800 when

---

[1] *Jane Austen's 'Sir Charles Grandison'*, edited by Brian Southam (Oxford University Press, 1981).

Anna might have been old enough to conceive the play, Jane Austen would
have had no hand in it. At that age the girl could have written it out for
herself.

Taken together, the literary evidence and the chronological circumstances point quite clearly to Jane Austen as the play's author. The manuscript itself provides more evidence. While the paper used for the later
sections is water-marked 1796 and 1799, and the style of the handwriting
looks right for a date around 1800, the handwriting of the opening section,
comprising the whole of Act One, on undated paper, is much less formed,
less mature. These pages were written some years earlier, possibly before
Anna was born.

Exit Anna as a dramatist, and enter Jane Austen, to the considerable enhancement, presumably, of the commercial value of
the document, and its much greater significance for students of
literature.

Among the winners on this occasion was Margaret Drabble, as
an interpreter of contemporary taste. She did not underestimate the
stir due to a new Austen work. Well before we could read the play,
we could hear tantalising snatches of it in a film which began by re-
enacting the Sotheby's auction — *Jane Austen in Manhattan,*
directed by James Ivory and scripted by Ruth Prawer Jhabvala.
Jane Austen's contribution to the film was admittedly slight to
begin with, and became wholly submerged, in what turned out to
be a subtle, ambivalent study of two rival producers of the play,
with very different aesthetic premises but a not dissimilar will to
manipulate their casts. Nevertheless, there could hardly be a greater
tribute to Jane Austen's 20th-century reputation. The international
film-going public was not only expected instantly to recognise her
name: it was expected to know her as a symbol, the acknowledged
classic of a mainstream cultural tradition.

Having seen the film, we can now read the book, either in Brian
Southam's businesslike inexpensive edition, or alternatively in a
three-coloured facsimile costing £150. And after the razzmatazz
there might, in fact, be the occasion for another kind of noise —
the sound of scholars breaking lances.

Some of the likely murmurs of complaint may prove a bit
churlish. Of course we should have preferred a novel, and a
polished performance rather than one written as a family
entertainment, and an original Austen work rather than one
initiated by Richardson. Yet, if it had to be an adaptation, no work
by another artist seems more appropriate and potentially more

significant than Richardson's last novel, which contributed more than any other single book to the tradition of social comedy, naturalistic yet deeply ethical, which Jane Austen inherited. Brian Southam, very much a critic at heart, orientates his edition firmly towards the literary reader, teacher or student, who normally is not concerned with technical problems of handwriting and dating, but will be interested in this discovery precisely for what it has to show about the relationship between one great literary intelligence and another. The deaths in recent times of F.R. and Q.D. Leavis might prompt us, with the coming to light of 'Grandison', to look again at one of their leading critical preoccupations, the handing-on of the English novel's Great Tradition. Southam's Introduction focuses strongly on this aspect of the manuscript — its relationship as a play to the novel which is its source. And after his edited version and transcript of the play, he provides a special series of notes relating 'Grandison' to *Grandison*, for those who are no longer likely to have the same familiarity as the Austen family circle with that seven-volume masterpiece.

Without this informed sense of its literary context, 'Grandison' on its own could prove a sad disappointment. It is a very literal transposition of the more memorable scenes from the novel's main plot, executed by a probably young and certainly not very practised dramatist. The first act is only unembarrassing on the assumption that the author is at most 12 years old; the rest has good touches, but is not overall so very much better, though Southam, perhaps moved a little by that handwriting, makes the best possible literary case for it. He is able to do so because of his hypothesis, already quoted, concerning the date at which the first act was written.

Everything turns, if Southam is right, upon the fact that 'Grandison', though eventually a coherent five-act play, is not a single manuscript. The first act and one cancelled page of a second were scribbled rather untidily on paper with no clear watermark, carelessly trimmed with scissors, and pinned and re-pinned on different occasions. The remaining three groups of paper have been neatly folded, in Jane Austen's characteristic adult manner, into small booklets, in which she has written Acts Two to Five. Not only does the handwriting and one watermark on this paper indicate a date after 1799: there is a reference in Act Three to a popular song, 'Laura and Lenza', which comes from a 'Fairy Ballet' first performed in London at the Haymarket in May 1800. The date of the longer and more accomplished part of 'Grandison', then, cannot be earlier than 1800, and might, for all we can feel sure, be some years later than that. But a date after 1800 is a bit of an embarrassment, and could even turn the discovered play from a rocket into a damp squib. In 1800, Jane Austen was 25, and she had already drafted versions of *Sense and Sensibility, Pride and Prejudice* and *Northanger Abbey*, with the latter two in sufficiently complete shape to be offered to publishers. She was no longer at a stage when she was going to school to the late Richardson.

Yet all is well if, as Southam supposes, the opening Act was written by Jane Austen on her own much earlier, most probably in 1791-2, when she was 16 or 17. In terms of her career as a novelist, this possibility is altogether more satisfying. The lamentable Act One becomes the key part of the play, rich in clues to Jane Austen's literary development. Now it need not matter that 'Grandison', as Southam frankly declares, is no masterpiece, not even a minor masterpiece. 'Love and Friendship' (1790) and 'The History of England' (1791) are much sharper burlesques of, respectively, sentimental novels and history-writing, each of them revealing a sharp eye for literary mannerism and (in a girl of about fifteen) a precocious literary intelligence. By placing 'Grandison' in a similar period, Southam incidentally encourages us to look out for evidence that Richardson's novel, too, is being affectionately sent up. It turns out that examples of what might be taken confidently for burlesque are few and scattered. No matter. Even 'Grandison's' general absence of sparkle becomes interesting, if like Southam we suppose the seriousness to be a symptom that Jane Austen was steadying herself for her productive early period of novel-writing. Thus, without making any inflated claims for the quality of his text, he has so placed it in Jane Austen's career as to maximise its literary importance.

All Southam's principal deductions are supported by Lord David Cecil, in a foreword written with that critic's customary charm, his inimitable blend of middlebrow thoughts in upper-class tones. Though he cavils gently at Jane Austen's taste for *Grandison* ('I cannot help sympathising a little with Miss Andrews in *Northanger Abbey*, who could not get beyond the first volume'), Lord David adds his authority to Southam's account of the play's authorship and nature: 'It is surely incredible that [Anna] should have been capable of the sustained literary effort involved in dramatising [Richardson's seven volumes]; all the more because this is done in a spirit of satirical burlesque intentionally unlike that of the book on which it is founded.'

Words like 'burlesque' and 'intentionally' dignify the play and imply that it is a knowing literary performance. But does 'Grandison' fit the description? Has the battery of experts, those who prepared Sotheby's catalogue as well as Mr Southam and Lord David, established beyond reasonable doubt that 'Grandison' is by Jane Austen at all?

It would be absurd for a reviewer who has not seen the manuscript to state categorically that it isn't. But before 'Grandison' becomes canonical, with all the expenditure of scholarly time that will entail, it is worth noting that some of the grounds of scholarly 'proof' are not all that strong. For example, *when* Jane Austen wrote down Acts Two to Five is not so settled as Southam and Lord David seem to think. There is no tradition that 'Grandison' dates from the time that Anna Austen was seven — that is, from 1800. The family authority on the play's inception is the third of Anna's six daughters, Fanny Caroline Lefroy: 'I have still in my possession, in Aunt Jane's writing, a drama my mother dictated to her, founded on *Sir Charles Grandison*, a book with which she was familiar at seven years old.' This carefully worded statement avoids setting a date on the play. Nor is it quite the case, as Mr Southam seems to think, that Anna could have had no motive for enlisting the help of an amanuensis and sympathetic adviser when she was, say, ten — by which time, as I shall be proposing in a moment, she could have been capable of substantially inventing the play we have before us. Jane Austen's departure from Steventon for Bath in 1801 is not really a bar to the collaboration in the next years, since she continued to visit her brother's family, and they her.

But the authorship of Acts Two to Five can wait, since Southam's case for a dominant contribution by Jane Austen turns on his hypothesis about Act One. The manuscript of the act looks different, so different that it could not have been written by Jane Austen at the same date and state of development as Act Two and the rest. Southam's edition reproduces four pages of manuscript, three of them from the 'early' group, and indeed the examples of dialogue, from page 1 and page 44, do not conform. Nor is Act One set out and written with the most marked personal characteristic of Jane Austen's later years — her celebrated neatness. But if the hand and the execution are as different as this, might it not follow that they are also sufficiently different to have been written by someone other than Jane Austen?

As the author of *Jane Austen's Literary Manuscripts* (1964), Brian Southam has a formidable knowledge of the variations in Jane Austen's early handwriting, and the problems of dating it. Perhaps page 1 of 'Grandison' is so like some of the pages of, say, 'Volume the First' as to account for his confidence in ascribing it to the teenage Jane Austen. Yet one would have like Southam at least to have considered the possibility that Act One was written by a different writer immediately before the rest of the play, since there is some internal evidence that there was no significant lapse of time between the composition of Act One and Act Two.

The evidence in question consists in the cancelled page, intended for the beginning of Act Two, which ends the first, 'early' bundle of papers. These lines represent two false starts at Act Two, which is to deal with much the most stageworthy sequence in the story, the abduction and attempted forced marriage of the heroine, Harriet Byron, by the villainous Sir Hargrave Pollexfen:

Act the 2d. Scene the 1st.
~~Colnebrook.~~
~~Enter Miss Grandison & Miss Byron.~~
Paddington Mrs Awberry's Parlour.
Enter Miss Byron, dragged in by Sir Hargrave Pollexfen.
Mrs Awberry & her two daughters.
Sir Hargrave brings Miss Byron a seat. ~~Miss~~ Awberry goes to a closet & ~~takes out a long cloak, attempts to put it round Miss Byron.~~ —

Southam devotes little attention to these false starts, but they must be highly significant. The first idea was to begin Act Two at Colnebrook, the home of Grandison's sister Lady L—, where Sir Charles took Harriet after rescuing her. (In the play as we now have it, Act Three will begin in this way.) The adapter's first notion, of immediately following Harriet's disappearance with a scene after her rescue, is easily explained when Richardson's novel is consulted. Since he was telling his story in letters, he had to follow a letter reporting Harriet's disappearance with a letter reporting her safe and well at Colnebrook; the exciting details of what had happened in between could be filled in only when Harriet herself was sufficiently recovered to narrate them. The inexperienced adapter thus first had the notion of sticking to the same sequence as the novel, even though it is out of chronological order. She quickly saw how undramatic that would be, and began again with a freer approach to the plot — which nevertheless still begins the scene with a not very material detail about Harriet's masquerade dress, a point Harriet harps on in the novel after she is rescued and before she tells her story. The angle of vision is still appropriate only for the novel, with its subjective way of telling; it is a nuance lost in dramatisation. The new Act Two, in Jane Austen's mature handwriting, begins instead by boldly selecting a dramatic moment from the middle of the abduction scene, when Sir Hargrave overhears Harriet trying to bribe his female aides into helping her to escape. This looks uncommonly like the analytical thinking of an experienced adult, brought to bear when a child arrives with a technical problem. The beginning of Act Two, revised version, could in all probability signal Aunt Jane's arrival on the scene.

In itself, Act One is no loss whatsoever from the Austen canon. As a dramatisation, it is inept; as literature, it has nothing to be said for it, not even as a skit. If Jane Austen's name had not got attached to it, we should surely have no difficulty in taking this much handled sheaf of paper, on which different hands have scribbled, for the record of a semi-improvised production by a group of children. But if that is all there is to Act One, just how strong is Southam's case for Jane Austen's authorship of the entire play? This rested in part on his belief that Anna must have been only seven when it was written: but it depended in practice rather more on his proposition that the first act was written by Jane Austen 'before Anna was born', which makes Jane and not Anna the true begetter of the project.

Putting the technical details aside, what is 'Grandison' most like? A burlesque of Richardson by a clever adolescent or even a practised young novelist? A play begun by a 16-year-old to be acted by her grown-up brothers and sisters, and her sophisticated cousin Eliza de Feuillide? These are Southam's suggestions. Or is it the ad-libbing of a child (or group of children), who happen to know the story of *Grandison*, some of its episodes and many of its verbal expressions, more or less by heart — perhaps from having the story read to them rather than from reading it themselves?

Scholars are not, surely, debarred from using common sense and common experience when the need arises. Children of between, say, eight and 11 cannot be supposed to act and think entirely differently from one century to another. Those of us who have, for our sins, taught in a school, or even been parents, may well have noted certain common characteristics in the child of ten (an age at which little girls often seem more brilliant than little boys). It is the phase of dressing-up; of play-acting; not (if children are left to their own devices) so much of learning some adult's script as of improvising their own. Before the scholars stepped in, the Austen family believed 'Grandison' to have evolved in just this kind of way. Rather than a burlesque, the play reads like a cross between a précis and a literal recapitulation. Its best lines are remembered from the novel. Its worst have the awkwardness and redundancy of children wondering what to say next or (especially) how to get themselves off the stage. There are many clever touches, and not much sense of purpose, especially towards the end. Many an indulgent parent must have sat through something like the following, from the end of Act Four:

MISS G. But come, is not it time to dress? [*looks at her watch*] Dear me! it is but four.
LORD L. You need not say 'But', Charlotte for you know we are to dine at half after four to-day.
MISS G. Indeed, my lord, my lady did not tell me so. Well, I will pardon her this time. Come, then, let us go, if it is time.
Exeunt ladies…
Enter a footman.
FOOT. Dinner is on the table, my lord.
LORD L. Very well.
Exit footman. Enter LADY L., MISS GRANDISON, MISS BYRON *and* MISS JERVOIS.
LORD L. Dinner is upon the table, my dear Caroline.
LADY L. Indeed. Come Harriet and all of you.
Exeunt.

Is this really the writing of one of our greatest novelists, at a stage in her development when she had already completed versions of *Pride and Prejudice* and *Northanger Abbey*? Some years before the date at which Southam proposes that she wrote Act One, she achieved in her fragment 'The Visit' in 'Volume the First' a broad caricature of the Richardsonian drawing-room situation which has more composure and more point than 'Grandison':

Enter the Company.
MISS F. I hope I have the pleasure of seeing your Ladyship well. Sir Arthur, your servant. Yrs Mr Willoughby. Dear Sophy, Dear Cloe, —
[*They pay their Compliments alternately.*]
MISS F. Pray be seated.
[*They sit.*]
Bless me! there ought to be 8 chairs and there are but 6. However, if your

Ladyship will but take Sir Arthur in your lap, & Sophy my Brother in hers,
I beleive we shall do pretty well.
LADY H. Oh! with pleasure...
SOPHY. I beg his Lordship would be seated.
MISS F. I am really shocked at crouding you in such a manner, but my
Grandmother (who bought all the furniture of this room) as she had never
a very large Party, did not think it necessary to buy more Chairs than were
sufficient for her own family and two of her particular freinds.
SOPHY. I beg you will make no apologies. Your brother is very light.

'The Visit' was written to be read, 'Grandison' to be acted.
Southam uses that point to account for the literary deficiency of
'Grandison', but it also helps to determine the date and the authorship. One Southam hypothesis is a stage performance by adults
in the mid-1790s, the infant Anna looking on. The best part, that
of Charlotte Grandison, might have been played by the now
widowed Eliza de Feuillide, who certainly acted at Steventon in
1787-8 and is said on less good authority to have done so again
in the mid-1790s. But what script does Southam mean us to understand that Eliza was using? Is he proposing an Ur-'Grandison'?
Four-fifths of the play he is editing could not have existed before
1800, and the introductory first act would not have been performed
on its own even by children.

'Grandison' is a five-act play — quite an undertaking to perform
— which even with much doubling requires at least seven actors; it
has in all 22 parts, 15 of which are for girls. Southam sees on the
manuscript the signs of a play in rehearsal. But he does not ask the
practical question: when were the Austen family and their friends
sufficiently numerous and theatre-minded to act it? Plays were
regularly performed at Steventon Rectory in the 1780s, while Jane
Austen's father, the Rev. George Austen, was Rector. The leading
spirits in the theatricals were the Rector's elder children: James,
born 1765, Edward (who later took the surname Knight), born
1767, Henry, born 1771. The younger children — Cassandra, born
1773, Francis, born 1774, Jane, born 1775, and Charles, born 1779
— almost certainly took lesser parts or acted as onlookers and
audience. The plays acted seem to have been all comedies, with the
exception of Thomas Franklin's tragedy *Matilda*; of the nine
known titles, seven were first produced on the London stage in the
1770s and 1780s. As far as we know, professional plays were always
chosen, though James Austen provided many of them with
prologues and epilogues. The most spectacular and from a literary

point of view interesting spate of theatricals began at Christmas 1787, when Eliza de Feuillide was staying at Steventon and, according to family tradition, flirting with the 22-year-old James and the 16-year-old Henry.[2] Eventually, after there had been some argument, the group agreed to perform Susannah Centlivre's *The Wonder: A Woman keeps a secret* (1714), in which the heroine (Eliza?) proposes to a man. The 12-year-old Jane Austen was presumably an observer of these fraught theatrical doings; in *Mansfield Park* she puts Fanny Price inarticulately in the same role, only substituting for Susannah Centlivre's bold play a work smacking of more up-to-date impropriety, Kotzebue's *Lovers' Vows*.

The Steventon theatricals are well-documented for the 1780s, when the Rectory was crowded with young people, the Rector's resident pupils supplementing his own family as they grew up. There are no such records afterwards, no extant prologues and epilogues, no references to acting in letters for any period in the 1790s, when the Rector had ceased to take in pupils, all the Austen sons except the mentally retarded George had left home, and only Cassandra and Jane among the younger generation remained. The literary efforts and fireside amusements of the 1790s — including Jane Austen's juvenilia — were, perforce, of a kind to be read rather than acted. There is, then, no evidence that Jane Austen wrote anything to be performed by her elder brothers. Indeed, there is a certain improbability in the idea that these polished actors, Oxford graduates and undergraduates, with literary pretensions of their own, would have condescended to learn lines written for them by a child.

Who could have written 'Grandison'? Who might have wanted it? In 1801 the Rev. George Austen retired to Bath, taking his wife and daughters with him. His eldest son, the Rev. James Austen — he of the theatricals — moved into Steventon Rectory with his wife and young children. Jane Austen was a good aunt to her many nephews and nieces, but proximity ensured she was closest to the Steventon family, who became in later years the chief source of biographical information about her. It was James's son, the Rev. J.E. Austen-Leigh (born 1798), who put together the family

---

[2]Much the fullest account of the Steventon theatricals and of James Austen's hitherto unknown Epilogues, will appear in George Holbert Tucker's forthcoming 'intimate history' of the Austen family, *A Goodly Heritage*.

Memoir of Jane Austen (1870), with the assistance particularly of his sister Caroline Austen (born 1803) and of his half-sister Anna, who since 1814 had been Mrs Lefroy. All three remembered their aunt as a great entertainer of children. Caroline recalled being told serialised fairy-tales, and being given clothes from Jane Austen's wardrobe with which to dress up. Anna was ten years older than Caroline, and on the whole in her recollections *she* told the stories, while Jane played the part of the encouraging or amused listener. When Anna was grown up and married she was still telling Jane stories: ridiculous versions of the novels she had borrowed from Alton circulating library, or her own attempt at a novel, which was to have been called *Which is the Heroine?* or *Enthusiasm.* To Anna's novel Jane Austen responded with amiable criticism: 'I wish you would not let him plunge into a "vortex of Dissipation". I do not object to the Thing, but I cannot bear the expression; — it is such thorough novel slang — and so old, that I dare say Adam met with it in the first novel he opened.'

Demoting Anna's part in 'Grandison' seems a bit of a shame. For an Austen, that 'large and clever family', she had what almost amounts to a deprived childhood. Her own mother, James's first wife, died when she was two, and Anna had to be sent to her grandparents and aunts at Steventon Rectory to be comforted. Part of the comfort over the next two years included being let in on the secret first readings of what was to be *Pride and Prejudice.* After James remarried in January 1797, Anna lived under the parental roof, but not happily, since she and her stepmother, the former Mary Lloyd, never got on. From Jane Austen's letters Mary emerges as a touchy, strong-willed, mean and narrow-minded woman, who came to exercise a strong influence over her husband which effectively cut out Anna. Jane Austen tried to intervene on Anna's behalf — for example, urging James to pay more attention to his eldest child; though Anna, moody, reckless and charming by turns, always 'doing too little or too much', was evidently an exasperating protégée. Jane Austen must have helped her more effectively by taking an interest herself: introducing her, perhaps, to the favourite reading of her own childhood, *Grandison*, encouraging her to write, telling her how the previous generation of children at Steventon Rectory had entertained themselves with theatricals. In those days Anna's father had been the leading light. Perhaps his neglected eldest daughter hoped to emulate him, and even to attract his attention, by getting her aunt to help her to stage a play.

Whether 'Grandison' ever was staged in its entirety may never be resolved. Many children in the same age-range gathered together when James Austen's children visited their Knight cousins at Godmersham in Kent, or when the Knights came to Steventon. Perhaps Act One spontaneously took shape on one such visit, and Anna then pressed her aunt to help her to write a complete script in time for the next opportunity — which may or may not have come. The two of them, niece and aunt, must have spent many hours together, at Bath or at Steventon, working out the form the play would take, with Anna evidently giving most attention to the part she identified with — that of Charlotte Grandison, Sir Charles's sprightly, rebellious sister. Charlotte's jokes in 'Grandison' are those of a bright, pert child, clearly a terror in a drawing-room.

LORD G. I am afraid I have been making you wait, gentlemen.
MISS G. Well, you need not be afraid any longer, for you most certainly have.

A bright child further expresses itself in faithfully retained verbal mannerism (Mr Selby's 'Adzooks!') and comic detail. Her aunt's taste is heard equally unmistakably in the discreet, mannerly tones of 'straight' characters, like the principals Harriet and Sir Charles Grandison, some of whose quiet rejoinders seem rebukes not directed to Charlotte alone. 'I will not be bribed into liking your wit, Charlotte.'

If this is the case, Jane Austen did not 'really' write 'Grandison' herself, while amiably letting Anna believe the play to be her own. Her contributions — the technical solution to staging Act Two, the more polite and adult lines of dialogue — unobtrusively rescued the play, but would not seem important to a child. They amount, surely, to less than joint authorship. In Anna's play, it was proper for Jane Austen to efface the continuous wit and literariness of her own writing, from childhood on. She maintained the same sympathetic, encouraging modesty when years later Anna was writing her novel: 'If you think differently, do not mind me.'

Such an interpretation extracts relatively little from 'Grandison' about Jane Austen the dramatist and Jane Austen the heir of Richardson. But it is not wholly without its insights. There are those who find Jane Austen the novelist and (especially) Jane Austen the domestic letter-writer a subtly unlikeable figure. Jane Austen the aunt emerges from the 'discovery' as an unmixed blessing.

The Prophet's Hair

Salman Rushdie

Early in 19—, when Srinagar was under the spell of a winter so fierce it could crack men's bones as if they were glass, a young man upon whose cold-pinked skin there lay, like a frost, the unmistakable sheen of wealth was to be seen entering the most wretched and disreputable part of the city, where the houses of wood and corrugated iron seemed perpetually on the verge of losing their balance, and asking in low, grave tones where he might go to engage the services of a dependably professional thief. The young man's name was Atta, and the rogues in that part of town directed him gleefully into ever-darker and less public alleys, until in a yard wet with the blood of a slaughtered chicken he was set upon by two men whose faces he never saw, robbed of the substantial bank-roll which he had insanely brought on his solitary excursion, and beaten within an inch of his life.

Night fell. His body was carried by anonymous hands to the edge of the lake, whence it was transported by shikara across the water and deposited, torn and bleeding, on the deserted embankment of the canal which led to the gardens of Shalimar. At dawn the next morning a flower-vendor was rowing his boat through water to which the cold of the night had given the cloudy consistency of wild honey when he saw the prone form of young Atta, who was just beginning to stir and moan, and on whose now deathly pale skin the sheen of wealth could still be made out dimly beneath an actual layer of frost. The flower-vendor moored his craft and by stooping over the mouth of the injured man was able to learn the poor fellow's address, which was mumbled through lips which could scarcely move; whereupon, hoping for a large tip, the hawker rowed Atta home to a large house on the shores of the lake, where a painfully beautiful girl and her equally handsome mother, neither of whom, it was clear from their eyes, had slept a wink from worrying, screamed at the sight of their Atta — who was the elder brother of the beautiful girl — lying motionless amid the funereally stunted winter blooms of the hopeful florist. The flower-vendor was indeed paid off handsomely, not least to ensure his silence, and plays no further part in our story. Atta himself, suffering terribly from exposure as well as a broken skull, entered a coma which caused the city's finest doctors to shrug helplessly. It was therefore all the more remarkable that on the very same evening the most wretched and disreputable part of the city received a second unexpected visitor. This was Huma, the sister of the unfortunate young man, and her question was the same as her brother's, and asked in the same low, grave tones: 'Where may I hire a thief?'

The story of the rich idiot who had come looking for a burglar was already common knowledge in those insalubrious gullies, but this time the girl added: 'I should say that I am carrying no money, nor am I wearing any jewels: my father has disowned me and will pay no ransom if I am kidnapped; and a letter has been lodged with the Commissioner of Police, my uncle, to be opened in the event of my not being safe at home by morning. In that letter he will find full details of my journey here, and he will move Heaven and Earth to punish my assailants.' Her extraordinary beauty, which was visible even through the enormous welts and bruises disfiguring her arms and forehead, coupled with the oddity of her inquiries, had attracted a sizable group of curious onlookers, and because her little speech seemed to them to cover just about everything, no one attempted to injure her in any way, although there were some raucous comments to the effect that it was pretty peculiar for someone who was trying to hire a crook to invoke the protection of a high-up policeman uncle. She was directed into ever-darker and less public alleys until finally in a gully as dark as ink an old woman with eyes which stared so piercingly that Huma instantly understood she was blind motioned her through a doorway from which darkness seemed to be pouring like smoke. Clenching her fists, angrily ordering her heart to behave normally, the girl followed the old woman into the gloom-wrapped house.

The faintest conceivable rivulet of candlelight trickled through the darkness; following this unreliable yellow thread (because she could no longer see the old lady), Huma received a sudden sharp blow to the shins and cried out involuntarily, after which she instantly bit her lip, angry at having revealed her mounting terror to whatever waited there shrouded in black. She had, in fact, collided with a low table on which a single candle burned and beyond which a mountainous figure could be made out, sitting crosslegged on the floor. 'Sit, sit,' said a man's calm, deep voice, and her legs, needing no more flowery invitation, buckled beneath her at the terse command. Clutching her left hand in her right, she forced her voice to respond evenly: 'And you, sir, will be the thief I have been requesting?'

Shifting its weight very slightly, the shadow-mountain informed her that all criminal activity originating in this zone was well organised and also centrally controlled, so that all requests for what might be termed freelance work had to be channelled through this room. He demanded comprehensive details of the crime to be committed, including a precise inventory of items to be acquired, also a clear statement of all financial inducements being offered with no gratuities excluded, plus, for filing purposes only, a summary of the motives for the application. At this, Huma, as though remembering something, stiffened both in body and resolve and replied loudly that her motives were entirely a matter for herself; that she would discuss details with no one but the thief himself; but that the rewards she proposed could only be described as 'lavish'. 'All I am willing to say to you, sir, since this appears to be some sort of employment agency, is that in return for such lavish rewards I must have the most desperate criminal at your disposal, a man for whom life holds no terrors, not even the fear of God. The worst of fellows, I tell you — nothing less will do!'

Now a paraffin storm-lantern was lighted, and Huma saw facing her a grey-haired giant down whose left cheek ran the most sinister of scars, a cicatrice in the shape of the Arabic letter 'S'. She had the insupportably nostalgic notion that the bogymen of her childhood nursery had risen up to confront her, because her ayah had always forestalled any incipient acts of disobedience by threatening Huma and Atta: 'You don't watch out and I'll send that one to steal you away — that Sheikh Sin, the Thief of Thieves!' Here, grey-haired but unquestionably scarred, was the notorious criminal himself — and was she crazy, were her ears playing tricks, or had he truly just announced that, given the circumstances, he himself was the only man for the job?

Struggling wildly against the newborn goblins of nostalgia, Huma warned the fearsome volunteer that only a matter of extreme urgency and peril would have brought her unescorted into these ferocious streets. 'Because we can afford no last-minute backings-out,' she continued, 'I am determined to tell you everything, keeping back no secrets whatsoever. If, after hearing me out, you are still prepared to proceed, then we shall do everything in our power both to assist you and make you rich.' The old thief shrugged, nodded, spat. Huma began her story.

Six days ago, everything in the household of her father, the wealthy moneylender Hashim, had been as it always was. At breakfast her mother had spooned khichri lovingly onto the moneylender's plate; the conversation had been filled with those expressions of courtesy and solicitude on which the family prided itself. Hashim was fond of pointing out that while he was not a godly man he set great store by 'living honourably in the world'. In that spacious lakeside residence, all outsiders were greeted with the same formality and respect, even those unfortunates who came to negotiate for small fragments of Hashim's great fortune, and of whom he naturally asked an interest rate of 71 per cent, partly, as he told his khichri-spooning wife, 'to teach these people the value of money: let them only learn that, and they will be cured of this fever of borrowing, borrowing all the time — so you see that if my plans succeed, I shall put myself out of business!' In their children, Atta and Huma, the moneylender and his wife had sought, successfully, to inculcate the virtues of thrift, plain dealing, perfect manners and a healthy independence of spirit.

Breakfast ended; the family wished each other a fulfilling day. Within a few hours, however, the glassy contentment of that household, of that life of porcelain delicacy and alabaster sensibilities, was to be shattered beyond all hope of repair.

The moneylender summoned his personal shikara and was on the verge of stepping into it when, attracted by a glint of silver, he noticed a small phial floating between the boat and his private quay. On an impulse, he scooped it out of the glutinous water: it was a cylinder of tinted glass cased in exquisitely-wrought silver, and Hashim saw within its walls a silver pendant bearing a single strand of human hair. Closing his fist around this unique discovery, he muttered to the boatman that he'd changed his plans, and hurried to his sanctum where, behind closed doors, he feasted his eyes on his find. There can be no doubt that Hashim the moneylender knew from the first that he was in possession of the famous holy hair of the Prophet Muhammad, whose theft from the shrine at Hazratbal the previous morning had created an unprecedented hue and cry in the valley. The thieves — no doubt alarmed by the pandemonium, by the procession through the streets of the endless ululating crocodiles of lamentation, by the riots, the political ramifications and by the massive police search which was commanded and carried out by men whose entire careers now hung upon this single lost hair — had evidently panicked and hurled the phial into the gelatine bosom of the lake. Having found it by a stroke of good fortune, Hashim's duty as a citizen was clear: the hair must be restored to its shrine, and the state to equanimity and peace.

But the moneylender had formed a different notion. All about him in his study was the evidence of collector's mania: great cases of impaled butterflies from Gulmarg, three dozen miniature cannons cast from the melted-down metal of the great gun Zamzama, innumerable swords, a Naga spear, ninety-four terracotta camels of the sort sold on railway-station platforms and an infinitude of tiny sandalwood dolls, which had originally been carved to serve as children's bathtime toys. 'And after all,' Hashim told himself, 'the Prophet would have disapproved mightily of this relic-worship: he abhorred the idea of being deified, so by keeping this rotting hair from its mindless devotees, I perform — do I not? — a finer service than I would by returning it! Naturally, I don't want it for its religious value: I'm a man of the world, of this world; I see it purely as a secular object of great rarity and blinding beauty — in short, it's the phial I desire, not the hair. There are American millionaires who buy stolen paintings and hide them away — they would know how I feel. I must, must have it!'

Every collector must share his treasures with one other human being, and Hashim summoned — and told — his only son Atta, who was deeply perturbed but, having been sworn to secrecy, only spilt the beans when the troubles became too terrible to bear. The youth left his father alone in the crowded solitude of his collections. Hashim was sitting erect in a hard chair, gazing intently at the beautiful phial.

It was well-known that the moneylender never ate lunch, so it was not until evening that a servant entered the sanctum to summon his master to the dining-table. He found Hashim as Atta had left him. The same, but not the same: because now the moneylender looked swollen, distended, his eyes bulged even more than they always had, they were red-rimmed and his knuckles were white. It was as though he was on the point of bursting, as though, under the influence of the misappropriated relic, he had filled up with some spectral fluid which might at any moment ooze uncontrollably from his every bodily opening. He had to be helped to the table, and then the explosion did indeed take place. Seemingly careless of the effect of his words on the carefully-constructed and fragile constitution of the family's life, Hashim began to gush, to spume streams of terrible truths. In horrified silence, his children heard their father turn upon his wife, and reveal to her that for many years their marriage had been the worst of his afflictions. 'An end to politeness!' he thundered. 'An end to hypocrisy!' He revealed to his family the existence of a mistress; he informed them of his regular visits to paid women. He told his wife that, far from being the principal beneficiary of his will, she would receive no more than the eighth portion which was her due under Islamic law. Then he turned upon his children, screaming at Atta for his lack of academic ability — 'A dope! I have been cursed with a dope!' — and accusing his daughter of lasciviousness, because she went around the city barefaced, which was unseemly for any good Muslim girl to do: she should, he commanded, enter purdah forthwith. He left the table without having eaten and fell into the deep sleep of a man who has got many things off his chest, leaving his children stunned, his wife in tears, and the dinner going cold on the sideboard under the gaze of an anticipatory bearer.

At five o'clock the next morning the moneylender forced his family to rise, wash and say their prayers; from that time on, he began to pray five times daily for the first time in his life, and his wife and children were obliged to do likewise. Before breakfast, Huma saw the servants, under her father's direction, constructing a great heap of books in the garden and setting fire to it. The only volume left untouched was the Quran, which Hashim wrapped in a silken cloth and placed on a table in the hall. He ordered each member of his family to read passages from this book for at least two hours per day. Visits to the cinema were also forbidden. And if Atta invited male friends to the house, Huma was to retire to her room.

By now, the family had entered a state of wild-eyed horror; but there was worse to come. That afternoon, a trembling debtor arrived at the house to confess his inability to pay the latest instalment of interest owed, and made the mistake of reminding Hashim, in somewhat blustering fashion, of the Quran's strictures against usury. The moneylender, flying into a rage, attacked the fellow with one of his large collection of bull-whips. By mischance, later the same day a second defaulter came to plead for time, and was seen fleeing Hashim's study with a great gash on his arm, because Huma's father had called him a thief of other men's money and had tried to cut off the fellow's right hand with one of the thirty-eight kukri knives hanging on the study walls. These breaches of the family's laws of decorum alarmed Atta and Huma, and when, that evening, their mother attempted to calm Hashim down, he struck her on the face with an open hand. Atta leapt to his mother's defence and he, too, was sent flying. 'From now on,' Hashim bellowed, 'there's going to be some discipline around here!'

The moneylender's wife began a fit of hysteria which continued throughout the night and the following day, and which so provoked her husband that he threatened her with divorce, at which she fled to her room, locked the door and subsided into a raga of sniffling. Huma now lost her composure, challenged her father openly, announced (with that same independence of spirit which he had encouraged in her) that she would wear no cloth over her face: apart from anything else, it was bad for the eyes. On hearing this, her father disowned her at once and gave her one week in which to pack her bags.

By the fourth day, the fear in the air of the house had become so thick that it was difficult to walk around. Atta told his shock-numbed sister: 'We are descending to gutter-level — but I know what must be done.'

That afternoon, Hashim left home accompanied by two hired thugs to extract the unpaid dues from his two insolvent clients. Atta went immediately to his father's study. Being the son and heir, he possessed his own key to the moneylender's safe, which he now used, and removing the little phial from its hiding place, he slipped it into his trouser pocket and re-locked the safe door.

Now he told Huma the secret of what his father had found in Lake Dal, and cried: 'Maybe I'm crazy — maybe the awful things that are happening have made me cracked — but I am convinced there will be no peace in our house until this hair is out of it.' His sister instantly agreed that the hair must be returned and Atta set off in a hired shikara to Hazratbal mosque. Only when the boat had delivered him into the throng of the distraught faithful which was swirling around the desecrated shrine did Atta discover that the relic was no longer in his pocket. There was only a hole, which his mother, usually so attentive to household matters, must have overlooked under the stress of recent events...Atta's initial surge of chagrin was quickly replaced by a feeling of profound relief. 'Suppose,' he imagined, 'I had already announced to the mullahs that the hair was on my person! They would never have believed me now — and this mob would have lynched me! At any rate, it's gone, and that's a load off my mind.' Feeling more contented than he had for days, the young man returned home.

Here he found his sister bruised and weeping in the hall; upstairs, in her bedroom, his mother wailed like a brand-new widow. He begged Huma to tell him what had happened, and when she replied that their father, returning from his brutal business trip, had once again noticed a glint of silver between boat and quay, had once again scooped up the errant relic, and was consequently in a rage to end all rages, having beaten the truth out of her — then Atta buried his face in his hands and sobbed that, in his opinion, the hair was persecuting them, that it had come back to finish the job.

Now it was Huma's turn to think of a way out of their troubles. While her arms turned black and blue and great stains spread across her forehead, she hugged her brother and whispered to him her determination to get rid of the hair *at all costs*: she repeated this last phrase several times. 'The hair,' she then declared, 'must be stolen. It was stolen from the mosque; it can be stolen from this house. But it must be a genuine robbery, carried out by a real thief, not by one of us who are the hair's victims — by a thief so desperate that he fears neither capture nor curses.' Of course, she added, the theft would be ten times harder to pull off now that their father, knowing that there had already been one attempt on the relic, was certainly on his guard.

'Can you do it?' Huma, in a room lit by candle and storm-lantern, ended her account with this question: 'What assurances can you give that the job holds no terrors for you still?' The criminal, spitting, stated that he was not in the habit of providing references, as a cook might, or a gardener, but he was not alarmed so easily, not by any children's djinn of a curse. The girl had to be content with this boast, and proceeded to describe the details of the proposed burglary. 'Since my brother's failure to restore the hair to the mosque, my father has taken to sleeping with his precious treasure under his pillow. However, he sleeps alone and very energetically: only enter his room without waking him, and he will certainly have tossed and turned quite enough to make the theft a simple matter. When you have the phial, come to my room,' and here she handed Sheikh Sin a plan of her home, 'and I will hand over all the jewellery owned by my mother and by myself. You will find...It is worth...You will be able to get a fortune for it...' It was clear that her self-control was weakening and that she was on the point of physical collapse. 'Tonight,' she burst out finally, 'you must come tonight!'

No sooner had she left the room than the old criminal's body was convulsed by a fit of coughing: he spat blood into an old tin can. The great Sheikh, the 'Thief of Thieves', was also an old and sick man, and every day the time drew nearer when some young pretender to his power would stick a dagger in his stomach. A lifelong addiction to gambling had left him as poor as he had been when, decades ago, he had started out in this line of work as a mere pickpocket's apprentice: in the extraordinary commission he had accepted from the moneylender's daughter he saw his opportunity of amassing enough wealth, at a stroke, to leave the valley and acquire the luxury of a respectable death which would leave his stomach intact.

As for the Prophet's hair, well, neither he nor his blind wife had ever had much to say for prophets — that was one thing they had in common with the moneylender's clan. It would not do, however, to reveal the nature of this, his last crime, to his four sons: to his consternation, they had all grown up into hopelessly devout fellows, who even spoke absurdly of making the pilgrimage to Mecca some day. 'But how will you go?' their father would laugh at them, because, with the absolutist love of a parent, he had made sure they were all provided with a lifelong source of high income by crippling them at birth, so that, as they dragged themselves around the city, they earned excellent money in the begging business. The children, then, could look after themselves; he and his wife would be off with the jewel-boxes of the moneylender's women. It was a timely chance indeed that had brought the beautiful bruised girl into his corner of the town.

That night, the large house on the shore of the lake lay blindly waiting, with silence lapping at its walls. A burglar's night: clouds in the sky and mists on the winter water. Hashim the moneylender was asleep, the only member of his family to whom sleep had come that night. In another room, his son Atta lay deep in the coils of his coma with a blood-clot forming on his brain, watched over by a mother who had let down her long greying hair to show her grief, a mother who placed warm compresses on his head with gestures redolent of impotence. In yet a third bedroom Huma waited, fully dressed, amidst the jewel-heavy caskets of her desperation. At last a bulbul sang softly from the garden below her window and, creeping downstairs, she opened a door to the bird, on whose face there was a scar in the shape of the Arabic letter 'S'. Noiseless now, the bird flew up the stairs behind her. At the head of the staircase they parted, moving in opposite directions along the corridor of their conspiracy without a glance at one another.

Entering the moneylender's room with professional ease, the burglar, Sin, discovered that Huma's predictions had been wholly accurate. Hashim lay sprawled diagonally across his bed, the pillow untenanted by his head, the prize easily accessible. Step by padded step, Sin moved towards the goal. It was at this point that young Atta, without any warning, his vocal cords prompted by God knows what pressure of the clot upon his brain, sat bolt upright in his bed, giving his mother the fright of her life, and screamed at the top of his voice: 'Thief! Thief! Thief!'

It seems probable that his poor mind had been dwelling, in these last moments, upon his own father, but it is impossible to be certain, because having uttered these three emphatic words the young man fell back on his pillow and died. At once his mother set up a screeching and a wailing and a keening and a howling so ear-splittingly intense as to complete the work which Atta's cry had begun — that is, her laments penetrated the walls of her husband's bedroom and brought Hashim wide awake.

Sheikh Sin was just deciding whether to dive beneath the bed or brain the moneylender good and proper when Hashim grabbed the tiger-striped swordstick which always stood propped up in a corner beside his bed, and rushed from the room without so much as noticing the burglar who stood on the opposite side of the bed in the darkness. Sin stooped quickly and removed the phial containing the Prophet's hair from its hiding place.

Meanwhile Hashim had erupted into the corridor, having unsheathed the sword inside his stick; he was waving the blade about dementedly with his right hand and shaking the stick with his left. Now a shadow came rushing towards him through the midnight darkness of the passageway and, in his somnolent anger, the moneylender thrust his sword fatally through its heart. Turning up the light, he found that he had murdered his daughter, and under the dire influence of this accident he found himself so persecuted by remorse that he turned the sword upon himself, fell upon it and so extinguished his life. His wife, the sole surviving member of the family, was driven mad by the general carnage and had to be committed to an asylum for the insane by her brother, the city's Commissioner of Police.

Sheikh Sin had quickly understood that the plan had gone awry: abandoning the dream of the jewel-boxes when he was but a few yards from its fulfilment, he climbed out of Hashim's window and made his escape during the awful events described above. Reaching home before dawn, he woke his wife and confessed his failure: it would be necessary, he said, for him to vanish for a while. Her blind eyes never opened until he had gone.

The noise in the Hashim household had roused their servants and even awakened the night-watchman, who had been fast asleep as usual on his charpoy by the gate; the police were alerted and the Commissioner himself informed. When he heard of Huma's death, the mournful officer opened and read the sealed letter which his niece had given him, and instantly led a large detachment of armed men into the light-repellent gullies of the most wretched and disreputable part of the city. The tongue of a malicious cat-burglar named Huma's fellow conspirator; the finger of an ambitious bank-robber pointed at the house in which he lay concealed; and although Sin managed to crawl through a hatch in the attic and attempt a roof-top escape, a bullet from the Commissioner's own rifle penetrated his stomach and brought him crashing messily to the ground at the feet of the enraged uncle. From the dead man's ragged pockets rolled a phial of tinted glass, cased in filigree silver.

The recovery of the Prophet's hair was announced at once on All-India Radio. One month later, the valley's holiest men assembled at the Hazratbal mosque and formally authenticated the relic. It sits to this day in a closely-guarded vault by the shores of the loveliest of lakes in the heart of the valley which is closer than any other place on earth to Paradise.

But before its story can properly be concluded, it is necessary to record that when the four sons of the dead Sheikh awoke on that morning of his death, having unwittingly spent a few minutes under the same roof as the holy hair, they found that a miracle had occurred, that they were all sound of limb and strong of wind, as whole as they might have been if their father had not thought to smash their legs in the first hours of their lives. They were, all four of them, very properly furious, because this miracle had reduced their earning powers by 75 per cent, at the most conservative estimate: so they were ruined men.

Only the Sheikh's widow had some reason for feeling grateful, because although her husband was dead she had regained her sight, so that it was possible for her to spend her last days gazing once more upon the beauties of the valley of Kashmir.

Bites from the Bearded Crocodile

G. Cabrera Infante

The decline of the so-called Cuban cultural renaissance started when Virgilio Pinera came down the ladder of the Czech airplane that brought him back from Brussels via Prague. He deplaned with mincing steps and, fluttering like a tropical butterfly suddenly sprung alive from a collector's case, stopped briefly and then kneeled and leaned forward to kiss the red Cuban soil — only to smack the tarmac instead. (This gesture proved to be some sort of near-miss-cum-hubris for, you see, the runway had recently been covered with a Russian blacktop.) Though it didn't really all begin then, but a few months earlier when *Lunes,* the literary supplement of the newspaper *Revolucion,* on which Virgilio Pinera was one of the principal collaborators (the word was usually meant in its second sense), was banned and closed down for good. Only it didn't begin then either, but when they censored and sequestered *PM*, a documentary sponsored by *Lunes* that didn't have any political content to warrant the seizure. That was really the beginning of the end. But let's start at the very beginning — which was when dictator Batista decided to flee instead of fighting and the 26th of July Movement took over the Government in the name of the Revolution, its martyrs and the poor people of Cuba.

Let's face it once and for all: it is true that there were more houses of ill repute than publishing houses in Havana before the Revolution — or more properly, Fidel Castro — seized power in 1959. But you can say the same of New York now, where, on a stroll down Broadway, you'll be able to meet more whores than writers and see more pimps than literary agents — no equation intended. If this happens in the metropolis, imagine the colonies. And Havana was the nearest Latin city to urban America — unless you want to insult Tijuana and call it a city. Before 1960 there were a few private houses but these mostly published textbooks. Other adventurous printers, whom you could equate with gigolos, were engaged in some kind of vanity publishing. Even Jose Lezama Lima, one of the true great poets in the 20th-century Spanish-speaking world, submitted to the extortion willingly, even gladly. It

275

was his rich friends who paid for the publication of such masterpieces as *Enemigo Rumor* ('Alien Rumour', 1941), *Aventuras Sigilosas* ('Adventures in Stealth', 1945) and *La Fijeza* ('Transfixed Beauty', 1949). It didn't matter that Juan Ramon Jimenez, the fastidious Spanish poet, a Republican refugee and future Nobel winner, had made seemingly extravagant claims about young Lezama's poetry. If he wanted to see his poems published, Lezama (or his patrons) had to pay for it. It was a flagrant literary mugging: your money or your silence. For Lezama, as for most Cuban writers, then, it was a question of perish to publish.

Of course there were real publishing houses then, not just one, as they have in Cuba now, run by the state at the service of party propaganda. The one they have now is the National Printing House where, under the rule of Alejo Carpentier (more later), 100,000 copies of *Moby Dick* were published — slightly abridged. The Cuban publishers had cleverly rewritten Melville. You had Ishmael, you had Queequeg, you had Captain Ahab, of course, you even had Father Mapple: but you couldn't find God in the labyrinth of the sea. Before the Revolution, some *ci-devant* publishing houses worked for the government in power, any government, even foreign ones. They would print Venezuelan authors in costly and garish editions, paid for not by the writers but by Venezuela herself, a country always rich in oil but poor in ink.

But there were other cultural achievements beyond printing deluxe editions of Cuban classics in the very young Caribbean republic. One must not forget that Cuba was the last colony in America to become independent from Spain. This happened only in 1902, and after that the small island was submitted to some sort of dependence on the United States until 1958. The strong links were only economic and political, though, and the American influence never really amounted to much in Cuban cultural life, which was oriented towards Europe, especially to France and Spain. Most Cuban writers could read and write French fluently, but very few had any English. The only thing American that was truly influential — and this only at a popular level — were Hollywood movies, as pervasive in Cuba then as they are in England now. Those remarkable achievements I mentioned before were in painting, architecture, the theatre and, of course, Cuban popular music: though actually extinct on the island, like the Cuban manatee, its irresistible song can be heard from Paris to Parana.

Believe it or not, the history of Cuban literature is one of the longest in America. It is not as long as the history of literature in England, of course, but there were poets writing and being published in Cuba before they named the American colonies New England. According to lore, the first Cuban poet was a Spaniard settled on the island who had the appropriate name of Silvestre de Balboa — his last name was fit for a conquistador, his first for silvan poetry. But Balboa wrote an epic instead. Published in 1605, *Espejo de Paciencia* ('The Looking-Glass of Patience') is a long poem that lay forgotten for more than two centuries, until it was rediscovered in 1834. It was about that time that Jose Maria de Heredia (cousin to the French Heredia, famous for his *Trophées*) wrote what is considered the first Romantic poem ever written in Spanish, 'The Ode to Niagara', conceived under the influence of Chateaubriand's prose and composed in exile in the USA. The 19th century gave us Jose Marti's powerful prose, written in exile in Spain and New York. Marti is perhaps the greatest prose-writer in all of the Spanish 19th century. A spell-binding novel, *Cecilia Valdes*, was written by Cirilo Villaverde in his exile in the 1880s in New York. Besides many minor poets, the Cuban 19th century produced a great poet, the subtly symbolist Julian del Casal, after Ruben Dario the greatest *modernista* poet ever. One should never confuse *modernismo,* with a small m, with Modernism in English, a quite different, later literary mood. The *modernista* was a strictly poetic movement, initiated in Latin America but taking off from the French Symbolists: ten poems that shook the Spanish-speaking world, mainly through the genius of Ruben Dario, the Indian poet from Nicaragua who sang of swans in Spain. Marti, himself a poet, was a precursor of *modernismo* without actually having to do with symbolism, French or otherwise. Marti was a true original. Unfortunately, he is only known today as the man who provided Pete Seeger with the lyrics for his apocryphal song 'Guantanamera'. The gospel according to Vanessa Redgrave is that Jose Marti, who died on a Cuban battlefield in 1895, is a close friend of Comandante Fidel Castro's. Of course anachronism is Miss Redgrave's forte, but this time she was dead right to show us how anachronistic it would be for a poet to be friends with Comandante Castro.

During the infamous Cuban Cultural Congress in 1971 (much more later), Fidel Castro said in his closing speech that before the Revolution there was only one theatre in Havana. He was lying, of course. But then the British reader might say that at least the man cared about culture. It would have been better if he didn't. One bit of learned advice to the British reader: if you hear Margaret Thatcher or her successor Big Benn speaking in the Commons on the state of the box-office in the West End, you'd better brace yourself because an English version of Dr Goebbels is surely limping his way down Whitehall — to take care of the Ministry for Public Enlightenment and Propaganda. The truth is that Fidel Castro never cared about the theatre or literature, or even mural painting, for that matter. He only cares about power and its total tool, propaganda. He is known even to have used Beckett's plays, to have said that *Waiting for Godot* showed the kind of capitalist-induced misery you'll never find in Cuba now. Godot forbids.

With all its political infirmities, and there were many, travellers to Cuba were surprised at what they saw. Even in 1958 somebody as alien as Sacheverell Sitwell enthuses over a song about Havana night life. As late as 1959, the British historian Hugh Thomas recognised that Cuba was one of the few tropical countries to have created a modern culture of its own. He also noticed that Fidel Castro owed his power not to guerrilla warfare, as he had believed before visiting Cuba, but to television. The way Castro used the television screen for his seizure of power was very similar to the use Adolf Hitler made of PA systems in Germany in the Thirties. At the time, 1960, Cuba had more TV sets than Italy, statistics that come as a surprise to many. In 1969 I was at a party in Hollywood at the house of a famous and wealthy film-maker, when he began asking me about life in Cuba. Those were the days of the war in Vietnam and Americans were regressing to the late Thirties, the decade when they suffered the vision of the blind in seeing Stalin as a saviour of civilisation as they knew it. Among the guests of this liberal director there was a well-known Austrian philosopher, now deceased. He had been a refugee from Nazi Germany since 1937. Both he and the movie director were Jewish. So was the director's beautiful wife. After hearing my story of dire needs and disasters the popular philosopher asked me in his still thick German accent: 'But isn't it true zat unter Doktor Castro de island has made a great progress in public health and education?' I'd heard the question before in many languages, with different accents, and I had a bitter double analogy on the tip of my logical, not ideological tongue: 'Mussolini made the Italian trains arrive on time for the first time since they were invented. Hitler, on the other hand, not only laid out the autobahns' — he grimaced at my plural — 'but lifted

Germany out of its economic and moral morass. At least, that's what my favourite great-uncle used to say over and over in my home town in Eastern Cuba. This happened before World War Two. Funnily enough, my great-uncle, a sweet soul, was a Nazi who became a vegetarian when he knew Hitler was one. Even funnier, Fidel Castro was born barely thirty miles away from us about the same time I was born. He could have been indoctrinated by my great-uncle. After the war, my great-uncle used to say over and over that Hitler was not dead. That was American propaganda. Hitler was alive and biding his own time to come back to power.

One day he stopped believing Hitler was still alive. I knew it because he dropped the Führer's name for good. When Fidel Castro came to power my great-uncle became a *fidelista*, but only after he saw that Castro was the typical tough tyrant. You see, my favourite great-uncle was a die-hard totalitarian. He also was the town's savant.' The professor, a survivor of the concentration camps and now a teacher of Marxian dialectics in Hollywood, saw I had a point when I hinted at a Hegelian *bon mot*: 'Even if the education programme was a success, which it wasn't,' I said, 'what good is teaching millions to read when only one man decides what you read, in Prussia as in Russia? Or in Cuba.'

In Britain, there is an ignorance of Cuba which is of the Right ('Please tell me,' I have been asked by a leading Conservative intellectual, 'is there any freedom of speech in Cuba?'): but British gentlemen of the Left, believe me, also ask stupid questions, full of political naivety signifying ideological ignorance. They often ask me eagerly about *samizdat* in Havana and how are Cuban dissidents faring. They, of all people, should know very well that *samizdat* (for a Cuban the very name is alien and it only makes sense in Spanish as an anagram for my cup of coffee) is a typically Soviet phenomenon of the Sixties. It exists now only because the present Soviet Government permits it. The same applies to Soviet dissidents, grandchildren of Khrushchev or sons of Brezhnev, who are expediently allowed to emigrate to Europe and America when Stalin, quite simply, would have sent them straight to Siberia. Who are the dissidents in East Germany or Bulgaria? Nobody, merely because the Communist governments in those countries cannot afford their existence. Writers in Czechoslovakia comply with Communist dicta or go to goal directly. Where are the dissidents in Albania? Nowhere, of course. Cuba, sad to say, has become a Latin American Albania, a deadly oxymoron. But few foreigners know this. Political hell is paved with the ignorance of strangers. The Holocaust was fully known only after the war. The gulags were publicised only after the death of Stalin. The atrocities of Castro, not all of them literary, will be known in full only after his demise, whenever that may be. Then people not only in England but everywhere, those of the Right as well as those of the Left, will know the true nature of the régime led by a man of infinite cunning and deceit, a beastly power-hungry egomaniac who is the bearded white double of Amin. It's not for nothing that he is Cuba's Commander-in-Chief, Secretary-General of the Party and President for Life. He also likes to be called a doctor when what he really is, again like Amin, is a crude actor playing his version of *Macbeth* to the largest captive audience in the Americas.

But when Fidel Castro entered Havana in January 1959 like a larger Christ (as Severo Sarduy wrote from Paris with love), some of us saw him as some kind of younger, bearded version of Magwitch, a tall outlaw emerging from the fog of history to make political Pips of us all. However, the outlaw never became an in-law, only a law unto himself: the Redeemer was always wearing a gun on his hip. When Castro took Batista's place there were three great older writers in Cuba: two powerful poets and a maverick belletrist. They were all strongly influenced by French literature. This holy, unholy trio were Jose Lezama Lima (1910-1976), Nicolas Guillen (1902—) and Virgilio Pinera (1912-1979). The first two were the poets — one popular, populist even, the other unpopular and hermetic. Later Lezama surprised everybody with the publication, in 1966, of his dense, impenetrable masterpiece *Paradiso,* a novel that is a confession and a memory and had a *succès de scandale* in Cuba for its intoxicating scenes of pederasty mixed with poetry in a prose that made Hermann Broch's look easy in comparison, if not facile. Virgilio Pinera was a short-story writer, a novelist and a playwright — and also a sometime poet. Nicolas Guillen, a mulatto who in the Twenties had written *poesia negra* (which had to do with Negro poetry what Shirley Bassey has to do with black music), fell under the spell of Lorca when he visited Havana in 1930 and shortly afterwards his Negro poetry was transformed into some kind of tropical flamenco. Later on, in the Thirties, he was writing so-called social poetry and became a member of the Cuban Communist Party — to his undoing. Guillen had a truly poetic gift, though in a minor key. In fact, he is, together with Cesar Vallejo and Pablo Neruda, the most widely translated Latin American poet of the century and has been nominated several times for the Nobel Prize. The musical connection is an apt one, for Guillen was a writer of pop poetry *avant la lettre*, the composer of soft song lyrics rather than of a powerful verse. His words cried for music and they got it. But it is really a pity that Pete Seeger was not around when Guillen wrote his early *sones* (a kind of rumba), to compose another 'Guantanamera' with Guillen's lyrics instead of Marti's verse, for Guillen was the true contemporary of these Cuban folk tunes that don't have to pay royalties to their real composers.

The fourth horseman of Cuban literature had not been living in Cuba for many years, if he ever lived there at all. Earlier, when he was young, he left Havana for Paris and didn't come back until the Nazis chased him out of France. His name was Alejo Carpentier (1904-1980). Born in Havana of a French father and a Russian mother, Carpentier was a failed architect, a dabbler in *poesia negra* (he even wrote a Negro novel dealing aptly with black magic, meaning Afro-Cuban *santeria*), a fine musicologist and finally a serious writer. But it was only when he moved to Venezuela in 1946 that he started writing his truly important novels, from *The Kingdom of this World* to *The Chase* and, perhaps his masterpiece, *Explosion in a Cathedral*, extravagantly praised by Dame Edith Sitwell (Ah those Sitwell siblings, meddling in things Cuban!) and Graham Greene and Tyrone Power. (Power wanted to write, produce and star in successive film versions of Carpentier's *Kingdom* and *Lost Steps* but he lost the crown to a coronary.) Something peculiar happened with Carpentier and Cuba: he loved the island but the island didn't love him. In Havana, he was just a journalist, almost a hack in posh magazines. Abroad, he became an all-round author and a true novelist. He even wrote in Paris the libretto for an opera composed by Edgar Varèse. This filled him with Parisian pride in a Varèse vein. Back in Cuba in 1940 meant for Carpentier, a vain man, back to journalism and the radio. But once established in Venezuela in the late Forties and Fifties, he wrote his best books. At the time he was the holder of a Venezuelan passport and was a cultural force to reckon with in Caracas. To his everlasting guilt, he even organised an international music festival sponsored by the Venezuelan version of Batista, Perez Jimenez. When he finally came back to Cuba for good — after the Revolution was safely in power — he became a bureaucrat (as manager of the only printing house in town); and though he was later promoted to France, for services rendered, as a de-luxe diplomat living in the Seizième, he never wrote another novel there — though he published at least five books with such a label on the cover.

Carpentier suffered from two lifelong obsessions, somehow interconnected: the art of the novel and the Nobel Prize for Literature. Chasing after the latter, he lost his writing steps and the kingdom of this world became a lethal tyranny that has finally done him in. As the Frenchman says: 'Nothing kills a man more quickly than to be forced to represent a country.' Carpentier, the poor son of a bitch, represented for twenty years a cause that he never believed in. In the end, ill with terminal cancer, Paris became a painful feat. He had to write in the early morning and later have breakfast and lunch and sometimes dinner with important French writers, with the exception of Sartre who despised him for being a civil servant with two masters. His output became meagre and his books grew poorer in style but richer in political content to please Havana and thus stay in Paris. He never got the Nobel Prize, by the way. Death got him first.

Those were the most representative names in Cuban literature when Fidel Castro came down from the mountains armed to his rotten teeth. (Then he wore tattered olive-green fatigues, now he wears a general's uniform and his teeth have been beautifully capped.) There were other writers, of course. Lino Novas Calvo, for example, one of the best short-story writers in Latin America, Hemingway's favourite translator and the man who first translated Faulkner and Huxley and Lawrence into Spanish when he was living in Madrid and collaborating with Ortega y Gasset on his *Revista de Occidente*, a review that changed a culture. And Fernando Ortiz, the anthropologist, the man who coined, among others, the word Afro-Cuban (after which Afro-American and Afro-Brazilian were formed) — a concept more than a word. And Lydia Cabrera, a white girl from a former rich family, the first woman to penetrate the sacred *santeria* cult and the *abakua*, originally a secret society for men only, with blood initiation rites which excluded, under threat of death, women and pederasts. Her work in what could be called anthropoetry was pioneering in America, where black cults of the occult, from Haiti to Brazil, are sometimes stronger than in Africa. The black continent didn't create voodoo: America did.

Other relevant artists of some international standing who were

born in Cuba and remained Cuban are Alicia Alonso, the dancer,
and Wilfredo Lam, the painter, and two great musicians, Amadeo
Roldan and Alejandro Garcia Caturla, probably better composers
than Brazil's Villalobos and the Mexican Carlos Chavez. Both died
too young to be known abroad, except in such recherché musical
circles as the coterie around Nadia Boulanger in Paris or by John
Cage's epigoni everywhere. Roldan, also a remarkable conductor,
died of a skin cancer in the face in his early thirties. Cruelly
deformed, in his last performances he had to climb the podium
wearing a silk mask. Caturla, a country judge who used to compose
even on the Bench, was killed by a thief on bail whom he had
refused to acquit the day before. Ironically, this petty criminal was
never pardoned and died in gaol — not because he had killed a
judge but because he had assassinated the Great Caturla.

Mme Alonso had been a prima ballerina with the American
Ballet Theatre since its inception in the early Forties. When she
decided to come back to Cuba and form a ballet company she was
sponsored by a local brewery and later by the Batista Government,
who thought her international star status was good propaganda
for Batista, who hated the ballet. Later she was adopted by the
Revolution as our dancing daughter. She has indeed been around a
lot and is still shuffling along at 70. Of all the artists mentioned
above, she is the only one who was trained in the United States and
belonged to the American school of dancing. Today her corps de
ballet dances *à la Russe* — in opposite steps to their prima ballerina
assoluta.

You cannot call Francis Picabia or Anaïs Nin Cuban. They
merely happened to have been born on the island, but were later
formed in France, where they made their reputation — whatever
that is. They were as Cuban as Jose Maria de Heredia. who at the
turn of the century dreamt of the coral reefs and azure seas and
verdant hills he saw in his native Santiago de Cuba — but wrote of
them in French Alexandrines in Paris. Or Italo Calvino, born in a
village near Havana but raised in Rome. But there have been some
important artists born in Cuba who stayed in the country, like
those painters who belonged to the Cuban school of painting of the
Forties and whose works can be seen in museums all over the
world. One of these painters was Fidelio Ponce de Leon. He
claimed to have been a descendant of the Spanish conquistador
who discovered Florida by chance when he was looking for the
Fountain of Youth. He died an old man at the age of 50 — the

painter not the discoverer, dreamers both. One of his best paintings hangs for ever on a wall of a smart, make-believe New York apartment, where it dominates the single set of Hitchcock's famous thriller *Rope*. Ponce, who was constantly asking friends and foes alike, 'Do they really know me in Paris?' never saw the film. He died, destitute and tubercular, before *Rope* opened in Havana in 1948.

The most famous Cuban artist ever was, of course, Jose Raul Capablanca, also known as the Chess Machine, considered by many to be the greatest chess-player who ever lived. Born in Havana in the late 19th century he has been buried in Cuba since 1941. Can anybody imagine how the Castro régime would have capitalised on the living legend Capablanca was? Fêted and filmed everywhere, the immortal story of his short, successful life is the stuff of which propaganda is made. Even Che Guevara mourned his death — twenty years later. Twelve facsimiles of Alicia Alonso dancing dozens of demented Coppelias wouldn't have meant so much to Communist Cuba.

I am not forgetting — how could I? — countless minor poets, bad poets, terrible poets and short-story writers by the dozen who thrived in the tropics with their small talents and enormous egos, opportunists all. It was in 1959, when editing *Revolucion* (which he founded clandestinely in 1956) that Carlos Franqui, then a revolutionary Cabinet-maker (four or five new ministers owed their jobs to him and not to Fidel Castro), decided that the paper needed a literary supplement. That's how *Lunes* was born — a goat child, a devil-goat, a scapegoat finally. A journalist since 1949, a movie critic from 1954 onwards and managing editor of *Carteles*, the second most popular weekly in Cuba and the Caribbean, I was appointed editor of *Lunes*. It would prove an almost fatal mistake for everyone involved.

Revolucion had been the voice from the underground of the 26th of July Movement, the organisation which did more to put Fidel Castro in power than the puny guerrilla he has made everybody believe did the job. Above ground now, *Revolucion* became a very powerful newspaper indeed, the first in Cuba and the only one that had access to the innermost recesses of power in the Government and in Cuban political life in general. Moreover, it had, for Cuba — at the time a country of some seven million people — an enormous circulation. *Lunes* profited from all this and became the first literary magazine in Latin America or Spain to boast of a circulation of almost 200,000 copies. *Lunes* had a lot of pull — and not merely literary punch.

My first mistake as an editor was to try and clean out the Cuban literary stables by sweeping the house of words with a political broom. That's called an inquisition, and it can induce writer's block by terror. The magazine, with the heavy weight of the Revolution and the Government behind it plus the 26th of July Movement's political prestige, literally blasted many writers into submission — or oblivion. We had the Surrealist credo as our catechism and Trotskyite politics as our aesthetics, mixed like bad metaphors — or heady drinks. From this position of maximum strength, we proceeded to annihilate respected writers of the past, like Lezama Lima, simply because he dared to combine in his poems the anachronistic ideologies of Gongora and Mallarmé, now joined in Havana to produce disjointed verse of a magnificently obscure Catholicism. We actually tried to assassinate Lezama's character. There were other, older casualties, like the Spanish dentist who wanted to be a Dantist and whose recently published novel was pulled from its Asturian roots, with no laughing-gas. At the same time, the magazine exalted Virgilio Pinera, a man of Lezama's generation, to the position of a Virgil out of double hell. He who had always been a pariah in his own country, a novelist who was terribly poor, almost destitute, became our favourite father-figure, the house-writer. Another mistake. Besides being an excellent short-story writer anthologised by Borges, a playwright of genius (he penned a play after the fashion of the theatre of the absurd when Ionesco hadn't yet staged *The Bald Prima Donna* and long before Beckett wrote *Waiting for Godot*) and a pleasant poet, Virgilio had a particular fault. As with San Andreas, it was a very visible one. Virgilio, like his Roman counterpart, was a pederast. Perhaps the epitome of the literary queen, a Cuban Cocteau known not for his plays but for his playmates. That was food for gossip in Paris, but this was revolutionary Havana and there was no room left for queens in a revolution. Instead of shouting 'Off with his head!', all Cuban queens ended up with no head, not even their own, especially not their own.

Third original sin in a row: there were too many talented people grouped around *Lunes*, each one supporting the Revolution in their fashion. Baragano, the Surrealist poet who came back from his exile in Paris where he was befriended by André Breton himself, who hated Sunday painters and minor poets, was pet poet and pet pest on the magazine. Heberto Padilla, born in the same town as Baragano (the funnily-named Puerta de Golpe in Cuban tobacco country: Puerto de Golpe literally means, as if Larry Grayson had named it, 'Shut the Door'), came from exile in the Berlitz Academy in New York, and cultivated an easygoing but mordant style of verse. Padilla was a powerful poet in *Lunes*. Both Baragano and Padilla, pugnacious poets, were out to get the older generation, many of them civil servants from Batista times and even before, as was the case with Lezama. Calvert Casey, who, in spite of his name and having been born in Baltimore, was not only a Cuban but a true *habanero*, delicate and precise in the exquisite concealments of his homosexual prose, though he had a mulatto lover, openly a couple. Anton Arrufat was a disciple of Pinera — and not only in playwriting. Pablo Armando Fernandez, a minor poet but an accomplished diplomat capable of extricating the magazine from any critical jam. He was our pint-size Sebastian, a moving target. He is still in Cuba, still a diplomat but no longer a poet, minor or otherwise. He is professionally dedicated to being host to political tourists from the United States, where he lived in a closet in Queens, before returning to Cuba, already married, in 1959. Like Padilla and Hurtado, I convinced Pablo to come back to Cuba from the States. Oscar Hurtado, also an economic exile in New York, a dear giant of a man, like the family elephant, but an incredible shrinking poet, inimical to Lezama and his *Origenes* group, who died not only unrecognised but unrecognising in an asylum, suffering silently and alone from a varicose brain. And, never allowed to leave the boat when it was listing (*Lunes* was on all the lists of the security service, the counter-espionage service and the police), there was I, who, though an inveterate smoker, couldn't share the peace pipe because I smoked cigars only then. The magazine, as you can see, was manned by a manic crew of pederasts (wait and you'll see why this fact of life became crucial to our demise), the happy few, as Che Guevara labelled us, who were not real revolutionaries, with a skipper who, no doubt due to myopia, saw the danger signals very, very late. Too late, in fact. He discovered that we had no true power when we hit what seemed a mere sectarian wave but was the tip of the totalitarian iceberg. *Lunes* should have been called the *Titanic*, for very soon we were in deep, cold waters. Before sinking, I saw clearly that we had tried to make the Revolution readable, therefore livable. Both tasks proved utterly impossible.

In its heyday, however, *Lunes* expanded quickly. Soon we had branched out into a publishing house (Ediciones Erre), whose first published book was *Poesia, Revolucion del Ser* ('Poetry, Being's Revolution', though, only a few months earlier, its author, Jose Baragano, still the Paris Surrealist, had titled it *Being is Nothingness*). This collection of poems was, in 1960, a rehashing of all the Surreal formulas of the preceding twenty years, but now sang a song to the Revolution and to the Heideggerian being for death. Though now, instead of nothingness, it offered everythingness. Opportunism, thy name is poetry. Then we had an hour, at peak time, on television, second channel to the left. We formed a record company, called Sonido Erre, or Sound R, R for Revolution. Our publishing venture — quite successful, by the way — was at the time the only independent publishing house left in Cuba. All the rest had already been nationalised. But it was no privilege, this solitary printing-press under private ownership. It was, in fact, as ominous as a smoke signal in Apache territory. It was then that I committed a mistake which proved to be a blessing in disguise. I helped Saba, my brother, with the completion of a documentary he was making with the cinematographer Orlando Jimenez — at the time the youngest photographer in Cuba, capable of handling a Cinemascope camera when he was 14, quite a film feat. The film was to be called *PM*, for obvious reasons. As its title suggests, it would be a view of Havana after dark: the camera peeping into the small cafés and bars and dives that were left, patronised by ordinary people, the common Cuban — workers, loafers, dancers of all sexes and races — having a last time before the night closed in. I liked the idea, for the so-called free cinema, invented in England, was the latest thing in movies at the time and practically unknown in Cuba. I gave them the money to edit the documentary, print two or three copies and design the titles. All this was done outside the Film Institute — that is, officialdom — in our TV channel labs, but quite openly. For its money, *Lunes* got the exclusive rights to show the picture on its programme, as soon as it was ready. We showed it without any problems at all. There was no censorship for us on television. As in the magazine, we were our own boss. After all, we were the offspring of *Revolucion,* the newspaper of the Revolution, the voice of the people. We were omnipotent, sort of.

But, naturally, a spectacle needs spectators, and the filmmakers wanted to show their little night film of music to a live audience. There were still two or three cinema theatres not yet nationalised in Old Havana, and one of them specialised in documentaries. The owner agreed to run the film: the next step was to obtain permission from the Comision Revisora to show the picture in public. The Comision Revisora was the same censorship office as in Batista's time and further back — from headquarters you could see *The Great Train Robbery* and Edison's *The Kiss*. In the past, what the censorship office did was to cut a bit of bare ass here or tit there in French films which were not even soft porn but were treated then as the hardest core. But, now, the Comision Revisora was under the control of the Film Institute, which is nothing like the British Film Institute but a state monopoly which controls everything that has to do with films, from making pictures to importing, distributing and exhibiting them. The Cuban Film Institute owns all the theatres, drive-ins and movie-houses in Cuba — and you must go to them even to get a roll of film for a snapshot camera. On top of that, they had a long-standing feud with *Lunes*, which they labelled as decadent, bourgeois, avant-gardist and, the worst epithet in the Communist name-calling catalogue, cosmopolitist. In turn, we saw them as despicable bureaucrats, a bunch of ignoramuses with artistically reactionary ideas and no taste at all. The director of the Film Institute, Alfredo Guevara (no relation to Che Guevara), was the worst Communist commissar to deal with films this side of Stalin's Shumyatsky. To take *PM* to the Film Institute for approval was a naive and daring thing to do — like Little Red Riding Hood testing the wolf's teeth. But, you see, it simply had to be done. Some time later, *Revolucion* was going to be killed and reborn under the name of *Granma* — and it has indeed shown big bad teeth since then. Nevertheless, we didn't expect such a brutal bite. The Comision Revisora not only refused to give any seal of approval to *PM*, but banned the film, which was accused of being counter-revolutionary and dangerous rubbish and licentious and lewd. Furthermore, they seized the copy sent for censorship.

This was more than we could stomach, even if there was to be a purge at the end of it. We had been expecting a showdown with the Film Institute. It was to become a shoot-out. The banning of *PM* occurred in June 1961, in what could be termed a period between two wars. In April that year the Bay of Pigs invasion took place. All the invaders had been impressively routed in less than 48 hours and, rather hastily, Fidel Castro had declared Cuba a socialist republic, though the country would be neither. The times were auspicious for the Communist Party (now merged with the remnants of the 26th of July Movement and the ghost of the Revolutionary Directory into one single party called ORI), so much so that its cultural committee had decided to stage a writers' congress in Havana and to invite a few foreign writers of note, such as Nathalie Sarraute, who were sympathisers of the Revolution but not necessarily Communists. In the meantime, in some kind of political montage (hooves of Klansmen's horses galloping, then cut to damsel in distress, then cut to threatening blackamoor), *Lunes* was seen busily collecting signatures to protest about the sequestering of *PM*, the little night film. This was going to have wider implications, with the Communist congress about to take place.

When they saw us coming and knew we meant business the Cultural Committee of the Party panicked. They asked us please not to turn the statement against the Film Institute into a manifesto by making it public. In turn, they promised to postpone their congress and wash our dirty linen indoors by orchestrating a meeting of all the factions concerned with Fidel Castro and almost the entire Government. It was a sneaky ambush, the varmints. They invited all the intellectuals involved — and then some. The meetings took place every Friday for three consecutive weeks and were held in the spacious hall of the National Library, a cultural palace built by Batista but claimed by the Revolution. The day of the first meeting came like doom. On the rostrum were Fidel Castro, President Dorticos (since deposed), the Minister of Education, his wife Haydée Santamaria, head of the Casa de las Americas (later a suicide), Carlos Rafael Rodriguez, then an influential Communist leader, now the third man from Moscow in Havana, his former wife Edith Garcia Buchaca (then the head of the Communist cultural apparat, who later lived under house arrest for 15 years), Vicentina Antuna, boss of the Cultural Council under the political spell of Buchaca, Alfredo Guevara, no Che Guevara but a tropical Macchiavelli giving advice not only to the Prince but also to the King. Then came the scapegoats, lambs feeding with lions: Carlos Franqui, editor of *Revolucion,* and I, as editor of *Lunes.*

President Dorticos, who thought then he was the president, declared the meetings open. The meetings that were to become proceedings of a trial. He announced, with the voice of the commodore of a yacht club which he had been, that everybody could speak his mind freely. Anybody could have their say now. Speak up comrades. Nobody did. We were all paralysed and gagged by such a panoply of political power. Suddenly, out of the red, a timid man with mousy hair, frightened voice and shy manners, slightly suspect because he looked frankly queer in spite of his efforts to appear manly, said that he wanted to speak. It was Virgilio Pinera. He confessed to being terribly frightened. He did't know why or of what, but he was really frightened, almost on the verge of panic. Then he added: 'I think it has to do with all this.' It seemed that he included the Revolution in his fear, though apparently he meant only the crowd of so many so-called intellectuals. But perhaps he was alluding to the life of a writer in a Communist country, a fear called Stalin, a fear called Castro. We'll never know, for Virgilio didn't say any more and meekly went back to his seat. Nobody was allowed to speak from his own seat: to have your say, as President Dorticos boomed his order, you had to stand in front of a microphone on a proscenium, facing the audience but taking good care that you didn't turn your back on Castro. Political distortions meant physical contortions. Everybody talked, even those who didn't know how, like Calvert Casey, a compulsive stammerer.

Suddenly, it became evident to everyone (defendants, prosecutor, jury, judge and witnesses) that this was a show trial held in private: it was not only *PM* but *Lunes* (and everything it stood for in Cuban culture) that was in the dock. Kafka in Cuba, Prague in Havana. Most of the people who took the stand were sworn enemies of the magazine — and some had reason to be. Like the fat woman who sent in some sonnets that were published in the magazine with the title: 'From the Fat Lady of the Sonnets'. The pained dentist who thought he was Dante *al dente* complained bitterly. And not only complained, but cried and prayed (he was a Catholic convert) and called us chartered murderers who assassinated writers as if they were so many characters. We were the hit-and-run men of culture. The Marxian Mafia? It was an impassioned though toothless speech — and he got what he wanted all along: a job as ambassador to the Vatican as a consolation prize. There were other witnesses, all for the prosecution, and a masked witness took off his mask for everyone to see his face: Baragano, the Surrealist poet who instigated all the attacks against Lezama and his disciples, had turned on us! There was an expected enemy, though: Guevara, by now a guerrilla speaker who couldn't say his r's, delivered a blow below the belt at both *Revolucion* and *Lunes*. Before I was an *Infante terrible*, now I was a babe in the wood. Fidel Castro himself talked to us. Characteristically, he had the last word. Getting rid first of the ever-present Browning 9mm fastened to his belt — making true a metaphor by Goebbels: 'Every time I hear the word culture, I reach for my pistol' — Castro delivered one of his most famous speeches, famous not for being eight hours long, but for being brief and to the point for the first time since he became Cuba's Prime Minister. His deposition is now called 'Words to the Intellectuals', and it ends with a résumé which Castroites everywhere claim to be a model of revolutionary rhetoric but which is really a Stalinist credo: 'Within the Revolution, everything,' he thundered like a thousand Zeuses. 'Against the Revolution, nothing!' Everybody applauded, some in good faith. Though not I. I *had* to applaud even when I knew full well what he meant by his slogan. It had been the case of a sentence without a verdict, through-the-looking-glass justice.

The outcome of the trial was that the Film Institute gave back the seized copy of *PM* to the directors, but the film remained censored. *Lunes* was banned, too, and barely three months later ceased appearing. There was an official explanation for the stay of execution: an acute shortage of newsprint — a likely story. Three more literary publications saw daylight after the meetings: *Union Review*, a monthly from the Writers' Union, dedicated to high Communist culture; *Gaceta de Cuba*, a weekly published by the Writers' Union that resembled *Lunes* like Cain resembled Abel; and an illustrated magazine issued by the Council for culture that looked like a tattered *Tatler*. Three red reviews all in a row. The Communists had their congress (why do they need congresses so much? Is it a fixation or a fix?) with foreign writers as guests. In a typical gambit I was made one of the seven vice-presidents of the newly-formed Writers' Union, so I wouldn't complain. I didn't. I never intended to. You see, I had been in the Soviet Union the year before and found out what happened to all the writers who dared displease Stalin, even *sotto voce*. A tropical version of Stalin, even behind beards, could be tropically lethal.

It was then that Virgilio Pinera came back from Brussels via Prague and missed kissing Cuban soil by about three feet. Some hubris. Early one morning, on militia duty at the gates of *Revolucion,* I had a phone call from him. I was surprised at first, then I was astounded. Virgilio was calling me from the local gaol at the beach where he lived. He told me he had been arrested on charges of being a passive P. 'But a capital P, you know.' I understood: Virgilio meant P, not for Pinera or for poet, but for Pederast. The night before there had been some sort of carnal *Kristalnacht* in Havana. A special branch of the police, called the Social Scum Squad, arrested on sight everbody walking the streets at night in Old Havana who looked to the naked eye like a prostitute, a pimp or a pederast. This police operation was called the Night of the Three Ps. But at the time Virgilio was miles away, in bed (he believed it was healthy to go to bed early and to rise early), in the shack he christened his big bungalow on the beach. How in hell was Virgilio in gaol?

The explanation lies in an infamous collective illness. The Government had and still has an obsession with queers, queens and kinks — in a word, all kinds of pederast. Five years later, they even built concentration camps for homosexuals, especially those with a cultural bent. In the Congress for Culture and Education of 1971 one of the main resolutions, which sounded more like a resolve, was not to allow homosexuals (now called 'infirms of a social pathology') to occupy positions from which they could pervert Cuban youth. (What about Cuban children?) They should have no prominent place in cultural circles or artistic activities, nor represent the Revolution abroad. (That was when Alicia Alonso's male corps de ballet took a step, a grand *jeté* from Prague to Paris.) It was Fidel Castro himself who closed the Congress with those words.

Why this 'pathological' aberration? Fidel Castro is, as gays in the United States like to say with terrible grammar, *mucho macho*. On the other hand, Che Guevara considered homosexuals to be sick people who must give way to the politically healthy 'new man' made by Communist Cuba. There are multiple levels of irony here. The other Guevara, Alfredo, was a notorious fag, protected by Fidel's own brother, Raul Castro. Che Guevara ended up as the name of a boutique in High Street Kensington. New Man is a brand of jeans made for boys and girls alike, while narrow trousers were prohibited wear in public in Cuba. A Castro convertible in New York is not a sofa-bed as advertised, but a man who goes either way — what Gore Vidal now calls a bisexual. A final irony is that the heart of the homosexual world is in San Francisco and is called Castro Street. Gay, yes, but with a vengeance.

Pinera the Pederast got out of gaol, thanks to the intervention of

Edith Buchaca, not out of pity but from political considerations. She knew the trouble a homosexual writer in gaol can make. She had read Oscar Wilde and she remembered the lines:

In Reading gaol by Reading town
There is a pit of shame.

She mispronounced 'Reading', but knew the ballad by heart. After the closure of *Lunes*, 'that pit of shame', most of the homosexuals on its payroll (Calvert Casey, Anton Arrufat and Pablo Armando Fernandez, my managing editor) went to work for Casa de Las Americas under Haydée Santamaria. This curiously contrary woman (whose personal and political contradictions led her to commit suicide last year) was a true *fidelista*. She was the only woman to take part in the attack on the Moncada barracks in 1953, where both her brother and her fiancé died after being tortured. She was forced to witness the torture. She had been with Castro's guerrillas in the mountains since 1956. But she had a 'weakness for culture', as she explained, while admitting that she was just an ignorant peasant woman. The first claim, being ignorant, was true, but not the second. She was a girl from a well-to-do family of the provincial bourgeoisie, which was not richer but more influential locally than its Havana counterpart. The rich in Cuban provinces elected mayors, selected high-society members and ran the local high schools. In tobacco country they were even more powerful — but they could be illiterate. Once she told me, not in the strictest confidence: 'What a coarse peasant ignorant woman I am! I always thought that Marx and Engels were a single philosopher. You know, like Ortega y Gasset.' More relevant, however, were Haydée Santamaria's revelations when she came back from her first trip to Russia and confided radiantly: 'I met Ekaterina Furtseva in Moscow. You know, the Minister for Culture. A beautiful woman!' — which she was — 'and so kind', which she wasn't, Old Steelsmile. 'You know what she did? Minister Furtseva explained to me, woman to woman, or rather, comrade to comrade, what happened to those writers and artists who died under Stalin — and why they simply had to die. They were not killed because they were hermetic poets, bourgeois novelists and abstract painters. Actually, they had to be shot because they were Nazi spies, not artists. Would you believe it? Hitler's agents all of them! They had to be exterminated. Do you understand?' I understood. Ah, what a naive and dangerous revolutionary woman she was! A gust of Russian cold crept up my spine.

Nevertheless, she allowed Arrufat to transform the *Revista Casa* into the best literary review in Latin America since *Sur*, edited by Victoria Ocampo and Borges. Until Anton ran into trouble for publishing a pederast poem by Jose Triana, a young playwright who has recently taken up exile in France incognito. The poem spoke obscurely of some innocent, not indecent, homosexual practices, like daubing themselves with KY, an emollient used for love-making, and asking naively how many flavours you could get abroad and which is the Flavour of the Month? Haydée Santamaria didn't know a thing about homosexual love — for her, heterosexuality and the missionary position were what the Revolution ordered. But she had to dismiss Arrufat on the spot because an envious poetaster, Roberto Retamar, formerly cultural attaché in Paris, personally informed President Dorticos of Arrufat's heineous crime against nature and the revolutionary people of Cuba. Arrufat was sacked and Retamar rewarded, as in any Soviet socialist realist novel, with the editorship of *Revista Casa*. Arrufat was even accused of the grave mistake of inviting Allen Ginsberg to Cuba. Ginsberg was a Communist from New York, but, being an Ur-gay, he was seen as less than pink in Havana. Furthermore, while in Cuba, he made some scandalous statements, such as claiming that Fidel Castro, that stallion (Castro's nickname in Cuba is El Caballo, the horse), that stalwart revolutionary hero, must, like most men, have been a homosexual some time in his long life. But the worst he did was to say in public that he found Che Guevara such a dish that he would like to go to bed with him, the sooner the better. Enough is more than enough in Castro's Cuba, and Ginsberg was held incommunicado in his hotel. Next morning he was put on a plane and sent packing to Prague, where he could find himself a Czech mate.

Meanwhile, in another consolation prize-giving (the closure of *Lunes* had left me without a job, vice-president of the Writers' Union or not), I was appointed cultural attaché in Brussels, just on the other side of the moon as seen from Havana, that dark secluded place Virgilio had come from. It was there that I found out all about the shenanigans of Retamar and the expelling of Arrufat from his haven by Haydée. I knew of the existence of UMAP, concentration camps behind their camouflaging acronyms: Units for Military Help to Agricultural Production. Apparently, the final solution for the homosexual population explosion was the sugar-cane plantation. As José Tura would have put it: 'Concentration camps for queers: we do the concentrating and they do the camping.' Even poor, peaceful Calvert Casey got into trouble when he dared tell a Mexican writer of the Left, just one more political tourist, that there were camps for homosexuals all over Cuba, and they were not exactly summer camps. This was a carefully guarded secret which Calvert knew about through the gay grapevine. Next morning, as in a guilty hangover, the Mexican tipped off Haydée Santamaria that she had counter-revolutionaries in her house, who told tales, very dangerous lies for Casa de las Americas. He whispered a gringo name, Casey. Calvert was severely reprimanded and demoted, but never sacked.

When I came back to Cuba for my mother's funeral, Havana seemed like the wrong side of hell. Virgilio, more than a guide to Avernus, looked as if he was playing the shivering old maid in one of his plays of the absurd. a queen playing canasta all the time. Lezama was secretly embroidering his *Paradiso* in the dark every night, telling nobody, not even his wife, in the morning: always cunning, being both Ulysses and Penelope. Huge Hurtado was now more shrunk than small Virgilio with his fear of breathing. Only Arrufat, impelled to follow in the wake of an alien, an Allen Ginsberg he never really met, wanted to take a band of gay desperados with buntings and streamers and screamers to shout out slogans before the Presidential Palace, the place where Dorticos lived. This was as suicidal as the kamikaze attack on the Palace, where Batista hid in 1957. To dissuade him from such follies, Virgilio had to tell him stories about what it was like to be a pederast writer, formerly from *Revolucion*, now in gaol: 'Counter-revolutionary thugs would simply tear you apart, child. They'll have you drawn and quartered for a cause that has ceased to exist years ago.' Arrufat finally saw the light (Virgilio was his master) and, instead of parading in front of the Palace, shut himself up in his room to write a play. It was based on *The Seven against Thebes*, with a Zeus who wore a black beard and thundered from Mount Olympus, in Spanish. for hours on end. Still eager to provoke, he wanted to call the play 'Death to the Infidel'. Virgilio then quoted the other Virgil: *'Facilis descensus Averni.'* With crocodile tears, I decided to leave Cuba. I had seen and been heard long enough and had made my mind up. I didn't tell anybody I was leaving for good, but I did.

Enter Padilla laughing. My novel *Three Trapped Tigers* had won Spain's most prestigious literary prize, the Biblioteca Breve Award, in 1965. The runner-up was *The Passion of Urbino*, by Lisandro Otero, who had been my classmate at the School of Journalism then: he was a staunch anti-Communist but he had become a paunchy bureaucrat at the Ministry of Foreign Affairs. Otero was a sometime friend of Padilla's, who used to call him La Belle Otero and other names and was always pretending that he lusted after Otero's wife, a Cuban ivory beauty, who had belonged to Havana high society and was now Haydée Santamaria's right arm at the Casa, but still a beauty. She knew how to spell Engels and could tell Karl from Groucho, gesturing amiably with her long white hands and even longer nails. She had exquisite manners too. We could all see what Lisandro saw in her: but what could she see in Ugly Otero? asked Padilla. *Pasion de Urbino* was published in Havana in 1967, and as Otero was such a big shot now at *El Caiman Barbudo*, Cuba's echo to the Russian *Krokodil*, they asked for reviews, or rather favourable opinions, from all and sundry. Padilla sent his — which was a vicious panning of Otero's novel and a paean to mine, just published in Spain after having a spot of bother with the Spanish censors. 'Scandal!' 'Slander' they cried at *El Caiman Barbudo,* which literally means 'The Bearded Crocodile'. Daggers flew from the bushy beard of the Communist cayman. Padilla had dared to praise a bad book by a counter-revolutionary living in exile in London, while failing to see the enormous merits of the excellent novel by Comrade Otero, a revolutionary living in Cuba — as he did when Batista was in power (my comment). The Padilla Affair had its roots in Communist dialectics: he who does not praise a Party member is an enemy of the Party. But Padilla, though not a Surrealist, sees the poet as a literary *agent provocateur,* his words a concealed weapon, wearing cloak and dagger. He never recanted. His enemies never relented, and in a Communist country, which lives and dies by the book, a war of words is considered warfare by other means. Silence is the last refuge of the class enemy and scepticism a dangerous deviation to the Right. Silence, rather than acquiescence, was what saved Boris Pasternak. Being outspoken or indiscreet, more than being relevant, was what lost Osip Mandelstam. Padilla, who had lived in Moscow, chose to be both poets at the same time. He could write

a poem deriding Fidel Castro and keep it quiet, playing a safe
Mandelstam, and, like Pasternak with Stalin, he would talk with
Fidel Castro on the phone as *l'enfant prodigue* of Cuban letters, a
wayward child of the Revolution who could always be chastised
and mend his ways — the Prime Minister playing the role of Cuban
Sugar Daddy.

Padilla was not Pasternak and Fidel Castro was not Stalin: the
poet became a case — known in Cuba and all over the Spanish-
speaking world and beyond as the 'Padilla Case'. But Padilla was
not going to be arrested by Scotland Yard and tried at the Old
Bailey. The totalitarian mind never bothers with what it calls
bourgeois justice: Fidel Castro was a lawyer by training, and so was
Dr Goebbels. In 1968 Padilla won a prize for poetry in a contest
sponsored by the Writers' Union in Havana and awarded by an
international jury. Among the jurors was J.M. Cohen, a British
critic, translator and anthologist of Spanish literature, then vaguely
connected with the Cuban cultural milieu. The title of Padilla's
book was *Out of the Game,* and this very name was anathema to
some members of the Writers' Union, especially its president, the
old Communist poet Nicolas Guillen, who tried to put pressure on
the jury to reverse their judgment. According to the dicta of
the Writers' Union, Padilla's poems were flagrantly counter-
revolutionary. But were they? The poem that gave the collection its
title was dedicated to Yannis Ritsos, a Greek Communist poet, and
began like this:

> Dismiss the poet!
> He has nothing to do.
> He doesn't play the game.
> He isn't enthusiastic.
> His message is muddled.
> Doesn't even think about miracles.
> He meditates all day.
> He always finds something to complain about.

Innocent enough lyrics, and the music was always by Theodorakis.
On top of that, Ritsos had been imprisoned in 1967 by the Greek
military junta. Obviously, this couldn't happen here. Other poems
were even less critical (if you can call the preceding lines critical).

Perhaps the most daring poem was 'To Write in the Scrapbook of a Tyrant':

Protect yourself from those who vacillate,
because one day they will know what they don't want.
Protect yourself from those who mumble,
Juan-the-stutterer, Pedro-the-mute,
because one day they shall find their strong voice.
Protect yourself from the timid and the frightened,
because one day they will not rise when you enter.

Is this the poetry that will launch an American invasion? Not bloody likely. At the time, in the frightful Spanish-speaking world of juntas and generals, in Franco's Spain, Blas de Otero was writing and publishing openly Communist poetry and getting away with it. He died in Spain. Nicanor Parra, in Pinochet's Chile, had been cryptically critical and nothing ever happened to him. He still lives in Chile. In Mexico, Octavio Paz, a strong voice for strong words, had resigned as ambassador to India as a gesture against the Tlatelolco Square massacre ordered by his President, but it was his own conscience that forced him to quit. He has always lived in Mexico. Meanwhile, in Communist Cuba in April 1971, Herberto Padilla was arrested *à la Russe*: in his house, early in the morning, stealthily but, a Cuban touch, having been given a quiet alarum by members of his block's Committee for the Defence of the Revolution.[1] Padilla remained barely a month in gaol, but this time, as didn't happen with the closure of *Lunes,* which was very cleverly staged, there was an international uproar. The mail carried private communiqués for discreet official eyes only and an open letter was sent to Fidel Castro himself. The missive from former friends was considered by the Cuban PM as an enemy missile. It was signed, surprisingly enough, by such leftist writers and sponsors of the Revolution as Jean-Paul Sartre and Simone de Beauvoir, Italo Calvino, Marguerite Duras, Hans Magnus Enzensberger, Juan Goytisolo, André Pierre de Mandiargues, Alain Jouffroy, Joyce Mansour, Alberto Moravia, Octavio Paz

---

[1] These Committees are para-police groups that operate in every large building, in every town or city, supposedly to protect the Revolution from its enemy within — the most powerful army in Latin America will take care of the enemy without. The members of Committees for the Defence of the Revolution are some two million Cubans, who engage in these activities willingly or not — though the Committees, like the People's Militia, are supposed to be strictly voluntary.

and some others who couldn't even pronounce the name of Padilla correctly, much less read his poems. It was a case of tit for tat. The European and Latin American intellectuals had been disillusioned with the Cuban Revolution for quite a while, and Fidel Castro was fed up with what he considered an intrusion into his personal domain. The truth is that the foreign writers and the Cuban dictator were no longer useful to each other.

For a moment, though, it looked as if the poet's head was about to roll. But Fidel Castro is a cunning version of Stalin, and Padilla, who wrote a poem about the tongue of the poet being requisitioned by the state, recanted and was released, though not before he had made a *viva voce* confession at the Writers' Union main lecture-hall. The trial of *Lunes* had been *in camera* and its verdict private. Now we had, not a quiet show trial, but a public confession that was quite a show. Padilla, not reading from any script but obviously following a scenario, in a very Orthodox Russian and un-Cuban Catholic way, confessed to all kinds of literary and political crimes, and even crimes against the state and the people of Cuba. He also named a few accomplices, among them the august, orotund figure of Lezama Lima, conspicuous that evening not only because he was publicly called a subversive poet but also because he was the second Cuban literary figure to be absent from the nicely set-up cultural soirée, obviously staged by State Security. The other absentee was also significant. It was the President of the Writers' Union, Nicolas Guillen, who conveniently pleaded illness.

After the Soviet-style confession — 'I know that my experience, comrades, is going to be an example. It must serve as an example for others' — there was an even more vehement and indignant letter to Castro, signed by yet more writers on the Left, like Nathalie Sarraute and Susan Sontag. The signatories were ashamed and angry at the outrage of a poet confessing to imaginary political crimes. They talked of the despicable indignity meted out to Padilla. They didn't, of course, say how many unknown workers and anonymous peasants had been forced to do the same all over Cuba in the past (since the inception of the Revolution, in fact) and how many more will one day find, *in corpore*, that Padilla's public recanting was no cruel and unusual punishment but a confession devoutly to be wished.

In Communist countries you have, as Milozc once said, the captive mind. But what about the captive body? Let me speak now of sadder, wiser men, like Valladares and Cuadra, poets in prison, captive minds in captive bodies. Armando Valladares, the poet in a wheelchair as he has been called in France, was condemned to 30 years in gaol in the early Sixties, when he was barely 20. In prison, as a result of ill-treatment and his various hunger strikes in protest against ill-treatment, he became an invalid. (By the way, many political prisoners have died in prison in Cuba, after suicidal hunger strikes directed at atrocious prison conditions. Not a single one of those who have died is known to the outside world, not even Jose Luis Boitel, the former Castroite student leader. International press agencies and the big newspapers of the Western world have not printed a single news item about those men: it is a lot easier to write interminably about Bobby Sands.) Angel Cuadra was sent to prison in 1960 as a convicted counter-revolutionary. He was released in 1976 and arrested again in 1977, without ever being allowed to leave the country. The second time round his crime was to have written poems about his miserable life and sent them abroad to be published. In England, nobody, except those in Amnesty, knows about these exotic people and their pathetic rather than poetic plight. They have suffered in Cuban gaols and in the process have learnt how to write poetry in silence. Their minds are not captive anymore, only their voices.

After Padilla confessed crimes that were as ludicrous as confessing to setting the Reichstag on fire, blowing up the battleship *Maine* in Havana harbour and masterminding the Gunpowder Plot, a season of calm came over the island. All was quiet on the Cuban cultural front — for a while. Lezama Lima, who couldn't publish anything after being implicated by Padilla, died. Death came to him as a Catholic. He died in obscurity, unrecognised in a public ward at the old hospital which before the Revolution was only for the destitute. The ward was curiously named Sala Borges. After Lezama's death, nothing was said about him for a while. Later, the state-owned National Printing Press published a prose poem by him about a dead poet called Licario, l'Icare, Icarus, the enraptured flyer who is killed by his own poetic flight. It was full circle for Jose Lezama Lima: from vanity publishing to vanishing print.

Then came Reinaldo Arenas, who looked a little bit like Lezama and a little bit like Padilla with a red head. He has read enough books to be able to spell trouble. Arenas (whose name means sands) was the only Cuban novelist who could be called a child of the Revolution: a poor peasant from Oriente province, now living in Havana. It was there that he published his first novel, with too much Faulkner in it but a truly remarkable first novel. Being a peasant (remember, this was supposed to be a peasant guerrilla revolution), he was adopted by the Writers' Union as the great red hope of the revolutionary novel. Not for him the Catholic erudition of Lezama or the degenerate decadence of Pinera's cadences or the cosmopolitan vices of a novelist exiled in Paris like Severo Sarduy, also young, also brilliant. But Arenas had, has they say in Cuba, *un defecto,* which sound almost exactly like 'disaffect' in Spanish. He was a homosexual — and a very obvious one, like a Havana *loca*, a mad girl. He didn't do anything to suppress or even to hide it. He belonged to the younger generation of homosexuals which produced the gay movement. Not that the Writers' Union didn't try to reform Arenas. They even proposed to him that he should marry, settle down into a Revolutionary household — and he would be left alone. They had successfully experimented with several actors who only liked to play the queen. This was a form of therapy closer to Pavlov than to Freud, more Russian than Viennese: a cure by marriage. But Arenas was a peasant and, like peasants everywhere, a stubborn man. He refused to comply, and went on with his gay ways. But then he wrote a second novel, the brilliant, original and successful *Hallucination*.

Suddenly, Arenas was gay but hot. Not in donkey's years had a young Cuban novelist still living on the island had such an international success, for him a *succès de folle*. It was, of course, the golden ass again. After his novel had been rejected by the Writers' Union, incompetent literarily but very competent politically, Arenas had sent the manuscript abroad — without consulting the Writers' Union, a publisher who, even when rejecting a book for ever, wants to know what happens next. Above all, *after* rejecting a book. Especially a book about a priest persecuted by tyranny. The priest was Mexican, tyranny universal. What came next to Arenas was not sucess but sudden recognition, disguised as a hideous nightmare. He lost his job at the National Library, a very minor post, he couldn't receive guests from abroad any more and he was carefully surveyed by State Security, a very literary bunch of cops. Finally, he was thrown in gaol, accused of corrupting a minor. At his trial, the *corpus delicti* was a hefty man of 25 with a fully grown beard and much taller than Arenas. (Arenas insists to this day that his partner was a Castro look-alike.) Be that as it may, Arenas was found guilty and sentenced to four years in gaol, for crimes against nature and against man. He served only one year, but in the Morro dungeons, a fortress that had not been in use as a prison since the English seized Havana in 1762! He survived his imprisonment for the same reason that he was in prison: he was a stubborn peasant.

When he was finally freed, 40 pounds thinner, he tried to leave Cuba come hell or high water. A pen pal from Paris sent him a rubber boat in the diplomatic pouch of a daring diplomat. They all belonged to the gay network — except the rubber boat. The inflatable raft worked perfectly on the beach when Arenas tried it one night — but once in the ocean its Mediterranean manufacture couldn't cope with the pull of the Gulf Stream and it split open. Arenas had to swim all the way back from the Stream through the shark-infested seas. Then he tried to swim (I could never find out how a peasant boy from the sticks became such an excellent swimmer in high water) across the Guantanamo Bay to reach the American Naval base at Caimanera, two miles away, a sanctuary for many lucky Cubans. Death or cruel punishment met those who couldn't make it: the whole no-man's-land, like the border between East Germany and West Germany, is jammed with self-manned machine-guns, touch-mines and electric traps, all triggered by electronic devices. Luckily, his escape intent was a non-event. Arenas was able to leave the lethal zone and steal himself back to Cuban soil — and the prospect of gaol again. Being fearful of coming back to Havana, he hid in Lenin Park, which is a wooded area outside the city limits. He stayed there for months, hidden in the heavily-guarded woods, Lenin a lenitive and a threat at the same time. Fortunately, he had a couple of faithful friends: twins so queenly and gentle that he called them the Brontë Sisters — Brontë with an *accent aigu* over the 'e'. It was thanks to them that he was able to survive at all and, a greater feat, to return to his flat undetected. His flat was actually a small room in an ancient and crumbling colonial hotel in Old Havana. He was there writing (and hiding what he wrote from the State Security's avid readers) when the assault on the Peruvian Embassy began. Some desperate Cubans took refuge there one day, including Arenas's missing lover. Three days later there were 11,000 people seeking asylum in the embassy compound, a feat without precedent in the history of diplomacy — not even the 55 days in Peking during the Boxer Rebellion could be compared with this. Arenas thought of seeking sanctuary too, but he told himself that his streak of bad luck would abort his mission before he attempted it.

Then came the boats from Miami, the Freedom Flotilla, to the rescue in the last reel, and with them the boat people trying to leave Cuba on anything that floated. Is this the island that Columbus once called Paradise Green? The Government, to justify their contention that only 'social scum' had sought asylum at the Peruvian Embassy, forcibly filled the privately-hired boats from Florida with all kinds of criminals, taken out of gaol, picked up on the streets of Havana and released from insane asylums. One day a delegate from the Committee for the Defence of the Revolution on the street where Arenas lived came to knock at his door, which was open anyway to exorcise the heat and snoopers alike. He was officially informed that he had to leave the country immediately, for he had been skimmed as scum — as it were, *la crème de la crème* of socialist degeneracy. For Arenas, it was a heaven-sent insult. He got dressed in a jiffy, ready to leave his room and ride down to Mariel, the port of departure for decadence, a Dunkirk for Cubans. Arenas had to wait for 48 long hours at the beach, come shine or come more shine. When his boat finally left, they were lost for two days on the dangerous Gulf Stream waters before they reached Key West, where he was locked in an American internment camp for undesirable aliens. But all this was paradise found for Arenas. Hell was left behind in Mariel, while he waited for his boat to come, fearing the Writers' Union Reading Committee might know he was leaving, for the vigilante Defence Committee had taken a decision at local level. On the beach, bleached white by the scorching white heat from a torrid sun, there were olive specks. This was not vegetation, but men: out of Doré or Dante, army personnel carrying enormous books in which every man or woman or child about to leave the island was carefully annotated — name, occupation, former address sounding like name, rank and serial number. To Arenas, this monstrous red ledger became a nightmare version of the Doomsday Book. Is this the reward for a writer? It seems to me like the wages of an unnamable sin. But I saw Reinaldo Arenas in New York in January, and he seemed the happiest man alive. A Happy Ending. Arenas reunited with his lover in Miami, both rescued by Arenas's uncle, a mean menace in mien but a lovable man in spite of being a Cuban city policeman. In New York, it was freezing outdoors. Not the kind of weather for a boy from the sticks in Cuba, but he took his shoes off and danced barefoot down those mean night streets. 'Look at me!' he shouted. 'Like Geene Kellee.' He was humming 'Singin' in the Rain'.

At the same time, almost to the day, Heberto Padilla left Cuba for good. American admirers had approached Senator Edward Kennedy to intercede in his favour with Fidel Castro. Senator Kennedy called Castro collect, and 24 hours later Padilla had an exit permit, two plane tickets and a lukewarm farewell from Fidel himself — as Padilla told everybody later. The story belongs in the universal history of infamous fathers. Padilla was summoned to one of Castro's many palaces hidden in Havana. After shaking hands, Castro told Padilla that he had heard the rumour that he, Padilla, wanted to leave Cuba. A sly look in his eyes, he asked: 'Is this true?' Then added: 'You know that this is your country and it will be yours until the day you die. The Cuban people is your people. You can go now and you can come back whenever you want. Your house will remain intact. Neither a brick nor a book, will be touched. I want you to know that.' Then the dictator dismissed the poet and sent him out of the game.

The Viennese philosopher and the Conservative thinker and the Hollywood director I'm sure will sing in a chorus: 'Ah but you see, the man really cares about poets.' So did Augustus with Ovid — and Stalin with too many poets to put in a ledger-book. Padilla did the right thing: he left the house and the city quickly and silently. In 1933, Joseph Goebbels saw a film by Fritz Lang. He thought it was Wagner in images. Knowing that Lang was one of the few great German directors still living in Germany who was not a Jew, he summoned him. In his enormous office, Goebbels told Lang that he wanted him to assume immediate care of the German film industry in the name of the Führer. Fritz Lang screwed his monocle, said that he wanted to think about it overnight, if Herr Doktor didn't mind and begged to leave, not forgetting to click his heels before exiting. Next morning, Lang left secretly on the first train to Paris. Like Lang, Padilla had learned the axiom of the plague years. It was formulated by Francesco Guicciardini, friend to Macchiavelli, and it says: 'A tyrant, like the plague, has only one remedy: to fly away as fast as one can — and as far away as possible.'

An American editor wanted to publish an anthology of Cuban writing and he came to me for advice. I mentioned several names in secret and added that he should include the writers left in Cuba. There were about five, I believe I told him. That was last year. Early this year he came back to me again: 'How many writers for my review are there left now?' I felt like a bookie but I had to tell him the truth: 'Well, Virgilio Pinera and Alejo Carpentier died. Edmundo Desnoes, Reinaldo Arenas and Benitez Rojas (who was Haydée Santamaria's answer to Carpentier) exiled themselves in the United States. Jose Triana, in some kind of *larvatus prodeo*, did the same in France. I reckon there's only one writer of international standing left in Cuba, Nicolas Guillen, and about five minor poets with unpronounceable names.' 'Not much, eh?' he said grimacing or perhaps grinning. I had to agree. No, not much, really. Not bloody much.

Alejo Carpentier died, as he wanted, in Paris, but not the way he wanted. Instead of the merciful heart attack in his sleep, he had a throat cancer and awoke in the dead of night. He had suffered a haemorrhage. Then he choked in his own unwise blood. Embalmed, he was sent back to Cuba to have a state funeral and a personal wreath from Fidel Castro: 'To the great writer of the people,' said the funeral inscription, and it lied. The only true writer of the people left in Cuba, Virgilio Pinera, died a different death.

The death of Virgilio didn't come swiftly or easily either. He was in his small flat in Havana and he felt ill. Somehow he managed to phone for an ambulance to come. Paperwork. A police state is primarily made of forms to be filled in and out. When the ambulance arrived, they found him downstairs, lying in the street, already dead. Alejo Carpentier, who wanted a heart attack, was almost eighty when he died. Virgilio Pinera, who didn't want any heart attacks, was 68. Carpentier's funeral was stately, pompous. Virgilio's funeral was another play of the absurd by himself. Rumour spread (in socialist countries, rumour runs, Party news crawls — and a running rumour is always trustworthy) that Virgilio had died. He was to lie in state in a humble *funeraria*. There was a small group of writers who looked queer — and queer they were. Virgilio had been their only true teacher, their mentor, their master in the *gai savoir*. There were fast-fading flowers and there was even a wreath from the Writers' Union, with no inscription.

There was everything you need for a funeral — except the body. Some people remembered having seen it very late the previous night. It had disappeared, though, taken away in the early morning. The explanation for sneaking Virgilio's body out was that he needed a second autopsy. Virgilio needed a second autopsy like he needed a hole in the head. He had died of cardiac arrest, everybody knew that. The real reason why the body disappeared as in a cheap thriller by Agatha Christie was that the Government (or the Writers' Union) feared a crowded funeral parlour, followed by a wake, finished with a riotous funeral procession. The body was bought back from the cold half an hour before the time the funeral procession was to take place — though the funeral procession never took place. Instead of driving the hearse at a walking pace (the custom in Havana, where funeral homes are never very far from the cemetery), as befits a decent funeral procession, the driver, following orders from the Writers' Union (or from the Government), sped away, as if he were racing in Le Mans, to elude any camp followers. But the disciples, a new school of Cuban queers, even newer than the school of Arenas, chased the hearse in cars, on bicyles and even on foot, running and grieving: 'Ay, Maestro, alas! You are being spirited away now but your spirit will remain with us! *Virgilio vive!*'

But Virgilio Pinera was dead as a doornail, and his body is still in his tomb (or must be) at the Colon Cemetry, one of the most sumptuous graveyards in the Americas, even bigger than the famous Recoleta in Buenos Aires, where Borges longs to be buried to dream that he is dead. Knowing the régime, I'm sure that Virgilio has been buried not in the Patriots' Pantheon but in what you could call a pauper's grave — though there are not supposed to be any pauper's graves in the land of socialism. All socialist dead are buried equally, but some are buried deeper. This doesn't pain me at all, because it wouldn't have bothered Virgilio in the least where his body lay to rest.

It is Pinera's writings that will live, twist and giggle for ever. I am truly worried about what happens to his body of work. I know that he will soon be out of print in Cuba and never be printed again. What was left unpublished remained for a while in his furnished flat, its door sealed by State Security, illiterate agents so strangely concerned with writers and their writings. His old flat will have new, anxious tenants ready to move in, eager to clean out. All the papers found there — Virgilio's last literary will and theatrical testament — will be put in a cardboard box and buried in one of the secret sections in the basement of the State Security building. That place, where Reinaldo Arenas's unpublished novels ended, is known by the State Security men who deal with Cubans of a literary leaning and a subversive bent (political, aesthetical, sexual) as

Siberia. This long, rambling article is an effort to show it all — the cellar, the State Security building, Havana and the island — as Siberia-in-the-tropics.

But I often wonder. Why was Virgilio so eager to kiss Cuban soil that he missed?